JONSONIAN DISCRIMINATIONS

JONSONIAN DISCRIMINATIONS

The Humanist Poet and
the Praise of True Nobility

MICHAEL McCANLES

UNIVERSITY OF TORONTO PRESS
Toronto   Buffalo   London

© University of Toronto Press 1992
Toronto   Buffalo   London
Printed in Canada

ISBN 0-8020-5955-4

Printed on acid-free paper

Canadian Cataloguing in Publication Data
McCanles, Michael
Jonsonian discriminations

Includes bibliographical references and index.
ISBN 0-8020-5955-4

1. Jonson, Ben, 1573?–1637 – Poetic works.
2. Nobility of character in literature.   I. Title.

PR2638.M33 1991   821'.3   C91-095060-1

Contents

Preface

The history of Ben Jonson's literary career exhibits his ambition, largely successful, to establish himself in traditional humanist fashion as adviser of prince and nobility, and the arbiter of public manners and political ethics. The scope and content of this ambition is registered somewhat differently in the three main genres of his literary output. The masques written for the court of King James attempt at once to educate the monarch in the virtues and responsibilities of rule, and to celebrate their achievement as a fait accompli. Some of Jonson's plays, such as *Every Man Out of His Humour, Cynthia's Revels, Poetaster*, and *Catiline*, explore various relations among court, aristocracy, and 'new men' of talent and ambition such as himself. In this connection Jonson brings to bear a long tradition of ideas about the nature of true nobility – *vera nobilitas* – which he inherited from classical and Renaissance sources. While vera nobilitas is present in these plays as one of many topics Jonson works out dramatically, in his nondramatic poetry he develops it most overtly and applies it to his own ambitions and career. More exactly, the poetry explores the inherently slippery and complex question of the authority and status the humanist self-made man of letters may justly claim vis-à-vis the aristocratic establishment he aspires to advise and serve.

In lieu of a major, total survey of Jonson's works which examines in detail the significant autobiographical component present in all of them, the current Jonson literature has produced several versions of 'Ben Jonson': the plain-style Jonson; the stoic Jonson; the psychologist's Jonson fixated on authority figures; the misogynist Jonson; and most recently the new historicist's Jonson as just the sort of figure he most abhorred, an envious and resentful sycophant. In order to avoid making still another contribution to these partial visions and versions, I have insisted on a systematic and integrative reading that leaves no poem unturned. This study gives an account of, or at the very least takes account of, every nondramatic poem Ben Jonson wrote that has survived.

Each poem is worth at least a glance, and most more than that. This total coverage includes all the poems in the three volumes of nondramatic poetry now canonically recognized: the *Epigrammes* and *The Forrest* (1616), and *The Vnder-wood* (1640), as well as the 'Ungathered Verse' included in the Herford and Simpson Oxford edition of Jonson's works, and Jonson's translation of Horace's *Ars Poetica*. It does not include the songs in the plays and the masques, a few poems dubiously ascribed to Jonson, and epitaphs in Latin. Groups of poems often slighted, such as his commendatory verse addressed to fellow authors and printed in their books, his lesser love poems, and the poetry written for King Charles and his family and circle, all take on upgraded importance in the context of his total poetic output. His translation of Horace's *Ars Poetica*, to which he gave a major significance, is examined and found to justify this significance.

The result is partly what was originally intended: a survey of Jonson's poetry which explores its dominant technical and thematic features. Technically, the feature of contrastivity, registered in the prosodic, semantic, and tropic components discussed in chapter 1, proves to be all-pervasive. At the level of content, contrastivity underwrites the discriminations Jonson derives from the tradition of the vera nobilitas argument, and develops as one of the argument's shrewdest expositors. Both features have been noted before in Jonson's poetry. However, no one heretofore has sought to survey all of Jonson's nondramatic poetic output so as to account for these features as what they are: dominant concerns of Jonson's poetic career from beginning to end.

And this foregrounds an aspect of this study not originally contemplated, but which has come to claim a significant part of its conclusions: this is also a study of how Jonson understood and sought to manage his career as humanist poet, and therefore is a contribution to his intellectual biography. Unlike Shakespeare's work, where the writer is present everywhere but visible nowhere (so goes the folklore), Jonson is both present and visible everywhere, and nowhere more so than in the nondramatic poetry. This study shows that Jonson understood the ideological and rhetorical dimensions of the vera nobilitas argument within an ongoing meditation on his own claim to status in the aristocratic establishment of early seventeenth-century England, which means that his poetry is a record of his thoughts on his own literary career and its ambitions.

Along the way I have also perforce had to invent revisionist treatments of the theory and history of the vera nobilitas argument, of epideictic rhetoric, and of the relations between the two. These treatments claim their own space in my argument and on the page. They have in turn required reexamination of Jonson's debts to some classical texts, and of the ideological and rhetorical features of these texts themselves. The result is a version of Jonson more complex and self-reflexive than has heretofore been discovered, more subtle, in some ways more genial, and even more sympathetic if not more lovable.

An earlier and expanded form of the discussion of Jonson's prosody in chapter 1 has appeared as 'Punctuation, Contrastive Emphasis, and New Information in the Prosody of Jonson's Poetry' *Language and Style* 19 (1986) 74–98. Permission to reprint portions of the material in this article is gratefully acknowledged from the editors of *Language and Style*.

The substance of this book was presented at a seminar at the Newberry Library, Chicago, during the fall of 1987.

I am grateful to the Graduate School of Marquette University and to its Graduate Research Committee for two Summer Faculty Fellowships which allowed me important time for research.

JONSONIAN DISCRIMINATIONS

CHAPTER ONE

The Poetics of Discrimination

1   Contrastive Emphasis in Jonson's Prosodic Practice

To begin where Jonson begins: with the first poem of *Epigrammes*, his first collection of nondramatic verse:[1]

> Pray thee, take care, that tak'st my booke in hand,
> To read it well: that is, to vnderstand.   (E1)

This is a powerful, and revealing, liminal gesture. It discloses a poet wary of misprision of his poetic utterances and rhetorical intentions, one who seeks to forestall incorrect and unwanted responses. Jonson here guides the reader both in understanding the epigrams to follow, and in recognizing what 'understanding' itself might mean. It is a gesture the poet repeats throughout the *Epigrammes*, as when, for instance, he hedges praise and blame against being mistaken for their perversions, flattery and malice.

It is also a gesture that Jonson repeats obsessively throughout the rest of his works: in prologues and dramatic dialogues instructing audiences how to respond to his plays; in marginalia appended to editions of plays and masques to forestall readers bent on detecting his scholarly ignorance; in quarrels with fellow artists who question the ethical purity of his literary career; in poetic lectures to women on the true locus of his aggressively masculine sex appeal. A gesture all the more profoundly defensive for masking as authoritative instruction, it declares the poet's not quite serene confidence in his power to control the direction of the reader's mental gaze.[2]

Jonson distinguishes three stages of acquaintance with this book, and one stage does not necessarily entail or imply the next: (1) taking the book in hand; (2) reading it well; (3) understanding it. He warns his reader not to be gulled into believing that merely taking his book in hand means reading well, or – more to the point – that 'reading well' means understanding.[3] The epigram requires the reader to discriminate understanding from an apparently synonymous phrase, 'to reade it well,' and in this it illustrates the discipline of reading which the epigram takes as its subject. Understanding this poem – and the rest of the epigrams – requires distinguishing what reading well might or should mean from what it does not. 'To read it well' is thus retroactively defined as something which, if it does not involve understanding, is not reading 'well' either.[4]

Jonson's poems habitually discriminate words and meanings that appear synonymous, while disclosing parallels between meanings apparently disparate or incompatible. This perspicuous discrimination of difference and likeness argues Jonson the forerunner of neoclassic poetic practice at the end of the century (Schelling 'Ben Jonson'). In Jonson's case such discriminations mark a dialogical transaction between reader and poem, founded on an ongoing dialectic between the statements available to the poet's argument, and those he chooses to write.

This dialectic is central to Jonson's rhetorical purpose. Since for Jonson the credibility of the humanist ethic rests on the capacity to discriminate the judgments possible on a given subject, the reader becomes an appropriate 'understander' of the poem by recreating the process through which the poet's judgments are arrived at and the poem composed. The reader discovers the meaning, validity, and import of the poetic statement to be a function of its having been progressively carved out of a limited repertoire of available statements.

This chapter investigates the orthographical, phonological, and semantic resources that create the discriminations that constitute the writing and reading of Jonson's poetry, and prefaces a consideration in later chapters of Jonson's humanist ethic. This first section examines the prosodic, semantic, and syntactical consequences of Jonson's eccentric punctuation. The contrastive prosodic emphasis that Jonson's punctuation creates imposes on his readers a complex process for recuperating his ethical concerns. Since it breaks up the syntax of his statements and marks points of juncture and emphasis in ways not easily understood today, this orthographical dimension of Jonson's poetry calls urgently for analysis.[5] One modern edition illustrates this lack of understanding by excising much of Jonson's own punctuation – exemplified in the two poetry collections brought out probably under his own direction in the 1616 Folio – in order to make the poetry more accessible to the modern reader.[6] Because the directions for performance that Jonson's punctuation delivers usually determine meaning, such editorial simplification often changes the meaning of Jonson's lines.

The remaining four sections of this chapter examine other dimensions of Jonson's poetry that create similar discriminations at the levels of syntax and meaning. Section 2 concerns Jonson's use of the incremental, paratactic list to impose upgraded emphasis on coordinate elements; section 3 deals with the interplay among homonyms and synonyms, section 4 with defining a positive value by negating its opposite, and section 5 with the interplay between metaphors and their literal meaning.

The import of Jonson's punctuation for prosody and meaning challenges the 'plain style' first proposed by Wesley Trimpi as an adequate description of Jonson's poetry, and accepted currently in the literature on Jonson's poetry.[7] Trimpi argues that syntactical and prosodic fragmentation within the individual line reproduces the conversation of congenial and learned men, and conveys an ethos of straightforward sincerity. For instance, in citing Seneca's prose style Trimpi says:

> The terse, epigrammatic statements [in Jonson's poetry] are like
> the *sententiae* in Seneca's letters, in both form and content, and the
> generalizations are based upon particular experience. The informal
> context of the personal relationship and the apparently unlabored,
> conversational diction and phrasing give the tone an intimacy
> which offers the reader an emotional assurance that what is being
> said is the truth. The emphasis upon both the author's and the
> friend's knowing himself is the Socratic and Senecan stylistic tradi-
> tion and accounts for much of the power of the poem. (142)

Trimpi's essential contribution was to discover in Jonson's prosody the formal justification for this supposed self-portrait. By conflating prosodic structure with tone of voice and presentation of self, Trimpi concludes that Jonson's poems project something like a dramatic presence: the poet's imitating himself speaking to an interlocutor identical with the addressee of the poem.[8]

However, if we read Jonson's poetry as Trimpi would have us do, we confront a verbal texture apparently static in structure and devoid of thematic complexity. The characteristics of Jonson's prosody that concern me here are exactly those which Trimpi slights and even mis-reads. Though he accurately cites Jonson's predilection for medial cae-sura, Trimpi denies a prosodic phenomenon that appears everywhere one looks: Jonson's habitual use of enjambment. This denial supports a larger insistence: that Jonson's lines are, despite their heavy medial pauses, metrically regular, and that this regularity contributes to and supports their ethical import. By supposing prosodic regularity the for-mal embodiment of ethical sincerity, Trimpi believes himself allowed to argue that static, conservative, and unproblematic ethical values call for prosodic regularity. As this chapter argues, this is not even to read Jonson's poetry well, let alone to understand it.

Punctuation's contribution to meaning is not a discovery of modern linguistics. In Shakespeare's *A Midsummer Night's Dream*, for instance, misinterpretation of points becomes an object of laughter. 'If we offend, it is with our good will. / That you should think, we come not to offend, / But with good will,' says Peter Quince as Prologue to the lamentable comedy of Pyramus and Thisbe (Neilson and Hill 5.1.108ff). Lysander comments: 'he knows not the stop. A good moral, my lord: it is not enough to speak, but to speak true.' The confusion lies in the fact that the same sequence of words may yield, when punctuated at different places, quite different and even opposite meanings.

Ben Jonson was no less punctilious when it came to such matters. In E58, 'To Groome Ideot,' he likewise insists that it is not enough to speak, but to speak true, that is, correctly. He prays not only that the groom 'forbeare / To read my verses,' but also insists that he himself must forbear to hear them:

> For offring, with thy smiles, my wit to grace,
> Thy ignorance still laughs in the wrong place.
> And so my sharpnesse thou no lesse dis-ioynts,
> Than thou did'st late my sense, loosing my points.

Jonson's concern with the punctuation of his poetic texts, both dramatic and nondramatic, has been discussed by A.C. Partridge and by Herford and Simpson.[9] We may readily presume that Jonson's objection to a performance of his poetry that ignores its punctuation is the same as that offered by Peter Quince's audience: to ignore the points is to lose the sense. And this is not a matter of syntax merely, but of performance. Since punctuation is not only a way of clarifying syntax, but also a notation for distributing junctures and emphases that convey this clar-ification in oral (or subvocal) performance, a reading is possible in which, as Theseus puts it, 'nothing [is] impaired, but all disordered.'

Punctuation becomes significant, in other words, because it directs intonation and intonation expounds meaning. The eccentricity of Jonson's punctuation is evident in three different configurations. The first two are syntactical and the third metrical: (1) coordinate and paratactic constructions; (2) problematic isolation by punctuation of phrases and clauses from their syntactical heads; (3) enjambment, which creates junctures similar to those enforced medially by punctuation.

The first configuration, called by Partridge the coordinate comma (2), is one of the commonest features of Jonson's punctuation, and is inserted between *and* and *or* in coordinate phrases and clauses. Typical examples throw a primary emphasis on what would otherwise be a prosodically downgraded ligature:

... [Camden] to whom my contrey owes
The great renowne, and name wherewith shee goes.   (E14, 3–4)

Queene, and Huntress, chaste, and faire, ...   (*Cynthia's Revels* 5.6)

And it is not alwayes face,
Clothes, or Fortune gives the grace;
Or the feature, or the youth:
But the Language, and the Truth,
With the Ardor, and the Passion,
Gives the Lover weight, and fashion.   (U2, *A Celebration of Charis in ten Lyrick Peeces* no. 1, 7–12)

In these cases, the punctuation is apparently at odds with the syntax. Either the two terms linked by *and* appear to be merely synonyms, as in 'renowne, and name'; or, as in 'Queene, and Huntress,' or 'the language, and the Truth,' the joined terms are given equal status in naming qualities that belong broadly to the same genus. The insertion of the coordinate *and* after the juncture created by the commas implies, however, that the second term is not at all necessarily implied by the first, and that, far from being mere repetition or redundancy, the addition of the second term is a connection consciously chosen to extend the argument in a significant direction.

The second distinctive use of punctuation occurs when modifying phrases and clauses are separated by punctuation from their syntactical heads, and, as in the case of coordinate conjunctions, they take on an upgraded emphasis. Several typical examples occur in the first eight lines of the song 'To Celia' (F5), which appears twice in the 1616 Folio: once in *Volpone* (3.7), and again as F5 in *The Forrest*:[10]

> Come my Celia let us proue,
> *While we may*, the sports of loue;
> Time will not be ours, *for euer.*
> He, *at length*, our good will seuer.
> Spend not then his guifts, *in vaine.*
> Sunnes, *that set*, may rise againe:
> But if, *once*, we loose this light,
> 'Tis, with vs, perpetuall night.   (emphasis added)

All seven of the units isolated by the punctuation are parenthetical elements that would normally receive only passing, downgraded emphasis in their unpunctuated versions. But because isolated by junctures before and after they receive upgraded emphasis. As with the coordinate *and* of the earlier examples, upgraded emphasis marks these units as possessing some thematic import that calls for explanatory interpretation.

The last configuration wherein Jonson creates junctures and emphases uncalled for in normal intonation is a metrical phenomenon, namely enjambment. Here, the break in syntactical structure created by the line end (often reinforced by a rhyme word) functions like punctuation, and for that reason punctuation is absent:

> So, justest Lord, may all your Judgments be
> Lawes, and no change e're come to one decree:
> So, may the King proclaime your Conscience is
> Law, to his law; ...
>
> > ('An Epigram. To THOMAS Lo: ELSMERE,
> > the last Terme he sate Chancellor' [U31] 1–4)

And there he lives with memorie: and *Ben*
> THE STAND
>
> *Jonson*, who sung this of him, e'er he went
> Himselfe to rest, ...
>
> > ('To the immortall memorie, and friendship
> > of that noble paire, Sir LVCIVS CARY,
> > and Sir H. MORISON' [U70] 84ff)

> *Hayward* and
> *Selden!* two Names that so much understand!
> ('An Epistle to Master IOHN SELDEN' [U14] 81–2)

All these examples have certain prosodic features in common: (1) the last syllable of the enjambed line invites a primary emphasis due to either normal phrase rhythm, or metrical pattern, or both; (2) the first word of the second line invites an even greater emphasis in order to allow this emphasis to stand out in contrast to the previous one; (3) the juncture between the two words throws upgraded emphasis on both of them. These passages stand for scores of similar ones in Jonson's poetry, and in general they are all alike in this: the reader is invited continually to pause in vocal and subvocal performance to emphasize words, phrases, and clauses isolated by punctuation and made to bear emphasis unaccountable solely for syntactical reasons.

In summary, my argument is the following: Jonson's punctuation introduces junctures and therefore emphases that would not normally occur without this punctuation. These emphases create contrasts, and contrasts mark the emphasized units as the information focus of their syntactical contexts, and therefore as points of new information. Contrast is of three sorts: phrasal, syntagmatic, and paradigmatic. Phrasal contrast occurs between the actual deviant phrase rhythm created by Jonson's punctuation, and an alternative, 'normal' rhythm of the same phrase read without that punctuation. Phrasal contrast in turn foregrounds the other two kinds of contrast. Syntagmatic contrast occurs between two emphasized units in the same text, while paradigmatic contrast occurs between an emphasized unit and another absent from the text but implied contrastively by the first. Syntagmatic and paradigmatic contrast mark the information focus of a specific section of the poetic text, and therefore the new or significant information of that section. Since new information is usually contrastively defined,[11] the reader is continually required to reconstruct the repertoire of words and ideas from which the actual text is a selection, and with which it implicitly contrasts.[12] Such points of juncture and emphasis as I have exemplified above become a series of fissures in Jonson's poems, through which the reader is invited to perceive the specific countertexts to the text at hand, and to recognize that the meaning of the text derives by contrast with the repertoire of other possible texts from which Jonson selected his own.[13]

This analysis will reveal that the structural dynamic of Jonson's poetry, the ethos this dynamic projects, and the rhetorical designs on the reader that both support are poetic phenomena entirely too complex for Trimpi's 'plain style' to explain. In place of Trimpi's metrical regularity I invite recognition of the complex play in Jonson's poetry among phrase rhythm, metrical set, and the deviant rhythm induced by unorthodox punctuation, juncture, and emphasis. In place of the mountainous poet phlegmatically defending his own monumentality by bludgeoning his readers with sincere (and sometimes trivial) *sententiae* (H&S 2:362–4) is revealed a poet cautious, self-critical, diplomatic, conscious of the nuances of meaning hidden in the simplest classical formula and the most routine social gesture, and seeking always to master the unpredictable ricochet of both; a poet who also must master the *ressentiment* of the new man compelled to make his way by his wits within an aristocratic establishment sometimes egregiously undeserving of its power and privileges, and who, almost alone among his contemporaries, has the grace, the tact, and the humour – by turns self-deprecating and aggressive – to ingratiate himself with the intellectual cream of the aristocracy, and finally with the king himself. And in place of traditional wisdom, uncomplicated because sound, and sound because readily acceptable to the reader, I seek to uncover a poetry that fairly leaps from the page with its agile dialectical play between meanings intended and rejected, present and absent, a poetry that strenuously engages the reader in writing the poem itself, a poetry which fulfils its humanist agenda in turn by reading and judging the reader.[14]

The first contrast to note here is phrasal: the contrast between the prosodic configuration which these syntactical units would exhibit in their unpunctuated versions, and that which they take on as a result of Jonson's punctuation. Hypothetical alternative versions of these coordinate phrases and clauses, because unseparated by punctuation, invite interpretation either as synonyms of each other, or as collectively defining a larger genus, or as simply constituting a paratactically structured sequence of words. Thus 'renown' means the same as 'name,' 'clothes' plus 'fortune' add up to the implied genus 'external gifts,' 'chaste and fair' constitute indifferently a catalogue of eulogistic epithets. In the passage from 'To Celia,' the marked phrases and clauses – shorn of their punctuation – become redundant specifications of the message already conveyed by main clauses: the exhortation *carpe diem*.

Phrasal contrast in turn foregrounds the other two kinds of contrast, namely, syntagmatic and paradigmatic contrast. In the case of the coordinate comma, the conjunctions create paradigmatic contrast, which means that they no longer function merely as coordinate or paratactical ligatures. On the contrary, contrastive emphasis on the conjunctions implies a hypothetical alternative conjunction, or the possibility that one may indeed have one of the linked terms without the other. And these implied contrasts solicit the reader's inquiry into the thematic reasons why these terms were chosen and so linked, what the possible alternatives were, and the relations among these choices. For instance, to speak of 'great renowne, and name' is to call attention to the following information: *renown* and *name* may not really mean the same thing; one may have the name but not its justification in true renown; and to have both is a greater achievement than to have only one.[15] In short, the coordinate conjunction *and* contrasts paradigmatically with the implied possible negative conjunction *and not*. The juncture and emphasis caused by the comma call attention to the fact that follow-up words, phrases, and clauses are not necessarily implied by the preceding, ones, that adding them is to add new meanings that do not merely redundantly repeat old meanings. The addition of new meanings becomes an information focus in its own right, and phonologically foregrounding this information focus requires assigning an upgraded emphasis to the *and* as well.[16] If one may possess language but not truth, be fair without being chaste, or have fashion without weight: then the significance of these terms' conjunction is defined against the possibility of their disjunction. And if this is the case, the reader may well inquire into the meanings of these terms and the human realities they refer to.

Similar comments are appropriate to the examples of enjambment. In the Ellesmere epigram –

> So, justest Lord, may all your Judgments be
> Lawes, and no change e're come to one decree:
> So, may the King proclaime your Conscience is
> Law, to his law ...   (U31)

– there is a syntagmatic contrast between judgment and laws, and between conscience and laws. Here Jonson plays off the breach between the normally uncertain subjective domain of judgment and conscience, and the public claims of laws, by asserting the unitive copula against this breach.

The *and* of the Selden poem, already upgraded by the exigencies of metre and rhyme, receives an even heavier emphasis in order to compensate for its otherwise normally downgraded status (an observation that applies to all the examples I have cited here). Jonson's insistence on praising the otherwise obscure companion of the famous Selden becomes itself a form of compensation. The Cary-Morison Ode uses enjambment as itself a thematic signifier, since the poem's significance concerns analogous links between two friends severed by death. At the stanza end 'Ben' joins with all those who keep alive the memory of Morison, only to suffer a radical shift in perspective with a break within his own name, within the same sentence and between two separate stanzas, to discover that everything he says applies to the poet as well, 'Who sung this of him ere he went / Himself to rest.' In this particular use of juncture and emphasis Jonson tropes these prosodic features in their own right.[17]

'To Celia' (F5) exemplifies Jonson's use of syntagmatic contrast in its clearest form. The isolating punctuation, which to modern eyes appears to turn these restrictive into nonrestrictive modifiers (Quirk et al 890–1), in fact serves another purpose altogether: foregrounding the syntagmatic contrast among the phrases themselves. The upgraded 'for ever' contrasts with the equally isolated and upgraded 'at length' in the next line, and with the 'once' three lines later. That one may spend time's gifts 'in vaine' implies that, though spending is inevitable, doing so vainly is not. 'Suns, that set,' contrasts unremarkably with 'may rise again' and more significantly with the 'with us' of the next line but one. The parenthetical 'While we may' of the second line in addition implies a paradigmatic contrast with the hypothetical alternative *may not*. Emphasized in this manner, these isolated units call contrastively to each other across the text of the poem and carry in epitome its thematic burden: the central distinction between what is and is not within human power. The lines of this poem, when read in their unpunctuated version, appear to render even more trivial the already well rehearsed exhortation of *carpe diem*.[18] By breaking the options down so precisely into what is and is not possible, the speaker of the poem invites the recalcitrant lady once again to consider with scrupulous precision the implications of her delay. As happens often in Jonson's poetry, he revivifies a classical topos by requiring the reader to recover the thought process that supports and continues to give that topos its enduring poignancy.[19]

The central importance of prosodic considerations in Jonson's poetry can be grasped in another way by glancing at poems whose unique metrical elements make them boundary cases: a poem such as 'Certaine Verses Written Vpon Coryats Crvdities' (M12) which is unmetrical to the point of being unscannable; and at the other extreme, the three poems of devotion that open *The Vnder-wood*, in which phrase rhythm and metrical pattern exactly correspond. The metrical dimension in both cases supports the contents of the poems, though it be deliberate nonsense in the one case and an unquestioning faith in the other.

Coryat's tall tales of misadventure easily get Jonson in the spirit of the thing, and he is quite willing to match Coryat in calculated gibberish. The clue to the part metrics plays in this farrago is indicated early: 'Mr. *Tom Coryate*, / Who, because his matter in all shoulde be meete, / To his strength, hath measur'd it out with his feet' (2–4). Jonson intends to match the wandering journey traced out by Coryat's feet with erratic feet of his own. I quote a short excerpt to indicate what Jonson could do when he set himself deliberately to creating metrical anomaly:

> How well, and how often his shoes too were mended,
> That sacred to *Odcombe* are there now suspended,
> I meane that one paire, wherewith he so hobled
> From Venice to Flushing, were not they well cobled?
> Yes. And thanks God in his Pistle or his Booke
> How many learned men he haue drawne with his hooke
> Of Latine and Greeke, to his friendship. And seuen
> He there doth protest he saw of the eleuen. (39–46)

Jonson has superposed on a five-foot line, which never quite attains iambic, a four-beat line that could be either dactylic or anapestic. The cross-currents of these two prosodic patterns turn the poem into the verbal counterpart of music by Charles Ives. In the majority of Jonson's poems the interplay of closure and disruption of closure, of continuity and discontinuity, of unexpected casesuras, linkages, contrasts, and the syncopation of rhythmic emphases: all of these become meaningful in the context of an established set of expectations, both metrical and phrasal, that are always kept intact. Here, there is simple unscannability, and the reader is not invited, as in Jonson's more metrically sophisticated poems, to recover a second sense that plays off and with the sense of the lines themselves.[20]

Similar remarks are appropriate to 'A Hymne On the Nativitie of my Saviour' (U1.3). Jonson deals here with a subject in which complicated choice has no place, and metrical and phrasal rhythms correspond exactly:

> I sing the birth, was borne to night,
> The Author both of Life, and light;
> > The Angels so did sound it,
> And like the ravish'd Sheep'erds said,
> Who saw the light, and were afraid,
> > > Yet search'd, and true they found it. (1–6)[21]

This poem exemplifies Jonson's experiments with doggerel rhythms in his later masques, such as *Christmas His Masque* (1616), *The Metamorphosed Gypsies* (1621), and *The Fortunate Isle* (1624), as well as one poem from a presumably lost entertainment that Herford and Simpson print among the miscellaneous poems: 'A Song of the Moon' (M45). Such boundary cases mark the limits of Jonson's usual metrical practice. They are significant in this context because they eschew the dialectic between normal and deviant phrase rhythms that create the paradigmatic and syntagmatic contrasts typical of his practice. In refusing the metrical and stanzaic resources that in his other poems evoke counterbalancing recognitions, Jonson signals here that the meaning of the nativity is beyond question.

That Jonson's notion of religious faith is not always so simple is indicated in several other poems from his slim religious output. In a late poem prefaced to a 1635 book of meditations on *The Femall Glory: or, The Life, and Death of our Blessed Lady, the holy Virgin Mary* (M41) Jonson sets forth a herbal 'ghyrlond' corresponding to the five letters of the name Marie, and exhibits a typically Jonsonian prosodic play: 'The fourth is humble *Ivy* intersert, / But lowlie laid, as on the earth asleep, / Preserved, in her antique bed of *Vert*, / No faith's more firme, or flat, then where't doth creep' (17–20). Donaldson (*Poems* 1975:331) gives us the normal phrase rhythm in his unpunctuated version of line 20: 'No faith's more firm or flat than where 't doth creep.' This version aligns metrical set and phrase rhythm, with the result that 'flat' and 'where't' receive a dominant emphasis, causing 'or' to be downgraded. In the correctly punctuated version, however, these proportions are reversed, and meanings become correspondingly denser. 'Or' severs 'firm' and 'flat' to signal that 'humble ivy' is firm because flat – 'flat' meaning humble in context of the preceding lines. The contrast is with a faith which though firm is not 'flat,' a discrimination that invites recognition that the strength of faith is only made perfect in the apparent weakness of humility.

Another, earlier poem on another Mary, namesake of 'heauens Queene,' exhibits Jonson using upgraded emphasis to move himself into a similar faith: 'On my first Davghter,' E22: 'Here lyes to each her parents ruth, / MARY, the Davghter of their youth: / Yet, all heauens gifts, being heauens due, / It makes the father, lesse, to rue' (1–4) The poignancy of the upgraded 'lesse' in line 4 responds to the isolated 'Yet' of the previous line, suggesting a fine discrimination of feeling. Since the daughter was owed heaven anyway, this makes the father to rue 'less,' but it does not destroy the sorrow. Jonson says that the daughter's reception into Mary's train is done 'In comfort of her mother's tears,' and this tells us, as does 'lesse' earlier, that sorrow is partially mitigated but nothing more.

Jonson uses orthographical isolation and the rhythmic upgrading it generates not merely to create binary contrasts, but to evoke undecidability between two meanings.[22] Leaving out the commas that isolate 'lesse' gives us the mitigation of sorrow but not its continued endurance, and this is just Jonson's point about consolations for death: that they leave us in a emotionally complicated space between different degrees and intensities of pain.

Ignoring deviant punctuation in other contexts can lead to other kinds of misreading. For example, in E57 'On Bavdes, and Vsvrers,' the absence of a comma changes the syntax:

> If, as their ends, their fruits were so, the same,
> Baudrie', and vsurie were one kind of game.

By placing a comma after 'so' Jonson highlights the parallel with 'as' earlier in the line. The meaning is the hypothetical supposition that bawdry and usury might be (but are not) the same in their results ('fruits') as they are in their purposes ('ends'). Leaving out the comma and reading the end of the line as 'so the same' makes 'so' merely an intensifier modifying 'the same,' with the consequent readings: 'so identical as to be the same kind of game.' But this is exactly what Jonson is not saying. Punctuating the line as he does, Jonson isolates identity and sets if off from the actual parallel he seeks to draw between pandering and usury. Both sell commodities that should not be sold – flesh and money – but the fornicator buys something that the borrower does not, namely venereal disease.

A similar determination of meaning in another epigram on gutter life occurs in E87, 'On Captaine Hazard the Cheater.' Jonson points the opening line of this epigram as:

> Touch'd with the sinne of false play, in his punque,
> HAZARD a moneth forsware his ...

Up to the first comma, it would appear that Hazard is the one 'touched' (tainted) by his cheating. When, however, the specifying phrase 'in his punque' (whore) is added, we retroactively rewrite the first half of the line to say that Hazard is 'touched' in the fencing sense of the word: scored upon or wounded. The first line including Jonson's comma can be paraphrased as: 'Hazard is tainted with the sin of cheating, and is in turn cheated by his whore.' Without the comma the first half of the line yields only the second meaning and thereby misses Jonson's point, namely that the cheater is not prepared to be cheated, and had not looked for that taint to infect his own mistress.[23]

In addition to E58 on the idiot who speaks his lines like a groom, Jonson declares his peremptory anger with poets (and others) who misunderstand and therefore neglect the importance of junctural pauses for specifying meaning: U29: 'A Fit of Rime against Rime.' In a poem where metrical set – often reinforced by rhyme – is foregrounded and dominates at the expense of phrase rhythm and therefore of meaning, the poet impudently attacks both devices. This is the direction of Jonson's attack in the poem's opening lines:

> Rime, the rack of finest wits,
> That expresseth but by fits,
>   True Conceipt,
> Spoyling Senses of their Treasure,
> Cosening Judgment with a measure,
>   But false weight.
> Wresting words, from their true calling;
> Propping Verse, for feare of falling
>   To the ground.
> Joynting Syllabes, drowning Letters,
> Fastning Vowells, as with fetters
>   They were bound! (1–12)

Sense is robbed by deceiving the reader's judgment with a measure that gives a 'false weight,' false emphasis to inappropriate words. The 'true calling' of words – meaning and truth, and also possibly pronunciation – is distorted to keep the lines from falling limp, like Jonson's exemplary line, 'To the ground.' When metrical set dominates, the normal junctures between syllables are obscured by elisions that ignore the meaning created by contrastive emphasis in spoken phrase rhythm.[24]

That Jonson has in mind his own practice of deviant medial juncture is indicated later in the poem, where he finds 'Vulgar Languages' are something '*Tyran* Rime hath so abused, / That they long since have refused / Other ceasure' (44–8). This seems a two-pronged attack: on endstopped lines as opposed to enjambed lines, and on endstopped lines distinct from those that employ medial caesura. It should be clear that Jonson's position does not set him against either rhyme or endstopped lines *tout court*, since he often employs both. Rather, he is concerned with the larger issue of how metrical pattern and phrase rhythm are related. I would suggest that Jonson is not calling for a counterpoint between metrical set and phrase rhythm, since this is not the prosodic fulcrum on which his own poetry balances, but rather between normal phrase rhythm ('Vulgar languages') and deviant phrase rhythm. Meaning is his prime concern, not rhythm, and meaning mediated through the contrasts created by the emphases articulated in turn by deviant punctuation and juncture.

Rhythm in the interest of a colloquial style projecting an ethos of stoic sincerity – the core of Trimpi's 'plain style' Jonson – is just not to be found here. Present instead is the poet's profoundly technical sense of the semantic resources of rhythm dissipated in false junctures and emphases created by adherence to metrical set. A case could be made that 'A Fit of Rime against Rime' is really a critique of poets ignorant of the art of creative punctuation. This case would have to acknowledge, moreover, that the junctures created by punctuation are not always contrastive, and that junctures become significant only in the context of larger and more complex syntactical and thematic levels of a poem's articulated meaning.[25] The fact that lockstep metrical set closes down such articulation is Jonson's real complaint in this poem.[26]

Enjambment as a means of creating juncture in Jonson's poetry can be illustrated by both positive and negative instances. The negative instances include verse samples wherein enjambment directs the reader's attention to emphases that do not seem to take on contrastive significance in their larger poetic context.[27] For instance the 1603 'Ode *Allegorike*' (M6) uncharacteristically employs stanzas of irregular line lengths in conjunction with extended syntactical periods. Such metrical asymmetry flattens out the peaks and valleys of semantic emphasis, just as it encourages the reader to push ever forward the unfolding of the syntax, riding over pauses toward the final closure. Enjambment in this context becomes nothing but a device to hurry the reader round the corner.

Enjambment, like syntactical closure in the middle of a line, always has the effect of deferring metrical closure. Medial closure still leaves the rest of the line to be filled out, while enjambment extends the syntactical group past the line end. And when a half-line created by caesura is itself enjambed with the one following in turn, the interplay between closures deferred and completed becomes intricate. In general, this interplay serves a typical Jonsonian dialectic between connection and disjunction. Enjambment forces continuity where disjunction is expected, becoming the mirror image of deviant punctuation, which creates disjunction where continuity would be expected. By refusing to allow readers to rest – and also by medial caesura causing the reader to rest 'too soon' – Jonson makes sure he remains alert to continual shifts of emphasis, to arguments that are still to unfold, and to arguments that are in fact closed decisively.

In U67, 'An Ode, or Song, by all the Muses. In celebration of her Majestie's birth-day,' where celebratory content is of prime importance, shifts of emphasis serve to highlight interplay of line- and syntax-closure for its own sake: 'Up publike joy, remember / This sixteenth of *November* / Some brave un-common way: / And though the Parish-steeple / Be silent, to the people / Ring thou it Holy-day' (1–6). Rather than being deemphasized by enjambment, rhyme is foregrounded because the irregular metrics of the lines cause the reader to look for an anchorage in the concluding or answering rhymes. What is deferred here is auditory chiming, and the reader is asked to look for nothing more syntagmatically contrastive than the second half of the rhyme.[28]

In other poems Jonson employs enjambment and rhyme to weight simple, relatively general words and phrases, such as 'to live,' 'state,' 'life,' 'true causes,' in E70, 'To William Roe.' In the first four lines these words become moments of stasis around which gather the other key terms of the argument: 'When *Nature* bids vs leaue to liue, 'tis late / Then to begin, my ROE: He makes a state / In life, that can employ it; and takes hold / On the true causes, ere they grow too old.' 'Late' makes all the more urgent discovering how to carve out one's 'state' in life, while 'hold' similarly links with state against becoming 'old,' which recalls 'late.' 'Then,' which opens the second line, takes on an upgraded emphasis to outweigh ''tis late,' already emphasized by metrical set. The paradigmatic contrast this upgrading creates between 'Then' and the implied 'now' both sums up the lines' argument, and is their most obviously contrastive moment. The rhyme words and the enjambed line-endings mark the syntagmatic movement of the argument, while remaining paradigmatic differentials both terms of which the wise person is advised to seize.

Enjambment marks both a continuity and a discontinuity, and does so in relation each to the other. If continuity means the expectation of further information entailed by the foregoing, discontinuity means that the entailment binding these two elements requires scrutiny. The poems in _Eupheme,_ the commemorative sequence addressed to Lady Venetia Digby (U84), contain a high incidence of enjambment, which in turn contributes to the density of their thematic import by directing the reader's attention to such borderline metrical and syntactical phenomena. The first poem, 'The Dedication of her CRADLE,' (U84.1), opens with a typical example. Those heads, like Venetia's, that 'Faire FAME' would crowne, 'ENVY would hold down / With her, in shade, / Of Death, and Darknesse' (3–5) The enjambment linking 'hold down' and 'With her' indicts the allegorized Envy not only of denigrating the deserving, but of trying to reduce the latter to its own level. In attempting to obliterate the gulf between the deserving and themselves, however, the envious unwittingly reaffirm that gulf by the discontinuity (line break) that separates 'With her' from 'hold down.' Enjambment marks the site of a paradox: logical continuity and discontinuity between the two phrases are both affirmed. The reader finds that 'With her,' receiving an upgraded emphasis at the beginning of a new line after a run-on, becomes new information. The enjambment here elicits the discovery that Envy at once denigrates those deserving of Fame by holding them down, and implicitly denigrates itself by holding them 'down / With her.'

The surprises that enjambment prepares can be as coy as those in the poem addressed to Lucy, countess of Bedford, in a copy of _Cynthia's Revels_ (1601). Jonson's muse threatens to disown the play unless 'if any way she do rewarde thee / But with a Kisse, (if thou canst dare it) / of her white Hand; or she can spare it' (8–10). At first, reward seems to be refused; then reward is granted, which is to be a kiss (on the lips?), which turns out not to be the case, but on the hand; which in fact is not a literal kiss after all, but the touch Lucy will bestow with her hand on the book when she accepts it. Enjambment works here to suggest closures of meaning that are always unclosed again with the addition of a further syntactical unit, which in turn retroactively changes the meaning or tone of the preceding.

Enjambment reflects and supports at the level of metrical boundary, that is, line end, a major Jonsonian poetic strategy apparent in larger structures as well. For example in a poem addressed, once again, to the countess of Bedford accompanying a copy of Donne's satires (E94), Jonson defines the perfect reader against successive obstacles that threaten – like line ends – to terminate the poem's progress. 'Rare poemes aske rare friends' (6), but satires read their readers in an unusually selective fashion. Since most of mankind are the subject of satires, 'fewest see' them (8) and very few readers are 'asked' by satires. This is because 'none ere tooke that pleasure in sinnes sense, / But, when they heard it tax'd, tooke more offence' (9–10). Lucy however is among the privileged readers who, though 'liuing where the matter is bred' [among sinful men], 'Dare for these poemes, yet, both aske, and read, / And like them too' (11–13). As usual, Jonson's isolating punctuation discriminates each segment, and raises the possibility that each successive verb (ask – read – like) could potentially be missing. Lucy, however, triumphantly rides to the very end of this disjunctive sequence: that she can ask these poems of the poet indicates that she 'must needfully, though few, / Be of the best: and 'mongst those, best are you' (13–14).

These poems demonstrate that enjambment, like deviant punctuation, creates moments of selection and choice where none would otherwise appear, and force readers to exercise their judgment in recreating these choices. Even in so apparently unproblematic a poem as E89, Jonson's epigram praising the actor Edward Allen, sharp discriminations introduced by unusually placed commas turn a simple complaint about the moderns versus the ancients into a complex dialectic: 'As skilfull ROSCIVS, and graue AESOPE, men, / Yet crown'd with honors, as with riches, then' (3–4). If men are rewarded with honours, what other possibilities are there? Men as distinct from gods? One remembers the deification awarded some Roman emperors, who may or may not have been as worthy of such honours as great Roman actors. But even if honoured now, 'then' great actors were also given wealth. Does this mean that the value of honours given today is diminished by the unwillingness to substantiate it with money as well? Are great actors, who are or may be honoured even as gods, in fact covertly denigrated instead?

Questions of this sort are raised everywhere one reads in Jonson's poetry, and not alone at the level of prosodic practice. As I have suggested, the disruptive effects of enjambment are paralleled by similar disruptions at higher, more complex levels of the poetic discourse, to which juncture and contrastive emphasis become only one, though a significant, contribution. These kinds of parallels can be distinguished into several classes, and exploring these classes will be the concern of the rest of this chapter.

2 Upgraded Coordinates, Disjunctive Sequences, and the Incremental List

Coordinate elements such as *and, or*, and *yet* can when prosodically upgraded serve a variety of contrastive uses. In the cases already examined *and* is made to contrast with an implied *and not*, thereby eliciting recognition that the words so connected are both separated, and united, by acts of discriminating judgment. Jonson's use of such coordinates in other poetic contexts reflects different thematic purposes. One of these is the disjunctive sequence, which is usually a list of items paratactically linked wherein the mere extension of the list calls it into question.

A witty example is E88, 'On English Movnsievr,' whose 'whole body' speaks '*french*, not he.' The result is a catalogue of markers signifying 'French fashion': 'That so much skarfe of *France*, and hat, and fether, / And shooe, and tye, and garter should come hether, / And land on one, whose face durst neuer bee / Toward the sea, farther then halfeway tree?' (1–6). The list of sartorial accessories is laid out metrically so that the pauses marked by the commas reinforce the dominant emphasis on each noun required by the iambic metre. The pauses created by the commas, however, suggest an alternative performance, wherein each *and* receives the dominant emphasis. The continuation of the list, as it proceeds past the line end (hurrying past one possible point of closure) well into the second line, contrasts with, and frustrates, the hopeful expectation of conclusion offered at each pause marked by the successive commas. This frustration is reinforced by another denial, whereby the accreted *ands* refuse with ever-growing insistence the pressure of the paradigmatically contrastive *and nots* that seem at every point about to halt the paratactic march of gewgaws. My own performance favours not only upgraded accent (rise in pitch) for the *ands*, but also a continual increase in stress (loudness) for each succeeding *and* unit as well:

<pre>
      2   1   3   2   4   3
    and hat, and feather, / And shooe, etc.
</pre>

By the time one reaches the second line, the *and not* becomes an implied countertext to the one at hand: [And not a shoe in addition to the feather] '*And* shooe' [And not a tie in addition to the shoe!] '... *and* tye,' and so on.

A similar outrage is generated in a brace of poems, U20 and U21, by similar means. In the first poem we encounter a sequence that looks at every pause as if it had gone as far as it could go, but which yet continues: 'I could forgive her being proud! a whore! / Perjur'd! and painted! if she were no more – , / But she is such, as she might, yet, forestall / The Divell; and be the damning of us all' (U20:21–4). Here coordinates are absent, but not the invitation to place ever-increasing emphasis on each succeeding epithet. Jonson mimics the speaker's incredulity by suggesting a still greater emphasis on the prosodically isolated 'yet,' that is outdone by the emphasis appropriate to 'be the damning of us all.' In the second epigram there is a similar build-up toward a false conclusion: 'there he was, / Proud, false, and trecherous, vindictive, all / That thought can adde, unthankfull, the lay-stall / Of putrid flesh alive! of blood, the sinke! / And so I leave to stirre him, lest he stinke' (U21:6–10). 'All / That thought can adde' seems to mark a closure in a catalogue that is yet topped by adding still further abuse.[29]

A similar violation of expectation created in the syntagmatic dimension coupled with a paradigmatically contrastive countertext occurs in the opening two lines of *A Celebration of Charis* (U2), 'His Excuse for loving':

> Let it not your wonder move,
> Lesse your laughter; that I love.

Here we have pauses of two lengths, the longer one marked by the semicolon in keeping with standard orthographical theory of the time (eg Daines 70–1). The consequent isolation of the clause 'that I love' from the rest of the line allows the dominant emphasis to fall on 'I,' rather than on 'love' as demanded by the metrical set. Accounting for the rest of these lines' carefully calibrated effect is the other pause, marked by both comma and line end, which suspends the reader over two distinct and incongruous possible reactions: what can possibly move both wonder, and still more (in contrast with 'lesse'), laughter? Wonder responds to magnitude and laughter to the absurd, and both join contrastively in the person of Ben himself: as large in his bulk as in his erotic expectations ludicrous. The fact 'that,' despite all, 'I love' stands in syntagmatic contrast with the putatively impossible union of wonder and laughter, and elicits wonder and laughter at these contrasts and unions as well. As in the case of 'The English Movnsievr,' a performance that responds to both the meaning and the phonology that mediates this meaning would conceivably involve an upward gradation of dominant emphases such as:

1		2		3		4
wonder	–	Lesse	–	laughter	–	I

Lists and sequences of this sort exemplify a kind of comic sublime, catalogued rhetorically in the figures of *hyperbole* and *auxesis*. Thomas Wilson describes *hyperbole* as 'mounting aboue the trueth,' and it occurs 'when wee doe set foorth things exceedingly and aboue all mens expectation, meaning only that they are very great' (Wilson 183). The notion that hyperboles are exaggerations that demand and expect deflation is matched, however, by John Hoskins' description of *hyperbole* that has the opposite effect: the naming a reality that is beyond the powers of language to express. It is a figure which 'expresseth a thing in the highest degree of possibility, beyond the truth, and that it descending thence may find the truth: sometimes in flat impossibility, that rather you may conceive the unspeakableness than the untruth of the relation' (Hoskins 29). The disjunctive sequence in Jonson's poetry has a similar effect: the indication that beyond statements already incredible lie statements still yet more so (McCanles 'Rhetoric'). Consequently, coordinates such as *and, or,* and *yet* when given upgraded emphasis may evoke by contrast not merely alternative conjunctions, but the demands and limitations of human reason and sanity.

A good example of the Jonsonian comic sublime is the well-nigh interminable catalogue of affectations in U15, 'An Epistle to a Friend, to perswade him to the Warres.' An excerpt from the middle of this catalogue will illustrate:

> Be at their Visits, see 'hem squemish, sick,
> Ready to cast, at one, whose band sits ill,
> And then, leape mad on a neat Pickardill,
> As if a Brize were gotten i' their tayle;

> And firke, and jerke, and for the Coach-man raile,
> And jealous each of other, yet thinke long
> To be abroad chanting some baudie song,
> And laugh, and measure thighes, then squeake, spring,
> itch,
> Doe all the tricks of a saut Lady Bitch ...   (68–76)[30]

Examples of the disjunctive sequence without benefit of explicit co-ordinates indicate Jonson's concern always to isolate for consideration and question the logical ligatures binding the units in the sequence. In E99, 'To the Same' (Sir Thomas Roe), such a sequence halts the reader's attention at just such points of linkage: 'That thou has kept thy loue, encreast they will, / Better'd thy trust to letters; that thy skill; / Hast taught thy selfe worthy thy pen to tread, / And that to write things worthy to be read' (1–4). The praise itself reflects Roe's consciousness of the distinct stages in the process of his own development, as important it would seem as the capacity to traverse these stages successfully. To understand the praise, however, the reader must understand these stages, which requires recognizing their disjunctive status in relation to one another, and consequently the distinct acts of conscious choice necessary to achieve each one.

3 Semantic Discrimination: Homonymy and Synonymy

Synonymy and homonymy are semantic rather than prosodic phenomena, but as Jonson uses them they work to the same ends as contrastive emphasis: to define the meaning of poetic statements dialectically, so that the reader participates in the acts of judgment and choice, of selection and rejection, that constituted the poem originally. A simple and paradigmatic example of synonymy is named such in E7, 'On the New Hot-Hovse':

> Where lately harbour'd many a famous whore,
>   A purging bill, now fix'd vpon the dore,
> Tells you it is a hot-house: So it ma',
>   And still be a whore-house. Th'are *Synonima*.

The poem documents the unremarkable discovery that a house that treats venereal disease – a 'hot-house' – is also a whore-house. The synonymous equivalence Jonson argues between 'hot-house' and 'whore-house' assumes that 'hot' may refer either to curative baths or to sexual heat. And so this transformation of the place of the cure into the place of the disease is already predicted by the homonymic pun linking the two senses of *hot*.[31] Being semantic mirror images of each other, homonymy and synonymy are related as two sides of the same phenomenon. The pun on *hot* (homonym) makes possible the witty identification of the same meaning (synonym) for both hot-house and whore-house. Theoretically this is a double resource of all words, at least in the context of a Saussurian, structuralist view of language. S. Karcevskij, a member of the Russian Formalists and the Prague Linguistic School, has argued in a notable article that every word is the intersection of two series: a series of different meanings (the same signifier taking on related but different signifieds), and a series of different signifiers related to the same signified: homonymy and synonymy respectively (Karcevskij; W. Steiner; P. Steiner). Karcesckij's argument assumes the Saussurian double articulation of the verbal sign into signifier and signified, and the definition of both within a system of phonic and semantic differences. In such a system both phonic signifier and semantic signified are determined by being the intersection of phonemic and semic elements whose identity is entirely a function of their differences from other similar elements.[32]

Being defined differentially at the levels of signifier and signified (physical word and meaning), the verbal sign implies at once all the other words that could have been used in a particular phrase or sentence to mean (more or less) the same thing – synonymy – and all the other meanings that might have occurred at that point – homonymy (W. Steiner 292). Contrastive emphasis creates moments in the text analogous to homonymy in marking the availability of several differentially defined meanings for the same 'slot' in the poetic text.

The homonymic slide from one meaning to a second in the epigram 'On the New Hot-Hovse' is one example, as is the pun on 'pay' in E12, 'On Lievtenant Shift.' Lieutenant Shift is a fictional representation of the out-of-service (demobbed) soldier, whose lack of funds does not deter his taking the pleasures of the city, for 'God pays'; that is, those whom he cheats by not paying will be rewarded by God in heaven. When the old bawd 'pays' Shift by giving him a pocky whore (22–4), the refrain of 'God pays' turns out to have a sinister second meaning, in that 'paying' also means 'paying home,' wreaking justice on someone.[33] The shiftless lieutenant is blindsided by the unpredicted second meaning of his own excuse: God, Jonson suggests, pays indeed, that is, punishes Shift; and he suggests further that one among many sins for which Shift is paid is just this ignorance of the differential possibilities latent in text of his own confidence game.[34]

The synonymic slide from one signifier to another is in turn made possible by the resources of homonymy. When the same signifier comes to have several meanings, or signifieds (homonymy), that signifier itself becomes one in a group of synonyms standing for these signifieds: different words with the same meaning (synonymy). E117, 'On Groyne,' exemplifies homonymy and synonymy enabling each other:

> GROYNE, come of age, his state sold out of hand
> For 'his whore: GROYNE doth still occupy his land.

By selling all his land for the money he pays his whore, Groin continues to occupy his land. Signifiers have shifted, but not the signified. That is, though Groin has shifted the sign of value from land to whore, the meaning of this sign remains the same: the money that his estate, and now his whore, represent. Consequently, 'state' and 'whore' have literally the same meaning, a synonymy that Jonson reinforces with the homonymic pun on 'occupy' as meaning at once economic and sexual possession.

Both synonymy and homonymy demarcate implied differences, and that is Jonson's point. Groin, like Lieutenant Shift, is victimized by unrecognized continuities and differences in the meaning of his own actions. If the reader can interpret what Groin cannot, this is because the reader, in recognizing the different meanings of 'occupy,' unmasks the supposed parity between *state* and *whore* that turned them, in Groin's case at least, into synonyms. Like contrastive emphasis, the intersection of different signifiers and signifieds leads for Jonson finally to marking discriminations rather than identities of meaning – and equally important, marking the differences between discrimination and identity.[35]

The varied uses of homonymy and synonymy also mark the difference between poems of blame and of praise. The former call attention to ironic identities between apparently distinct meanings, while the latter are concerned with discriminations among apparently identical or similar meanings. If the epideictic mode is shown in this study to commit Jonson to oscillating between homonymy and synonymy as two devices for marking contrastivity, it is apparent that the satirist delights in spying out covert liaisons and the eulogist equally hidden discriminations.

E91, 'To Sir Horace Vere,' for instance, concludes as follows: 'Humanitie, and pietie, which are / As noble in great chiefes, as they are rare. / And best become the valiant man to weare, / Who more should seeke mens reuerence, then feare' (15ff). The distinction between reverence and fear is important to Jonson as one of several paradigms for distinguishing respect for true nobility from the fear created by class oppression and the desire to overawe: 'To Penshvrst' (F2) applies the distinction to relations between country nobility and tenants, the 'Panegyre' to the king's relations with his subjects.

This paradigm is evoked at a distance by a similar distinction drawn at the end of E96, 'To Iohn Donne,' which Jonson sends along with a copy of his *Epigrammes*.[36] Jonson announces that he desires a fit audience though few: 'A man should seeke great glorie, and not broad' (12). The distinction here extends along an axis of opposition separating literal and metaphorical meanings, another mode of discrimination that Jonson found fruitful, and which I discuss later in this chapter. The point of intersection between these apparent synonyms is the semantic marker + *extension*. The upgraded emphasis that 'great' and 'broad' accrue renders them syntagmatically constrastive. Distinction becomes itself a point of new information, and the reader is invited to invent, that is, discover, the markers that distinguish the two terms. Glory may be extensive in space ('broad') but not great in significance or intensity. To understand this, however, is to understand further that naming a reputation 'great' is both to call upon a physical dimension for metaphorical purposes, and to call that physical dimension into question. Thus: 'great glorie' depends upon a metaphorical transference from 'broad' and its synonyms, while the propositional content of the line itself insists on cancelling this transference and emphasizing instead an 'extension' that is wholly immaterial.

Jonson's main ethical concern was just such slippages of meaning: in verbal language, and in the codes that constitute the elaborate social and political signs of nobility and power.[37] Where the collective signifier of noble status – fashionable clothes and manners, inherited titles, coats of arms, genealogies, manor houses – fails to signify the true nobility for which it is culturally encoded, this slippage of signification turns aristocratic establishments into complex homonymic signs that mean more than one thing. While putatively signifying the possession of true nobility, they can be read ironically to signify its absence. In calling for a true assignment of ethical signifieds to political signifiers, Jonson was committed to unmasking such slippage as part of his career's campaign for revising the semiosis of aristocratic status.

The extent of Jonson's concern with such discriminations, its informing even the more evanescent details of his poetic output, will become apparent in the chapters that follow. As a preface to the thematic dimension of Jonson's poetry supported by metrical and semantic contrastivity, I conclude this section with the opening lines of a poem that defines humanist virtue by discriminating the meanings of its own language: F11, 'Epode.'

Jonson defines the humanistic ethic as a potentially unstable compound of ethical and psychological elements, the significance of whose joining is measured by their vulnerability to being driven asunder. The opening four lines summarize this ethic in both its apparent simplicity, and its consequent instability. The first two lines – 'Not to know vice at all, and keep true state / Is vertue, and not *Fate*' (1–2) – allow the *and* in the first line only uncontrastive conjunctive force, and permit the assumption that the line's two halves tautologically imply each other: ignorance of vice and keeping 'true state' would both indifferently specify the generic condition of virtue. However, the upgraded emphasis invited on the *and* contrasts paradigmatically with the implied negative conjunction, and this raises the other contingency, namely that ignorance of vice may be incompatible with keeping true state. The emphasis on the conjunction gains significance by denying this contingency, and asserting instead that true virtue involves specifically maintaining that true state which might otherwise be threatened by ethical ignorance. In other words, the two degrees of emphasis available to the conjunction cause the opening line to have two mutually exclusive meanings: that ignorance of vice may entail either possession of virtue, or its loss.

This interpretation is confirmed retroactively when Jonson explores in lines 3–4 the alternative situation, namely knowledge of vice: 'Next, to that vertue, is to know vice well, / And her blacke spite expell.' Here, the *And* of line 4 defines contrastively once again the other possibility: that to 'know vice well' may also leave one unable to repel it. Taken together, the two couplets raise – by overtly setting aside – the paradox that ignorance as well as knowledge of vice may both entail one's falling victim to it. There being no safe or secure linkage between virtue and either knowledge or ignorance of vice suggests that neither condition can be an ethical shield unless it is understood how both can fail.

The nature of safety and security is in fact one of the central concerns of the whole poem. Virtue's conditions, so transparent to the classical stoicism that identifies it with human freedom as distinct from fate, are in fact highly problematic. The paradox by which vice may result from both ignorance and knowledge is of course unpredictable and unexpected. It calls attention to itself as new information requiring much care to elucidate, and this elucidation is in fact the rest of the poem.

The immediately following lines expand the ways in which knowledge of vice may have the effects of ignorance, 'since no brest is so sure, / Or safe, but shee'll procure / Some way of entrance' (5–7). The watch-fulness Jonson exhorts is rendered both necessary, and problematic, once it is understood that the mind's virtuous fortifications become penetrable through the very confidence in safety such watchfulness creates. The apparently tautological pair 'so sure, / Or safe' reminds us of how surety may work against safety. And 'to watch, and ward' (8) invites us to recognize that watching is not necessarily the same as warding (guarding), and in fact reliance wholly on the 'watch' of conscious virtue may well lead to relaxation of one's guard.

Needful is the alertness of 'wakefull reason, our affections king: / Who (in th'examining) / Will quickly taste the treason, and commit / Close, the close cause of it' (13–16). To commit something 'close' in Renaissance locution means to put it under guard or in prison. It also means something kept disguised and secret. The two meanings flow together in order then to be disjoined to the perspicuous eye of the truly virtuous reader. To commit close is to bring into the castle of the mind and to confine it there ('close' as a noun being also an enclosed section of a castle). Such confining is intended to avoid another kind of intrusion, that by which the vicious object, having been unwittingly allowed within, secretly works to subvert. The emphasis on the first *close*, deriving from the enjambment, is upgraded to match the emphasis given the second *close*, thereby calling attention to an identity as well as a crucial difference between the word's two meanings: 'Thus, by these subtle traines, / Do seuerall passions [still] inuade the minde, / And strike our reason blinde' (28–30).

Later in the poem Jonson similarly distinguishes true and false ways of maintaining marital fidelity. Typically, he proceeds by negatives: excluded are those who are impotent, or who fear discovery because they 'Cannot so safely sinne' (81), who have vowed abstinence, or who are chaste only through fear of punishment. The only true fidelity exists on the part of him who understands Jonson's last line: 'Man may securely sinne, but safely neuer.' The difference between *security* and *safety* here is not merely between the external security of closed doors and the internal safety of the soul guarded against sin. The difference restates once again the complex contrasts of the opening lines: one is never safe as long as one believes that safety and security mean the same thing.

To assume that warding within necessarily constitutes watching without is to repress recognizing that what you 'commit close' within may be your close, that is, secret, sin. Consequently *security* can never with certitude equal *safety* for the sinner, or for the virtuous either.

4   Boundary Crossing and Negative Definition

Homonymy and synonymy are local effects and focus attention on the interaction between two words or phrases whose play of meaning usurps the whole court of play. Syntagmatic contrasts, while being essentially semantic, nevertheless extend the discriminations at issue onto the more complex level of whole poems: complete poetic discourses the argumentative structures of which turn upon several related differentials and weave them into denser patterns of meaning. It is at this level that Jonson's dialectical habits are most clearly displayed.

Sometimes such habits, particularly in the poems from *The Forrest* on, yield textures of meaning characterized by unexpected subtlety. At other times, particularly in the satirical epigrams, such differentials entice the reader's double take, nothing more. In E42, 'On Giles and Ione,' Jonson takes acerbic delight in the concluding lines: 'If, now, with man and wife, to will, and nill / The selfe-same things, a note of concord be: / I know no couple better can agree!' (16–18), because this 'agreement' means their mutual understanding that neither can stand the other. A similar form of coarse amusement is available in E50, 'To Sir Cod,' who is advised to treat his syphilis with something stronger than 'burnt gummes' and 'fumie clysters,' namely arsenic. Since arsenic is also a poison, it would either cure him or kill him, thus in either case making him more 'fit for societie' (3). Unforeseen discriminations of meaning always wait to ambush the unwary: Hornet (E78) uses his wife to draw men to be his own customers:

> Hornet, thou hast thy wife drest, for the stall,
> To draw thee custome: but her selfe gets all.

Names are destiny in Jonson, and the 'horn' lurking in the 'hornet' who waits to sting customers cuckolds him instead.

One difference for Jonson between the ethically insightful and the ethically obtuse is that the first are capable of appropriate choices based on precise discriminations, whereas the latter are condemned to Hobson's choices, where choice becomes double-bind. E38, 'To Person Gviltie,' shows Jonson expanding the one-shot epigrammatic differential into a progressively unfolded skein of self-entanglement. In an earlier epigram (E30) Jonson had informed 'Guiltie' that complaining about satire is unwittingly to betray one's own sins. Evidently Guilty has taken Jonson's advice to heart, since he now seeks to ward off such betrayals by applauding Jonson's satires louder than anyone else: 'You laugh when you are touch'd, and long before / Any man else, you clap your hands, and rore, / And crie good! good!' (3–5). But Jonson here has Guilty coming and going. As the poet points out, at least Guilty's earlier, adverse reaction displayed shame, whereas now even shame has abandoned him. Seeking to co-opt Jonson's game by applauding satirical attacks on himself, Guilty has only succeeded in confirming their accuracy. The irony is that Guilty believes that he, along with the poet, ought to be able to reap the benefits of differential structure, and to avoid one side of an opposition by embracing the other. Instead, Guilty falls victim to the undisclosed synonymies in the text of his own dubious moral identity: opposite reactions end up signifying and disclosing the same guilt.

Nevertheless, as his poetic art matured still further beyond the 'ripest' of his studies, the *Epigrammes* (H&S 8:25), Jonson's poetry exhibited differential structures operating both at the local level marked by contrastive emphasis, and at the level of more extended passages. My analysis of the 'Epode' demonstrates this expansion in one case. This poem is one example in *The Forrest* which shows that this volume represents a major step in this maturation. Another example is F12, 'Epistle: To Elizabeth Covntesse of Rvtland,' the opening lines of which are exemplary:

> Whil'st that, for which, all vertue now is sold,
>   And almost euery vice, almightie gold,
> That which, to boote with hell, is thought worth heauen,
>   And, for it, life, conscience, yea, soules are giuen,
> Toyles, by braue custome, vp and downe the court,
>   To euery squire, or groome, that will report
> Well, or ill, onely, all the following yeere,
>   Iust to the waight their this dayes-presents beare;
> While it makes huishers seruiceable men,
>   And some one apteth to be trusted, then,
> Though neuer after ... (1–11)

This poem was a New Year's gift sent, as the opening lines aver, in lieu of gold. At some points the punctuation opens to the reader's view multiple relations among the words thus isolated. One example is lines 6–7: 'that will report / Well, or ill, onely, all the following yeere.' By isolating 'well,' 'ill,' 'only,' and 'or' Jonson allows the reader to consider how a bribe renders the bribed servant at once pliable in the variety of tales he is willing to tell, and obedient in telling only the one for which he is paid.

An extension of a similar effect to the opposite allegation occurs at lines 10ff: 'And some one apteth to be trusted, then, / Though never after.' The isolating punctuation paces the line and highlights the briber's own dawning recognition of his action's consequences. 'Then' read without the preceding comma merely specifies the bribe's effect: having been bribed, *then* the usher is apt to be trusted. The isolation of 'then,' however, allows it to equivocate in its contrastive function, from *then* vs *previously*, before the bribe, to *then* vs *afterwards*, after the bribe. This semantic spin on 'then' pinpoints the briber's belated discovery that the trust he pays for lasts no longer than the moment the money is delivered.

Other play among the meanings of different words is highlighted by the punctuation of the opening four lines. Without the punctuation that isolates 'for which,' the metrical set and the information focus of line 1 would emphasize 'virtue.' The text as punctuated, however, invites emphasis on 'all' at least as strong as that on 'virtue.' Jonson's intent is revealed in the next line, where 'all vertue' is paired off with 'almost every vice,' the suggestion being that there are some vices that even money can't buy. The morpheme *al-* is repeated a third in time in 'almightie gold,' and the reader is left to conclude that if gold is at the top of this perverse scale of values, then virtue must rank below even vice, since some vices are beyond price, though no virtues are. A similar progression is marked out in line 4, where 'soules' receives a dominant emphasis relative to those on 'life' and 'conscience,' because of the juncture marked by the comma after 'yea.'

In a softer, elegiac mood the poet discriminates subtle shadings of meaning and emotion, as in E45, 'On my First Sonne.' The concluding discrimination between love and liking is the culmination of cognate differences that only gradually emerge as the poem unfolds: 'For whose sake, hence-forth, all his vowes be such, / As what he loues may neuer like too much' (11–12). Gardiner has aptly noted the 'effect of correction, restatement, surprise' characteristic of the poem's progress (*Craftsmanship* 46). She finds such additions particularly telling in the opening lines, where the poet recognizes the impersonal fate which took the seven-year-old boy away from him: 'Farewell, thou child of my right hand, and ioy; / My sinne was too much hope of thee, lou'd boy, / Seuen yeeres tho'wert lent to me, and I thee pay, / Exacted by thy fate, on the iust day' (1–4). Jonson registers his acquiescence in the harsh justice of his 'paying' the boy 'lent' by the fate, and his lamentation for having to do so. The fundamental poles to which the poet's emotions oscillate are the impersonal facts and meanings of the boy's death, and the sense of profound loss that acquiescing in these can never mitigate.

The bitterness of the poet's loss can be partially measured by a bitter parallel with the epigram preceding this one, namely E44, 'On Chvffe, Bancks the Vsvrer's Kinsman':

> CHVFFE, lately rich in name, in chattels, goods,
>   And rich in issue to inherit all
>   Ere blacks were bought for his owne funerall,
> Saw all his race approach the blacker floods:
> He meant they thither should make swift repaire,
> When he made him executor, might be heire.

Chuff disinherits his children, a commodity ('rich in issue') that he apparently is willing to part with, in choosing for his executor his usurer kinsman. Since disinheritance is treated in the poem as tantamount to severing paternal kinship, his children's early death turns out to fulfil in essence his original intention. The contrasts between two fathers' reactions to their children's deaths turn on the identification of child with wealth. Chuff's children are a form of riches, while the poet is required to 'pay' his dead child to the fate, which exacts this payment 'on the iust day' and becomes a usurer like Bancks, Chuff's executor, and finally his heir.[38]

The 'logic' of repayment extends into lines 5–8, where the poet seeks consolation in the equally logical conclusion that early death has saved the young boy from 'worlds, and fleshes rage, / And, if no other miserie, yet age.' This equivocal consolation is introduced by a disorienting connective: 'For why / Will man lament the state he should enuie?' Initially appearing a logical extension of the preceding outburst, the 'For why' statement encompasses at once the evils the boy will escape, and the fact that the father will continue nevertheless to lament. This is because his son's escape from the miseries of age entails his attaining no more age at all. Consequently, the poet would wish to lose 'all father, now,' because being a father condemns him to divided emotions of this sort.

The son is exhorted to 'Rest in soft peace,' in contrast both to the future 'rage' the boy has escaped, and to Jonson's own restless emotion. The concluding distinction between love and like forces the reader to perceive exactly, that is differentially, the nature of Jonson's sorrow for what he has lost. 'Like too much' catches up the second line: 'My sinne was too much hope of thee, lou'd boy,' where Jonson implies that in loving his son he was too possessive, and too unwilling to recognize the just claims of time, or of fate (a justice cited in the opening lines as well). Like the Marschallin in Hofmannsthal's libretto for *Der Rosenkavalier*, Jonson comes to understand that the only proper way to hold anything is loosely, in full recognition of its evanescence:

> Leicht muss man sein,
> mit leichtem Herz und leichten Händen
> halten und nehmen, halten und lassen ...

The last line of the poem, then, yields discriminations amid identities that are never wholly obliterated. Vowing never to like too much what the logic of time will tear away from him, he seeks to sunder love and liking, relegating love to a domain of emotion beyond logic. So much the discriminations between the meanings of apparent synonyms tell us. They also tell us that such discriminations – the attempted compartmentalizing of fact and emotion – are ultimately futile, and to love is always to like too much.

Jonson's capacity to extend the resources of contrastivity beyond the local level by building larger structures out of smaller is illustrated in a later poem, a translation of a fragment of Petronius (U88). Its total removal from the emotions of the lament for his son makes the similarities between the two stand out the more sharply:

> Doing, a filthy pleasure is, and short;
> And done, we straight repent us of the sport:
> Let us not then rush blindly on unto it,
> Like lustfull beasts, that onely know to doe it:
> For lust will languish, and that heat decay.
> But thus, thus, keeping endlesse Holy-day,
> Let us together closely lie, and kisse,
> There is no labour, nor no shame in this;

This hath pleas'd, doth please, and long will please; never
Can this decay, but is beginning ever.

The poem contrasts the brevity of consummated, and the protraction of unconsummated love. The poem argues the Shakespearean insight that the pleasure of appetite is prolonged by refusing its indulgence. The opening couplet mimics the ephemeralness of sexual pleasure and the speaker's 'short' dismissal of it. The heavy caesuras that link 'and short' with 'and done' likewise mimic the brief interval linking act and completion, and mirror the disjunctive sequence exemplified earlier. Closure is repeatedly breached, like each moment of the sexual act which though complete yet yields on the instant to the next, and all in a short space of time.

The rhythm opens up in the next three lines. Lovers who do not understand the truth of the first two lines are 'lustful beasts' and 'rush blindly.' For what the poet advocates is not chastity, but a sexual play that, being more refined, is not self-destructive. Anatomizing the tenses of 'do' discloses lovers 'that onely know to doe it,' and know nothing of succeeding moments. Did they so, they would know also that 'lust will languish, and that heat decay.' 'Thus, thus' suggests the intimacy of the speaker's physically demonstrating what he wants even as he defines it. In contrast with 'and short' of the first line, 'keeping endless Holy-day' defines the meaning of another kind of love-making before the speaker names it. The final isolated foot that ends the next line – 'and kisse' – echoes the 'and short; / And done' of the first two lines, and names alternative pleasures that, because lesser, need never end.

The final couplet revises the war between the tenses, substituting continuity for abrupt segmentations that isolate successive moments: 'This hath pleased, doth please, and long will please.' Such love-making 'never can ... decay,' which delays the rapid slide of 'doing' into 'done' in the opening lines. And something else happens here: 'long will please; never / ...' contains just the hint, before the reader rides over the enjambment, that 'never' modifies 'please.' In that case we have a perfectly poised, Keatsian recognition of the exigencies of such love-making, which are simply that it can never please completely, but also 'never / Can this decay.'

In other cases, not many, we find Jonson exploring contrasts of a less resonant sort in genres and subjects that are more characteristic of other poets. U3, 'The Musicall strife; In a Pastorall Dialogue,' is sufficiently un-Jonsonian to call attention to the poet's conscious imitation of the late Elizabethan polished rusticity found in Marlowe, Sidney, and Drayton, among others (Parfitt [*Complete Poems* 519] cites *England's Helicon*). This poem plays across the traditional chain of being: the two lovers evoke and humanize animals, stones, rivers, woods, while calling down angels to themselves or raising themselves to the angelic state. Jonson schematically exhausts a limited repertoire of possible combinations: First the voices are to 'war,' then they are to 'mix,' then each is to sing alone, then neither, and finally 'Nay, rather both our soules / bee strayn'd / To meet their high desire; / So they in state of Grace retain'd, / May wish us of their Quire' (25ff). By comparison with the poems already discussed, the choices here lack significance, which suggests that while differences make choices inevitable, not all choices make a difference.

Choices similarly explored to similar lack of significance occur in the following poem, U4, 'A Song,' which opens with the line 'Oh doe not wanton with those eyes.' Indeed, the poem exists to tell us that there is nothing the lady can do with her eyes that will not cause the speaker amorous pain. Whether wantoning or shamefast, angry or kind, whether tearful or fearful: all ocular moods become so attractive that differences cease to differentiate.

Several Donnian exercises in paradox follow in U5, U6, and U7, which highlight some interesting parallels and, finally, divergences between the two poets' use of dialectical reasoning. U6, for instance, 'Another [Song Apologetique] In defence of their [women's] Inconstancie,' imitates several poems of Donne, as well as one of his prose paradoxes of the same name. As with Donne, the arguments appear at once rational and outrageous, the application of sober reasoning to justify promiscuity. The implication is that men's sexual freedom possesses a meretricious logic denied women. The central matter is a rational argument favouring a frivolous use of reason. If the argument is allowed, then it comes under the same test, with the result that the lady can call rationality into question, along with logical arguments against female promiscuity. Whether the rational advocacy succeeds or fails, promiscuity remains the winner.[39] Dilemma is also the mode of U7, 'A Nymphs Passion.' She must choose between telling the nymphs of her love and fearing that 'they'd love him too' (4), and keeping silent. To elicit their envy she decides to tell; but if she tells and he forsakes her the other nymphs will pity and scorn her. She suspects that others know of him and love him already; yet he seems to her faithful.

For Jonson choice is not dilemmatic, where for Donne it often is, since Donne is very much interested, as Jonson is not, in the crises of thought where two mutually exclusive, yet irresistible, arguments meet head on (McCanles *Dialectical* 57–74). For Jonson choice is in the end unequivocal enough; its problems lie rather in clarifying what choices are actually at issue, that is, in perceiving the significance of what is said in negative terms, by contrast with what is not.

The differences are even more apparent in another Donne imitation, one of the 'Elegies,' U18. This poem illustrates how well Jonson understood Donne's method of stringing out the thought of a poem. Thus: the lady's beauty elicits fear as well as love, and the lover suspects that he fears rather a creation of his own thoughts. (The comparison to the stick that appears bent in water is a tolerably Donnian touch.) Fear requires a boldness that depends equivocally on the blind errors of love and fortune ('you / Can have no way but falsehood to be true?' Donne asks in 'Womans Constancy' [Donne *Elegies*, Gardner ed]). If Donne uses the principle of noncontradiction against itself, so that the act of choosing one alternative always risks choosing the other as well, Jonson's Donne imitations exploit the format of this dialectic without evoking its metatextual resonances.

Jonson did not lack interest in Horace, whom he portrayed as an alter ego in *Poetaster*, and whose *Ars Poetica*, which he translated, became a major model for his own life. He was obviously intrigued with Horace's poetry, since selections from him constitute the largest number of poems by a single author among the handful that Jonson noted as translations. No one pretends that Jonson translated Horace with much degree of artistic success, and aesthetically the two translations of the *Ars Poetica* are monuments to little save the poet's perseverance. Nevertheless, these *essais* are instructive in the same way as Jonson's Donne imitations: they point out by deflection the true line of Jonson's poetic wit, and illustrate Jonson's continuing attempts to refine that wit by exercising it in styles that for him generally resisted success.

The translation of the ninth ode from book III, the 'Dialogue of Horace, and Lydia' (U87), exemplifies how little Jonson could make of Horace's discriminations while sedulously pursuing his own. The pathos of this poem depends on the reader's savouring its emotional ambiguities. Both lovers recall their former love for each other, affirm commitment to their present lovers, and acknowledge the possibility of renewed love in some hypothetical future. The lovers cannot move either away from or toward each other: Horace will love Lydia if Lydia will love Horace, and vice versa.

Hor. But, say old Love returne should make,
    And us dis-joyn'd force to her brazen yoke,
    That I bright *Chloe* off should shake;
    And to left-*Lydia*, now the gate stood ope.
Lyd. Though he be fairer then a Starre;
    Thou lighter then the barke of any tree,
    And then rough *Adria*, angrier, farre;
    Yet would I wish to love, live, die with thee. (17–24)

If they love each other, then they are like each other; and if they are like each other, then part of this likeness lies in their both having other lovers. The tenuous balance between the two speakers is the poise between two opposing attractions: the pull of present love against that of a past – and possibly future – love. Neither lover yields and each is held in this tensive moment of stasis by the stasis of the other, which is why Horace uses the dialogue form.

It is possible to read Jonson's translation and extract the core of the poem's poignancy, but one has to labour at it. Leaving aside the awkward lines, such as lines 2, 6, and 18 – partially redeemed by a final line not unworthy of Horace's 'tecum vivere amem, tecum obeam lubens' (Horace 82) – the main problem is that one can read Jonson's version and miss what is going on. Lydia says to Horace exactly what Horace says to her, a mirror-imaging that is highlighted by Lydia's repeating phrases and syntactical patterns in Horace's first two stanzas:

> [Horace:]
> me nunc Thressa Chloe regit,
>   dulcis docta modos et citharae sciens,
> pro qua non metuam mori,
>   si parcent animae fata superstiti.
> [Lydia:]
> 'me torret face mutua
>   Thurini Calais filius Ornyti,
> pro quo bis patiar mori,
>   si parcent puero fata superstiti.' (5–12)

Jonson's insistence on a literal, almost line-by-line translation does not, however, extend to reproducing this striking feature of the original. Horace's suggestion that Lydia mimics – even mocks – Horace by echoing him is consequently almost wholly lost in Jonson's version.

One has the feeling that Jonson was not oblivious to the keen points of emotional stress in the poem; rather, the scan of his instruments for defining the complexities of difference simply did not take them in. The present statement is defined by other possible but absent statements: such is the typical Jonsonian process. In Horace's practice, however, the movement is often in just the opposite direction: the gradual unfolding of an often casual and unequivocal assertion toward a moment of logical or emotional complexity. Horace's poetry is full of such local paradoxes (Commager 101–5), and, being in this like Donne, Horace is not like Jonson.

5   The Literal and the Metaphorical

Jonson's fascination with metaphor and its capacity for literalizations comic and perverse links these with the other boundary crossings I have explored in this chapter. In general, such literalizations are poetic solecisms that violate and focus attention on the frontiers between the literal and the metaphorical. They are analogues of homonymic and synonymic slides, and demarcate from yet another perspective precise discriminations of meaning.

From the beginning to the end of his playwright's career Jonson delighted in characters who literalized the metaphors constituting their names. The first version of *Every Man in His Humor* has Cob ('herring'), who laments the necessity imposed by fasting days of eating fish:

A fasting day no sooner comes, but my lineage goes to racke, poore Cobbes they smoake for it, they melt in passion, and your maids too know this, and yet would haue me turne *Hannibal* [cannibal], and eat my own fish & blood: my princely couze [*pulls out a red herring*], feare nothing; I have not the heart to devour you ... (3.1.184–9; H&S 3:237–8)

The double-takes and rapid recalculations demanded by this passage are paradigmatic of this sort of thing wherever it occurs in Jonson. Cob is a human being bearing the name of a fish, a walking homonym that focuses initial attention on the two diverse references of the word itself. Difference is then confounded when Cob insists that he is indeed a member of the herring family, but neither so much a member that he can't eat a herring for dinner, nor so removed that eating a herring for dinner will not constitute cannibalism. This play across the gap separating not only man from fish, but identity from difference, dissolves in farce when Cob pulls a fish out of his pocket and addresses it as a royal relative.

The different meanings of Cob's name are sustained throughout the passage as the constants which make the comic pretence to obliterate these differences possible. It is just this kind of category violation that allegory also invites, where allegorical characters literalize the details of their own metaphoricity. In *The Staple of News*, for instance, one of the women in the entourage of the allegorical Pecunia is soft and will stick to your lips if you kiss her, because her name is Wax (2.5.73–5; Wilkes 4:293).

In another instance, the character Argurion in *Cynthia's Revels*, the stream of *double entendres* divides into parallel channels of meanings that resonate with each other:

> *Cupid*: ... A nymph of a most wandering and giddy disposition, humorous as the air, she'll run from gallant to gallant, as they sit at primero in the presence, most strangely, and seldom stays with any ... She takes special pleasure in a close obscure lodging, and, for that cause, visits the city so often, where she has many secret true-concealing favourites. When she comes abroad, she's more loose and scattering than dust, and will fly from place to place, as she were wrapped with a whirlwind. (2.3.145–54; Wilkes 2:31–2)

This passage defines by contrast exactly where the solecisms in the Cob and Wax passages lie: in meanings that cannot be transported without absurdity across the frontier dividing the literal from the metaphorical. With Argurion, however, Jonson invites us to marvel not only at the droll transgressions such demarcations make possible, but also at the wit which allows two different meanings for the same words to sit uncannily at ease on both sides of these demarcations. The flightiness of the nymph herself can without wrenching become the evanescence of money, and finally both meanings fuse at the point where social and monetary fickleness meet and feed each other.

For this reader, such easy recuperations hold less interest than the teasing undecidabilities of Cob and Wax, or Vulcan in U43, 'An Execration upon Vulcan.' Jonson here simultaneously addresses him as a god and demythologizes him as literal fire. Much of the poem's humour depends on attributing to one the characteristics of the other: fire is given human motivations, while a human figure is thrust into lanterns and forges. A similarly enticing loop binding two frames of meaning occurs in E133, 'On the Famovs Voyage,' where the literal/metaphorical differential circulates, transforming literal into metaphorical and vice versa. The preface to the poem says that whatever ancient poets feigned about visitations to Hell by Hercules, Theseus, Opheus, and Ulysses is to be found literally in contemporary London. The imagery of Hell is appropriate to the movement of sewage through the Fleet Ditch, for if Hell possesses any specific details they derive from man-made places of foulness, which in turn can be appropriately troped by being compared to Hell itself: Hell tropes London and London tropes Hell. The mock-heroic dimension, in which Fleet Ditch appears diminished by comparison to the Hades of the epic poets, becomes exemplary of the this-world origin of Hell, in which case the opposition between heroic and mock-heroic disappears, reinscribed as displaced mimesis or replication.[40]

Jonson distrusts metaphor and conducts an unrelenting campaign to demystify it by deliberately violating its rules. Thus *The Alchemist* employs alchemy as a metaphor for human fantasy and desire, which becomes comical and reprehensible the moment the gulls believe they can realize these fantasies literally in the real world (Kernan 174, 184).

The politics of meaning, soon to break out in open quarrel between Jonson and Inigo Jones, is incipiently present in the printed texts of the early masques, such as *The Masque of Blackness* and of *Beauty, Hymenaei*, and *The Masque of Queens*. What Jones presented on stage, as Jonson was increasingly to perceive, were costumes and stage sets that literalized metaphorical icon and symbol in palpably physical and nonverbal form. What they 'meant' was up to the poet to clarify by unmetaphoring iconographical representations, which then pointed past themselves to the immaterial literal meaning rendered in the poet's words. Jonson enforces this recuperation in scrupulous accounts of the sources and meanings of these iconographical figures. So for instance in the text of *The Masque of Queens*:

> Here, the Throne wherein they sate, being *Machina versatilis*, sodaynely chang'd; and in the Place of it appeard *Fama bona*, as she is describ'd, in Iconolog. di Cesare Ripa. attir'd in white, with white Wings, hauing a collar of Gold, about her neck, and a heart hanging at it; which *Orus Apollo* in his *Hieroglyp.* interprets the note of good fame.   (H&S 7:305)

In the world of the printed text, where the poet held sway, this vector of interpretation could be preserved, and Jonson sedulously explains every jot and tittle of costume and action to ensure that this remained the case. For the royal and aristocratic audiences, however, such did not remain the case, to Jonson's chagrin and ultimate eclipse.

In place of literalized metaphor Jonson offers unmetaphored metaphor, deliberately encouraging metaphor's capacity to play itself out at absurd, self-demystifying extremes.[41] In such instances, violations of the rules of metaphor function analogously to the violation of normal phrase rhythm: both momentarily disrupt the orderly flow of meaning in the interest of marking necessary discriminations. In another example taken from the masques, Robin Goodfellow in *Love Restored* complains:

> 'Tis that Imposter PLVTVS, the god of *money*, who ha's stolne
> LOVE'S ensignes; and in his belyed figure, raignes i' the world, mak-
> ing friendships, contracts, mariages, and almost religion; begetting,
> breeding, and holding the neerest respects of mankind; and vsurp-
> ing all those offices in this Age of gold, which LOVE himselfe per-
> form'd in the golden age.   (H&S 7:382)

The distinction between the age of gold and the golden age is clearly between two value systems, one pecuniary and the other ethical.[42] Less clear but more interesting is Jonson's highlighting the dialectics among several different relations between literal and metaphoric gold. The 'age of gold' is called such by metaphorical extension of literal gold's great material value, a metaphor inviting literalization as 'an era of high human virtue.' Meanwhile, the literal gold at the base of this metaphor generates a second, and opposed, metaphorical meaning, which is 'an era of pecuniary rapacity.' Jonson, in other words, uses the first transference of meaning to throw into relief by contrast a second which inverts it. The play of meaning is similar to the homonymic and synonymic slides discussed in section 3, such as the differences in meaning between *safe* and *secure* in the 'Epode' (F11). When the distinction is not between different meanings as such, but between homonyms within a metaphorical transference of meaning, something more complicated happens. And this is a transference where the literal meaning of *gold* both supports and undercuts its own metaphorical meaning.[43]

The goal is, as always in Jonson's dialectical practice, to discriminate different meanings within apparent identities and equivalences. And Jonson sees such discriminations particularly necessary in those cases where men and women victimize themselves with metaphors for their heart's desires, having forgotten or effaced their metaphoricity. Jonson uses the comic, perverse extremes to which literalized metaphor may extend to call by contrast for a return to clear distinctions between fantasy and reality, between image and idea, and between meaning and meaning.

A return to some simpler examples, this time wholly from the non-dramatic poetry, will help to clarify. In E31, 'On Banck the Vsvrer,' 'travail' literally means locomotion as well as labour by metaphorical extension: 'BANCK feels no lameness of his knottie gout, / His monyes trauaile for him, in and out: / And though the soundest legs goe euery day, / He toyles to be at hell, as soone as they.' Banck compensates for the gout indigenous to usurers by having his money travel for him, and the poet asserts that the travail of Banck's money will bring him just as fast to hell as would his own legs. The pun on *travel*, which marks two apparently different meanings, turns out to be no pun at all: labour and locomotion fuse into a single form of toil, the final end of which is damnation, and the jolt of the epigram lies in discovering this equivalence.

When such wit is not used for comic ends it may yield pathos. Jonson concludes F1, 'Why I write not of Love,' with the line 'When *Loue* is fled, and I grow old' (12). The flight of love is literalized in the wings of Cupid, which bear him away from the poet's attempts 'to binde him, in my verse' (2). Because 'Into my ri'mes' Cupid 'could ne're be got,' the poet's 'numbers are so cold' (9, 11). Jonson moves between literalizing the metaphor – love = Cupid = a boy with actual wings – and unmetaphoring this metaphor – Cupid = boy who flies away = loss of erotic activity. Significantly, *Cupid* is absent from the poem, his place taken by the semantically polyvalent '*Loue*.' When at the end '*Loue* is fled' Jonson has already played through, and against, a literal attempt to fetter him/it, and the poet's loneliness is finally credited to the unsatisfactory explanation that Venus' son wished to escape the fate of his mother caught in the net with Mars: an explanation that does not explain what cannot or perhaps ought not be explained.[44]

Finally, literalizing metaphor serves more serious purposes in Jonson's poetry, and these have to do with issues I shall expand upon in later chapters: the complex affiliation between the outward, visible signs that constitute Inigo Jones' mythic, and James I's real world of aristocratic and monarchal status, power and privilege; and the inner meanings, necessarily immaterial and verbal, that ground whatever signification these signs may justifiably claim. I shall close this section with a poem that points toward such larger issues, U24, 'The mind of the Frontispice to a Booke.' The book is Sir Walter Ralegh's *History of the World*, and Jonson's poem is part of the work's prefatory commendations.

As in the masques, the visual element in the frontispiece is already verbal in inspiration, being a complex emblem including six human figures (one a skeleton: 'Mors') with Latin titles assigned to them. In the centre of the picture 'The Mistresse of Mans life, grave Historie' (2) is shown 'Raising the World to good or evill fame' (3), who are represented by two figures facing each other and labelled 'Fama Bona' and 'Fama Mala' respectively. At the top of the picture, presiding over the round globe, is an open eye, marked 'Providentia.' The purpose of history, set by a 'Wise Providence' (5), is 'that nor the good / Might be defrauded, nor the great secur'd, / But both might know their wayes were understood.' (7). Both are illumined by two figures: 'the beamie hand / Of Truth' (9–10) 'guided by Experience, whose straite wand / Doth mete, whose lyne doth sound the depth of things.' (11–12). The globe of the world is supported as well by four pillers, whose Latin titles Jonson translates to conclude the poem: 'Times witnesse, herald of Antiquite, / The light of Truth, and life of Memorie' (17–18).

There would seem to be no question that for Jonson the verbal is the privileged code, in which alone can be articulated the truth of visual signs. In his poems on Inigo Jones and on visual signs in general, including the collective signs of aristocratic status, Jonson emphasizes the necessity of the verbal text to make these signs intelligible and even visible ('speake that I may see thee,' *Discoveries* [H&S 8:625]). Visual signs in all of these cases are meaningless until articulated in the verbal texts demarcating the differentials that make meaning possible.

The temple entitled 'The History of the World' is upheld by four columns labelled in the picture 'Testis Temporum,' 'Nuncia Vetustatis,' 'Lux Veritatis,' and 'Vita Memoriae.' When Jonson's poem unmetaphors the literalized metaphors in the emblem, we discover that the emblem has only rendered spatially the fact that History requires the 'support' of verbal testimony and 'witness' that the poem has been enacting all along. The emblem presents encoded in spatial juxtaposition the syntagmatic and semantic elements of meaning rendered in the poetic discourse itself. Thus the visual derives from the verbal and is in turn dependent on the verbal to assign its meaning. Jonson's point here, as in other statements about all visual signs of human meaning, is that they always and ever encode, however covertly, verbal texts, and to make them independent of these is to make them nonsensical.

The resources of contrastivity that I have explored in this chapter are the instruments the poet employs to make such discriminations as these. At the phonological level of juncture and emphasis, at the semantic level of synonym, homonym, and metaphor, Jonson calls upon the reader not merely 'to reade' well but 'to vnderstand.' Understanding for Jonson encompasses a complex process of discrimination, judgment, and choice, in which the linguistic features of his texts evoke, support, and are in turn validated by, the fundamental ethical identity of poet and his reader. The act of discrimination appears as the hallmark of Jonson's life and career, and is therefore registered at every level of his writing, from the lowly comma and semicolon up to the large discriminations between reality and appearance, human power and weakness, ethical respectability and depravity, and the true and false public signs of these, which collectively constitute the major concerns of all of his writings. To understand these things in Jonson's poetry is indeed to read it well.

CHAPTER TWO

Jonson and 'Vera Nobilitas'

1 History and Structure of the 'Vera Nobilitas' Argument

An early vector of Jonson's literary career appears near the beginning of the first play he was willing to acknowledge by publication, *Every Man in His Humour*. In its first version, Lorenzo Senior lectures his nephew Stephano on the emptiness of pretence to self-importance based on gentle birth. Stephano is advised: 'Let not your cariage and behauiour taste / Of affectation, lest while you pretend / To make a blaze of gentrie to the world / A little puffe of scorne extinguish it' (1.1.68–71; H&S 3:199). He is told that he should 'Stand not so much on your gentility' but rather 'entertain a perfect real substance.' Stephano of course ignores this advice and mindlessly pursues whoever appears able to teach him the catch-phrases and gestural tics of fashion to fill out the 'substance' of gentility Stephano's snobbery discloses him aware of lacking. In this earlier version of the play, Stephano's snobbery about his gentle birth is subordinated to his display of general frivolity, making him the perfect target of the little puff of scorn that Lorenzo warns him of.

In the second version, with which Jonson opens the 1616 Folio of his *Workes*, the earlier Stephano's snobbery is filled out, and becomes the mark against which both Jonson's and Edward Knowell's shafts are aimed. This shift in Jonson's design is highlighted by an addition to Edward Knowell Senior's expostulation with Stephen: 'Nor stand so much on your gentility, / Which is an airy and mere borrowed thing, / From dead men's dust and bones; and none of yours / Except you make or hold it' (1.i.80–3; Wilkes 1:186). The senior Knowell dips briefly into a long tradition of statements about the foundions of true gentility, to inform him that gentility cannot be inherited from the dead, but can only be achieved by one's own labours and self-discipline. It is a subject that Jonson was never to cease exploring, and we have here probably its first appearance in his *oeuvre*.[1]

The tradition old Knowell alludes to extends back to fifth-century Athens, and develops through Pindar and Theognis to Aristotle and Isocrates, through Sallust, Cicero, Horace, Seneca, Pliny the Younger, and Juvenal to Claudian in Latin literature, to be picked up by Boethius and transmitted to Dante, the writers of the *Roman de la Rose*, Chaucer, and finally to full development and flowering among Italian and English humanists of the Renaissance.[2] Treated in classical Greek writing under the name *areté*, in Latin literature as *virtus*, and by Chaucer called *gentillesse*, this tradition is summarized in the writings of fifteenth-century Florentine humanists under the phrase *vera nobilitas* (Skinner 1:236 and passim). This phrase names a coherent yet historically shifting and evolving set of arguments that concern the true foundations of aristocratic status, which Renaissance humanism derived mainly from classical sources and reframed to serve its own educational agenda. There is little that Jonson says on the subject that does not betray a similar indebtedness, and indeed because he appears to be repeating commonplaces his concern with vera nobilitas has passed with little comment in the literature on Jonson's works.[3] The reasons for this neglect are important for understanding the concept itself, its history, and its surprising endurance through Western writing up to the Renaissance.[4]

The vera nobilitas argument lies at or near the centre of most subjects and themes Jonson treats in his nondramatic poetry. He foreshadows this treatment when he dedicates the *Epigrammes* to an aristocratic patron, William Herbert, earl of Pembroke: 'My Lord. While you cannot change your merit, I dare not change your title: It was that made it, and not I' (25). Pembroke's title, in the words of the epigram 'To Sir William Iephson' (E116), was 'made' by his merit, 'not entayl'd on title,' because '*Nature* no such difference had imprest / In men, but euery brauest was the best: / That bloud not mindes, but mindes did bloud adorne: / And to liue great, was better, then great borne' (9–12). The oppositions and equivalences in this epigram are typical of the vera nobilitas tradition in general. Noble titles derive from merit, not the other way round – or at least that is the way the case should be, which is why Jonson praises Sir William for reversing the usually reversed priority. The distinction between noble 'bloud' and 'minde' makes the latter a synecdoche for intellectual cultivation, and discloses Jonson's humanist bias. Where classical Greek and Roman definitions of vera nobilitas emphasize acts of remarkable statesmanship or valour performed in the public domain, Renaissance humanism bent the classical emphasis toward the attainments of humanist scholarship as the true justification of aristocratic privilege.

The second distinction in this epigram sets high birth against living greatly. This antithesis has clearer classical antecedents, and declares that each scion of a noble family retains that nobility not by inheriting it but by recreating it anew. Noble birth contributes nothing to true 'greatness,' that is, noble status, and is consequently redundant. No one says this in Jonson's time or before. In fact, Jonson as well as other Renaissance humanists make just the opposite point: the desirable norm is an established aristocracy composed of individuals who have in addition achieved vera nobilitas by their own labours.

However, writing during the years following Jonson's death, Blaise Pascal in a brief treatise entitled 'On the Condition of the Great' marked the end of the vera nobilitas argument as it had developed from fifth-century Greece to Jonson's own time. When Pascal says that 'there are in the world two kinds of greatness: for there is greatness of institution, and natural greatness' (380), he is merely repeating the distinction historically fundamental to the vera nobilitas argument. Nevertheless, Pascal breaks decisively with its history when he concludes that these two kinds of greatness have nothing to do with each other. For Pascal aristocratic status depends on an external political structure, and this status may exist independent of the inner virtues that make natural greatness. He acknowledges to his noble addressee that he owes 'the ceremonies that are merited by your quality of duke ... But if you were a duke without being a gentleman, I should still do you justice; for in rendering you the external homage which the order of men has attached to your birth, I should not fail to have for you the internal contempt that would be merited by your baseness of mind' (381).

Pascal's treatise closes the traditional debate on true nobility by relegating 'greatness of institution' and 'natural greatness' to dividend and distinguished worlds. In doing so he relinquishes the attempt laboured intensively by those before him (including Jonson) to construct a political and social semiotic in which the outer signifier of public honour designates accurately an inner signified of personal virtue and achievement.[5] Instead, he no more believes that those who possess noble privileges must develop capacities to exercise these responsibly than he believes those possessed of natural greatness should need or expect public honour through noble status commensurate with that greatness.

Pascal foreshadows the eighteenth century's more radical assault on title and privilege. Tom Paine's branding 'pompous titles bestowed on unworthy men' an 'absurdity' at which 'Virtue is inflamed' and which 'sober reason calls ... nonsense' (Paine 409) has little to do with vera nobilitas arguments advanced up through the Renaissance. The 'meritocracy' that dominates twentieth-century thinking has rendered so commonplace the evaluation of men and women for their personal accomplishments that it is difficult for modern scholars to comprehend the powerful political, ideological, and personal urgencies that prolonged the vera nobilitas debate for two millennia. In this latter-day context its insistent repetition in earlier times has lent it an aura of triteness so pale as to make it practically invisible.[6] We have, to be sure, the illuminating studies of Werner Jaeger, Ruth Kelso, Fritz Caspari, Curtis Watson Brown, John Major (on Sir Thomas Elyot), Quentin Skinner, and Lauro Martines, in which the history of vera nobilitas is thoroughly explored, and my own work is much indebted to theirs. These works collectively establish vera nobilitas as a commonplace from the dawn of Western civilization (and as such duly noted by E.R. Curtius [179–80] whose time never decisively arrived for the simple reason that it was never absent from the scene.

Contrary to one myth about the vera nobilitas argument, it is democratic or egalitarian in neither idea nor intent, nor is it consciously subversive of aristocratic establishments. I say 'consciously,' because the concept of vera nobilitas was intrinsically subversive, and its endless repetition never made it less so. The vera nobilitas argument both supports and subverts aristocratic establishments, and this ambiguity generated a indigenous core of contradictions among the positions historically constituting the argument itself. It was just these fissures within the ideology of aristocratic establishments that the concept of vera nobilitas was used to unmask, and in the process it replicated them as well. As a consequence the vera nobilitas argument displays an underlying coherence among notions linked to each other as corollaries and yet paradoxically inconsistent with one another, a coherence which is more dialectical than univocal or deductive. Jonson's poetry rendered an unparalleled articulation of the argument's explosive instability, and discussion of it must begin by examining its capacity for self-subversion as Jonson himself received it from his sources.

A survey of the vera nobilitas argument yields three distinct oppositional or differential formats within which it could be and was historically advanced:

(A) Inherited status versus personal achievement.
(B) Outer signs of status versus inner virtue.
(C) Talent versus education.

Differentials (A) and (B) summarize the two conceptions of true nobility identifiable as the Greek and Roman viewpoints respectively. Differential (C) could serve to generate arguments in favour of aristocracies either of birth or of merit, as it did for the poet Pindar and for the fourth-century Sophists.

The first two oppositions in turn can be opened out into a four-proposition matrix that makes explicit the minimum essential positions on the basis of which the vera nobilitas argument was constructed between classical times and the end of the Renaissance:

(1) Aristocrats possess true nobility.
(2) Aristocrats ought to possess true nobility.
(3) Those who possess true nobility ought to be aristocrats.
(4) Those who possess true nobility are aristocrats.

Propositions (1) and (2) state the Greek notion that those who are aristocrats should possess true nobility because the latter is necessary for political responsibility. The second two propositions (3 and 4) assert the Roman position that those who possess true nobility should receive aristocratic status as a just reward for personal achievement.

Possession of *areté* for the Greeks was a concomitant of political responsibility, and could mean several things. The *areté* of the Homeric hero consisted of pride in military exploits (Jaeger 1:5), but it could also mean 'intellectual sovereignty' (8). The point for Jaeger, and for us, is that *aristos* during the Homeric age was usually employed in the plural to denote the nobility. Jaeger argues in addition, however, that possession of *areté* which places one among the *aristoi* must be continually renewed with each generation: it is in short the product of education (21).[7] When, during the ascendancy of the city states in the fifth century, aristocratic *areté* comes to mean the virtue of every citizen who understands the laws of the city and the necessity for obeying them (106), *areté* can no long be reserved for members of aristocratic families. On the contrary, it is something that can be taught and learned. The symmetrical alignment of personal capacity and public power was based on the unexceptionable assumption, made explicit by Sophists and followers of Plato alike, that the offices of leadership would most satisfactorily be discharged by those most able to do so. The Isocratean agenda of the education of princes thus logically extended the originary demand that the *aristoi* consist only of those possessed of *areté*.

The assertion (1) that 'aristocrats possess true nobility' sums up the position of the Homeric age idealized nostalgically by Theognis and Pindar.[8] It also states the originary myth which the vera nobilities argument always takes as normative. Cicero in *De officiis* (93) cites Herodotus for the notion that the Medes first appointed kings on the basis of personal virtues, and G.B. Nenna in his *Nennio, or a Treatise of Nobility* (the title of the English translation published in 1595 of the 1542 original) likewise draws 'the register of noblemen' from those 'that were good, the most wise, the most prudent, the most iust, and of most vnderstanding' (Aa1v).[9] John Selden's *Titles of Honor* (1614), to which Jonson contributed a dedicatory poem containing a major statement of his own position on true nobility, says that the 'Dignities [aristocracies and monarchies] were so made, that the first deserving, and his begotten heires, such only as were deserving, should enjoy it' (B4v).

The vera nobilitas argument always assumes this originary grounding of noble status on personal ability and achievement, and any justification of aristocratic privilege will argue that it is founded on true, that is, inner nobility. It is against such a norm that the vera nobilitas argument measures such deviations when it distinguishes true nobility from 'false' nobility (the 'gentle ungentle' of the anonymous sixteenth-century *Institucion of a Gentleman*; Caspari 150). By contrast, the moment it became possible for Pascal to argue in the seventeenth century that noble status need no longer signal true nobility, the complex tensions internal to the vera nobilitas argument from the Greeks down to his time are dissolved, and 'true nobility' as a central issue of debate ceased to exist. All that remained were the inevitable evolution of an ideology of merit, and the political and social revolutions necessary to implement that ideology.

The second proposition – 'Aristocrats ought to possess true nobility' – contains an equivocation. On the one hand, the negative implied by 'ought' means merely that those born into inherited positions of power should be trained in the virtues that allow them to confront these responsibly. This is Isocrates' position and the position of the *de regimine principum* genre generally. As Jaeger points out, the Sophists' 'aim was to transcend the aristocratic principle of privileged education, which made it impossible for anyone to acquire *areté* unless he already possessed it by inheritance from his divine ancestors' (1:287). The Sophists displaced 'aristocracy of race' by an 'aristocracy of intellect' (289), a significant move, because it led to identifying teaching ethical virtue with teaching knowledge (290–2).

The Sophists initiate the philosophical and political splits which the vera nobilitas argument builds on and seeks to heal. With personal achievement (read: education in *areté*) separated from inherited status, talent for such achievement is no longer the privileged possession of a noble class but is distributed to human rationality in general. Plato in *The Republic* returned to the Pindaric position to the extent of founding leadership on breeding,[10] and this great *locus classicus* in the history of education in the West is finally less significant for the vera nobilitas argument than the agenda of the 'education of princes' developed by Plato's great antagonist Isocrates.[11] Isocrates' fusion of the Pindaric encomium with the Sophists' educational program directed to ruling princes (Jaeger 3:33–7) provides Jonson's poetry of praise its earliest prototype.

On the other hand, the 'ought' in the assertion that 'aristocrats ought to possess true nobility' suggests that membership in the *aristoi* was by no means a sign that one possessed *areté*, and it discloses the subversive implications in the Isocratean teacher's claim to educate kings in the practices of kingship. In the earliest example of the *de regimine principum* genre, Isocrates advises the young ruler Nicocles that education is necessary if a king is to become worthy of his office and responsibilities.[12] Such advice implies that kings, being not born but made, may very well be the worse for not being made well. The teacher who can teach kingship has put himself, as Jaeger says, 'on a higher plane than the monarch himself,' and this because he represents 'a higher order of things, which deserves respect simply because of its moral truth' (3:86). By extension, Jonson's addresses to royalty and nobility exhibit the diplomacy of a man who realizes that any advice recommending the development of vera nobilitas implies its lack.

This reinterpretation of the split between outer status and inner true nobility, implicit in the Greek formulation, was historically realized during the tumultuous climax of Roman conflicts between patricians and plebeians in the first century BC, and gave rise to the position summed up in proposition (3), which argues that only those who possess true nobility should be awarded aristocratic status. Where the Greek concept rests aristocratic establishments on the virtues that make for political responsibility, the later Roman version concerns the semiotic dimension of noble status as a signifier of inner virtue. The first perspective envisions status as a means of government, the second status as a form of just reward for achieved merit.

The argument that 'those who possess true nobility ought to be aristocrats' receives its inaugural statement with unrestrained acerbity in the speech Sallust writes for Marius in *The Jugurthine Wars*. Having been elected consul, Marius delivers an extended oration that makes his own case representative of the larger ideological conflicts between plebeians and patricians. Marius contrasts his self-reliance with those who 'rely for protection on their ancient lineage, the resources of their relatives and marriage connexions, and their numerous dependants' (117).[13] Unlike those 'who have merely assumed a mask of virtue in order to procure advancement,' he does not need such a mask, having 'spent all my life in honourable pursuits.' Marius leaps easily to larger ideological issues to back up his argument. Insisting 'that all men are partakers of one and the same nature, and that manly virtue is the only true nobility' (118), Marius attacks patricians who scorn self-made men, but draw their own aristocratic status from ancestors of the same stripe (119). Marius is hot on the trail of semiotic contradiction: 'The privilege they claim on the strength of other people's merits, they will not allow me in right of my own merits, just because I have no family portraits to show and am a newcomer to the nobility of office.' We have here something very much like the insight that Jonson labours to articulate: a semiotic of noble titles that at once depends upon, mocks, and is mocked by true nobility. Marius calls for a system of rewards that truly reflects true nobility, and makes explicit the vera nobilitas argument's stake in a semiotic of noble titles.

This all-important shift from aristocratic status as a political reality to aristocratic status as a semiotic function is particularly marked in the Renaissance, and is a major source of Jonson's obsession with the masks behind which the intellectually and morally bankrupt hide their lack of true nobility. The question for Jonson was not so much whether the monarchy and aristocracy of England were fit to rule, as whether they were fit to possess the powers and privileges of rule. As humanist poet Jonson had no personal claim to make on the basis of the first kind of argument, but he saw a crucial connection between his career and the implications of the second.

If the first two propositions support aristocratic establishments, proposition (3) subverts that support, calls such establishments into question, and leads logically to the fourth proposition – 'those who possess true nobility are aristocrats.' This was an argument that only began to be made in the late Renaissance (by G.B. Nenna and Robert Burton, for instance), but could not be pursued until the political climate was appropriate for undercutting the hierarchical conception of political and social structure root and branch. Certainly it is implied in Pascal's 'On the Condition of the Great.' This proposition is useful in this discussion because it suggests the logical and historical teleology, as it were, of the vera nobilitas argument, and makes explicit the position that writers like Jonson were always skirting but could never allow themselves to venture into overtly.

Jonson's classical sources, in addition to Sallust, include Cicero, Horace, Seneca, Pliny the Younger, and Juvenal. Tacitus, Suetonius, and Dio Cassius should also be mentioned in this context because, although not bequeathing significant statements on vera nobilitas, they delineated the ideological ambiguities of the principate during its first hundred and thirty years, when the vera nobilitas argument developed some of its most serpentine possibilities.

Cicero extended into the domain of practical political power Isocrates' fusion of learning and political wisdom, joining the adviser of princes with the political leader himself. Cicero's argument that his own election to the consulship restored an ancient Roman practice means that the vera nobilitas argument has reverted to the Greek concern with admitting to high office persons whose abilities most warranted it. What Marius claimed by reason of military feats Cicero claimed by force of eloquence: the right to the highest Roman office, the consulship.[14] Cicero was of course the model for Renaissance humanism's claim to power on the basis of learning and eloquence, and Cicero's speech in defence of Murena states that 'the choice of a consul' has traditionally been awarded those possessed of 'the ability to influence, by means of wise advice and eloquence, the minds of the Senators, the people, and those who act as jurors' (*Nine Orations* 176). The Ciceronian model was in fact activated only once in the pre-democratic history of the West: quattrocento Florence and the humanist chancellors Salutati, Bracciolini, and Bruni.

Cicero contributed to the vera nobilitas argument the notion of virtue personally laboured for, as distinct from the gifts of fortune, such as beauty, health, and wealth, which one may receive without earning or deserving them. True nobility requires the four cardinal virtues that alone a man may possess without fear of loss because only he can bestow these on himself (*Tusculan Disputations* 465–75; *De partitione oratoria* 2:365–68; *De inventione* 327). This distinction will recur numerous times in Renaissance writing on vera nobilitas, and is important here because it links the value which for Jonson labour confers on literary production (Maus 12) with the nobility that a man's achievements confer on himself.

Seneca's version of the opposition between goods of fortune (clothing, inherited estates and titles, and 'deceptions of fortune') and inner virtue takes on a typically stoic bias.[15] When he reorients the argument toward the semiotic matters of outer signifier and inner signified and away from Cicero's focus on political power, Seneca breaks down the liaison between inner person and outer circumstances – including the panoply of noble status – and argues the dominant value of the first. In a classic statement of the vera nobilitas argument Seneca insists that 'a man's condition' should not 'lessen the value of a service,' and that instead 'the very value of the service [should] exalt the man's condition ... no man is more noble than another except in so far as the nature of one man is more upright and more capable of good actions' (*De beneficiis; Moral Essays* 3:177). Elsewhere Seneca finds noble status a form of clothing that deceives the eye: 'But when you wish to inquire into a man's true worth, and to know what manner of man he is, look at him when he is naked; make him lay aside his inherited estate, his titles, and the other deceptions of fortune; let him even strip off his body. Consider his soul, its quality and its stature, and thus learn whether its greatness is borrowed, or its own' (*Ad Lucilium Epistulae Morales* no. 76; 2:167).

To the degree that stoic virtue shuns honours and praise, and holds outer signs of power insignificant, Seneca's stoic agenda rejects the notion that those with true nobility ought to be aristocrats, and Jonson parts company with it.[16] It is important to distinguish carefully where Jonson's debt to Senecan stoicism stops, because the contention that Jonson adopted the agenda of stoic withdrawal necessarily entails the conclusion that he also adopted Seneca's totally negative valuation of the outer signs of true nobility which constituted aristocratic status. On the contrary, the central import of Jonson's *oeuvre* belies any contention that Jonson like Seneca completely severed inner moral reality from involvement in the public political world. That Jonson did not model his ideal of the 'centred self' on Seneca is indicated by his conviction that the aristocratic establishment of England should in fact be left wholly in place, but transformed: a system of outer signs whose meanings have been radically altered from within.[17]

In the *Panegyricus*, which Pliny the Younger addressed to the emperor Trajan, Jonson found a document that was to exert a major influence on him. It provided the model for an early treatment of the links between humanist poet and monarch: 'A Panegyre on the Happie Entrance of Iames, Ovr Soveraigne to His first high Session of Parliament in this his Kingdome, the 19. of March, 1603.' In addition, Jonson discovered in Pliny's *Panegyricus* the only fully developed model for the epideictic agenda of his nondramatic poetry: (1) an example of how the rhetoric of praise could establish its own credibility by distancing itself from flattery; (2) a description of the alignment between inner virtue and imperial office which defined itself against the various misalignments to which the vera nobilitas argument was vulnerable. The popularity of Pliny's oration during the Renaissance has been noted (Garrison 24), but recent examinations of Jonson's classical debts (for example, Peterson and Maus) make nothing of this particular one. Pliny alone in the history of the vera nobilitas argument before Jonson displays an analytic intelligence sufficient to grasp the pitfalls and traps, rhetorical and ideological, that this argument entails.

A fuller consideration of Pliny's oration will occur in chapter 4, where Jonson's treatment of epideictic rhetoric is discussed. The *Panegyricus* explores the possibility of an imperial status justifiably awarded on the basis of merit. Pliny ties Trajan's ascendancy to the ideals of the republic, arguing that the republic alone awarded high status on the basis of merit.[18] The central argument of Pliny's praise of Trajan rests squarely on the assertion that only those who possess true nobility deserve imperial titles: 'Others accepted that title [Father of the country] from the start along with that of Emperor and Caesar, on the first day of their principate, but you waved it away until even in your own grudging estimate of your services, you had to admit it was your due. Thus you alone have been Father of the country in fact before you were in name' (Pliny 2:369). The achievement of merit precedes its public acknowledgment, and consequently Pliny can assert that 'in fact, you were emperor, but did not know it' (345), which asserts the fourth proposition of the vera nobilitas matrix: those who possess true nobility are aristocrats.

In comparison with Pliny and Seneca, the other two later Roman writers who carried on the vera nobilitas tradition are of diminished relevance both to this tradition and to Jonson. The later of the two, Claudian, shows exactly how the concept of vera nobilitas can be reduced to pale and invisible cliché. In praising the emperor Theodosius,

Claudian finds that 'Virtue suffers no eclipse by poverty,' that it considers 'merits not their place of birth, what their character not whence their origin,' that 'the path to fortune is open to genius' ('On Stilicho's Consulship' bk 2; 2:11). Claudian's treatment of the vera nobilitas theme is useful here because, in lacking any resonance of the dialectics inherent in it, it highlights by contrast this resonance in his model Pliny.

To the vera nobilitas arguments advanced earlier by Sallust, Cicero, Seneca, and Pliny, Juvenal's eighth satire adds a wealth of personal and disgusting detail. The objects of his attack are not merely idle patricians, as they were for Sallust's Marius: they are shown in addition gambling, whoring, drinking, and vomiting in the gutter egalitarianism of the stews. Juvenal says in effect that people who disgrace themselves cannot hope to recuperate this disgrace by pointing to noble ancestors (8:125ff). Though Jonson draws this concern with symbolic details as much from Martial as from Juvenal, it is Juvenal who makes ideological capital out of aristocratic debauchery, and it is Juvenal, rather than Martial, who offers Jonson a method for establishing a complex conception of vera nobilitas through purely negative, satiric means.

Quattrocento Florentine statements on true nobility occur in a particularly rich political and cultural setting. For this reason it is impossible to establish a single provenance for the civic humanists' claims to political power based on classical learning and skill in rhetoric. Certainly the external threat posed by Visconti imperialism at the beginning of the fifteenth century is one major cause of Florence's constructing a republican ideology for itself, as Hans Baron and George Holmes have put the case. Equally important is Lauro Martines' discussion of the liaison between Florence's leading merchant families and humanist scholars (*Social World*), a liaison that can be traced back to the mercantile Commune's struggle with feudal tyranny (Becker).

Italian writing on true nobility before the quattrocento includes Brunetto Latini's *Li Livres Dou Tresor* and the *Convivio* of Latini's pupil Dante. Latini cites Juvenal, Cicero, and Seneca to support a nobility founded on virtue as distinct from noble lineage (295–6; Skinner 1:45–6). Dante contrasts the opposing authorities of the emperor and of reason. If the emperor says that he is noble who is born of a noble family, Dante replies that reason tells us something else: 'Wherever virtue is, there is nobility. But virtue is not always there where nobility is' (192). Dante takes the vera nobilitas argument with unswerving literalness: if nobility cannot be inherited and is wholly a God-given personal possession (262), then in no way does it concern social and political status: thus he refuses the Senecan etymology that derives *nobilis* from *noscere* (251–2), while extending the Senecan argument to its logical conclusion.

Certainly Florentine civic humanism of the fifteenth century reverses this relegation of true nobility to the private sphere. Lauro Martines' analysis of the symbiosis between emergent mercantile political power and humanist scholarship marks a still further development in the inner dynamics of the vera nobilitas argument. The result of this symbiosis is that 'Humanism spoke for and to the dominant social groups' (*Power* 191). Humanist scholars married into important mercantile families, and otherwise availed themselves of the resources and opportunities which Florence offered to become personally wealthy and politically prominent (Martines *Social* 263ff). Florentine humanists internalized the oligarchic values of the dominant mercantile families, thereby upholding the proposition that aristocrats possess true nobility.

However, while so doing these humanists always managed to reverse the perspective when arguing vera nobilitas. Like Pliny praising Trajan, they treated noble persons as if they already possessed the humanist virtue which they could not possibly possess until obliging humanists taught it them. And since this impossibility is itself part of humanist doctrine, it follows that Renaissance humanists supported established aristocracies in the process of implicitly calling them into question. The history of vera nobilitas in the Renaissance is the history of writers like Jonson who attempt to lay out rhetorically to aristocratic gaze a program of education in humanist virtue as if such a program only supported the aristocratic status of its patrons and did not implicitly subvert it. The study of Jonson's life and career is largely a study of the strategies that Jonson evolved for doing just that.

Italian treatises relevant to the discussion of true nobility and translated into English during the English Renaissance include those of Montemagno, Castiglione, Nenna, Guazzo, and Romei. The direction of the indigenously English tradition begins, however, with Sir Thomas Elyot's *Boke named the Governour* (1531) and concerns the need for a ruling class to be humanistically educated. English humanism mainly pursued arguments for vera nobilitas as the foundation of political responsibility, as distinct from polemics over political justice and the semiotics of social prestige dramatized in the Italian dialogues that English men and women read during the sixteenth century.

Typical of the latter was Buonaccorso da Montemagno's *Controversy about Nobility* (1428), which John Tiptoft translated in 1460 and Caxton printed in 1481. This dialogue matches Roman members of the patrician and plebeian orders, with the latter arguing that 'noblesse ... is excercised in connyng and vertu. And he that is endued with suche a courage deserueth best to be called noble, whorshipful, & excellent' (234). This dialogue was dramatized in Henry Medwall's *Fulgens and Lucrece* (1497) in the context of the new Tudor government's promotion of new men to replace the aristocracy killed off by the civil wars (Bevington 42ff).

Castiglione's main contribution to the vera nobilitas argument is the highly ambiguous and potentially explosive notion of *sprezzatura*, the capacity to practise a difficult art with such ease and nonchalance as to convey the impression of natural talent. This is in effect an educative ascesis aimed at achieving the appearance of its opposite, and its own effacement or disguise. Count Ludovico discusses this capacity when arguing that talent is natural and cannot be communicated by education, but only conveyed by blood, that is, noble birth. True nobility becomes a gift of nature, 'because nature in every thing hath deeply sowed the privie seed, which giveth a certaine force and propertie of her beginning, unto whatsoever springeth of it' (269–70). If common consent assigns *sprezzatura* to the talented, and the talented are identified with the scions of noble families, then the purpose of education in *sprezzatura* is to allow the low-born to learn how to look like nobility.[19] The whole concept of *sprezzatura* therefore validates gracious self-presentation as the guarantee of nobility, and in this Castiglione counsels the very thing that Jonson attacks: false simulation of true nobility.[20]

Stefano Guazzo's *Civile Conversation* was published in England in George Pettie's translation of the first three books in 1581, the fourth and last book appearing in 1586 translated by Bartholomew Young. In his Preface, Pettie criticizes the identification of true nobility with natural gifts that one need not labour to achieve, and insists that the attempt, implicit in Castiglione's *sprezzatura*, to disguise one's labours is to call one's own achievements into question: 'Therefore (Gentlemen) never deny your selves to be Schollers, never be ashamed to shewe your learnyng, confesse it, professe it, imbrace, honor it: for it is it which honoureth you, it is only it which maketh you men, it is onely it which maketh you Gentlemen.' (9)

Guazzo's treatise opens up a strain of the vera nobilitas argument that leads directly to one of Jonson's concerns: his refusal to efface the traces of labour in his own literary production. This emphasis on labour is present throughout Guazzo's discussion of vera nobilitas, and is directly linked with the question of how to interpret the outer signs of noble status. Guazzo's spokesman in this dialogue says: 'Consider now that gentry by byrth costeth you nothing, but that you have it by succession, mary gentry by vertue you have gotten hardly, having first passed thorowe the pykes, and a thousand daungers' (1:178). Labour in turn is defined as intellectual labour, and this betrays the humanist bias which equates the virtue which is true nobility with intellectual merit as distinct from public, that is, political and military achievements.

Guazzo's perspective on the vera nobilitas argument focuses on the unstable semiosis of noble status. Guazzo's interlocutor raises a question radically underlying the whole vera nobilitas argument, when he asks of 'Gentlemen more uncivill then the Clownes themselves,' 'If they be uncivill, howe are they Gentlemen? And if they be Gentlemen, howe are they uncivill?' (175) Guazzo's response discriminates between true and false signs of nobility by measuring these against the possession of true nobility or its lack. He argues that the signs constituting noble status can conceal their falsity behind the communally shared belief that such signs are usually true. They simulate true nobility, dissimulate this simulation, and are therefore doubly lies. By discriminating true signs of nobility from the false, Guazzo typifies the frustration of sixteenth-century writers who sought to heal the breach between outer sign and inner reality in the face of political and social systems in which the two appeared irreconcilable.

Giovanni Battista Nenna published *Il Nennio* in 1542, and in 1595 William Jones brought out his English translation under the title *Nennio, or A Treatise of Nobility*. Three years later in 1598 *The Courtiers Academie* of Count Annibale Romei was published in the translation by one I.K. These two works display a more developed and extreme polarity between the main terms that constitute the vera nobilitas argument than do similar treatises written England following Elyot's *Book of the Governor* and Ascham's *Schoolmaster*.

Both Nenna's and Romei's dialogues make the double argument that noble families train their offspring in noble virtues, and those who are trained in noble virtues constitute the true nobility. Nenna's representative of base-born true nobility, Fabricio, asserts that nature has 'equally framed vs all, shee fashioned the minde of man pure and cleane equally in all men,' and from this deduces the conclusion that 'the mind of man, is apt by nature to receiue either vertue, or vice: if thou traine it vp in vertue, it will become vertuous and Noble' (N1r). The nature/ nurture differential balances delicately here between supporting either inherited or achieved nobility. Varano in Romei's *Courtiers Academie* defends the first position with an argument that repeats Fabricio's defence of its opposite. He makes explicit the mystified belief in transmission of noble virtues through male semen assumed in all defences of aristocratic establishments, calling it the 'onely secret vertue of seede,' and then goes on to insist that 'also reason doth instigate a man, to immitate the reuealed vertue of his progenitours, not to shewe himselfe altogether vnworthy of their splendor and glory' (196). In short, the same argument supports opposed positions.

More significant are the semiotic ambiguities of outward noble status that underlie much of the debate in the *Nennio*. Speaking *in propria persona*, Nenna compares the false aristocrat to a whited sepulchre who, though 'descended of noble bloud, ... at the first sight he seemeth gratious, & pleasing,' there is found in him neither grace nor pleasure. He 'is farre different from him, whose minde is fraught with vertues, because that hee holdeth not an apparance of true Nobilitie, but the verie essence thereof' (x1v). This passage foreshadows Jonson's insistent critique of visual manifestations of inner human moral qualities, a critique present in the poems attacking Inigo Jones, and in the complex uses, literal and metaphorical, to which Jonson puts human clothes. It also turns the vera nobilitas argument away from the question of locus (inherited vs achieved) and toward the question of public signs (truth vs falsity). This new orientation is further specified by the distinction between simulation and dissimulation: simulation of true nobility and dissimulation of its absence.

The debate on true nobility in Nenna's dialogue spins off another of vastly greater importance, a debate about the credibility of an aristocratic and monarchal political system itself. One resolution to this debate is an antinomianism that rejects outer signs *tout court*, the Pascalian alternative that Nenna does not flinch from. He insists 'that if we will effectually comprehend the true essence of man ... he should cast off all his habilitie, depriue himself of honour, forsake the goodes of fortune, lay aside his costly apparell ... Thus shall we know whether he bee noble, or ignoble; good or euill, if in regard of his Nobilitie, he hath need of that which is his own, or of that which other men possess' (v2v–v3r). Jonson would not favour the utopian rigours exemplified here. His aspiration to a place in an English aristocracy turned aristocracy of humanist virtue meant that, after all, he wanted its outer structure kept very much in place.

The beginning of the humanist agenda for education in England is not properly English, but is included here because of its author's influence. I refer to Erasmus' *The Education of a Christian Prince*, which contains most of the standard topics that, scattered throughout discussions classical, medieval, and Renaissance, collectively constitute the vera nobilitas argument. Erasmus is important because he links the two main directions in which the vera nobilitas argument moved: toward political justice and political responsibility respectively. It is unusual to find both topics present together in the same work, since they assume mutually exclusive premises. The argument for political responsibility, which is the main concern of Tudor humanism, presumes that aristocrats already possess true nobility; while the first, springing from the proposition that those who possess true nobility ought to be aristocrats, implicitly calls the second into question. Erasmus shows later sixteenth-century writers how to turn the argument from political justice into a support for the aristocratic status quo. Having outlined the virtues the prince should have, Erasmus asserts: 'But if the prince has none of these qualities, these symbols are not ornaments to him, but stand as accusations against him.' Since actors may wear 'a scepter, [and] royal purple robes ... What is it that distinguishes a real king from the actor? It is the spirit befitting a prince ... The crown, the scepter, the royal robes, the collar, the sword belt are all marks or symbols of good qualities in the good prince; in a bad one, they are accusations of vice' (152).

Erasmus goes a step beyond Nenna in finding the signs of royalty not merely the possible simulation of true nobility and the dissimulation of its absence. In a further move that Jonson will pick up, the failure of signs of nobility to signify truthfully transforms them into signs of this failure. The result is an argument for justice to true nobility that supports a call for political responsibility. In this way, without violating diplomatic tact, Erasmus manages to inform a prince, whose only claim to power is inheritance, that true nobility is independent of inherited status.

More's *Utopia* presents in some ways the most radical variant to be found in the entire history of the vera nobilitas argument up through the Renaissance. Caspari views the book as an 'experiment' wherein More wanted 'to see how a society could be organized on the basis of reason alone, and ruled by those who possessed it in the highest degree' (50). By eliminating 'such factors as property, inherited, social position' (50), More in effect privileges 'those of superior mental ability' who alone 'are eligible for the higher offices' (65). Utopia is a paradise of vera nobilitas, in which the logical implications of the argument are driven to their final destination. Utopia is, in short, governed by those who possess true nobility, and true nobility is specifically defined against inherited noble status. More splits the vera nobilitas argument wide open along a fault line deeply engrained in it. The four-proposition matrix that constitutes the argument concludes with the proposition that those who possess true nobility are aristocrats. More's radical vision literalizes this proposition and its implications, but of course finds that this literalization exists nowhere.

More's vision is important for Jonson because it embodies one extreme to which Jonson's own development of vera nobilitas could have led had not Jonson taken pains to head it off. Jonson unashamedly falls into the same class which Skinner defines by the examples of Erasmus, Vives, and Elyot: one which 'tended to adopt a thoroughly genial attitude towards the ruling classes' (259). Jonson likewise offered himself as a 'therapist ... to help them adjust to the unfamiliar world of the Renaissance. More, by contrast, never addresses himself to the "great lords" and "governors" of his age except to insult them' (259–60). In these remarks Skinner focuses Jonson's problem exactly: how to address the lords and governors of the Stuart monarchy on the subject of true nobility without insulting them.

Actually, the rest of the sixteenth- and early seventeenth-century writers I shall touch on in this section demonstrate that the margins for manoeuvre on this score were rather wide. Jonson's poetry and masques in fact cap an ever-swelling body of treatises and exhortations addressed to prince and nobility in sixteenth-century England, and they support the conclusion that prince and nobility were always willing, if not eager, to listen. Caspari, Kelso, Simon, and Stone record the unqualified success enjoyed by the humanist educational agenda in its campaign to place itself at the centre of Tudor bureaucratic power (Kelso 146ff; Simon 170; Stone 672ff). And not a little of this success lay in the diplomatic mixture of deference and admonition with which this agenda was set forth.

The model of this diplomacy is Sir Thomas Elyot in *The Governor*, which is the true fountainhead of the vera nobilitas argument in sixteenth-century England. Much of *The Governor* can be read as Elyot's attempt, like Jonson's, to make his true nobility argument without calling into question the hierarchical English political system. Elyot says in effect that if noble houses claim privilege and power on the basis of natural hierarchy, then they must perforce admit vera nobilitas as the foundation of this claim. Elyot here both supports a traditional aristocracy, and grounds its existence on the true nobility of trained intellect:

an aristocracy is one of talent and achieved virtue, or it is not an aristocracy at all (4ff). Like Erasmus, he combines the arguments for political responsibility and for political justice, but does so in a unique way, making the awarding of power to the aristocracy a matter of equity (Major 122, 201).

Mervyn James perceives that 'Elyot had embarked, with remarkable effectiveness, on the task of restating the honour code in terms of the popularized humanism of the age' (27). In this view Elyot's project conflates what would in other contexts be kept apart: the code of the 'honor community' of established aristocrats, who alone validated the claims of that community's members, and the notion of true nobility founded on learning and validated by those learned in humanist virtue. James sees Elyot asserting what Jonson was to assert later on: there was not and could not be a conflict with the honour community, because honour was historically founded on the inner virtues of true nobility.[21]

At mid-century appeared the anonymous *The Institucion of a Gentleman* (1555), which explored the significant tripartite distinction between those possessed of inherited status, of achieved status, and of both, all signified by oxymoron and tautology that renders in little the inner contradictions of the vera nobilitas argument. The author divides the gentry into the 'gentle ungentle' (Ciir) and the 'ungentle gentle' (Ciiiir): those possessed only of inherited status and the truly noble respectively. These oxymorons make possible and necessary the tautology 'gentle gentle' (B[vi]v), who possess both inherited and achieved status. The point of course is that this is not a tautology, that 'gentle' is in fact a homonym that refers to two distinct paradigms of gentility. But these two paradigms exhibit a breach that the author, obeying the imperatives of the vera nobilitas argument, seeks to heal. And the fact that he is constrained by the nature of the case to distinguish 'gentle' and 'gentle' in the act of identifying them is a semantic gesture that reveals nothing so much as their separation.

Contemporary with Jonson, but representing the Pascalian blade which will cut the Gordian knot of the vera nobilitas argument that Jonson set himself patiently to untie, is Robert Burton's virulent rejection of aristocratic establishments in *The Anatomy of Melancholy*. Burton proclaims that 'Of all vanities and fopperies, to brag of Gentility is the greatest; for what is it they crack so much of, and challenge such superiority, as if they were demi-gods?' (500) ... 'For learning & virtue in a Nobleman is more eminent, and, as a jewel set in gold is more precious, and much to be respected, such a man deserves better than others, and is as great an honour to his family as his Noble family to him' (507). Burton's attack merely repeats those which Lawrence Stone has chronicled (748ff) through the early part of the seventeenth century, marking a radical breakdown in respect for inherited noble status represented by Pascal in the seventeenth century, and in the next by Thomas Paine.

The history of vera nobilitas is not a random collection of arguments pro and con aristocratic establishments or 'new men.' Rather, the vera nobilitas argument is a matrix of four logically interrelated propositions that collectively constitute the argument itself. The radical ambiguity of this argument lies in its capacity to generate opposed and mutually exclusive ways of obeying its central imperative, namely that inner ability and outer power should be symmetrically matched. This imperative made it possible to derive claims that subvert aristocratic establishments from arguments that support them, and bequeathed to a writer like Jonson a set of propositions collectively problematic in their logical interrelations and unstable in their consequences. As a result, Jonson in writing on the subject always risked being led by his argument in directions contrary to his original premises and overt intentions, and his poetry foregrounds the logical and rhetorical strategies he called upon to deflect these implications.

It is clear that Jonson had no truck with revolution, and the poetry addressed to Charles I, his family, and his favourites during the early 1630s is an embarrassing record of Jonson's willingness to toe the line of Caroline absolutism. However, this late poetry is uncharacteristic of Jonson's complex accommodations of aristocratic status in earlier years. It is rather in this earlier poetry, written from the accession of James in 1603 to his death in 1625, that Jonson thoroughly developed his versions of the vera nobilitas argument. It was for Jonson a necessary and significant heritage, because it enabled him to articulate the ambiguities of his social situation where they intersected his literary ambitions.

2   The Great and the Good

The originality in Jonson's treatment of the vera nobilitas argument lies in his discovering that any one of its four constituent statements implies the other three. This means that praising an aristocrat for true nobility implies the possibility of its absence; that exalting personal merit as the only justification for aristocratic status both supports and subverts this status; that aristocratic establishments can be read as merely redundant supplements to the true nobility of personal achievement; and that the humanist poet who claims patronage, prestige, and status on the basis of his own true nobility commits his ambition to these ambiguities and inevitably risks seeing his claim frustrated by them.

In the rest of this chapter I shall examine those poems in which Jonson seeks to give true nobility a positive definition. Necessarily, the dialectics of the vera nobilitas argument required Jonson to hedge this positive definition against its own perversion. Much of what he says about vera nobilitas is consequently to be found in the many poems where he anatomizes satirically the signs of aristocratic status that, far from manifesting the presence of true nobility, in fact (attempt to) disguise its absence. Such poems complement those which define and praise its true versions.

A major object of Jonson's attack are all forms of clothes, literal as well as metaphorical, such as titles, fashionable dress, pretentious manor houses, coats of arms and genealogies, that one can assume in order to signify falsely one's possession of aristocratic status. The Jacobean practice of selling knighthoods and titles is exemplary of this sort of false signifying, something which Jonson attacks in E46, 'To Sir Lucklesse Woo-All,' who buys a title in order to woo a rich lady. Though failing that, 'he weares his knight-hood euery day' (6). The ironic literalizing of a knight-hood as clothing makes it something anyone can buy. Obviously, if a knighthood can be bought and sold irrespective of merit, then its signifying function is worse than meaningless. It retains its politically validated and socially accepted capacity to signify such merit truthfully, only employed now to signify falsely. As the following epigram (E47) states, Sir Luckless' wooing of all widows means that he 'will get none' (2). The poet suggests that passing one by may change his luck, since luck devoid of merit is all he has to depend on.

This chapter should be understood as one half of a two-chapter composite, the second half of which is chapter 3, wherein I examine Jonson's dyslogistic, satiric treatment of the vera nobilitas argument's perversions. The alternation between poems of praise and poems of blame in the *Epigrammes*, as well as their later fusion in the same poem, indicates more than the intention to juxtapose the mean and magnificent, virtuous and vile, as Edward Partridge makes the case ('Jonson's *Epigrammes*' 173). Such an argument assumes that Jonson makes precise, sharp (and ultimately trivial) ethical distinctions between those he approves and those he doesn't, when in fact he isn't simply performing, as Don E. Wayne has called it, 'an official social function' in his praise, and in his satire showing us 'the way he really perceived his society'

('Poetry and Power' 88). Jonson's ethical perceptions are essentially dialectical, and not merely the accidental product of a humanist poet's programmatic exploring the twin resources of epideictic rhetoric. On the contrary, for him the significance of the vera nobilitas argument depends radically upon isolating and pinpointing its perversions. No praise of true nobility is possible independent of attack on those who do not possess it, who pretend to it, and who therefore pervert it. Like Juvenal, Jonson cannot choose but write satire.

Jonson's links with the history of the vera nobilitas argument are clearest in those poems where he explores the relations between the 'great' an the 'good.' Jonson develops this liaison between noble birth and achieved nobility in the 'Epistle. To Katherine, Lady Avbigny' (F13): 'For he, that once is good, is ever great.' The good/great differential Jonson inherited from Seneca, along with the notion that true greatness could only be founded on goodness ('To Novatus on Anger'; *Moral Essays* 1:163). Exemplifying Roman stoicism in the first century of the principate, Seneca like Jonson poses inner greatness of private virtue against an outer greatness awarded by the fickleness of political fortune. Certainly the tutor of Nero knew whereof he spoke.

Jonson spins out this position in an uncharacteristically direct and traditional manner in the epigram E116, when he says that Sir William Jephson was 'the first, mad'st merit know her strength, / And those that lack'd it, to suspect at length, / 'Twas not entayl'd on title. That some word / Might be found out as good, and not *my Lord*' (5–8), and that 'to liue great, was better, then great borne' (12). The meanings of 'great' and 'good' often depend on the context in which they occur. For example, E66 praises Henry Cary, who has made his family 'both great, an glad' because Cary 'to vpbraid the sloth of this our time, / Durst valour make, almost, but not a crime' (4–6). Cary's military valour occupies the slot opposite 'great' and exemplifies the mythic origins of noble houses posited by some Renaissance versions of the vera nobilitas argument: a greatness founded on an originary act of virtue.

Like 'good' and 'goodness' the word 'virtue' is a kind of cipher whose lack of precise meaning allows Jonson to define it contextually against various opposed terms. This generality is a central problem when one investigates the virtues that different writers on vera nobilitas themes define as the source of true nobility. The equation of true nobility with virtue defined as moral habit, as distinct from public service or humanist learning, occurs at various points in its history. Cicero means by *virtus* the four cardinal virtues of wisdom, justice, temperance, and fortitude

(*Tusculan Disputations* 463–71; *De inventione* 327; *De officiis* 10), and this meaning is taken up mainly in English writing under the Tudors. Elyot and More in *Utopia* extend the properties of aristocratic public responsibility to include Christian virtues, as does Lawrence Humphrey at mid-century (*The Nobles, or of Nobilitye* [1563]). Jonson may oppose 'virtue' to 'vice,' as in E102, 'To William Earle of Pembroke': 'Nor could the age haue mist thee, in this strife / Of vice, and vertue; wherein all great life / Almost, is exercis'd' (5–7). 'Vertue' in the context of this poem is allied with 'noblêsse' (13), and takes on a specifically religious meaning when both are set against 'vice.'

However, the 'good' and 'virtue' usually have for Jonson a meaning rather social or broadly political than religious or moral. The 'virtue' Jonson praises derives from a humanist matrix of values, and is equated with the expense of labour and energy in perfecting personal talents. 'Virtue' is thus defined by Jonson, as by the majority of Renaissance writers on vera nobilitas, against inherited aristocratic status, and as such it concerns less moral goodness than the achievements that assign intrinsic worth to the human being.[22] The various meanings which 'virtue' accrues in discussions of vera nobilitas down through the Renaissance always depend on what conception of inherited nobility it is being defined against.

It is important to isolate the meanings 'virtue' has in Jonson's poetry in order to highlight the issue of vera nobilitas which would otherwise be obscured if terms such as 'virtue' and 'goodness' are understood in a strictly religious or ethical manner. It will become apparent that Jonson's reputation as a 'moralist' poet who deals with ethical discriminations between human good and evil needs major revision. In place of the moralizing poet appears the humanist poet dominated by a concern with the problematic place of self-made 'new men' in a society equivocally bent on rewarding such men and keeping them in their place. Jonson's attempt to define an aristocracy of humanist virtue may well have the good of his own society as its goal, but if so this is because Jonson had no less at heart a concern with his own career in the context of that society.

Jonson most extensively develops identifications of virtue with true nobility in the late set of poems gathered under the title *Eupheme*, the elegiac celebration of the deceased Venetia, wife of Sir Kenelm Digby. The eighth poem (U84.8) is addressed to their sons Kenelm, John, and George: 'Boast not these Titles of your Ancestors; / (Brave Youths) th'are their possession, none of yours: / When your owne Vertues, equall'd

have their <u>Names,</u> / 'Twill be but faire, to leane upon their *Fames*' (1–4).
Jonson argues here a textbook example of the vera nobilitas position.
The Digby sons are exhorted to look to their lineal ancestors not for
titles, which are names belonging only to those who merited them by
their virtues, but to the virtues themselves, for only by renewing these
may they claim the titles that are transmitted to them by blood: 'Hang
all your roomes, with one large Pedigree: / 'Tis Vertue alone, is true
Nobilitie. / Which Vertue from your Father, ripe, will fall; / Study
illustrious Him, and you have all' (20–3).

A similar argument occurs in F14, 'To Sir William Sydney, on His
Birth-day':

> Nor can a little of the common store,
>   Of nobles vertues, shew in you;
>   Your blood
>   So good
> And great, must seeke for new,
> And studie more:
>   Not weary, rest
>   On what's deceast.
>   For they, that swell
>   With dust of ancestors, in graues but dwell. (31–40)

Contrastive emphases articulate these traditional sentiments and make
them live again as thoughts to be scrutinized and tensive in the mind's
grasp. Being a scion of the Sidney family, Sir William has presumably
inherited no 'little of the common store, / Of nobles vertues.' However,
possessing 'blood / So good / and great' he must refuse to rest satisfied
with such an inheritance. Jonson cunningly avoids tacit insult to Sir
William, by arguing that to inherit greatness means to renew this greatness in his own virtuous labours. The noble status of the Sidney family
validates itself by transmitting a criterion of family membership dependent on pursuit of true nobility alone, and the true heir of the Sidney
name establishes his genealogy by acting as if he has inherited no status
at all.

One way of dividing Jonson's poems about true greatness is to distinguish addresses to those born into titled families from those who
achieved titles.[23] The former include William Sidney, and also such
aristocrats as Venetia Stanley, her husband Sir Kenelm Digby, Lucy

countess of Bedford, the earls of Pembroke (dedicatee of the *Epi-grammes* and *Catiline*) and Newcastle (also the notorious Somerset), the countesses of Rutland and Montgomery, as well as Lady Aubigny and her husband Esmé Stuart, to give only a partial list of Jonson's addressees. Faced with retroactively justifying de facto aristocratic status on the basis of personal achievement, Jonson wrote poems to aristocrats that involve complex rhetorical and ideological strategies. Poems on the other hand addressed to knights, and those such as the Cecils and Bacon who had reached from obscure origins as high as the privy council, need not cushion aristocratic sensibilities, but remain nevertheless concerned with merit rewarded delicately poised on the edge of aristocratic pretension.

The poem on her husband addressed to Venetia Stanley when she was alive (U78, 'To my MVSE, the Lady *Digby*, on her Husband, Sir *Kenelme Digby*') finds him uniting the scholar, courtier, and soldier in a paragon out of Castiglione, as well as the four cardinal virtues Cicero calls the marks of one deserving praise for personal achievement. Like Jonson's assertion to Sir Kenelm's sons in *Eupheme* U84.8 that ''Tis Vertue alone, is true Nobilitie' (21), the four cardinal virtues are a formula the poet apparently feels unconstrained to develop. As such they show Jonson's thought resting at the lowest common denominator that links all writing on true nobility wherever it is found. A similar unwillingness to ruffle the waters of commendation appears in 'An Epigram on WILLIAM Lord Burleigh, Lo: high Treasurer of England' (U30), and is doubtless due to the occasion of the poem itself: an inscription on a gold plate to be given by Burleigh's son, Robert Cecil. Here, Burleigh is called 'the grave, the wise, the great, the good, / What is there more that can ennoble blood?' (5–6). What more indeed, unless it be a rhetoric probing enough to turn these words into something more than ciphers? The thematic flatness of this catalogue serves, nevertheless, to highlight by contrast those many poems wherein Jonson gives the 'great' and the 'good' dense significance by pitting their various meanings against one another.

Jonson's emotional aloofness here marks the difference between these poems and those in which he explores with shrewdness and acuity the achievements, and temptations, of self-made men. With these Jonson is in his element, for they offer the reader mirrors of the norms and values by which the poet measured himself. For instance, the epigram addressed 'To Sir Thomas Overbvry' (E113) concerns the changes wrought at the royal court by a man of letters, and here the mirroring is direct: 'Nor may'any feare, to loose of their degree, / Who'in such ambition can but follow thee' (11–12). Those ambitious for 'degree' can achieve it only by pursuing the virtues exemplified in the addressee. What started out in the poem as mutual exclusion between virtue and status ends as mutual implication.

Jonson's interest in excavating the history of vera nobilitas is demonstrated (as is much else) in one of his major poems on the subject, his 'Epistle to Master IOHN SELDEN' (U14), which prefaces Selden's *Titles of Honour* (1614), a historical study of royal and noble titles in various ancient and modern cultures. Selden's interests are antiquarian and archaeological, and one looks in vain for much discussion in it of the vera nobilitas argument.[24] This does not deter Jonson from finding the book a sharp appraisal of the reasons and justifications for the titles that constitute established aristocracies: 'What fables have you vext! what truth redeem'd / Antiquities search'd! Opinions dis-esteem'd! / Impostures branded! and Authorities urg'd! / What blots and errours, have you watch'd and purg'd / Records, and Authors of! how rectified / Times, manners, customes! Innovations spide! / Sought out the Fountaines, Sources, Creekes, paths, wayes / And noted the beginnings and decayes!' (39–46). Selden's critical examination of the origins of titles becomes for Jonson an examination of other origins: not historical so much as ethical and philosophical.

As reward for Selden's success Jonson says ''Mongst thy Titles showne / Of others honours, thus, enjoy thine owne.' This statement adumbrates a topic taken up later in this book, namely aristocratic status and titles as a form of epideictic rhetoric, with the epideictic rhetor as himself a bestower of titles. The first part of the poem (to line 28) probes the problematic nature of epideictic rhetoric, so 'that my Reader [may be] assur'd, I now / Meane what I speake' (27–8). Concern with praising Selden's book on the basis of merit replicates Selden's concern with cognate questions in the history of ranks and titles. In another related direction, Jonson praises Selden for matching the book's style to its subject matter: 'But to the Subject, still the Colours fit / In sharpnesse of all Search, wisdome of Choise, / Newnesse of Sense, Antiquitie of voyce!' (58–60) Jonson finds in Selden the stylistic characteristics he cultivates in his own writing, where acute perception of difference makes possible wise discrimination in fitting the colours of rhetoric to inner meaning: the central issue of vera nobilitas.

Selden was one who, among those who achieved greatness, Jonson most admired. Among those born great, Katherine, the wife of an early patron, Esmé Stuart Lord d'Aubigny, elicited one of Jonson's most thoroughly developed examinations of how merit may justifiably be ascribed to a person who inherits noble status: the 'Epistle to Katherine, Lady Avbigny' (F13).

The opening forty-four lines anatomize praise and flattery, and the poet's authority to declare, as well as Lady Katherine's capacity to understand, her unique virtues. Praise lacks credibility in its own time because no one believes anyone good enough to deserve it. Jonson defends himself against 'the vicious, / Such as suspect them-selues, and thinke it fit / For their owne cap'tall crimes, to'indite my wit' (12–14). The poet must defend his readiness to praise 'euery vertue, wheresoere it moue, / and howsoeuer; and I am at fewd / With sinne and vice, though with a throne endew'd' (8–10). The judgment that calls all praise flattery implicitly calls into question the virtues of noble persons, as it does the poet who praises them. As in the poem on Selden, the credibility of poet and of addressee stand or fall together, and Jonson well understood the unacknowledged accusations of self implicit in all attacks on others.

Lady Katherine can expect to 'Looke then, and see your selfe' (29) in the glass Jonson holds up to her, and she will see there not a painted face, because 'That askes but to be censur'd by the eyes: / And, in those outward formes, all fooles are wise' (35–6). In discriminating between cosmetics and the face behind them, the poet prepares her for discriminations which 'all fooles' are incapable of making: between inherited status and true nobility. Lady Katherine needs a false glass as little as she needs the cosmetics of either face paint or inherited status: 'No lady, but, at some time, loues her glasse. / And this shall be no false one, but as much / Remou'd, as you from need to haue it such' (26–8). Jonson's thought here is acute. The false glass of flattery is the false poet's response to the noble person's conviction that she needs such in order to mask her deficiencies of beauty or virtue. Needing or demanding the false glass of flattery or cosmetics, or of noble status, discloses the very lacks one seeks to hide; just as accusations addressed to others are futile attempts to distance the self from evils of which one thereby accuses oneself. As in the song early in *Epicoene*, where much painting and elaborate dress hints that within 'all is not sweet, all is not sound,' masking oneself behind noble status discloses a conviction that one has something to hide. Jonson says that Lady Katherine's willingness to hear the truth about herself licenses him to tell it, and therefore what she hears from him will necessarily be such.

Jonson goes on to celebrate 'your happy fate, / ... that mixt you with a state / Of so great title, birth, but vertue most, / Without which, all the rest were sounds, or lost. / 'Tis onely that can time, and chance defeat: / For he, that once is good, is euer great' (47–52). The *but* marks a point at once of contrast and continuity: continuity between 'so great title, birth' and 'vertue,' an achievement all the greater than greatness because it contrasts paradigmatically with the other meaning of *but* available in this context, which marks the potential separation between greatness and virtue. A similar double meaning occurs in the line ''Tis onely that can time, and chance defeat.' The information focus on *that* brings into question its syntactical status: presuming 'that' refers to 'vertue,' then 'time' and 'chance' are the objects of 'defeat' by virtue. On the other hand, the intervening line 'Without which, all the rest were sounds, or lost' by extension suggests that 'that' can refer to 'title' and 'birth,' which become the object of 'defeat' by 'time' and 'chance.' The point of this syntactical ambiguity is, of course, that birth, title, and virtue must hang as it were together, or they will hang separately.

Jonson's central rhetorical problem is sharply broached here: how to avoid casting doubt on the value of inherited, outward status in the process of contrasting it with 'vertue' as the only true foundation of human worth. If praising Lady Katherine for true greatness implies the possibility that she (and her peers) may not possess it, then praise on these terms comes perilously close to blame, radically calling into question the whole class system founded on the assumption that members of the aristocracy are by nature the true *aristoi*, those who possess *areté*. Jonson neutralizes this dangerous potential by engaging his aristocratic reader in tracing inherited nobility back to the true nobility of virtue. Lady Katherine cannot look askance at the implication that she is not endowed with true nobility at birth, because that would be to reject the originary proposition which she must nevertheless agree to, namely that nobility is founded on virtue. Therefore her own ideology renders her complicitous with that of the humanist poet.

Understood in the context of the vera nobilitas argument, specifically the possibilities of blame and subversion lurking at its margins, this poem discloses a rhetorical and ideological tension that would otherwise be invisible. The elaborate self-reflexive prologues in this and similar poems, wherein Jonson raises for consideration, and rejection, alternative meanings implied dialectically by those he intends, reveal his felt need to guard both poems and himself from such subversion. Consciousness of the history and dialectics of the vera nobilitas argument would seem to have been for Jonson a continual burden.

3 Discriminating True Nobility

The good/great differential remains throughout Jonson's poetry the model of all other contrastive definitions of true nobility. There are no terms of these definitions afforded by the history of vera nobilitas that Jonson does not employ in one poem or another, and the poet's adherence to this model is likewise an adherence to this history. A brief consideration of 'An Ode to IAMES Earle of Desmond, writ in Queene ELIZABETHS time, since lost, and recovered' (U25) will serve to introduce this section, in which the good/great differential is expanded to generate other versions of itself.

The subject of the poem was an unfortunate pawn in the English government's struggle with the Irish rebel, his cousin, who had assumed the earldom of Desmond and who continued the rebellion previously led by James' father. James was lodged in the Tower from 1584 to 1600, when he was created earl of Desmond by the queen in a propaganda effort to disinherit his cousin (H&S 11:62). The poem is uncharacteristic in exploring none of the resources available in the irregular Pindaric stanza for contrastive emphasis. By comparison, the much later Ode to Cary and Morison (U70), which will conclude this section exhibits a sharpening of Jonson's understanding of the Pindaric stanza.

The Desmond Ode turns on the parallels among several differentials. In the second stanza, for instance, Jonson sets in opposition Desmond's 'True noblêsse' and the appearance of downtrodden fortune, which true judgment can nevertheless discriminate. However, the rest of the poem contains the implicit warning that this differential will work in Desmond's favour only as long as he himself maintains a parallel distance between fortune and his inner virtue. The next stanza (27ff) opposes the 'glad Innocence, / Where only a mans birth is his offence' (31–2), to those who seek to 'practise upon honours thrall' (35). Jonson's point is of course that as long as Desmond maintains his innocence, the fact that he is imprisoned for his family connections is of minor importance. Jonson reveals much about his own attitude toward aristocratic status, when he says that there is nothing wrong with Desmond save his high birth.

The next stanza develops the stoic notion that he is never hurt who refuses to be hurt: 'For fury wasteth, / As patience lasteth. / No armour to the mind! He is shot-free / From injurie, / That is not hurt; not he, that is not hit' (46–50). The last stanza tells all in its final lines: 'O then (my best-best lov'd) let me importune, / That you will stand, / As farre from all revolt, as you are now from Fortune' (63–5). In other words, to engage in revolt, as did his father and cousin, is to commit himself to outer fortune, which is to cross the boundary separating the various differentials Jonson has been lining up throughout the poem.

The Desmond Ode shows the kind of poetry Jonson, or anyone else, could write were they to versify formulas transmitted by the vera nobilitas tradition. Only Jonson, on the eve of major transformations in Western thinking which changed everything else as well as the direction and content of the vera nobilitas argument, perceived its inner contradictions. And a measure of his distance from his predecessors is epitomized in the distance he travelled from the Desmond Ode in the main body of his poetic treatments of the subject.

This distance is measured in an epigram where the Jonsonian strategy of dialectical definition becomes itself the topic of discussion: E102, 'To William Earle of Pembroke.' William Herbert is the dedicatee of the *Epigrammes* and was one of Jonson's major patrons. The poet suggests at the beginning that the epigram form can be used to 'open out' the 'implicit' meaning of a person or a subject: 'I doe but name thee PEMBROKE, and I find / It is an *Epigramme*, on all man-kind; / Against the bad, but of, and to the good: / Both which are ask'd, to haue thee vnderstood' (1–4). One way of approaching Jonson's notion that the name of a person connotes specific vices or virtues is through the modern linguistic problem of whether proper names, as distinct from common nouns, have any connotations. That is, do they only point to an individual, and therefore have reference without meaning (Martin 35)? In response, Graham Dunstan Martin argues that 'the extension of a proper name is in virtue of the connotations possessed by a particular use of it; and without such connotations its extension would be totally inexplicable' (36).[25]

Jonson's practice creates such meanings in the manner that Martin specifies. Naming William Herbert *Pembroke*, as Jonson's epigram asserts, is to assign the name meanings the poet finds in his character. Names and titles do not confer meaning, but take on only the meaning given them by the inner virtues of those who bear them: linguistic anomaly enters the service of the vera nobilitas argument.[26] Understanding what *Pembroke* means, that is, understanding the kind of person Pembroke is, requires understanding the complex relations between virtue and vice: 'Nor could the age haue mist thee, in this strife / Of vice, and vertue; wherein all great life / Almost, is exercis'd (5–7). The purpose is to define Pembroke's virtue without tying it negatively to vice and thereby suggesting that Pembroke is virtuous simply because he is not vicious. Jonson gets round this problem by first openly announcing this definition, and then posing it against his own definition of Pembroke's virtue.

Jonson registers this discrimination contrastively. 'In this strife / Of vice, and virtue' allows an upgraded emphasis on *and* that negates the expected 'strife' between opposed ethical qualities. The emphasized *and* suggests instead that there are in fact two strifes, one involving virtue and the other vice. If this is so, then one is not constrained to measure virtue only in opposition to vice, which is exactly how some understand the matter: 'and scarse one knowes, / To which, yet, of the sides himselfe he owes' (7–8). The upgraded *yet* sets up a paradigmatic contrast that is syntagmatically picked up by the equally upgraded 'for reward, to day' of the following lines: 'They follow vertue, for reward, to day; / To morrow vice, if she giue better pay' (9–10). For these people the strife between vice and virtue is a debate regarding which is going to pay best. *Yet* here suggests a suspension of decision up to the very last moment, as contrasted with Pembroke, who has already made this decision once and for all. If there is to be a 'strife / Of vice and virtue' (that is, reading with the punctuation removed), then this strife is waged by those who 'are so good, and bad, iust at a price, / As nothing else discernes the vertue or vice' (11–12). The upgraded emphasis on *and* suggests multiple contrasts: with *and not* (I will be good and not bad today), with *or* (I am capable of being either good or bad), and finally with the normal emphasis allowed by suppressing the punctuation (in waging this strife I am both good and bad).

The strife of virtue that Pembroke wages, on the other hand, eschews this dubious complicity generated by a false strife between virtue and vice, and favours instead maintaining an unmoved moral stance: 'But thou, whose noblêsse keeps one stature still, / And one true posture, though besieg'd with ill / Of what ambition, faction, pride can raise; / Whose life, eu'n they, that enuie it, must praise' (13–16). Jonson's point here is that if one cannot define either virtue or vice without defining both together, then one must discriminate between these two ways of making this definition.[27]

Jonson again marks this contrast between two different versions of the same opposition in the E119, 'To Sir Raph Shelton,' in a manner less subtle than in the epigram to Pembroke, but hardly less telling. And it is typical that Jonson should second-guess his own praise of Shelton by recognizing the possible implication that he rejects the mob and the court despite his own preference: 'No, SHELTON, giue me thee, canst want all these, / But dost it out of iudgment, not disease' (7–8). Such second-guessing is present in all the poems addressed to nobility and represents a dominant reflex in Jonson's thinking, an awareness that discrimination doubly entails exclusions that imply each other as well as some that don't; and that the more challenging discriminations are those that articulate the difference.

Contrasts between apparent synonyms, already discussed in chapter 1 as a favoured mode of contrast, enable precise definitions of true nobility. The epigram 'To Sir Horace Vere' (E91) praises the military hero for private virtues such as 'Humanitie, and pietie, which are / As noble in great chiefes, as they are rare. / And best become the valiant man to weare, / Who more should seeke mens' reuerence, then feare' (15–18). The distinction between fear and reverence Jonson would have found in Pliny's *Panegyricus* (Briggs 'Epigrams' 177), and he makes the same distinction in his 'Panegyre' addressed to King James in 1603. To evoke fear modulated into reverence is to link military qualities with the private virtues of humanity and piety, rather than to exclude them. The distinctions and liaisons between apparent synonyms that Jonson invites the reader to grasp are exactly those that Jonson praises Vere for having already articulated to himself as an ethical principle of his life.[28]

The examined life is of course a central Jonsonian topic and one that he always develops contrastively. Vera nobilitas arguments provided him with the categorical framework for this development, and many of the specific differentials underpinning particular poems as well. The evanescence of a life well lived is, however, not a topic traced in the history of vera nobilitas, but one that evoked in Jonson a level of feeling that he rarely displays on other occasions. It is the more significant that Jonson should explore the topos of the well-lived brief life as if it were still another version of the vera nobilitas argument, in the most significant poem he wrote on the subject: U70, 'To the immortall memorie, and friendship of that noble paire, Sir LVCIVS CARY, and Sir H. MORISON.' Here, the short life of Morison is compared favourably for its achievements with that of a hypothetical 'peere,' whose long life was yet too short for any significant accomplishment.

Before examining this ode, for comparison I will briefly touch on another poem dealing to some extent with the same subject, a translation from Martial's epigram 77 from book 8 (U89). The sense of evanescence is rendered in the contrast between the 'eternall Flower' and the man who dies amid the pleasures of life. The 'rosie garlands' (4) are evanescent, but the 'old *Falernian* wine' is not, even though it 'Dark thy cleare glasse' (5). Everyone looks after Liber (1), for he is the 'sweetest care' of his friends. Present is the *carpe diem* motif, wherein images of eternity become images of fleeting time. But 'Hee, that but living halfe his dayes, dies such, / Makes his life longer then 'twas given him, much' (7–8). The rhyme 'dies such' – 'much' summarizes the poem's exhortation: to compress more intensity of life into a shorter span than normal. The difference between saying only 'Make his life longer' and 'Making his life longer ... much' is the difference between the statement of a mere paradox (a short intense life is as long as a long dull life), and the assertion that such a life is in fact longer. The intensifier, isolated by both punctuation and syntax, suggests that the price of this form of living is not a mere trade-off, that this life is even to be preferred.[29]

The Cary-Morison ode, by comparison, sidesteps any hint of *carpe diem*, though some of its paradoxes echo those in the Martial translation. I am speaking of images, motifs, and particularly of enjambment, a metrical phenomenon that maintains a borderline existence and whose significance always looks in two directions. But *carpe diem* motifs are as far from this poem as they are from one of Jonson's main sources for the poem's subject, namely Seneca of the Moral Epistles: 'Show me that the good in life does not depend upon life's length, but upon the use we make of it; also, that it is possible, or rather, usual, for a man who has lived long to have lived too little' (1:329).[30]

Morison exemplifies the perfection of the short life, measured not 'by the space, / [But] by the act' (21–2): 'All Offices were done / By him, so ample, full, and round, / In weight, in measure, number, sound, / As though his age imperfect might appeare, / His life was of Humanitie the Spheare' (48–52). The perfection of Morison's life is also compared here to the perfection of poetic verses, something Jonson reinforces later: 'for Life doth her great actions spell, / By what was done and wrought / In season, and so brought / To light: her measures are, how well / Each syllab'e answer'd, and was form'd, how faire; / These make the lines of life, and that's her ayre' (59–64).

If the art of living is like the art of verse, then this ode is a treatise on enjambment. Enjambment is various literal and troped forms is one of the major features here, so that this poem becomes a discussion of enjambment considered as a metaphor for the decisive 'turns' of human life.[31] The Latin word *versus*, which means turn, is literalized in the poem's run-on lines at decisive turns of its argument, as it is in Jonson's naming the Pindaric stanzas 'The Turne,' 'The Counter-turne,' and 'The Stand.' All this suggests that the act of writing poetry, and in particular this poem, in turning lines 'turns' oneself, as Jonson puts it in his poem on Shakespeare (M26): 'And, that he, / Who casts to write a liuing line, must sweat, / (Such as thine are) and strike the second heat / Vpon the *Muses* anuile: turne the same, / (And himselfe with it) that he thinkes to frame' (58–62).[32]

The self-reflexive allusion to the poem's composition is fused with the enjambment that splits and unites the poet's own name across the stanza boundary separating the counter-turn and the stand:

> Of which we *Priests* and *Poets* say
> Such truths, as we expect for happy men,
> And there he lives with memorie; and *Ben*

> *The Stand*

> *Jonson*, who sung this of him, e're he went
> Himeselfe to rest ... (82–6)

Similar tropings of the poem's verbal dimension are scattered throughout. For example, the two friends were 'Each stiled, by his end, / The Copie of his friend' (111–12), where the stile (stylus) that writes creates *copia* in the process of drawing the two friends as mirror reflections of each other.

The important thing here is that Morison's life is intriguingly like enjambment. Enjambment combines and contrasts a bridge across the discontinuous with a rupture of the continuous. Like Wittgenstein's duck-rabbit, which Hollander cites in this connection (104), a run-on line is available to being read both ways, though not at the same time. When Jonson says 'Hee leap't the present age,' it is tantamount to saying that Morison's life span, like a run-on line, was complete in itself, and yet broken off at a point of rupture to be completed after the 'turn' marked by that rupture: leaping across an ending to continue life in 'that bright eternall Day' (70, 81). To this extent, much of the poem directs the reader to understand how ruptures prepare for continuities, and short lives prepare for completion across the turn that divides life from death.

Literal and metaphoric enjambments fuse when Jonson refers to Cary and Morison as

> these twi-
> lights, the *Dioscuri* (92–3)

As Hollander observes, 'here the meter imitates the action of death by cutting the word apart even as death divided the two men' (123). Actually the run-on here does more than sever the word 'twilight' at a morphemic boundary. The first half of the word thus isolated gestures toward doubleness, before it turns toward a second meaning, namely the boundary between day and night that also marks a turning point of transition between the two. The Dioscuri were the brothers Castor and Pollux, who after Castor's death oscillated as the constellation Gemini in tandem between the heavens and the infernal world, the one rising as the other set (Donaldson *Ben Jonson* 1985; 704). In a stunning act of wit Jonson invites the reader in processing these lines to behold ruptures turning into continuities and vice versa.

But if death, like enjambment, marks a rupture as well as a continuity, then Jonson must also confront the fact that Morison's premature death was a true closure. The question the poem asks in this connection is nothing other than the central humanist question 'What constitutes the perfect human life?' The answer the poet gives is a version of the vera nobilitas argument that wholly assimilates its definitions of virtue and merit to an exalted vision of life lived at once in time and in eternity, and transcending in its perfection the boundary between them.

The 'Brave Infant of *Saguntum*,' whose instantaneous turn from life back into its mother's womb opens the poem, announces in epitome the problem the poem poses, and its solution as well. As liminal narrative, it tells the story of a 'summ'd ... circle' so tiny in its circumference that finding its 'Center' teases us out of thought. The problems the infant's tale raises include the reason for its rejection of the world, on which the poet speculates in the following counter-turn. But more centrally, this problem lies rather in determining 'what is life, if measur'd by the space, / Not by the act?' (21–2). If, as the counter-turn says, the infant was drawn back to the womb by 'wiser Nature' because of 'the horrour of that sack[,] ... Where shame, faith, honour, and regard of right / Lay trampled on' (11–14), the implicit question is, then, 'Which is better: the brief but perfect life of the infant, or a life lived amid horrors typified by the sack of his city?'

It is this line of thought that leads immediately to the 'antimasque' of the poem, the satirical portrait of the aristocrat who lives fourscore years to no purpose: 'He purchas'd friends, and fame, and honours then, / And had his noble name advanc'd with men: / But weary of that flight, / Hee stoop'd in all mens sight / To sordid flatteries, acts of strife, / And sunke in that dead sea of life / So deep, as he did then death's waters sup; / But that the Corke of Title boy'd him up' (35–42). The meretricious deceptions wrought by the external signs of nobility are conflated with the deceptive appearance of a life which seems significant in being merely long. The opposition that Jonson poses here is patent: empty titles and honours signify a long but sterile life just as (in the following stanza) Morison's virtues constitute a life perfect though short.

Though the territory looks familiar, Jonson here turns the vera nobilitas argument to new uses. At issue is the discrimination not simply between true and false nobility, but between two conceptions of human life, and in this poem true nobility merits not membership in an aristocracy of humanist virtue but immortality. For this reason the poet deliberately catches himself up in the act of asserting that Morison 'fell young' and affirms by contrast that 'Hee stood, a Souldier to the last right end, / A perfect Patriot, and a noble friend, / But most, a vertuous Sonne' (45–7). Death becomes less the closure of life than the final arc whose addition completes the perfect sphere of humanity.[33]

The agenda in this poem is hidden to the extent that the significance of Morison's life is hidden from those who do not know how to read it. This agenda is to affirm a life perfectible in the achieved harmony of its constituents: 'for Life doth her great actions spell, / By what was done and wrought / In season, and so brought / To light: her measures are, how well / Each syllab'e answer'd, and was form'd, how faire; / These make the lines of life, and that's her ayre' (59–64). There are three enjambments in as many lines, and each articulates contrasts both paradigmatic and syntagmatic. Jonson finds that the structure of Morison's life corresponds to the structuring of his own verse. As in the 'twi-/ lights' run-on, trope is literalized in the form of the verse – or the verse is troped as a metaphor for human life.

Life 'spells' great actions not only 'By what was done and wrought' but by its having been done 'In season.' Paradigmatically *in season* contrasts with the implied *out of season*, thereby establishing the choice between these two possibilities as the information focus of the whole phrase: the significance of an action depends on a decorum that matches it to its appropriate place in a temporal scheme. As a consequence, 'In season' syntactically subordinates 'done' and 'wrought,' transforming them from absolute verbs – as read before the run-on – into specifications of itself. 'Brought / To light' fuses three distinct meanings: (1) bring to completion and perfection; (2) end one's life; (3) go to a greater light. The run-on break here throws contrastive emphasis on *to light* so as to invite the reader's bringing to light these various meanings as well.

The remainder of the stanza identifies Jonson's conception of poetry with the humanist norm of the perfect human life as the embodiment of vera nobilitas. 'Measures' here means 'criteria' and 'her' refers back to 'life.' There is, of course, the second meaning of the word as prosodic measure. 'Answer'd' I interpret to mean that each syllable corresponded to or was aligned with all the others. By querying how each 'syllab'e answer'd, and was form'd,' the reader discovers the judgments and choices that constituted the composing process itself. We have here a statement of one of the major arguments of this book. The 'lines of life' assimilate the construction of poetry to the construction of a human life: both involve conscious choices, selections that are also rejections, and both must occur under the impetus of a teleology, the ultimate goal of which is a line and a life that is 'ample, full, and round, / In weight, in measure, number, sound' (49–50).

The contrast between 'bulke' in the next stanza and 'small proportions' yields a notion of 'just beauties' characterized by appropriate distribution and arrangement of parts. The long-standing 'Oake' harks back to the 'Stirrer' buoyed up by 'the Corke of Title,' long-lived but empty of true nobility. As I shall show in chapter 4, those who mask the lack of true nobility behind the public signs of nobility flee the discriminations that self-judgment imposes, while unwittingly unmasking themselves in their need for such masks. Poetry and life may both be perfect in short measures because Jonsonian measures eschew at every point this lack of discrimination, this failure to call each part of the whole to account for itself.

The most remarkable enjambment in the poem – perhaps in all of Jonson's poetry – occurs at 'Ben / Jonson,' where the enjambment runs from the end of the Counter-Turn into the Stand: 'Who Sung this of him, e're he went / Himselfe to rest, / Or taste a part of that full joy he meant / To have expressed, / In this bright *Asterisme*' (85–9). At the end of the previous stanza 'Ben' completes the rhyme of 'Such truths, as we expect for happy men, / And there he lives with memorie: and Ben / ...' (83–4). This enjambment places the poet himself in two domains of thought and reality. As 'Ben' he is one with that group of '*Priests*, and *Poets*' who affirm 'that bright eternall Day: ... Such truths, as we expect for happy men.' But as 'Jonson,' the poet himself enters into and becomes part of the process of greatly living and dying that he evokes for Morison. It is a riveting strategy, one that without preparation suddenly thrusts on the poet everything the poet has asserted of his subject. The break-plus-continuity in the enjambment epitomizes the links that join the poet and his subject across the disjunction between the two. In this way Jonson commits himself to 'Such truths' as he speaks to Morison: Ben is the one who remembers, and Jonson is the one whom, along with Morison, he must remember.34

4 The Achievement of Merit

The notion that merit alone justifies aristocratic titles and privileges is so basic to the vera nobilitas tradition, and to Jonson's own development of this tradition, that a separate section devoted to the subject may appear redundant. However, Jonson's perspective on the merit component of this tradition opens out and foregrounds unusual aspects that deserve attention. For instance, Jonson emphasizes a parity between merit and personal labour that is only implicit in classical and Renaissance conceptions of true nobility, particularly the Greek sophists' belief in the perfection of talent by education, as well as Horace's identification in the *Ars poetica* of the arts of poetry with the arts of ethical discrimination. Renaissance humanism directs personal effort into learning and finds in its pursuit the road to ethical perfection. Jonson in some poems distinguishes the idleness of the high-born and the man-hours of sweat required of the base-born new man, with scorn and approbation distributed accordingly.

Jonson valued the labour involved in personal achievement almost for its own sake (Maus 13), an ideal that Peterson shows Jonson could have found in Horace (160, 193), but which bears witness to a longer and more complex genealogy in the vera nobilitas tradition. Pindar may have questioned the significance and efficacy of mere labour in the absence of inborn talent, but in the Renaissance Bruni praised Florence for being 'so outstanding for its talents and industry.' This is because the 'hope of honor is in fact held out, and these energies are in fact released, amongst all the citizens of our city' (quoted in Skinner 1:80).

In Nenna's dialogue, the spokesman for vera nobilitas says 'who know-eth not this, that without great labor, a man cannot attaine to anie worthy action, or laudable deed' (P3v–P4r). There is finally George Pet-tie's pointed insistence that learned gentlemen should not be ashamed to show their learning, a rejection of the *sprezzatura* that disguises the efforts behind one's achievements that Castiglione called for (Guazzo 1:8–9).

In Jonson's case personal labour characterizes a specific activity: the acts of judgment and choice that Jonson demands of himself, of his readers, and of the recipients of his praise. Jonson says in the *Discoveries*: 'Indeed, things, wrote with labour, deserve to be so read, and will last their Age' (H&S 8:638). This is an intellectual labour whose phonological, semantic, and syntactical coordinates I have sketched in chapter 1, and which enables discriminations that are finally ethical as well as discur-sive.

More broadly, it is important to isolate those poems that feature the argument for merit in order to fill out some of the details of what Jonson meant by the 'good' in distinguishing it from the great. It is, after all, notoriously difficult to determine with precision what Renaissance hu-manism meant by true nobility. I have indicated in the first section of this chapter that the contents of 'true nobility' and 'inner virtue' are usually defined dialectically, that is, their meanings depend on what they are defined against. This is no less true for Jonson's own uses of the vera nobilitas argument.

It is also true that the values Jonson espouses are generally thought to be either difficult to extract from his poetry, or elusively simple. Stanley Fish speaks for some interpreters when he says that 'the power of his poetry ... depends, paradoxically, on the determined reticence of that poetry, on its unwillingness to open itself to inspection, on its often-proclaimed inability to specify or describe the values that inform it, ...' (40). Similarly, George Parfitt avers that Jonson's achievement 'depends upon the reduction of moral complexity to simplified clarity. A feature and tool of this simplification is a use of language in which association and paradox are reduced to a minimum, in favor of precision and local meaning' (Parfitt 'Ethical Thought' 133).

By now it should be evident that Jonson's poetry does not withhold the ethical coordinates that underpin his praise and blame, nor are these coordinates as simple as Parfitt finds them. The meanings Jonson gives the notions of merit, achievement, and personal labour are central to these arguments, because on their basis alone can he justify the supreme place he claims for true nobility in an aristocracy of humanist virtue. And the paradoxes throughout Jonson's verse are partly the result of his need to make his vera nobilitas arguments dialectically, by differential, contrastive definition.

One relatively straightforward way into Jonson's conception of merit is the epigram 'Of Life, and Death' (E80): 'The ports of death are sinnes; of life, good deeds: / Through which, our merit leads vs to our meeds. / How wilfull blind is he then, that would stray, / And hath it, in his powers, to make his way!' (1–4). Jonson rarely appeals to otherworldly norms to justify his ethical discriminations; just as, similarly, he is less concerned with the virtue-vice differential than with that which poses virtue as true nobility against inherited title. In this epigram, however, merit acquires the meaning of heavenly reward, and Jonson criticizes those who are 'wilful blind' in refusing to understand the proportion between both 'rewards' with which death presents us.

As usual, things are not as simple as they seem, and they begin to become complicated with the phrase 'wilfull blind.' Any person who has it 'in his powers, to make his way' and yet strays can only be understood to be not simply blind but wilfully blind, deliberately refusing to see the way. The phrase is interesting because it hovers between two traditionally opposed readings of men's ethical choices. On the one hand the Socratic notion holds that evil results from ignorance: no person is evil willingly, and he who chooses evil is blind. On the other, the Pauline and Augustinian reading emphasizes the will infected by the fall of man, and finds that evil results from conscious choice (Hoopes).

Jonson's interpretation seems to combine both views. 'Wilfull' blindness refuses not so much self-knowledge as the undesired information about the self such knowledge supplies, and so becomes blind to its own blindness. This refusal is for Jonson a moral act because it depends upon informed decision, which is why the wilfully blind is he that 'would stray,' that is, wills to do so, when he 'hath it, in his powers, to make his way!' It entails, in short, mental and moral laziness, the refusal to make the effort, and 'Meeds' are the just rewards for our conscious choice to labour on our own moral education. Those who do so confront death 'as men might iudge vs past it' (7), as if it were no longer a threat to be confronted.

Merit is then for Jonson earned by intellectual labour, an unsurprising conclusion given his commitment to humanist conceptions of true nobility. The object, content, and goals of this labour, however, Jonson defines with considerably more precision than we come to expect from

late Renaissance writing on true nobility, where exhortation to the four
classic cardinal virtues and sundry Christian virtues usually exhausts
such specification. Jonson defines merit differently for those who have
risen by it than he does for the nobly born. In the latter case, where
Jonson is constrained diplomatically to skirt the embarrassments attending such praise, he lauds aristocrats for possessing true nobility
primarily because they have laboured to achieve it when they didn't
have to. Understandably, however, Jonson most identifies with new
men, those who have laboured and been rewarded accordingly.

A group of epigrams beginning with E63, 'To Robert Earle of Salisbvrie,' addresses just such men: born to the middle-class or the gentry,
whose greatness is significant precisely because achieved. Robert Cecil,
the son of the great Burleigh of Queen Elizabeth's time, was of course
the paradigm of great place won by talent. The three successive epigrams
on Cecil – assuming that the 'retraction' in E65 'To My Mvse' refers to
Cecil as well – present a particularly sensitive facet of Jonson's attitude
toward men who fulfilled his humanist ideal of merit rewarded: an
attitude of approbation laced with hostility, issuing in poems that reveal
these ambiguities mainly in the contorted rhetoric Jonson uses to hide
them. These and similar poems will be discussed in the final chapter
of this study, where I examine the autobiographical implications of
Jonson's poetry.

Other epigrams in this group, where this hostility is absent and Jon-
son's understanding of merit is therefore reflected undistorted, include
E70, 'To William Roe'; E74, 'To Thomas Lord Chancelor [Egerton]'; E95,
'To Sir Henrie Savile'; and E116, 'To Sir William Iephson.'

The epigram to Jephson, examined in an earlier section of this chapter, makes a relatively general statement of the vera nobilitas argument
and reflects with little addition some commonplaces in the argument's
history. E70, addressed to William Roe, is an early, undeveloped version of the Cary-Morison Ode: 'When *Nature* bids vs leaue to liue, 'tis
late / Then to begin, my ROE: He makes a state / In life, that can employ
it; and take hold / On the true causes, ere they grow too old' (1–4).[35]
Jonson here praises an aggressive appropriation of the principles of
success ('makes a state / In life'), and the man who knows to do this
in season. The difference between Roe and those who literally surround
him on the pages of the *Epigrammes* – Pertinax Cob, the Covrt-Parrat,
the Covrt-ling, and Fine Grand (E69, E71, E72, E73 respectively – is,
however, not this aggressiveness, but his knowing 'the true causes' of
such state.

The poems addressed to the Lord Chancellor, Thomas Egerton, and to Sir Henry Savile are more specific. E74 concerns the poet's judgment of Egerton when he hears and perceives his various acts of wisdom and fairness as a judge. It is possible to be skilful in the laws without being wise, a fact that makes Egerton all the more remarkable in being both. 'Whil'st thou art certaine to thy words, once gone, / As is thy conscience, which is always one' (7–8). Egerton weighs his words, so that the 'certainty' of his choice is aligned with the self-assurance of his conscience. The virtues of judgment that Jonson predicates of Egerton turn out to be those Jonson claims for himself and demands of his readers. Jonson praises Egerton because he, like the poet in the poem on Shakespeare, necessarily 'turns' himself in turning his discourse.

Acts of speaking and writing proclaim just as much as do public acts in the social, political domain the moral character of the man, and for this reason Jonson praises Sir Henry Savile's translation of Tacitus' *Histories* (1591): 'Although to write be lesser then to doo, / It is the next deed, and a great one too' (24–5). For Jonson the historian must possess the same virtues as the men whose acts he describes. He must be able to 'speake of the intents, / The councells, actions, orders, and euents / Of state, and censure them'; he must know to 'write the things, the causes, and the men'; and finally he must possess the courage to write the truth (31ff).

Moving backward in the poem from this conclusion, one notes that Jonson compares Savile as a historian to Sallust, who was first a soldier under Caesar and later a historian. Savile, 'That liu'st from hope, from feare, from faction free; / That hast they brest so cleere of present crimes, / Thou need'st not shrinke at voyce of after-times' (18–20), becomes like the statesman himself subject to 'censure' of later ages. Like Machiavelli, Jonson would seem to hold that there are writers who lack nothing of the prince save a principality.[36] He would also seem to agree with Machiavelli that the same kinds of talents needed for success in the political world are needed to write about the political world (McCanles *The Discourse* 40ff and passim). In this Jonson states his version of the humanist commonplace Jaeger discovers first among the Greek Sophists, namely that he who would teach those who move public events must possess the intellectual virtues that move public events well.

This is not a usual theme for Jonson, since, of the two distinct orientations of the vera nobilitas argument discussed in section 1, Jonson is more concerned with aristocratic status as the reward of true nobility than with true nobility as a condition of public service. It is significant then that Jonson's praise of these men and others like them considers their public service less a result of their verbal skills than a reward for them.

A paradigmatic example is U33, 'An Epigram to the Councellour that pleaded, and carried the Cause.' If the subject of this poem is Sir Anthony Benn (the end of line 6 being a blank in the 1640 folio and requiring a proper name rhyming with 'men' [H&S 11:65]), then Jonson's identification with him is not surprising. Herford and Simpson quote a contemporary account:

> MR. ANTHONYE BEN, a reader of the Middle Temple, stepped in to be recorder of London. He was a citisen's son of London, well enoughe spoken, but his spokesman to this businesse was the king's letters, procured by a great one about him, to wit, the earl of Buckingham.

The first fourteen lines declare that Jonson will no longer tolerate others satirizing lawyers, since Benn has convinced him that lawyers can be honest and worthy men. Benn 'dost vexe, and search' a cause to see if he can defend it. If not, 'Thou hast the brave scorne, to put back the fee' (19, 22). Benn exhibits the kind of discrimination that Jonson can admire: 'What use, what strength of reason! and how much / Of Bookes, of Presidents, hast thou at hand! / As if the generall store thou didst command / Of Argument, still drawing forth the best, / And not being borrow'd by thee, but possest' (24–7). Benn's authority derives from his mastery of the legal arguments afforded by precedents, and this mastery depends in turn on the strength of his judgment.

A similar genealogy of powers Jonson discovers in the leading legal figure of the age, Sir Edward Coke, in the epigram addressed to him 'when he was Lord chiefe Iustice of England' (U46). In Coke Jonson finds that 'Integritie, / And skill in thee, now, grew Authoritie' (9–10). If the only true authority is that which cannot be conferred, but which results instead from 'integrity' and 'skill,' the contrastive emphasis on 'now' implies at least two things: (1) authority and these virtues do not often go together, and (2) the ideal legal system is one in which inner authority is recognized and confirmed by status in the system itself. For this reason Jonson can open the poem by stating 'He that should search all Glories of the Gowne, / And steps of all rais'd servants of the Crowne, / He could not find, then thee, of all that store / Whom Fortune aided lesse, or Vertue more' (1–4).

The virtues Jonson praises in the poems discussed here are those fostered in the public domain where verbal discrimination is of primary importance: political affairs and the law. Jonson's fullest poetic statement of the poet's public responsibilities outside of the *Discoveries* is his translation of Horace's *Ars poetica*. 'Horace His Art of Poetry' was clearly an important document for Jonson, although the nature of that importance is not equally clear. He translated it twice, once in 1604, and a second time after 1610, the date of Daniel Heinsius' edition of Horace's works, which contains a rearranged version of the *Ars Poetica* that won Jonson's acceptance (H&S 11:110–12). Jonson read his translation to Drummond in 1619, and it survived the fire that destroyed many of his papers in 1625. Both versions exist in different volumes printed in the 1640 Folio.

Horace's treatise in verse was in the Renaissance a primary classical source text for humanist poetics, along with Aristotle's *Poetics* and *Rhetoric*, Quintilian's *Institutes*, and the relevant treatises of Plato and Cicero. The nature of its influence presents problems, however, partly because the exact intention and subject of the treatise were (and are) in dispute, and partly because it was read through the double lenses of Aristotle's *Poetics* and of rhetorical theory. Bernard Weinberg's survey of late Italian literary criticism documents these problem areas (1:71–249). D.A. Russell's comment is applicable to all attempts at any time to render a definitive interpretation of Horace's purposes: 'Lines and sections read quite differently according to what you hold in mind from the context, and whether you look forwards or back ... Anyone who undertakes to guide a party round the poem is likely to be pointing out things that are not there, and missing things that are' (116). Depending on where one starts and the uses to which one wants to put the *Ars poetica*, it can be seen as a discussion of decorum, verisimilitude, audience reception, fictional characterization, style, genre, or the qualities that constitute a true poet. Furthermore, the apparently random manner in which these topics are organized induced Heinsius to reorder the text and Jonson to revise his first translation accordingly.

Given the general importance of the treatise in the Renaissance and to Jonson in particular, it is worth considering his translation in the context of the dominant concerns of his poetry. In this context Jonson's translation yields up aspects of Horace's argument that differ markedly from those Weinberg finds interesting to the Italian literary critics,[37] and which suggest that Jonson read it as a treatise concerned less with rhetorical effect and poetic decorum than with the ethical discriminations of the poet that underlie and are reflected in his artistic choices.[38] Horace domesticated in Jonson's poetic *oeuvre* comes, not unexpectedly, to the defence of the poet as humanist scholar.

A major significance of the *Ars poetica* occurs for Jonson in those passages which concern vera nobilitas, and the ethical discriminations fundamental to its possession, which this study has found dominant in Jonson's poetry at large. In the final section of Horace's poem, a passage which delineates the qualifications of the poet (295–476),[39] and in which Horace contrasts himself with poetic pretenders, Jonson translates as follows:

> But I cannot buy
> My title, at their rate, I'ad rather, I,
> Be like a Whet-stone, that an edge can put
> On steele, though 't selfe be dull, and cannot cut.   (431–4)

Horace will teach his poets 'Their Charge and Office, whence their wealth to fet, / What nourisheth, what formed, what begot / The Poët, what becommeth, and what not' (436–8), because 'The very root of writing well, and spring / Is to be wise' (440–1).

Horace like Jonson localizes the issue of the true poet as a question of titles which may be bought, whether or not they are deserved. Consequently, 'what becommeth and what not' translates 'Quid deceat, quid non' (308), where the verb *decere*, 'what is appropriate,' appears carrying with it a major focus of the whole poem, namely the concept of decorum. It is this appearance, plus its reinforcement in this and following passages, that link this section on the discriminating poet with the formalist and rhetorical slants on decorum dominating earlier sections.[40] In other words, the true poet is defined for both Horace and Jonson as one whose capacity for true ethical discrimination – *areté* – is registered in artistic decorum: knowing what is decorous – *decere* (*to propon*): 'to be appropriate.' This identification is made explicit in the final statement above, which makes *sapere* the source of *scribendi rectè* and a matter of ethical understanding rather than technical training (338).

Of equal interest to Jonson the humanist poet is a passage that follows almost immediately, and which renders the *Ars poetica* a contribution to the humanist agenda for the poet as adviser of public men: 'Hee, that hath studied well the debt, and knowes / What to his Countrey, what his friends he owes, / What height of love, a Parent will fit best, / What brethren, what a stranger, and his guest, / Can tell a States-mans dutie, what the arts / And office of a Judge are' (445–50). In the context of a treatise on poetry, what is 'owed' ('Quid debeat,' 312) to these various individuals means the poet's knowledge of what is appropriate, what is decorous, which he draws for the purposes of poetic composition from his study of the actual cases (Brink 340ff). Jonson would appear to be following Horace in conflating such ethical judgment with ethical judgment per se. The next lines confirm this conflation: 'And I still bid the learned Maker looke, / On life, and manners, and make those his booke, / Thence draw forth true expressions' (453–5). This is not a matter of artistic imitation only – as if the poet's main function for Horace (and Jonson) were only verisimilitude – but rather of mastering the ethical dimension of human actions in order to express them truly in language. This is probably Horace's intention, if Brink's commentary is to be accepted; it is certainly the agenda of Jonson's humanism.[41]

Jonson was also sensitive to those passages in Horace's poem that concern the poet's status vis-à-vis aristocratic establishments. Horace (396ff) mimics those who, without training or talent, believe their social status enables them to write poetry: 'Yet who's most ignorant, dares Verses make. / Why not? I'm gentle, and free-borne, doe hate / Vice, and, am knowne, to have a Knights estate' (570–2). Merit, we are not allowed to forget, means here poetic talent. Jonson also follows Horace in warning the reader against flattery: 'When you write Verses, with your judge do so: / Looke through him, and be sure, you take not mocks / For praises, where the mind conceales a foxe' (620–2). 'Looke through him' is borrowed from preceding lines ('quem perspexisse laborant') about kings who use wine to distinguish true from false friends. The notion that false praise is really a form of mockery is Jonson's contribution. Compared with the Latin original, Jonson's version widens the gap between outside and inside, as well as the compensating need to 'look through' appearances.

Jonson sought to make ethical discrimination the foundation of poetic decorum, and this connection he found in the *Ars poetica*. It is therefore not surprising that discussions in earlier sections of poetic decorum, verisimilitude, genre, and characterization become in effect discussions of the poet's powers of discrimination. If Jonson interpreted these earlier sections as advice on training the judgment of the poet under the guise of prescriptions for poetic form and content, then his reading was a startlingly original one, either for his own time or our own.

A typical example advises the poet to recognize the limits of his powers and not to reach for or pretend to greater: 'So, shunning faults, to greater fault doth lead, / When in a wrong, and artlesse way we tread' (43–4). This is developed a little later:

> Take, therefore, you that write, still, matter fit
> Unto your strength, and long examine it,
> Upon your shoulders. Prove what they will beare,
> And what they will not. Him, whose choice doth reare
> His matter to his power, in all he makes ... (53–7)

This advice grounds artistic self-knowledge on ethical reflection. For Jonson, the artist who neglects this prescription makes himself vulnerable to the satiric judgments to be discussed in chapter 4: attacks on those whose refusal to come to terms with their limitations results in attempts to hide behind pretensions that ironically disclose them.[42]

Later lines of this passage distinguish two recognizably Jonsonian forms of selection and rejection: that which selects from what is deferred, and that which selects from what is simply rejected, which forms of choice correspond to syntagmatic contrast and paradigmatic contrast respectively:

> Now, to speake; and then differ
> Much, that mought now be spoke: omitted here
> Till fitter season. Now, to like of this,
> Lay that aside, the *Epicks* office is. (61–4)

This passage, and similar ones on the need to match one's poetic ambitions to one's talents (124–5, 178–82, 195–9, 349–54), illustrate not merely the analogies binding together the decorums of art and life, but also the multiple applications of the same sentences and phrases to one or the other, with complex overlaps and diversities of meaning arising accordingly.

Horace's claims for the privileges of poetic talent over gentle birth take on expanded meaning in the context of the vera nobilitas argument; while Jonson's central concern with the poet as praiser of true nobility, who justifies himself by mastering the discriminations between true and false nobility, amplifies Horace's insistence on the need for the poet to cultivate the ethical dimension of his art. As such, Jonson's reading is in closer touch with Horace's purpose than are those Renaissance commentators who saw it primarily in rhetorical or formalistic terms. Jonson here gives us a lesson in humanist imitation of classical texts: specifically, in how meanings latent in the original emerge in new contexts, or meanings already obvious expand in new directions.

5   The Act of Discrimination

Discrimination as a topos of praise becomes itself the overt subject of some of Jonson's poems. In E86, Jonson praises Sir Henry Goodyere for making just the kind of choices he elicits from his readers. The poet, who 'would know' Goodyere (1), begins by observing 'thy wel-made choise of friends, and bookes' (2). Knowledge then leads to love – the same process the poet will assign to himself at the poem's end – which in turn breeds a sympathy through which the poet may 'behold thy ends / In making thy friends bookes, and thy bookes friends' (3–4). Goodyere loves his books because he understands them, and understands his friends because he loves them. The subject of this poem is praise rendered suspect of partiality because inspired by love. The closing couplet of this poem defines the problem negatively in the contrasts which it implies: 'Where, though 't be loue, that to thy praise doth moue, / It was a knowledge, that begat that loue' (7–8). The poet is willing to concede that love inspires his praise, if he can qualify the former by saying that it depends in turn on knowledge.

The poet's voice, which is the poem at hand, both praises Goodyere's capacity to unite love and knowledge, and speaks that union on its own: the one who can praise justly and knowledgeably is the praiseworthy person. The circularity of the poem, returning at the close to the topic of the opening, replicates the self-reflexivity mediated through this praise, which foregrounds the acute discriminations of the speaker himself.

Reading one's friends as books is a rubric that subsumes many of Jonson's poems. His lifelong determination to make writing and reading, speaking and hearing metonymies for his society's systems of signs and communication can only make sense in a context where the latter are ever available for becoming the vehicles of false representation. In the *Discoveries* he returns repeatedly to these matters and the equivalences that undergird them. For instance:

Language most shewes a man: speake that I may see thee. It springs out of the most retired, and inmost parts of us, and is the

Image of the Parent of it, the mind. No glasse renders a mans forme, or likeness, so true as his speech. (H&S 8:625)

Jonson's strong humanist strain would naturally make 'speak that I may see thee' a touchstone of his social transactions. In the next two chapters I shall examine Jonson's insistence on words, rather than graphic representation (for example, one's 'glass'), as the true tellers of truth in a world where the signs of high status can hide the lack of true nobility. Jonson demands a semiotics of social, political signs that features a direct, undisplaced and undistorted reflection in outer signs of the moral state of the inner person – the demand of the vera nobilitas argument for a perfect symmetry between true nobility and aristocratic status. If language tells the truth because 'it springs out of the most retired, and inmost parts of us, and is the image of the parent of it, the mind,' then we must take seriously Jonson's radical assumption of a founding, trans-discursive human subject, out of whom issues speech that can bear either a true or false reflection of that subject, and who can accordingly be held to account for this speech.

The sequence of three epigrams, E121, E122, and E123, addressed to Benjamin Rudyerd, exhibits comparable discriminations repeated at several levels of the poems' address. In E121 Jonson confronts once again the issue of how to render credible the praise of friends, and typically he makes the issue part of the poem's statement: 'Yet is the office [praise] not to be despis'd, / If onely loue should make the action pris'd: / Nor he, for friendship to be thought vnfit, / That striues, his manners should precede his wit' (5–8). In acknowledging the reader's scepticism regarding the praise of friends, these lines envision a loving praise ('manners') that 'precedes' witty judgment only in the sense of being courteous. The poet here discriminates between praise that is objective as well as loving, and praise that cannot be both.

In the opening quatrain Jonson's praise of Rudyerd's 'learned *Muse*' is compared to great ladies being greeted by lesser. Jonson's putatively 'lighter' muse emulates Rudyerd's, with the result that 'Shee learnes to know long difference of their states' (4). In the second quatrain the poet manages at once deference to Rudyerd's poetry (published in 1660; H&S 11:27), an assertion of the justice of both his praise and his friendship, and a subtle recuperation in his own favour of the difference between them. It is an example of the tact Jonson exhibits throughout his poetry in praise of lesser writers who are also friends.

The second epigram addressed to Rudyerd (E122) gestures toward a utopian semiotic aligning inner truth and outward show. The differential governing the poem poses assaying and empirical testing – 'know,' 'trie,' 'set,' and 'touch' – against superficial or inaccurate knowledge. The objects of this testing are forms of simplicity and primitive purity conventionally associated with the age of Saturn that may never have existed, and consequently require rigorous investigation to see if they can be reacquired: 'pure gold' (4), 'wise simplicitie' (4), 'virtue ... as shee was yong' (5), 'holiest friend-ship, naked to the touch' (7), where *touch* means also *assay*. Benjamin Rudyerd, the addressee of this epigram, however, 'prou'st, all these were, and againe may be' (10): if fables true, only here.

The opening couplet becomes now intelligible:

> If I would wish, for truth, and not for show,
> The aged SATVRNE's age, and rites to know ...

In question is the syntactical construction of the first line. Without the first comma, the verb 'wish' becomes 'wish for,' with 'truth' and (negatively) 'show' its objects. The insertion of the first comma makes the line syntactically problematic until one reaches 'TO KNOW,' which retroactively parses 'for truth, and not for show' as a parenthetical unit. *For* comes to mean 'for the purpose of,' in the interest of; and to know the age of Saturn becomes the object of the wish. The two revisions dovetail to make the following statement: I wish the return of the age of gold, in effect to know truth and not mere appearance. I am aware that this return may be merely a 'show,' since the age of gold may be only a fiction, but I intend it in this poem seriously: a true return of the age of truth.

The final epigram of the Rudyerd series, E123, retains the general topic of the first two: the relations between friends who are also writers, and the trials and possible dislocations of truth and friendship that may accompany that double relationship: 'Writing thy selfe, or iudging others writ, / I know not which th'hast most, candor, or wit: / But both th'hast so, as who affects the state / Of the best writer, and iudge, should emulate.' This epigram makes homologous two differentials: writer/critic and wit/candour: wit the virtue of writers, candour of critics. Rudyerd always acts as both, thereby at once writing himself, judging himself, and writing and judging others. Jonson telescopes seemingly distinct acts of construction and judgment, and insists that success in any one of these depends on success in all.

Friendship, manners, wit, truth and appearance, writing, judging both self and others: these terms refer to essential components and activities of human society. In all three epigrams these terms of ethically weighted significance stand to one another in mutually implicative and exclusive relations. Discriminations abound throughout, but they are to some extent unlike most that I have described heretofore. The discriminations here are more complex because they operate on several levels at once, recursively reappearing within one term already distinguished from a second, or setting one manner of distinguishing two terms over against another. They present a picture of Jonson the poet unfamiliar to many of his readers and critics: a poet interested in hedging his ethical state-ments by tracing out the boundaries between the different meanings lurking within apparently simple oppositions and equivalences.[43] The poet he is most like in this respect is Milton of the last major poems. Both present a discursive surface deceptively free of overt ambiguities, yet radically ambiguous because the simple oppositions and equiva-lences with which both deal always contrastively imply other possible relationships. If, as Roland Barthes has argued (S/Z 44–5), the ambiguities of irony are usually solvable for simple, unironic meanings, the strategies of Milton and Jonson work the same observation in reverse: richness of meaning is derivable from apparently simple, unambiguous meaning.

I shall conclude this chapter with an examination of several poems wherein discriminations within and among shades of ethical excellence are the point of focus. These include E128, 'To William Roe'; and two contiguous poems from *The Forrest*, F10 and F11, the latter being the 'Epode,' the partial examination of which begun in chapter 1 I will complete here.

The final half line of the epigram on Roe – 'This man hath trauail'd well' (14) – is what the whole epigram is about (Peterson 33–4). Roe goes 'Countries, and climes, manners, and men to know, / To 'extract, and choose the best of all these knowne, / And those to turne to bloud, and make thine owne' (2–4). This is a typically Jonsonian disjunctive se-quence, indicative of successive stages where choices are to be made, things selected and rejected at each step. This epigram establishes a kind of paradox, where the ideal traveller is at once changed and not changed by his travels. What he experiences he turns 'to bloud,' makes it part of himself, and consequently comes back at once the same man of discrimination and judgment he left, and a man expanded in his learning assimilated precisely by this discrimination and judgment. The result is 'Thy selfe, with thy first thoughts, brought home by thee' (10). Roe's friends may greet a 'selfe' whom they can recognize, maintained by the integrity of Roe's 'first thoughts': 'there, may all thy ends, / As the beginnings here, proue purely sweet, / And perfect in a circle alwayes meet' (6–7).

The ideally travelled Roe becomes like the epic hero Aeneas, who having travelled through the world 'Came back untouched' (14). Lying behind this poem are other Jonsonian discussions of travellers, like that on the English Mounsieur (E88), who reverses Roe by travelling not at all, but becoming nevertheless an affected pastiche of foreign fashions. Of the same stripe is Amorphus in *Cynthia's Revels*, whom Mercury describes as 'a traveller, one so made out of the mixture of shreds of forms, that himself [Amorphus] is truly deformed' (2.3.77–8; Wilkes 2:29). Obviously, for Jonson there are good and bad ways of travailing, and of assimilating one's travels.

F10 and F11 were both printed in Robert Chester's *Loues Martyr* (1601), the same volume in which Shakespeare's 'The Phoenix and Turtle' appeared. The two poems taken together match each other as, respectively, a negative statement of the subjects the poet refuses to write about, prefacing a major statement of Jonson's ethical discriminations. F10 exists in two different versions, one of which is unfinished and called in manuscript 'Proludium.' The finished text of F10 is a humorous response to the poet's reluctance to 'sing,' which is carried further into a reluctance to call upon classical subject matter of pagan gods and goddesses:

> And must I sing? what subiect shall I chuse?
> Or whose great name in *Poets* heauen vse,
> For the more countenance to my actiue *Muse*?
>
> HERCVLES? alas his bones are yet sore,
> With his old earthly labours. To 'exact more,
> Of his dull god-head, were sinne. Ile implore
>
> PHOEBVS. No? tend thy cart still. Enuious day
> Shall not giue out, that I haue made thee stay,
> And foundred thy hot teame, to tune my lay.

Nor will I beg of thee, *Lord of the vine*,
To raise my spirits with thy coniuring wine,
In the greene circle of thy Iuy twine.   (1–12)

These gods are treated with jocular familiarity, in the vein of Anacreon or Lucian, which means that Jonson insists on literalizing the elaborate metaphors these mythic figures take on in the mythological and emblematic handbooks that he knew well.[44] The full significance of this rejection depends on what it is made in favour of, which include the ethical treatise that is the following poem and, in another direction, the poet's inspiration by his own muse: 'Nor all the ladies of the *Thespian lake*, / (Though they were crusht into one forme) could make / A beautie of that merit, that should take / My *Muse* vp by *commission*: No, I bring / My owne true fire. Now my thought takes wing, / And now an *Epode* to deepe eares I sing' (25–30).

The incomplete 'Proludium' sets up the axes of opposition along other lines: 'An elegie? no, muse: yt askes a straine / to loose, and Cap'ring, for thy stricter veyne' (1–2). Here, the poet sets in opposition the elegy and the epode, genres identifiable with Ovid and Horace respectively, and refuses in addition the poetry of lustful love for that of virtuous love. Suggestive in this connection are similar oppositions in *Poetaster*, which was performed in the same year in which *Loues Martyr* appears: the lustful Ovid versus the high-minded Horace, and the banquet of the gods in which Ovid and his friends literalize (and debase) mythological deities, versus Augustus Caesar's impassioned speech in act 4, scene 3 of that play condemning such debasement.

Poetaster is a major document in the history of Jonson's understanding and direction of his literary career. The alternatives, which move between the gods as inspirers of virtue and the same gods literalized as comic *farceurs*, parallel the oppositions between the 'Epode' and the two poems that Jonson wrote to preface it. The 'Epode' registers an identification with Horace that poses Jonson and the chaste virtue of that poem against the licentiousness of the Ovidian elegy and by extension of the fad of Ovidian poetry in the 1590s (Donno; Hallett Smith 64–130). Equally important are the suggestions, overt in *Poetaster*, of the poet's making an important career choice, when he seeks to identify himself with the monarchal establishment via Horace's attachment to and approval by Augustus Caesar. In this early stage of his career Jonson already envisions himself an arbiter of the court's manners and morals, a fantasy literalized in his preceding play, *Cynthia's Revels*. It is obvious that the dramatic portrait of the Roman emperor embodies Jonson's ideal of a political hierarchy open to appreciating and advancing men of learning and creativity, a portrait of vera nobilitas yearnings almost embarrassing in the details of its wish-fulfilment.

The opening lines of the 'Epode' (F11) have already been examined in chapter 1 to illustrate certain aspects of contrastivity typical in Jonson's poetry. Here the intention is to complete that analysis by exploring the ethical discriminations foregrounded by the poem's phonologically induced contrasts.

In that chapter, the distinction between *security* and *safety* is extended back into the poem from the final line:

> Man may securely sinne, but safely neuer.

The opening lines prepare for this discrimination between meanings of apparent synonyms, by moving the reader through a complex series of attendant discriminations, the conclusion of which is that the virtuously provident are perhaps never so vulnerable to seduction as when convinced of their invulnerability. The poem's finally disclosed subject turns out to be not virtue but the self-knowledge that makes virtue possible. The treasons that subvert ethical purity lie in the self, and Jonson calls upon allegory of the medieval 'castle of man' variety to enact a cautionary version of such betrayals:

> But this true course is not embrac'd by many:
>   By many? scarse by any.
> For either our affections doe rebell,
>   Or else the sentinell
> (That should ring larum to the heart) doth sleepe,
>   Or some great thought doth keepe
> Backe the intelligence, and falsely sweares,
>   Th'are base, and idle feares
> Whereof the loyall conscience so complaines.
>   Thus, by these subtle traines,
> Doe seuerall passions still inuade the minde,
>   And strike our reasons blinde. (19–30)

Extending the castle allegory, Jonson moves here from malfeasance in the ranks to bickering among the officers. Either one's affections rebel, or even worse the mind's 'sentinell' is asleep, lulled, as line 8 suggests, by the assumption that *ward* (protection) is necessarily entailed by careful *watch*. That line's upgraded emphasis on *and* contrastively foregrounds the differences between being watchful and guarding oneself. This difference is rendered explicit in the brief satire on 'some great thought' who (being more great than good) suppresses 'the intelligence,' just as great men suppress intelligent men who are necessary as a 'loyall conscience' to teach the collective human person of the commonwealth how to guard itself against the evils that assail it.

The poem moves next to consider love as the 'first' of the 'vsurping rancke' of passions requiring such warning. Jonson contrasts two kinds of love, one being the 'blinde Desire' that he deals with in the cancelled 'Proludium.' On the other hand, 'Now, true Loue / No such effects doth proue; / That is an essence, farre more gentle, fine, / Pure, perfect, nay diuine' (43–6). In contrast with the self-divisions that subtly may fissure even the most guarded mind, Jonson gives us a community of two people in perfect harmony.[45] This community in turn generates the charge of 'Some vicious foole' who says that such perfect love is impossible. Harmony is once again tested by the centrifugal forces that threaten to disrupt it from within, and this leads Jonson to consider the reasons why this marriage will survive. These are defined by contrast with various forms of enforced chastity and fidelity, which Jonson wants to set aside in order to open a space for exploring a marriage grounded on mutual esteem alone:

> Much more a noble, and right generous mind
>   (To vertuous moods inclin'd)
> That knowes the waight of guilt: He will refraine
>   From thoughts of such a staine.
> And to his sense obiect this sentence euer,
> *Man may securely sinne, but safely neuer.*

The poem has wound back to the discriminations of the opening lines, but we have not arrived at where we began. The Phoenix-husband can now be expected to remain faithful to his Dove to the degree that he internalizes the ethical discriminations evolved through the poem. The 'noble, and right generous mind' is one whose recognitions of virtue and vice depend on each other, and whose capacity to guard the first from the second – at risk in the poem's opening lines – depends on his capacity to think through the discriminations the poem makes and understand them. And these discriminations are all versions of those made in the opening and closing lines between words and phrases with apparently identical meanings. If enjambment becomes a trope for the central thematic concerns in the Cary-Morison Ode, the discrimination between apparent synonyms is the governing trope in the 'Epode.' The reader is repeatedly required to make such discriminations, and to understand what they mean by understanding why they are made. The difference between *security* and *safety* is finally between a virtuous form of security which is also safe, and a vicious form of security which is not. And the reader's capacity to achieve the first and avoid the second depends on his or her capacity to see the difference. Ethical choice is only enabled by the skills of precise writing and reading, and herein lies the heart of Renaissance humanism's identification of rhetorical training and ethical education.

CHAPTER THREE

Signs of Nobility and the Nobility of Signs

1 Of Simulation and Dissimulation

 The vera nobilitas argument originated in attempts to align inherited privilege with native talent, to prepare the nobly born for shouldering the responsibilities of government, and the writings of Elyot, Ascham, Humphrey and others during the sixteenth century represent the last significant attempt to match noble birth and political responsibility, to implement in effect the *regimen principum* originating with Plato and Isocrates. The other direction in which the vera nobilitas argument moves during its history is summarized by Marius' speech in Sallust's *Jugurthine Wars*, which argues not merely that the most competent should take on the burdens of government, but that they should be rewarded with the titles of such responsibility as a just public recognition of this competence. Where the first argument seeks to march responsibility with competence, the second would align signs of status with inner merit. And because the signs of aristocratic status may ascribe a nobility that members of the aristocracy do not possess – arguably the case with Robert Carr, the earl of Somerset, and George Villiers, duke of Buckingham in James I's later years – the crisis of the vera nobilitas argument becomes a semiotic crisis because it concerns the semiotics of hierarchical political structures.

This semiotic crisis is in turn part of the 'crisis of the aristocracy,' as Lawrence Stone has called the progressive loss of prestige the English aristocracy suffered during the hundred years straddling 1600. In particular, the 'enormous inflation by King James in the numbers of all ranks' (Stone 185) meant in effect 'the granting of titles of honour for cash not merit, in too great numbers, and to too unworthy persons' (748). Reflecting the belief that signs of aristocratic status confer nobility, both the old nobility and those newly created inverted the vera nobilitas argument by searching out – or inventing – extensive genealogies proving their noble ancestry.[1] Conspicuous prodigy houses added to the expansion, inflation, and exhaustion that overtook the signs of aristocratic status. In thus shamelessly exploiting them, the aristocracy unwittingly foregrounded the double capacity of these signs to disguise the lack of true nobility as well as manifest its possession.

'Inflation' is an accurate metaphor, because it articulates the nation's dwindling confidence in the truthfulness of the signs of aristocratic status. The assumption that such signs confer value in their own right obscures their true condition as mere signs whose significance depends entirely on the true nobility of those who display them. And it is on this displacement that Jonson's negative definition of true nobility focuses.

Jonson deals with prodigy houses as displays of unmerited status in 'To Penshvrst,' and *The Staple of News* makes comedy out of pretentious genealogies. In general, however, Jonson is concerned less with these splashier displays of false nobility than with private deportment and the transformation of speech and clothes into signs intended to declare one's putative virtues, and to hide from others – and oneself – the fact of their nonexistence. The failure of the aristocracy to exercise political power and privilege responsibly was less Jonson's concern than its failure to justify its power and privilege in the first place. For Jonson such justification would have meant development of the mind's capacity finely to discriminate ethical choices, the Renaissance humanist criterion of true nobility.

The capacity of humanly constructed signs to lie rests on their capacity to tell the truth, and Jonson localizes this dual potentiality in the clothes, both metaphorical and literal, that disguise the wearer's lacks through the same semiotic powers that allow them to manifest his or her virtues. However, deception by the visible is matched for Jonson by the ear's power to pierce that deception. He invites us to 'see' a person by hearing him speak, and the genius of Jonson's comedies lies partly in their wealth of fools and knaves who betray themselves by the pretensions of their speech. Clothes on the other hand include all form of masking that appeal to the eye – including masques reducible to mere spectacle – which pass untested by the ethical discriminations that speech makes

and invites. Jonson privileges verbal speech over visible display as the
truer measure of both true and false nobility, and this will be one topic
this chapter investigates.

Some of Jonson's poems are critical of men and women who like
himself were born into the class of tradesmen and artisans, yet who
aspire beyond their class on grounds that for Jonson are without merit.
On the other hand, recognition of Jonson's merits by aristocratic friends
and patrons is valuable only to the degree that their judgments are
informed by the capacity to discriminate true from false merit. And
since this capacity is in turn identical with the possession of true nobility,
Jonson must labour to summon up an aristocratic audience that possesses this capacity. Such an aristocracy alone is worth aspiring to, and
it alone can confer on inner true nobility public rewards that truly signify
it.

When Jonson attacks false pretensions to true nobility he takes the
perspective of the aristocracy itself and judges such pretensions by its
own values. His desire to become a member of the aristocracy is thus
proleptically fulfilled by identification with its elitist values against undesirable versions of his own ambitions. Such attacks are an identification, such as Kenneth Burke speaks of, with the ideology of the class
that excludes him.²

In this first section I shall discuss poems drawn mainly but not exclusively from the *Epigrammes*, wherein Jonson explores the capacity
of publicly acknowledged signs of prestige and status to simulate personal achievement, and thereby dissimulate its absence. Jonson in these
poems reverses the logic of simulation by showing how it reveals itself
unwittingly and transforms the signs of personal virtue into signs of its
lack.

The second section focuses on Jonson's favoured metaphor for such
simulation, namely clothes, which include all the ways in which men
and women dress themselves in the garments of ethical respectability
or aristocratic prestige. This section will concern clothes also as a social
code for signalling membership in one's class, their consequent capacity
to assert such membership falsely becoming the object of Elizabethan
sumptuary legislation.

Section 3 will extend this discussion by dealing with the rest of Jonson's poems that examine other misused signs of aristocratic status.
This section isolates in particular one Jonsonian strategy for carrying
out this critique: signs of status as versions of homonymy. Like words

with more than one meaning, such signs convey both false and true information about their users.

Finally, it becomes apparent that outer display can fail to reflect inner virtue in two opposite respects. One the one hand self-presentation can disguise the lack of inner virtue, and on the other its possession. In the first case outer signs tell more than the truth, and in the second less. Section 4 shows Jonson attempting unsuccessfully to break out of the hermeneutic circle in which the semiotics of the vera nobilitas argument binds him, a semiotics which validates outer sign by inner truth, and inner truth by outer sign.

A classical text paradigmatic for Jonson's explorations of the gaps and ligatures between inner person and outer man occurs in the *Rhetorica ad Herennium*. The writer exemplifies the trope of Comparison which Jonson will literalize:

> Let us imagine a player on the lyre who has presented himself on the stage, magnificently garbed, clothed in a gold-embroidered robe, with purple mantle interlaced in various colours, wearing a golden crown illumined with large gleaming jewels, and holding a lyre covered with golden ornaments and set off with ivory. Further, he has personal beauty, presence, and stature that impose dignity. If, when by these means he has roused a great expectation in the public, he should in the silence he has created suddenly give utterance to a rasping voice, and this should be accompanied by a repulsive gesture, he is the more forcibly thrust off in derision and scorn, the richer his adornment and the higher the hopes he has raised. ([Cicero] *Ad Herennium* 381)

Several things become apparent here. First, there is a sharp indecorum in the disproportion between visual and audible signs, and we may have here the ultimate origin of Jonson's demand, recorded in the *Discoveries*, 'Speak that I may see thee.'[3] If language issues, as Jonson says elsewhere in the *Discoveries*, from the inner man, then it cannot disguise as successfully as visible display the lacks of the inner man. Secondly, implicit in both the *Ad Herennium* example and Jonson's sententia is an anthropological model of surfaces and depths, of outsides and insides, appearances and realities.

Thirdly, this description (which reads before the fact like the emperor Nero in performance) forms one half of a comparison, the other half being none other than a version of the vera nobilitas argument. The passage in the *Ad Herennium* continues:

> In the same way, a man of high station, endowed with great and opulent resources, and abounding in all the gifts of fortune and the emoluments of nature, if he yet lacks virtue and the arts that teach virtue, will so much the more forcibly in derision and scorn be cast from all association with good men, the richer he is in the other advantages, the greater his distinction, and the higher the hopes he has raised.

This comparison transforms both clothes and wealth into signs that signify falsely. Both take on semiotic functions by entering a public code in which fine clothes and wealth putatively signify 'dignity' in the case of the singer, and 'virtue' in the case of the wealthy man. Pursuing these semiotic implications of the vera nobilitas argument leads Jonson to demand outer signs that accurately reflect inner realities and commits him to discounting the former in order to penetrate to the latter. This agenda is implied in one of Jonson's most incisive statements of the clothes motif, the song 'Still to be neat' from *Epicoene:*

> Still to be neat, still to be dressed,
> As you were going to a feast;
> Still to be powdered, still perfumed:
> Lady, it is to be presumed,
> Though art's hid causes are not found,
> All is not sweet, all is not sound.
>
> Give me a look, give me a face,
> That makes simplicity a grace;
> Robes loosely flowing, hair as free:
> Such sweet neglect more taketh me,
> Than all the adulteries of art;
> They strike mine eyes, but not my heart.
>
> (1.1.80ff; Wilkes ed 3:131)

Disguises reveal the need to disguise, raising suspicions of the presence of the hidden. 'Art's hid causes' sums up two hidden realities: an art that in concealing its artfulness attempts to look like nature; and the causes of the its use – the deficiencies to be hidden – which are obscured as well. Because the artifice dissimulates its own dissimulation, the poet is moved to pierce it. Indeed, because he has done so he suspects that 'All is not sweet, all is not sound.'[4]

The second stanza of Jonson's poem concerns not the body beneath the clothes, as in Herrick's rewrite ('Delight in Disorder'), where the kindling clothes and erring lace hide and disclose the naked body underneath, but the person behind the disguise. Externals appeal to what registers externals, and such disguises strike the poet's eye but not his heart. What does strike his heart is 'simplicity,' but simplicity that is a 'grace,' that is, ornament, not simple-mindedness. Jonson turns the art/nature differential, which includes the covert collusions between the two terms that it invites, on its head twice in the poem. If the lady in the first stanza seeks to hide her art by making it appear natural, the lady in the second makes naturalness itself a form of art.

Jonson seeks to discriminate here not the artful and the natural, but two different relations between art and nature. Art becomes an adultery – literally an admixture debasing an otherwise pure substance – when it seeks to disguise itself. The 'naturalist' in the poem is neither the poet nor the lady with the flowing robes and loose hair, but the lady in the first stanza. It is she who, in setting human artifice and human natural imperfections at odds, seeks to hide the latter with the former. But in fleeing the natural for artifice she discloses an equal distaste for the artificial, attempting to 'hide' its causes as well, by projecting a meretricious naturalness. The adultery here lies in the muddle that results: a lady at once artificial and artificially natural, at home with neither and consequently displaying to the suspicious eye of the poet a self-accusation that admits her own sense of deficiency.[5]

For Jonson, those who disguise their deficiencies always disclose them, and in this lies the semiotic homonymy of such disguises: their capacity to signify both high value and low value. This is Jonson's point in E16, 'To Brayne-Hardie,' who 'damns himselfe' (10) by boasting of his prowess in quarrelling and brawling.

There are several unmaskings here. First, Hardie is shown to hide his cowardice behind the mask of quarrelling oaths, which bring him into numerous fights, all of which, however, he avoids: 'So, in short time, th'art in arrerage growne / Some hundred quarrells, yet dost thou fight none' (5–6). His cowardice is manifested by the number of brawls his swearing commits him to, since the greater the number of unfulfilled oaths the greater the cowardice these oaths must compensate for. Then there is the second unmasking. By such swearing Hardie risks damnation, thereby reclaiming seriously what he swears only in pretence (though he deceives himself in believing he swears in earnest), namely, his true courage: 'He that dares damne himselfe, dares more then fight' (10). In the end, Hardie's attempts to convince others of his courage prove successful.

Jonson's ironies are convoluted because they trace through the complex swerves impelled by Hardie's self-recognition, a self-recognition at once admitted and denied, and both in the same act of boasting. It is, however, one thing to victimize oneself by unwittingly displaying not only one's cowardice, but one's admission of and fear of one's cowardice in trying to mask it. It is something else to be told that the mask itself is a form of courage, being a disclosure both of the cowardice one fears to disclose and of the damnation one risks in addition to all the rest.

Such paradoxes of self-evasion are central to Jonson's acute analysis of the simulations and dissimulations constituting pretensions to status.[6] Self-evasion presupposes both self-recognition and self-delusion, a paradox of consciousness that has been described by Jacques Lacan under the term *méconnaissance:*

> What in fact is the phenomenon of delusional belief? It is, I insist, failure to recognize, with all that this term contains of an essential antinomy. For to fail to recognize presupposes a recognition, as is manifested in systematic failure to recognize, where it must obviously be admitted that what is denied is in some fashion recognized. (Lacan *Language* 96)

Jonson lays bare before Hardie the labyrinthine process of his moral self-evasion. The labour of self-evasion is proportioned to the self-condemnation that generates it; and it is finally self-condemnation that Jonson excoriates in much of his work.

A briefer epigram to similar purport is E20, 'To the Same Sir Cod':

> Th'expence in odours is a most vaine sinne,
> Except thou could'st, Sir COD, weare them within.

Sir Cod would seem in need of more sweetening than that afforded by mere perfumes. If 'odours' are intended to hide character lacks of a more substantial sort, then their only true efficacy would be to 'sweeten' the failings of the inner man. But of course, perfume cannot do this in any literal fashion, and that fact points up the vast gulf between Sir

Cod's true lacks, and the perfumes with which he seeks to hide these lacks, or to compensate for them.

The satirical epigrams share something with the riddle, in challenging the reader to discover the hidden joke. They hide the connections, equivalences, and differentials that make sense of their surface statements and in this respect the reader conspires with the poet in writing the epigram. When the reader perceives the wit and can explain the epigram, at that moment he or she also comes to share the writer's judgment as well.[7] The satirical epigram evokes this information by mimicking, and unmasking, the hidden human, moral reality which is the epigram's content. In describing Hardie's and Sir Cod's gestures of simulation and dissimulation, Jonson gives them a structure and a logic like those of censorship in dreams for Freud. Each has a self-revealing logic of its own. And it is this logic that the epigram inscribes, while it conceals – as its subject conceals – the motivational source ('art's hid causes') that generates that inscription, and renders it revealingly incomplete.[8]

That which reveals itself by being incomplete is the subject of several epigrams that Jonson writes attacking poetasters who have lifted *mots* from him and passed them off as their own. In E53, 'To Old-end Gatherer,' the plagiarist hides both the author he stole from and his own theft, leaving only the name of a patron on the title page. The pun on 'pill'd' (2), that is, both stolen and compiled, reveals the thief's poverty of mind: he must steal to make a book, and when he makes a book it is only stolen (compiled) from another. Consequently, putting in the name of the patron is an attempt to confirm the book's originality, like the witness at a Puritan baptism who turns out to be the father as well: 'It was as if thou printed had'st an oath, / To giue the world assurance thou wert both; / And that, as *puritanes* at baptisme doo, / Thou art the father, and the witnesse too' (5–8). Jonson suggests that the anonymous author at once disclaims his literary larceny and displays his consciousness of it.

E56, 'On Poet-Ape,' makes the purveying of literary fragments a sign of the theft that collected them which anyone can read: 'Foole, as if halfe eyes wil not know a fleece / From locks of wooll, or shreds from the whole peece?' (13–14). The poet-ape 'takes vp all, makes each mans wit his own. / And, told of this, he slights it' (8–9). The ambiguity of 'slights it' evokes mutually exclusive attitudes: the poet-ape exhibits both shame in denying, and shamelessness in admitting, his thefts, each stance complicit with the other.

Finally, we have an epigram that records Jonson's sale of *vers de circonstance* 'To <u>Fine Grand</u>' (E73), and his presenting him with the bill for payment, an itemized account that makes up the bulk of the poem which the poet publishes because 'The world must know your greatnesse is my debter' (4). Fine Grand's 'greatness' is small enough – easily satisfied to support itself with 'a faire *greeke* poesie for a ring' or 'your mistris *anagram*, 'i your hilt' (10, 16) – but Jonson insists nevertheless on broadcasting the poet's power to thrust greatness even on such unpromising material. This epigram contains a vertiginous oscillation between great and trivial valuations. Clearly, Fine Grand fancies his wit and prestige greatly enhanced by his purchase of Jonson's baubles. This in turn enhances the poet's ego, or might do so were he not sardonically aware that he must write 'most vile verses,' which 'cost me more paine, / Then had I made 'hem good, to fit your vaine' (19–20). Fine Grand's need to buy verses witnesses personal lacks that in his own eyes must appear peculiarly trivial, since they require such trivial compensations to mask them. And it is not lost on Jonson that Fine Grand's campaign to convince the world of his wit leads him to one of the wittiest poets of the age – to be satisfied, as it were, with nothing less than the best – only to purchase trifles from him. Jonson demands quick payment, 'or Ile pay you' (22), a demand that reduces the sharpness of poetic wit to monetary payment, an equivalence that Jonson is sure Fine Grand will understand.

The fragments and shards of discourse become likewise objects of desire in another quarter: inside information about political manoeuvre and intrigue serves to confer on the bearer a specious importance proportional to the callowness of the eager listeners whom this information gulls. 'Captayne Hvngry' of E107, a demobbed soldier, is one Jonsonian version of this type, as is Sir Politick Would-Be in *Volpone* another. Sir Pol's description of the intelligence-monger conveys to Peregrine a non-ironic and straight-faced version of the type Jonson portrays in several poems:

> First, for your garb, it must be grave and serious;
> Very reserved and locked; not tell a secret,
> On any terms, not to your father; scarce
> A fable, but with caution; make sure choice
> Both of your company and discourse ...   (4.1.12–16; Wilkes ed)

The illusion of importance conveyed by possessing privileged information betrays the impostor's dependence for his self-identity wholly on his listener's lust to penetrate the raw appearances of things to a reality intriguing because hidden from view.

As for Sir Pol, for Captain Hungry news and dinner go together. The captain is in fact empty of everything except lies, with which he pays for his meals: 'Tell the grosse *Dutch* those grosser tales of yours, / How great you were with their two Emperours; / And yet are with their Princes: Fill them full / Of your *Moravian* horse, *Venetian* bull. / Tell them, what parts yo'haue tane, whence run away, / What States yo'haue gull'd, and which yet keepes yo'in pay' (5–10). Pieces and shards of the soldier's conversation appear in the underlined place names, which, though names of real countries, are curiously transformed into mere words to be conjured with, empty signifiers encoding reference to nothing but empty pretensions. Consequently in the following passage, 'your *Ville-royes*, and *Silleries*, / *Ianin's*, your *Nuncio's*, and your *Tuïlleries*, / Your *Arch-Dukes* Agents, and your *Beringhams*, / That are your wordes of credit' (21–4), such names of persons and places become purely fictional and no different from palpable concoctions such as *Shieterhuissen* (privy), *Popenheim*, and *Hans-spiegle*, which in this context take on a specious geographical authenticity.

The following epigram 'To Trve Sovldiers' (E108) is presumably addressed to soldiers who took offence at the previous epigram. Jonson distinguishes true and false captains, and says that it is the latter who wrong the true soldiers, not the poet himself: 'Strength of my countrey, whilst I bring to view / Such as are misse-call'd Captaynes, and wrong you; / And your high names' (1–3). He concludes by saying that 'He that not trusts me, hauing vow'd thus much, / but's angry for the Captayne, still: is such' (9–10). This is consistent with Jonson's conviction that the truly virtuous need not fear taint by satire, and only those complain who fear such an attack, displaying in the process their own vulnerability.[9]

A fuller version of E107 is E92, 'The New Crie.' Here Jonson unmasks intelligence-mongers whose cryptic remarks and elaborately evasive gestures hide nothing but the fact that there is nothing to hide. They 'talke reseru'd, lock'd vp, and full of feare, / Nay, aske you, how the day goes, in your eare. / Keepe a *starre*-chamber sentence close, twelue dayes: / And whisper what a Proclamation sayes' (17–20). Jonson may have remembered here Donne's fourth satire, in which a courtier plays a similar game with the poem's speaker:

He takes my hand, and as a Still, which staies
A Sembriefe, 'twixt each drop, he nigardly,
As loth to enrich mee, so tells many a lye.
More then ten Hollensheads, or Halls, or Stowes,
Of triviall houshold trash he knowes ...

Like Jonson, Donne has also caught the trick of the courtier's voice:

He knowes
When the Queene frown'd, or smil'd, and he knowes what
A subtle States-man may gather of that ...   (94–100, Grierson ed)

Both poets have in mind the same phenomenon, but Jonson's agenda
is different from Donne's: to unmask not only the 'ripe statesmen's'
simulation of being privy to state matters, but their dissimulation of
this simulation. Their facility with invisible writing, with covert violation of seals (25ff), their portentous innuendoes ('And they know, / If
the *States* make peace, how it will goe / With *England*,' 29–31), all are
mutedly ostentatious flourishes of elaborate concealment, intended to
mask not only the fact that there is nothing to hide, but the masking
itself.

Such elaborate simulation, dissimulation of simulation, and finally
dissimulation of dissimulation cannot be assaulted frontally, as can the
less sophisticated fortifications of the Captain Hungrys of the world.
Rather, like a spell that can be undone only by being read backward,
Jonson must elaborately retrace each twist and turn of self-evasion generated by the *méconnaissance* of one's deficiencies. Such impostors have
already recognized the deficiencies signalled by their need to disguise
themselves, and seek to forestall in advance, as it were, decipherment
and detection. The espionage game, which such intelligence-mongers
claim to have decoded, replicates their own game of hide-and-seek with
themselves and with others. And to unmask that game Jonson must
patiently remove layer after layer of disguise, thrusting into the light of
day every tactical move of self-effacement.[10]

One conclusion seems inevitable: Jonson knows too much about these
tactics, he pursues too unerringly such prey past the blinds set up to
deflect those less adept in the ways of moral self-delusion. This is not
to agree with Alvin Kernan that Jonson is, like the figure of the satirist
in Renaissance satire, complicitous with the evils he attacks. It is rather
to suggest that Jonson has earned the capacity, and therefore the right,

to pursue with such knowledgeable self-assurance the moral *méconnaissance* of others because he has pursued the same thing with equal rigour in himself.

Another conclusion that is perhaps less certain but no less suggestive has to do with courtship, defined by Kenneth Burke as 'the use of suasive devices for transcending social estrangement' (*Rhetoric* 208). Intelligence-monitoring, like most other confidence games played by figures in Jonson's poetry and plays, is an attempt to win acceptance by an alien Other ensconced across a barrier of social or ethical inequality. In E107, 'To Captayne Hvngry,' the erotic parallel is made overt: 'Giue your yong States-men, (that first make your drunke, / And then lye with you, closer, then a punque, / For newes) your *Villle-royes*, and *Silleries*' (19–21). In this respect courting of acceptance parallels Jonson's own agenda of courtship, and for him such parallels typically threaten to displace his own version; or – which comes to the same thing – he sees that his own version risks being transformed into such malign versions of itself. Satire of the sort in E92 represents Jonson's need to co-opt courtship by analysing the rhetoric of the falsely pretentious, forestalling it, and distancing it from his own.

One poem where Jonson turns a critical eye most overtly on himself is U45, 'An Epistle to Master Arth: Squib,' which sets the poet's agenda directly in the opening lines: 'What I am not, and what I faine would be, / Whilst I informe my selfe, I would teach thee, / My gentle *Arthur*; that it might be said / One lesson we have both learn'd, and well read' (1–4). The poem queries what characterizes true friendship, and Jonson's method is typically dialectical, beginning with negative qualities. Testing friends for their authenticity is like testing money; counterfeits lead to consideration of deceit, which leads into the clothes motif:

> Men have Masques and nets,
> But these with wearing will themselves unfold:
> They cannot last. No lie grew ever old.
> Turne him, and see his Threds: looke, if he be
> Friend to himselfe, that would be friend to thee.
> For that is first requir'd, A man be his owne.
> But he that's too-much that, is friend of none. (18–22)

The poet's opening promise to examine himself as he examines the meaning of friendship is thus linked with the end: friendship with others requires self-knowledge.

The core of this self-examination is whether a person is 'Friend to himselfe,' a central component implicit in Jonson's critique of pretensions to self-importance. Equally implicit is the connection between self-contempt and fruitful deceit, which in hiding a man from himself signals a self that, in being not 'his owne,' cannot be given a friend. He invites young Arthur to test him by these criteria, and implies that Jonson would test him likewise, implying in addition that examinations of self and of other are mutually implicative, and neither can proceed alone.[11]

There are a few poems in which Jonson indulges the Juvenalian vein of Donne, Marston, and Hall. One of these is U15, 'An Epistle to a Friend, to perswade him to the Warres,' in which Jonson recites still more extensively the qualities he demands of the person who loves himself and therefore has no need of masking. The main body of the poem includes the expected catalogue of types inhabiting this 'hell on earth: where flatterers, spies, / Informers, Masters both of Arts and lies; / Lewd slanderers, soft whisperers that let blood / The life, and fame-vaynes (yet not understood / Of the poore sufferers) where the envious, proud, / Ambitious, factious, superstitious, lowd / Boasters, and perjur'd, with the infinite more / Praevaricators swarme' (163–70). Specific portraits include 'the grave, sower, and supercilious Sir / In outward face, but inward, light as Furre, / Or Feathers,' who is 'Honour'd at once, and envi'd (if it can / Be honour is so mixt) by such as would, / For all their spight, be like him if they could' (19–26). Jonson finds 'Pride, and stiffe Clownage mixt / To make up Greatnesse!' (43–4), while 'Stallion' causes 'his Court-bred-fillie' to 'fall upon her back / In admiration, stretch'd upon the rack / Of lust, to his rich Suit and title, Lord' (47–51). Clothes become for her a sexual fetish: 'To do't with Cloth, or Stuffes, lusts name might merit; / With Velvet, Plush, and Tissues, it is spirit' (57–8).

The poem's addressee, one Colby otherwise unidentified, is on the other hand admonished

> Goe, quit' hem all. And take along with thee,
> Thy true friends wishes, *Colby*, which shall be,
> That thine be just, and honest; that thy Deeds
> Not wound thy conscience, when thy body bleeds;
> That thou dost all things more for truth, then glory,
> And never but for doing wrong be sory;
> That by commanding first thy selfe, thou mak'st
> Thy person fit for any charge thou tak'st;

That fortune never make thee to complaine,
But what she gives, thou dar'st give her againe;
That whatsoever face thy fate puts on,
Thou shrinke or start not, but be alwayes one;
That thou thinke nothing great, but what is good,
And from that thought strive to be understood.   (175–88)

In the context of the preceding catalogue, these stoic arguments take on a recognizable vera nobilitas import, concerned less with moral oppositions between virtue and vice than with false pretensions versus stoic honesty. Colby is advised that command of fortune originates with 'commanding first thy selfe,' which means freedom from the vacuous self's need to be filled with others' regard and honour.

Jonson's command of himself was sorely tested throughout his career, but perhaps nothing, not even the failure of *The New Inn*, seems to have shaken him more than his gradual but irreversible displacement in the favour of the court by Inigo Jones. It was a running battle almost from the beginning of their collaboration on the production of court masques, but Jonson's final judgment on Jones' ascendancy was to take the matter beyond questions of poetry versus spectacle in deciding the priorities of the masque form. In 'An Expostulacion with Inigo Iones' (M34) the conflict between the spoken word and visual spectacle becomes a metaphor for an issue even closer to Jonson: the relation of the self-made artist to the aristocracy of England.

Inigo Jones' class origins seem to have been much like Jonson's, Jones being 'the son of a weaver [who] had begun life as a joiner' (H&S 1:277; Summerson 15ff). Like Jonson he was ambitious for status and recognition, and Jonson accuses him of aspirations to a title in M35, 'To Inigo Marquess Would be A Corollary' to the preceding 'Expostulacion.' Jones like Jonson used his art to achieve status at court and patronage from the king and the nobility. What incenses Jonson about the man is the same thing that incensed him about Jones' contributions to the masques at court: both are mere outsides without either depth or intellectual content.

This poem summarizes the series of connections I have examined in this section, between Jonson's strictures on social pretensions constructed wholly from external show, and his insistence that only those capable of the ethical discriminations afforded by verbal discourse can possess the understanding which marks the member of the true nobility of humanist virtue. The 'Mighty showes' (39) that Jonson attacks are thus at once Jones' stage scenery and Jones himself: 'What need of prose / Or Verse, or Sense t'express Immortal you? / You are the Spectacles of state! Tis true / Court Hieroglyphicks, & all Artes affoord / In the mere perspectiue of an Inch board!' (40–4). We have here the classic Jonsonian scenario: a set of signifiers – in this case, the whole panoply of stage design, costume, and music – without signifieds, without the meaning supplied for Jonson only by language. It is Fastidious Brisk of *Every Man Out* all over again, the false courtiers of *Cynthia's Revels* and social snobs of *Poetaster*.

Indeed, the situation was worse than that. The masques at court were never mere spectacles, for Jonson poured out a never-ending stream of verse in all forms and styles, not to mention humanistic classical learning and mythology by the yard, only to see the court (and its correspondents, including the ubiquitous ambassador of Venice) award Jones' increasingly ingenious deployment of stage machinery and perspective the whole of their attention. Inigo Jones thus became for Jonson in his last years a summation of all that he inveighed against. And Jones capped this function by usurping Jonson's own place and standing in the one locus wherein Jonson hoped to reap the rewards of his own labour: the court itself. The full significance of the attacks on Inigo Jones can only appear in the context of Jonson's blueprint for an aristocracy of title transformed into an aristocracy of humanist virtue.

Jones is, first of all, a man of 'titles': 'By all your Titles, & whole style at ones / Of Tyre-man, Mounte-banck & Iustice Jones, / I doe salute you! Are you fitted yet? / Will any of these express your place? or witt? / Or are you soe ambitious 'boue your peers! / You would be an Asinigo, by your ears?' ('Expostulacion' 15–20). Jones having 'growne rich? & proud' is told that 'your Trappings will not change you. Change your mynd. / Noe veluet Sheath you weare, will alter kynde' (24–6). Jones' scene designs require 'noe more then certenyne politique Eyes' – which Jonson can provide:

> Eyes that can pierce into the Misteryes
> Of many Colours! read them! & reueale
> Mythology there painted on slit deale!
> Oh, to make Boardes to speake! There is a taske
> Painting & Carpentry are the Soule of Masque.   (45–50)

This scenery projects the illusion of hidden depths which tempt the eye to pierce into mysteries projected in painted perspectives that turn out to be no deeper or thicker than wooden planks. These planks mimic speech and are planted with 'Musick which noe eare can reach!' as well as 'Attyre the Persons as noe thought can teach / Sense, what they are!' (53–5). Jones' spectacle aspires to take over the roles of music and fable (63), and in comparison Jonson asks 'What Poesy ere was painted on a wall / That might compare with thee?' (97–8).[12]

Implied in this poem is a homology that Jonson pursues with varying degrees of explicitness throughout his poetry, and in particular the poems considered in this chapter – language : picture :: true meaning : false meaning :: inner person : outer show. By querying the capacity of Jones' scenic constructions to speak and tell a story, Jonson highlights what for him is the indispensable component of meaning: verbal language. Jonson's position strikingly previews the paradox of modern semiotics, where human verbal language, while being itself one code out of many, is yet the privileged code in which the meanings of all other codes are mediated and inscribed.[13] Particularly relevant is Jonson's articulating meaning in differential structures which, as I have suggested in chapter 1, invites analysis by application of a structuralist model in which meaning is entirely a system of differences.[14] In the case of those like Jones and the other examples discussed in this section, outer show is a visual presentation aimed at blocking penetration, and it lies in the discourse of the satirical poem itself to bestow a momentary plenitude on the emptiness of those pretending to importance, as that discourse inscribes the dodges and swerves of the *méconnaissance* that constitute that plenitude.[15]

2 The Semiotics of Aristocratic Status

Jonson's attitude toward the masques he produced with Inigo Jones must surely have been deeply ambiguous and troubling from the beginning. His laboured allegorizations of myth and spectacle appended to the early quarto editions registered suspicions that were confirmed in the end: that the 'illusion of power,' as Stephen Orgel calls it (*Illusion*) – the sheer visual impact of spectacle and stage machinery – would always exert hypnotic power over courtly audiences, and so obliterate the immaterial meaning lying behind them, the work not of the painter but of the poet.[16] Jonson feared and respected the power of signs, the material, visible panoply of status and dominion: the power of signs of power. And there is perhaps a sense in his poetry of exorcising this fear by the strategy of insisting that such signs are empty and impotent unless supported by the inner virtue of true nobility.

In this regard Jonson committed himself to a double agenda: dismantling of signs of power considered as pure illusions, the mere outer panoply of power; and the replenishing of these signs with the humanist values that alone conferred vera nobilitas. It soon becomes obvious that the double thrust of this agenda pulled in different directions. This is because any critique of an aristocratic semiotic in the name of allegiance to it must always risk subverting it.

Another way of elucidating this anomaly is to examine the play of meanings in an aphorism of Chateaubriand, embedded in his *Memoirs*, on the logic governing the decay of aristocracies, and its relevance to Jonson's own analyses:

The aristocracy has three successive ages: the age of superiority, the age of privilege, the age of vanity; once it has left the first behind, it degenerates in the second and expires in the last. (4)

François-René de Chateaubriand, born of noble lineage before the Revolution and sometime servant of it after, was well placed to make this observation. It is a belated expression of the vera nobilitas argument, and articulates how signs of power can enable and conceal the evacuation of their own meaning.

Privilege signifies superiority (true nobility) only as long as superiority exists to give it meaning. But since privilege can also mask the disappearance of superiority, the vanity which preens itself in the superiority putatively signified by privilege ironically discloses its absence. It is, in other words, just this exploitation of the signs of power that constitutes vanity, and which invites the critical eye to unmask a privilege unfounded on superiority. Chateaubriand's epigram therefore inscribes a paradox: because each successive stage assumes the previous one, each successive stage can undercut the previous one.

In this section I propose a semiotic restatement of a problem which the vera nobilitas argument historically addressed in philosophical and ethical terms. This argument constructed an implicitly semiotic analysis when it asserted that the outer signs of aristocratic status are incomplete when they do not refer to true nobility. And a brief examination of this analysis in semiotic terms will illuminate its peculiar instability which Jonson laboured to articulate.

The fundamental structure of the sign in modern semiotics is its bipartite division into signifier and signified. In the various classic developments of semiotics out of Saussurian structuralism set forth by Louis Hjemlslev, Roland Barthes, and Umberto Eco, material signifier and its signified (meaning) only come into existence simultaneously, both parts of a system of signifiers and signifieds respectively which together constitute the semantic repertoire of the sign system itself. Furthermore, the process of code construction can be repeated recursively, so that codes of signs collectively become a set of signifiers in still another code, in which they take on still other, secondary meanings. This last point, which Barthes (*Elements*) following Hjelmslev calls connotation (89) and Eco overcoding (129), refers to ways in which cultures take over sign systems that already exist complete and articulated in their own sphere, and employ them as signifiers for meanings additional to and different from those they originally have.

The codes of epideictic rhetoric, clothes, architecture, heraldry, and genealogical tables have the capacity to become signifiers in a secondary sociopolitical code, in which they collectively signify 'high status,' 'privilege,' 'power.' And this code can be 'overcoded' yet again, signifying in turn 'possession of true nobility.' However, since each of these codes is already a sign system complete in its own right, there is no semiotic necessity that requires it to be overcoded and enter a new code such as one in which 'aristocracy' or 'true nobility' are the signified. In practical, concrete terms, the signifiers of noble status need not refer to a signified of noble status, nor need noble status signify true nobility, and this lack of obligation registers semiotically the same lack which the vera nobilitas argument historically sought to remedy.

In chapter 2 it became apparent that the vera nobilitas argument could subvert or support established aristocracies because the assertion that aristocrats possess true nobility generates dialectically the assertion that they do not, and the assertion that those who possess true nobility are not aristocrats elicits arguments that they are. Viewing aristocratic establishments as rich and complex semiotic systems uncovers one ground of these paradoxes, and serves to clarify the argument's capacity to generate different conclusions that contradict one another.

In a related direction, a semiotic model illuminates Chateaubriand's discovery that privilege may signify either the possession of superiority or its lack. Chateaubriand's epigram yields five distinct but related semiotic possibilities. The semiotic system of aristocratic status has the multiple capacity to (a) manifest possession of true nobility, (b) simulate its presence, (c) dissimulate its absence, (d) disclose its absence, (e) dissimulate its dissimulation. In Chateaubriand's terms, privilege can (a) manifest possession of superiority, (b) simulate its possession, (c) privilege dissimulates the absence of superiority, (d) vanity in turn ironically announces the absence of superiority, and (e) seeks to dissimulate its dissimulation.

These multiple semiotic relations reflect the double supplementary status of aristocratic status itself.[17] On the one hand, such status supplements true nobility as something merely added on, a publicly recognized sign of nobility which is not otherwise essential to it or constitutive of it. On the other, the system of signs that constitute aristocratic status may come to constitute the only substantive reality there is, thereby supplementing true nobility in a new way – as that which is necessary to complete it, to bring it into existence: the supplement as that which supplants.[18] Obviously, the vera nobilitas argument lauds the first sort of supplementation and inveighs against the second. Chateaubriand pinpoints for readers of Jonson just this capacity of aristocratic status to supplement true nobility in both senses. It is this dual semiotic capacity by which signs that signify truly are also able to signify falsely, this double supplementary function of signs themselves, that both the French and the English writer bring into high relief.

Jonson employs clothes as a central trope for all external signs (or signifiers) by which men and women disclose and dissimulate their inner selves.[19] In this he follows the mainstream vera nobilitas argument. Seneca, for instance, sought to pierce behind the clothes to the soul,[20] and in the Renaissance Giovanni Nenna distinguishes rhetorically: 'And what if some times the first were but meanlie apparelled, and the latter did weare costly garmentes, wilt thou say that hee were more noble, or more accompt, and worthy of more estimation? no surely as I thinke' (Q1v). Clothes derive their capacity to simulate high rank and dissimulate inner lacks from their being encoded to signify class status.

A manuscript 'Book of Precedence' dating from the early Renaissance in England specifies the clothing and behaviour appropriate for each rank of the major and minor peerage ('Precedence'). Violations of clothing codes, and complaints about these violations, were commonplace during the sixteenth century. One of Guazzo's interlocutors, for instance, speaks of 'many riche Pesantes, who are not ashamed to attire themselves like Gentlemen, to weare weapons by their side, and suche like ornaments, which are proper only to gentlemen' (1:196). By contrast, he says, you shall not see this disorder and confusion in Fraunce, where, by ancient custome severall apparell is worne, according to everie ones calling. So that by the garments only, you may know whether a woman be the wife of an Artificer, a Merchant, or Gentlemen: And which is more, by the apparel, you shall knowe a difference betweene Gentlewomen themselves, for some attire is proper to Ladies, and those that attende in the court uppon some Queene or Princesse, likewise to the wives of Presidentes, Counsellours, and principal Magistrates, which neverthelesse is not allowed to everie Gentlewoman. (1:197)[21]

The need to maintain 'a common rhetorical code for registering elite status' (Whigham 155) was enforced by Queen Elizabeth through sumptuary laws, and a 'Homilie against Excesse of Apparell' was read in churches against violating this code. Whigham cites a 1577 indictment whose details suggest 'that most of the discriminatory enforcement was aimed at denying and punishing pretensions to gentry status' (162).

I cite the kinds of social encoding that clothes underwent in Jonson's own time (and such codes certainly predate the Renaissance) in order to define by contrast Jonson's similar, but finally very different position on clothes as signifiers that can simulate and dissimulate. Sumptuary laws and homilies on clothing assume that clothes encode, and can be mapped onto, the class system of hierarchical status – that clothes in fact reflect this status. However, Jonson's critique of clothes (and of all coded signs of status) operates on an axis of opposition that cuts across that assumed by sumptuary decorum. Whereas within the perspective of sumptuary legislation putting on the 'wrong' clothes disguises lack of class status, for Jonson putting on the wrong clothes disguises the lack of inner virtue that alone justifies such status. Sumptuary laws treated the social status that clothing styles were supposed to signify as a natural and God-given fact of political structure (Elyot 2ff). Clothes could therefore become merely an additional code supplementary to class status. For Jonson, however, clothes were themselves part of the semiotic system that constituted class status, which was in turn supplementary to true nobility. Consequently, while sumptuary laws tested the appropriateness of clothing against a person's birth, Jonson in true vera nobilitas fashion tested both against personal achievement.

The arbitrariness with which the clothes code could be made to signify secondary meanings elicited an equally arbitrary response, namely laws intended to fix and stabilize the code's possible meanings: a semiotic system by fiat. The semiotic-cum-legislative laws insisting that aristocratic clothing signify aristocratic status made possible the simulations and dissimulations that Jonson anatomizes in his poetry and plays. Because clothing can not only simulate and dissimulate, but also disclose both simulation and dissimulation, we may expect in the poems discussed in this section to treat clothes as at once disguises and manifestations of inner poverty, and the latter because the former.

This ambiguous and ironic semiotic phenomenon Jonson renders mainly by causing inner and outer to change places, so that the inner person comes to consist in nothing but layers of clothes. In the epigram 'On the New Motion,' that is, puppet (E97), the poet confronts a courtier so overdressed that he is unable to determine what sort of thing it is. This question motivates the poem: 'What then so swells each lim?' (19). The poet ticks off various fashionable and courtly activities in order to demonstrate that the Motion is 'swelled' by none of these. This 'new motion' is just that: a puppet literally made up of layers of clothing: 'Onely his clothes haue ouer-leauen'd him' (20). There is no distinction between inside and outside, because inside consists only of outsides.

Jonson ironically mimics attempts to create self-importance out of clothes by literalizing the transformation of the inner person into nothing but clothing. Such a literalization occurs in E15, 'On Covrt-Worme':

> All men are wormes: But this no man. In silke
>   'Twas brought to court first wrapt, and white as milke;
> Where, afterwards, it grew a butter-flye:
>   Which, was a cater-pillar. So't will dye.

This is a tiny allegory, in which the progress of the courtier's advancement at court is literalized as a development from worm to caterpillar and finally to butterfly. This literalization is motivated by the double association of silk with both caterpillar and the courtier's clothing. The courtier, having defined himself entirely by his clothes, turns into nothing but a silkworm, who can look forward to a span of court favour as evanescent as his life.[22]

In a manner similar to that in the 'Expostulacion,' Jonson finds that clothes project the illusion of hidden depths, which turn out to conceal nothing at all, save layers of illusion, of simulation. Literalizing the penetration these illusory depths invite, Jonson turns clothes into a sexual fetish. In *The New Inn* Pinnacia Stuff describes her tailor husband's employing her as a kind of sex doll which he dresses in clothes ordered by gentle ladies:

> When he makes any fine garment will fit me,
> Or any rich thing that he thinks of price,
> Then must I put it on and be his countess,
> Before he carry it home unto the owners.
>
> (4.3.66–9; Wilkes 4:444–5)

Similarly, in the two epigrams 'On Sir Volvptvovs Beast,' E25 and E26, Sir Voluptuous compels his wife to dress as and act out the roles of his various pederastic partners, including a boy and a goat. His wife dressing herself in the forms projected on her by her husband's fantasies, becoming an adulteress and consequently 'her own cuckqueane' (5), that is, her own cuckold. And there is a kind of perverse logic in these transformations. In the opening line Jonson discriminates contrastively the two qualities of Beast's wife: she is 'faire, and innocent.' Her innocence creates the malleability by which she can become in fantasy at once dutiful spouse, male whore, a goat, and the adulteress who cuckolds herself. The fact that, as Jonson says in the second epigram, Beast no longer 'knows' his wife, because 'He'adulters still: his thoughts lye with a whore,' derives from his dressing her in his sexual fantasies. Sexual congress in turn produces its own impossible perversities, where penetration proceeds into a hidden depth consisting of nothing but surfaces.

U15, 'An Epistle to a Friend, to perswade him to the Warres,' examined briefly in the previous section, refers to the 'Court-bred-fillie' who lusts 'To do't with Cloth' (48, 57). Jonson expands such sexual fetishism to pornographic detail in U42, 'An Elegie,' which, unlike other poems with the same title in *The Vnder-wood*, seems clearly authorial. Its central subject is poetry's power to praise beautiful women, or more precisely, its capacity to articulate sex appeal. The body of the poem satirizes the clothes fetishism of poetasters, and Jonson in this replicates a central point of his *Charis* sequence (U2): that the true lover is he whose poetry addresses the lady herself and not her clothes.

Jonson launches into this by insisting that 'No Poets verses yet did ever move, / Whose Readers did not thinke he was in love' (3–4), and then claims that his love poetry will convince so effectively that London citizens will fear his seductive power over their wives and daughters. An extended description follows of the city husbands' own erotic fantasies spun around 'a Velvet Petticote, or Gowne, / Whose like I have knowne the Taylors Wife put on / To doe her Husband's rites in, e're 'twere gone / Home to the Customer' (38–41). Jonson works up a full-scale scenario in which the footman

> did make most solemne love,
> To ev'ry Petticote he brush'd, and Glove
> He did lay up, and would adore the shooe,
> Or slipper was left off, and kiss it too,
> Court every hanging Gowne, and after that,
> Lift up some one, and doe, I tell not what. (53–8)

Then there is the poetaster 'That chanc'd the lace, laid on a Smock, to see, / And straight-way spent a Sonnet' (66–7). Of course, the seductive poetling and the fearful citizen secretly share this sexual fetish and de-serve each other. Jonson concludes by asking 'why / Thou art jealous of thy Wifes, or Daughters case [dress]: / More than of eithers manners, wit, or face!' (86–8).

The city husband, the lovesick groom, and the poetaster all attest at once to their sexual perversion, snobbism, and sense of class inferiority by projecting women's clothes as the vessel of their desirability. Like Nick Stuff in *The New Inn*, the tailor makes love to his wife dressed in clothes that he will after deliver to a great lady, and the footman makes love to gloves and slippers. Clothes, which are here a sign of courtly status aped by city wives, become the object of a desire at once sexual and social. If clothes signify noble status, then one hides one's naked inferiority by putting them on, and turning social snobbery into sexual desire.

This displacement overcodes a sartorial code of noble status with a secondary code in which clothes conceal and reveal sexual mystery. Kenneth Burke's suggestive linking of erotic courtship with the court-ship practised between those separated by class boundaries touches on Jonson's complex semiotic analysis here.23 Common to both analyses is estrangement and the resultant mystery that generates desire. Jonson discloses in this poem how lover and beloved – the class that courts and the class that is courted – cooperate in transforming the system of signs that mediates a mysterious interiority into the substantial em-bodiment of this interiority.24 If the signifiers of noble status refer to an inner 'mystery' of true nobility, penetration to possession of this mystery is displaced onto sexual penetration, which seeks to possess the mysteries hidden and revealed by clothes.[25]

Furthermore, the desirability of clothes is linked with the capacity to write poetry in which this desirability is verbalized and articulated. The city husband was 'ore-joyed to peepe / In at a hole, and see these Actions creepe /. From the poor wretch, which though he play'd in prose, / He would have done in verse, with any of those / Wrung on the Withers, by Lord Love's despite, / Had he'had the facultie to read, and write!' (59–64). The servant who 'would have done in verse' is in turn linked with the 'Songsters' who seeing 'the lace, laid on a Smock ... / straight-way spent a Sonnet.' Verse in this perspective both articulates and displaces sexual activity, thereby doubling the displacement of female sexuality onto their clothes. An appropriate voyeurism reinforces this displacement: the footman who lifts 'up some one' skirt is viewed in turn by a city husband who was 'o're-joy'd to peepe / In at a hole' to watch the footman masturbating with his collection of female finery.

The overcodings in this poem which link class snobbery with sexual desire provide Jonson a thematic matrix within which to attack aristocratic semiosis as fetish under both aspects. The sexual snobbery of the footman replicates that of the tailor who makes love to his wife dressed in milady's gowns. Equally central for Jonson, however, is that both forms of fetish depend on poetic discourse to verbalize them, to articulate the semiotic relays that transform clothes into a code mediating social/sexual desirability. The songsters, the city husbands, and the infatuated grooms are all bad poets, who create a poetics of clothes in which clothes metriciously hide the fact that they veil nonexistent penetralia enshrining nonexistent objects of desire.[26]

3 *Méconnaissance* of the Self

If clothes for Jonson, as for many of his contemporaries (including a government that sought to enforce sumptuary legislation), constituted a semiotic code signifying noble status, the poet did not limit his scrutiny to these alone. Conspicuous consumption as the mark of status was commonplace during Elizabeth's and James' reigns, and testimonies to greatness were writ large for all to see. Prodigy houses, huge retinues, and lavish entertainment (usually of the monarch) joined displays on a more human scale such as ritual ceremonies and coats-of-arms.[27] Jonson's satirical agenda, superficially similar to that of Juvenal in its acerbic commentary on outrageous pretensions, is in fact *sui generis*. Where

Juvenalian satire is directly accusatory in unmasking the vices behind such pretensions, Jonson's satire unmasks and displays the accusations that the objects of his judgments direct against themselves and seek to escape. Jonsonian satire discovers the depth of inner abjectness to be directly proportional to the pretensions required to compensate for it. Jonsonian satire is constituted from, and attacks the *méconnaissance* of self which both acknowledges self-hatred and evades such acknowledgment.

For this reason Jonson insists that those who criticize his satire proclaim publicly adverse readings of their own moral worth. Jonson reasons that the one who feels himself its object is the only person who rejects satirical attacks, and that to criticize satire is tantamount to admitting that one is satirizable.[28] The stinking Sir Cod, for instance, becomes 'Sir Cod the Perfvmed' in E19: 'That COD can get no widdow, yet a knight, / I sent the cause: Hee wooes with an ill sprite.' Sir Cod would seem to have no spirit, only breath, and that an 'ill sprite,' bad breath, something announced by the perfume intended to cover it up. Elsewhere Jonson flaunts his unwillingness to name names as a threat, daring 'Person Gviltie' (E30 and E38) to disclose himself by accusing Jonson of traducing him. In 'A little Shrub growing by' (U21) the poet refuses to name the person attacked for two reasons: he does not want to name him because he is so evil; and naming him will only induce him to come forth: 'And so leave to stirre him, lest he stinke.' The refusal to name thus becomes still another insult. In chapter 2, section 2, I discussed those poems where Jonson explores the meaning given proper names by the virtues of the person named. Here this situation is reversed: the persons Jonson satirizes remain nameless unless and until they announce themselves in rejecting Jonson's charges, thereby admitting their accuracy.[29]

Self-denigration in a stratified society is available in many forms, not the least of which involves internalizing the snobbism of those above, and venting one's *ressentiment* by relaying that snobbism to those below. E28, 'On Don Svrly,' cuts both ways: having been himself the object of aristocratic insult, Surly internalizes along with self-debasement the belief that such behaviour constitutes greatness: 'DON SVRLY, to aspire the glorious name / Of a great man, and to be thought the same, / Makes serious vse of all great trade he knowes. / He speakes to men with a *Rhinocerotes* nose, / Which hee thinks great' (1–5). Surly becomes at once sadist and masochist, a master and slave who relays to and evokes in others a divided identity identical with his own. Chateaubriand's sequence Jonson renders as a double series of relays: an aristocracy of vanity that claims privilege only by coercing from inferiors acknowledgment of its own superiority; and these inferiors who, by aping the privileges of aristocratic superiority, disclose the vanity behind both, and the self-denigration behind the vanity.

One of Jonson's finest extended satires explores the dialectics of *méconnaissance*: 'A speach according to Horace' (U44). Jonson here attacks both middle-class pretensions to noble status, and aristocrats' relinquishing this status by resting on the prestige of inherited title. In ceding their military function in the state of the social-climbing bourgeoisie, the aristocracy are complicitous with the latter's play-acting at nobility. The hierarchical relations between the two estates are reversed when London citizens aspire to noble rank, and aristocrats go into trade. As a result neither's pretensions square with inner reality.

The opening lines (1–10) mimic the sanguine boasts of the citizen trained bands, volunteer soldiers who mobilize on weekends to parade and fight mock battles:

> Why yet, my noble hearts, they cannot say,
>   But we have Powder still for the Kings Day,
> And Ord'nance too: so much as from the Tower
>   T'have wak'd, if sleeping, *Spaines* Ambassadour,
> Old *Aesope Gundomar*: the French can tell,
>   For they did see it the last tilting well,
> That we have Trumpets, Armour, and great Horse,
>   Launces, and men, and some a breaking force.   (1–8)

The 'craftie Clerke, and Knight, Sir *Hugh*' reads out Aelian's *Tactics*; the city argues whether he or Tilly be the greater general; they fight famous sieges over again with blanks, and enrol their names among those who have fought England's battles in the past: 'O happie Art! and wise Epitome / Of bearing Armes! most civill Soldierie! / Thou canst draw forth thy forces, and fight drie / the Battells of thy Aldermanitie / Without the hazard of a drop of blood.' (43–6).

Next, a complacent aristocrat confirms the aristocracy's dependence on inherited title for its status, and its willingness to yield the offices of the commonwealth to the middle class: 'let Clownes, and Tradesmen breed / Their Sonnes to studie Arts, the Lawes, the Creed' (73–4). He asks what 'need we know, / More then to praise a Dog? or Horse? or speake / The Hawking language?' (70–7). His present concern is with 'so much land a yeare, or such a Banke, / That turnes us so much moneys' (76–7). Cooperating perhaps too egregiously with the poet's design, the aristocrat descants on his own loss of true nobility:

> Let poore Nobilitie be vertuous: Wee,
>> Descended in a rope of Titles, be
> From *Guy*, or *Bevis*, *Arthur*, or from whom
>> The Herald will. Our blood is now become
> Past the need of vertue. Let them care,
>> That in the Cradle of their Gentrie are;
> To serve the State by Councels, and by Armes:
>> We neither love the Troubles nor the harmes.   (79–86)

The references to hunting and hawking might have come from attacks on aristocratic irresponsibility in the previous century, when the axis of opposition on which current opinion split posed aristocratic leisure and clerkly education (Caspari 136–7). Exhortations addressed to the nobility that they uphold their political responsibilities can be found in the anonymous *Institution of a Gentleman* (1555) and Lawrence Humphrey's *The Nobles or of Nobilitye* (1563), as well as in the more familiar treatises by Elyot and Ascham.[30] But Jonson is referring here to a specifically seventeenth-century phenomenon: increasing aristocratic debt to middle-class financiers and merchants, which involved members of aristocratic families in trade as a way of life (Wright 23–4).

Jonson does not appear to believe that the merchant middle class has any business (except business!) in aspiring to noble status. In this he agreed with Philip Stubbes, whose *Anatomy of Abuses* (1583) had complained about the same thing (Wright 20). However, the aspirations that Jonson mocks in this poem were real and vocal enough among citizens themselves (21ff), and the fact that he attacks specifically middle-class ambitions highlights his own investment in distancing himself from what he saw as reprehensible forms of social climbing.

Both critiques, that of the ambitious middle class and that of the declining aristocracy, meet in the vera nobilitas argument. The nobility's cession of political responsibility to the middle class and its retreat to claiming status by descent 'from whom / the Herald will' mark exactly what galls Jonson in all of this. Middle-class pretensions are represented, significantly, by just that domain of service which the aristocracy traditionally dominated, namely the military (James 3). Jonson's sarcasm implies that all the mock battles in the world will not make a merchant noble, while acting like merchants is exactly that which makes the nobility ignoble – that and their cynical recourse to aristocratic status founded on dubious genealogies fabricated by the College of Heralds (Stone 23).

The conclusion seems inevitable that Jonson equated a faltering aristocracy with a merchant middle class possessing questionable qualifications for taking its place. The poem's positive message defines the qualifications under which a member of the middle class might justifiably aspire to aristocratic status, and these qualifications are exactly what the aristocracy has rejected and what the middle class never had in the first place: a true nobility defined by intellectual achievement. And Jonson knew just the man who could fill the bill.[31]

This poem is linked with a group of poems conspicuous for another typical Jonsonian device of satiric unmasking: homonymy and synonymy. An extension of the contrasts these devices mark includes those among the five signifying functions possible in an aristocratic semiosis (already discussed in section 2 of this chapter). Where Jonson is concerned more broadly with attempts to simulate self-approbation and dissimulate its absence, the same five functions occur. Clothes, language, behaviour, and manners – the collective codes that can signify personal worth – (a) manifest possession of this worth, (b) simulate its presence, (c) dissimulate its absence, (d) ironically announce its absence, (e) dissimulate this dissimulation.[32]

Homonymy occurs when, for instance, the same sign fulfils two or more of these functions. A relatively uncomplex example is E82, 'On Cashierd Capt. Svrly,' which turns on the double meaning of 'keep.' Jonson writes in affected amazement that Surly's 'old whore' yet swims in 'new silks.' This is remarkable because Surly has been 'cast,' that is, cast off, and yet 'keepes her well.' But in fact the real situation is just the reverse: 'shee keeps him.' The pivot of meaning here turns on the keep/cast differential, which initially defines 'keep' to mean 'continued possession.' But because Surly has no money it turns out that she keeps him in the sense of support or maintenance, and does so by keeping herself in 'new silkes.' The indignities Svrly suffers multiply when 'keep' in the sense of possession gives way to a situation in which he instead is kept, that is, supported by her whoring.

Synonymy unmasks instead a supposed change of meaning behind a change in signifiers. 'On Mill my Ladies Woman' (E90) calls for a similar analysis in that both epigrams require the reader to adjust to unstable relations between signifier and signified. Mill's fidelity to her lover through his metamorphosis from pubescent page to rotund steward would be praiseworthy, did not Jonson assimilate her blindness to her lover's physical deterioration to the legendary Milo's lifting a calf every day until it becomes a bull: 'And it is hop'd, that shee, like MILO, wull, / First bearing him a calfe, beare him a bull' (17–18). 'Calfe' means a callow youth, while 'bull' takes on sexual overtones that spill over onto 'bear' as well. Mill, like the wrestler Milo, remains unaware of the gradual increment of weight in her lover. Synonymy names Mill's perceiving the same attractions signified by a series of changing (and deteriorating) signifiers: 'Nay, his face growing worse, / And he remou'd to gent'man of the horse, / MILL was still the same' (11–13).

As synecdoches for all the ways in which men and women may hide from others and themselves their own inner poverty, homonymy and synonymy of course enable the disclosure of what they hide as well.[33]And such disclosures take the form of discriminations that the poet makes for them, since they are patently incapable of making them for themselves. Consequently, poems in which Jonson disambiguates homonymical and synonymical slides praise those the moral value of whose lives is displayed in the discriminations they achieve, and damn those who fail.[34]

There are, finally, those who for one reason or another cannot or ought not to be named. In 'To one that desired me not to name him' (E77) Jonson attacks the pretension that one does in fact have publicly 'so good a fame' (1) that he fears 'my booke should speake thy name' (2). Jonson replies: 'For, if thou shame, ranck'd with my friends, to goe, / I'm more asham'd to haue thee thought my foe' (3–4). Jonson accuses his victim of naive ignorance of all the possible inferences that claiming a name, that is, public reputation, can imply. Assuming his reputation is a good one, and that he can only be hurt by being named in Jonson's poetry, he opens himself up to being told roundly that (1) his reputation is not as good as he thinks; (2) the poet may give his own – low – valuation to naming him; (3) diffidence about one's 'name' (as reputation) may imply a pretentiousness that naming one's 'name' (as appellation) can only disclose; and (4) the word 'name' may evoke the rhyming echo 'shame' from more than one perspective. The result is that the poet reaches an accord with his addressee not to name him, and thereby gives a meaning to 'not-naming' that the latter would never have thought of.

The complementary notion that silence about a name may be a charity is explored with controlled pathos in one of Jonson's more enigmatic epitaphs: 'Epitaph on Elizabeth, L.H.' (E124). The poet suppresses the family name of the poem's subject, and that fact is the poem's true subject.[35] In this poem Jonson seeks to display the dead woman's virtues while hiding her family name, possibly because of some scandal that public knowledge of that name would bring on the family itself. If this is the case, then Jonson has succeeded indeed in saying much 'In a little' (2). He has in effect severed the Christian name from the surname, stating the virtues that supply meaning to the first, while hiding the 'fault' (7) that might wound the meaning of the second. It is an act of discrimination that, like the epigram to the person who feared to have Jonson name him, unfolds still further discriminations: (1) Jonson asserts that a person may have personal virtues that are not diminished by suppression of family name; (2) that suppression registers obeisance to public respect for that name, a respect which the poet putatively shares; (3) nevertheless, by announcing this suppression the poet also announces his refusal to sacrifice one exigency to the other. By discriminating justice to the person and justice to her family, Jonson registers in a gesture of unusually subtle tact his commitment to the full range of the vera nobilitas argument's potentiality for both supporting the individual's possessing value by reason of family connections, and subverting that connection.

4 Signs of Inexpressibility

The incapacity of language to express virtues transcendent in their greatness is a figure of epideictic rhetoric, namely the inexpressibility topos. Jonson sometimes uses this topos as a strategy for adding credibility to his praise, and as such it will be discussed in the next chapter. There are, however, poems in which Jonson celebrates forms of true nobility that outer signs belie or misrepresent. Two groups of these poems address women whose beauty or pock-marked plainness both fail adequately to represent their inner virtue: Venetia Stanley, the wife of Sir Kenelm Digby (Eupheme, U84); and (possibly) both Lady Mary Sidney, mother of the poet (F8), and Anne Clifford, countess of Dorset, Pembroke, and Montgomery (U34).[36]

'To Sicknesse' (F8) decries the injustice that venereal disease should attack a chaste lady when so many promiscuous men and women actively pursue it. Jonson pretends the pox is a god or patron whose favours must be sedulously sought, so that disease becomes an external signifier accurately reflecting an inner signified of personal achievement:

'These, *disease*, will thee deserue: / And will, long ere thou should'st starue, / On their beds, most prostitute, / Moue it, as their humblest sute, / In thy iustice to molest / None but them, and leaue the rest' (43–8). The logic of the vera nobilitas argument has seldom been used to argue so rigorous a form of social justice.[37]

'An Epigram. To the small Poxe' (U34) also anthropomorphizes disease, links it with dubious cosmetics, and employs a vera nobilitas argument to criticize those devoted to both. Belief that external beauty determines personal value means that external plainness constitutes its lack, a conclusion that entails an obsession with cosmetics that announces the absence of merit in the act of affirming its presence. The lady praised in the poem escapes this enervating dialectic by refusing to tie her sense of importance to her beauty: 'She never sought / Quarrell with Nature, or in ballance brought / Art, her false servant' (5–7). Both beauty's possession and consequently its loss affect nothing that was not already an inalienable possession. The smallpox, and the beauty it destroys, are both 'scorn'd' (18), and the scorn is itself part of this spiritual possession.[38]

The logic of these two poems suggests that for Jonson coexistence of beauty and virtue is a feminine version of the correspondence between noble birth and true nobility. This is confirmed by the epigram addressed 'To Mrs. Philip Sydney' (E114), a daughter of Sir Robert Sidney and niece of the poet. Cupid plays a typically Jonsonian semiotic game, recuperating the signifier after first grasping the signified that gives it meaning: 'For CVPID, who (at first) tooke vaine delight, / In meere outformes, vntill he lost his sight, / Hath chang'd his soule, and made his obiect you' (3–5). Cupid's blindness creates sight again, but only after the god comes to see that the beauty which he saw with his eyes signifies something he could perceive only when blind, namely the lady's virtue. The gods too need educating in the truths of the vera nobilitas argument.

Venetia Stanley, wife of Jonson's friend, fellow scholar, and patron Sir Kenelm Digby, is one of the prime examples in Jonson's poetry of a woman who joins nobility with virtue. In this she belongs with a select number of women, including Lucy countess of Bedford, Lady Mary Wroth and various other female members of the Sidney family, and the wives of some of Jonson's patrons: 'All Nobilitie / (But pride, that schisme of incivilitie) / She had, and it became her!' (U84.9:159–61). The uncompleted sequence *Eupheme* (U84) written on her death represents Jonson's most sustained examination of the semiosis of aristocratic status, while it revises the terms of this examination in earlier poems.

Jonson distinguishes outer signs of virtue, such as the body and portraits which can reflect only the body, and verbal speech which alone articulates the ethical meaning of these signs. The third and fourth stanzas of U84.4, 'The MIND,' summarizes Jonson's point. The painter 'could make shift to paint an Eye' (9), an eagle, the sun, or the sea, 'But these are like a Mind, not it' (12). 'To expresse a Mind to sense' (13) requires something 'of kinne to whence it came' (16), namely 'a Heavens Intelligence' (14). Jonson has made these points before and they are unexceptionable. However, in the final 'Elegie' language as well as spectacle fails before the beatific vision, and Jonson reaches toward an unmediated manifestation of inner nobility that indicts all signs of inadequacy because capable of falsification. Far from merely revising the semiosis of aristocratic status, this sequence repudiates mediating signs altogether.

Eupheme, sent to Digby in 1633 (H&S 11:103), is contemporary with the poems attacking Inigo Jones, and reflects their central concerns. In both groups Jonson flirts with the fourth proposition in the vera nobilitas argument: those who possess true nobility are aristocrats. This argument breaks radically with the imperative that inner merit should be reflected in outer status, and implies that the signs of aristocratic status are meaningless. As Jonson approached the end of his life he may well have despaired of any fulfilment of that imperative. Certainly the disappointments inflicted on him by Inigo Jones' successes as stage designer and architect in the service of Charles I seem the symptoms of such a despair. The quasi-Platonism of *Eupheme*, quite uncharacteristic of earlier Jonsonian arguments, sunders political signifier and ethical signified. If Venetia Stanley was his poetic muse, as number 9 avers, she represented rather a late inspiration that compensated for defeats and disappointments, than one who might have urged a younger and more aggressive poet to seize the intellectual hegemony rightfully his by reason of his intellectual powers and achievements.

'The Dedication of her CRADLE' (U84.1) contrasts 'a Song of her Descent; / And Call to the high Parliament / Of Heaven' (29–31) with the rattles that 'Take little Infants with their noyse' (18). This poem also banishes Envy, which seeks to 'hold downe' Venetia 'With her, in shade / of Death, and Darkenesse' (3–5). The poet's claim, in contrast with noise-makers that strike the senses, that 'here are no such Trifles brought' (25), argues a praise that looks through such distractions. If Envy degrades the noble, then no less do ignoble conceptions of nobility that tie it to trifles appealing to the eye and ear.

'The Song of her DESCENT' (U84.2) promised by the previous poem invites the 'bold PENATES' that preside over the two houses of Northumberland and Stanley to speak of her great family, and to 'Tell, testify the grand / Meeting of Graces, that so swell'd the flood / Of vertues in her, as, in short, she grew / The wonder of her Sexe, and of your blood' (9–12). It was her 'flood / Of vertues' that dignified the lines of her descent and family. The argument here Pliny developed in his *Panegyricus* addressed to Trajan: the correspondence of high birth with merit, where the latter retroactively justifies the former.

Jonson launches into a new development of the vera nobilitas argument in the following poems. The mind-body antinomy opposes poet and painter, and ultimately inner virtue and outer signs. The mind and its virtue shine through the bodily and sociopolitical signs that but imperfectly mediate them. A similar usage occurs in *Cynthia's Revels*, where in dedicating the play to the royal court Jonson says:

> It is not powdering, perfuming, and every day smelling of the tailor, that converteth to a beautiful object: but in mind, shining through any suit, which needs no false light either of riches, or honours to help it.   (Wilkes 2:[vii])

'Shining through' pivots on two scrupulously discriminated meanings – appearing both through and despite the mediation of clothing – and Jonson intends both meanings. If clothing can successfully mimic true nobility, as the frivolous courtiers in *Cynthia's Revels* believe, the virtuous mind may well be constrained to 'shine through' its clothing to distinguish itself from those whose virtues are coextensive with their clothes.

In *Eupheme*, as in the poems on Inigo Jones, this semiotic complexity is rearranged, so that the mind (of Venetia in this case) becomes a reality itself almost physically palpable in its perfection, thereby overgoing physical signifiers in their own domain. U84.3, 'The Picture of the BODY,' substitutes not mind for body or clothes, but one semiotic relation for another. This poem is a prototype of the 'instructions to the painter' satires written at mid-century and after, to which Andrew Marvell contributed. Jonson's advice moves the painter out of the picture altogether, and supplants both with verbal language which alone can mediate the virtues of the mind. Venetia's beauty appears as the sun's light gradually breaking through a cloud: 'Draw first a Cloud: all save her neck; / And, out of that, make Day to breake; / Till, like her face, it doe appeare, /

And Men may thinke, all light rose there' (13–16). Instead of a literal picture of Venetia's body, Jonson gives us an emblem in which Venetia's face is fused with the starry universe.

> Last, draw the circles of this Globe,
>   And let there be a starry Robe
>   Of Constellations 'bout her horld;
>   And thou hast painted beauties world.   (25–8)

Jonson's instructions to the painter reinscribe the palpably visual in metaphors expressing immaterial beauty breaking through the barrier of the flesh, where the face is first the sun and then the cloud itself, which the beams of the universe disperse in turn. That is one way of recuperating lines 13ff, and it leads to the figure of Venetia resituated within a frame of constellations. These images are obviously inconsistent when read with schematic literalness. They exhibit a depth receding away from the viewer, which is the painter's manner of suggesting an interiority that paint's commitment to surfaces can only counterfeit. One is reminded of Jonson's highlighting in the 'Expostulacion with Inigo Jones' the painter's attempt to make boards speak and mimic the resources of language. In both cases Jonson announces the obligation of visual spectacle to give way to verbal discourse, and he does this by requiring that the first perform the office of the second, and then allowing it to fail.

In U84.4, 'The MIND,' Jonson banishes material representation altogether, along with the painter whose 'hand will never hit, / To draw a thing that cannot sit' (7–8). It is the thing itself Jonson professes to desire: 'Sweet Mind, then speake your selfe, and say, / As you goe on, by what brave way / Our sense you doe with knowledge fill, / And yet remaine our wonder still' (17–20). Jonson's task is to explain how this mind manifests itself 'through' material signifiers whose capacity to counterfeit the presence of mind may obscure it altogether.39 Once again Jonson yields to his dearest fantasy: a semiosis in which signifer and signified, because symmetrically aligned, cannot subvert each other:

> Or hath she here, upon the ground,
>   Some Paradise, or Palace found
>   In all the bounds of beautie fit
>   For her to 'inhabit? There is it.   (49–52)

The distribution of emphases in this stanza is typical of those throughout this poem. In place of a complex dialectic between the present and the absent, Jonson evokes a mind whose beauty is sensually present in the music of her voice; and it is this music that the poem imitates, to the point where Venetia's voice becomes a model of Jonson's own verse. Her voice is 'Musique to the eare' (35), as if 'what it spoke, it planted there. ... And, though the sound were parted thence, / Still left an Eccho in the sense' (36, 38–40). The echo of Venetia's voice is literally reproduced in the pun on *sense*, where the word's acoustic effect as rhyme echoes its meaning. Her musical voice replicates the meaning of what she says, and both are echoed in the ear of the poet who answers these echoes with musical verse.

The final poem of this truncated sequence is Jonson's 'Elegie on my Muse' (U84.9). Its central motif is sight: things seen and not seen, things visible only to purified sight, things visible only in heaven after the last judgment, things seen in meditation. The poet's opening lament gives way to envisioning her in heaven 'where *Love* is all the guest! / And the whole *Banquet* is full of *God*!' (64–5). The poet then reverses himself, saying that he 'violates the God-head' who seeks to pry 'with rude, / Dull, and prophane, weak, and imperfect eyes, / [and to] Have busie search made in his mysteries!' (74, 78–80). The poet imagines the meeting of friends and family in heaven, where 'each shall know, there, one anothers face, / By beatifick vertue of the Place' (115–16). Finally, he imagines that 'In this sweet *Extasie*' of meditation 'she was rapt hence' (225), which meditation is treated as a series of visions.

The reference to Christian doctrines of the beatific vision is an element new in Jonson's poetry, and a significant one. U83, 'An Elegie On the Lady JANE PAWLET Marchion: of Winton' likewise introduces a fully developed eschatological element. The similarities between this elegy and *Eupheme* highlight Jonson's latest thoughts on the semiotic problems that had concerned him throughout his career.

Like Lady Venetia the Lady Jane Pawlett is envisioned rapt with the beatific vision:

> And now, through circumfused light, she lookes
>   On Natures secrets, there, as her owne bookes:
> Speakes Heavens Language! and discourseth free
>   To every *Order*, ev'ry *Hierarchie*!
> Beholds her Maker! and, in him, doth see
>   What the beginnings of all beauties be;

And all beatitudes, that thence doe flow:
Which they that have the Crowne are sure to know!   (69–76)

The opening of the poem has the poet seeing the unseeable, and being turned to marble as a consequence. His inability to speak becomes the inexpressibility of the lady's soul: 'I, or my trump must breake, / But rather I, should I of that part speake! / It is too neere of kin to Heaven, the Soule, / To be describ'd!' (27–30). Labouring to express Lady Jane's true virtues, he dismisses the titles that might be inscribed on her tomb: 'Shee was the lady *Jane*, and *Marchionisse* / Of Winchester; ... / Earle *Rivers* Grand-Child.' But this is insignificant praise – 'the Heralds can tell this' – compared to the soul he seeks behind these titles. These are mere 'formes,' in place of which he invites 'good Fame' to 'Sound thou her Vertues, give her soule a Name' (19ff). Jonson discovers, however, that in seeking to name her soul he has reinscribed the *insolubilium* which the vera nobilitas argument had originally posed: how to render signs of status adequate to reflecting the soul of the noble person.

Inexpressibility reverses the hierarchy in which Jonson usually ranks words over pictures. The final poem of *Eupheme* makes this reversal overt by contrast, because it occurs in a sequence which reiterates Jonson's insistence that the virtues of the mind can be mediated only by verbal discourse. What are we to understand, then, when Jonson deprecates speech in this final elegy, as in the poem on the marchioness of Winton, and in its place praises the vision that sees souls and souls' virtues naked?

Several displacements occur here. The first reverses the attempts of Inigo Jones to make pictures speak and two-dimensional boards do the work of words. In these late poems, by contrast, vision 'speaks' what words cannot. Secondly, Jonson here repudiates the claims of all forms of signification to reflect inner true nobility, and this repudiation extends to verbal discourse as well. The eschatological allusions may be taken literally – Jonson despairs of any just reward for humanist achievement short of heaven. Or they may be taken as conveying his final thoughts on the limits to which critiques of true nobility and the signs thereof can extend, and how little they can finally achieve.[40]

If I am right, and in these late poems Jonson repudiated all attempts to align inner virtue and outer expression, then this repudiation is already implicit in the negative critiques discussed in this chapter. The poet's subtle and extensive probing of the semiotics of noble status discovers no means of confirming discriminations between the noble and the ignoble in the domain of public recognition that are proof against fools, or knaves. Having spent his career seeking to create a semiosis of true nobility, it would seem that the critiques the poet found necessary to hedge this semiosis against perversion had finally undermined his faith in its possibility. Venetia Digby died in 1633 when Jonson was himself sinking gradually toward death (in 1637), and there is some reason for believing that this poem, which links her death with his, and with the death of his poetic powers (*The Magnetic Lady* was written in 1632), is intended as concealed autobiography. Jonson extends the failure of his expressive powers to a more radical failure, namely his own death:

> 'Twere time that I dy'd too, now shee is dead,
>   Who was my *Muse*, and life of all I sey'd,
> The Spirit that I wrote with, and conceiv'd;
>   All that was good, or great in me she weav'd,
> And set it forth; the rest were Cobwebs fine,
>   Spun out in name of some of the old *Nine*!   (U84.9:1–6)

The failure of the Jonsonian enterprise is signalled by the poet's celebrating a beatific vision that transcends the sight that deceives as well as the verse that does not.

CHAPTER FOUR

'Vera Nobilitas' as a Theory of Epideictic Rhetoric

1 Epideictic Rhetoric and Credibility

Jonson says in the *Discoveries* that 'It is as great a spite to be praised in the wrong place, and by the wrong person, as can be done to a noble nature' (H&S 8:568), and in this statement he states by negation the agenda of his nondramatic poetry. True praise of those whose true nobility merits it by a poet whose authority establishes the credibility of both: this describes not only the purpose of much of Jonson's poetry but its central subject as well.

Praise in this poetry has been much discussed recently, with emphasis on Jonson's use of Roman models (Peterson *Imitation*), the voices of his poetic personae (Greene 'Accommodations'), and the poet's reactions to the political and courtly contexts of his time (Goldberg *James I*, Helgerson *Self-Crowned*, Fish 'Authors-Readers,' Wayne 'Poetry and Power' and *To Penshurst*, Marcus *Politics*, Riggs, Evans, and Rowe). These studies are important for understanding specific uses to which Jonson put epideictic rhetoric, but they do not account for the fact that the nature of epideixis itself, and its intimate connection with the object of his praise, vera nobilitas, are often Jonson's main subjects. While the history of epideictic rhetoric in its impact on Renaissance literature has been well established in the studies of O.B. Hardison, James Garrison, and Barbara Lewalski among others, its intimate linkages with the vera nobilitas argument in both Jonson and its history at large remain to date unexplored territory.

It will be necessary to reexamine the theory of epideixis in the classical and Renaissance periods, in order to reclaim Jonson's own understanding of these linkages. For classical rhetoric the proper object of praise and blame is not only, or even primarily, moral virtue and vice respectively, but rather true nobility and its lack. This orientation Cicero drew from Aristotle and bequeathed to later ages. Renaissance writings on vera nobilitas in turn indicate that aristocratic status is essentially a mode of epideictic rhetoric: the public recognition of, and bestowal of praise on, those who possess true nobility.

This reexamination will take up section 2 of this chapter. Sections 3, 4, and 5 survey the large number of poems and passages in which Jonson explores the nature of epideixis and the issues it raises. These issues turn out to be three fold: (1) the credibility of praise, (2) the merit of the praised, and (3) the authority of the poet. For Jonson, true praise stands to the possession of true nobility as flattery to its lack, and the credibility of the former depends on discriminating the two. Further discriminations bear on the poet's authority, where he confronts possible charges of both sycophancy and arrogance in addressing his noble readers, partisanship in judging his fellow writers, and envy and malice in satirizing those whose pretences to true nobility he has penetrated.

It is obvious that the authority of the poet is intimately connected with he merit of the person praised, and both affect the credibility of the praise.[1] Credibility is also an issue for the vera nobilitas argument, which asks two potentially explosive questions: 'Do hierarchical class structures have any credibility? And if not, under what conditions may they come to possess it?' If aristocratic status is in effect a form of epideixis, then those who praise are those who award aristocratic status. And that means that the epideictic poet claims for himself the office of arbitrating who does and does not truly possess it. Jonson's most famous poem of praise, 'To the memory of my beloued, The AVTHOR Mr. William Shakespeare: And what he hath left vs' (M26), links these issues of credibility for poet, poem, and subject, and this poem will introduce this chapter's main concerns.

Ascertaining the true subject of Jonson's eulogy of Shakespeare is critical to understanding what the poem says. S. Schoenbaum's remark that 'Jonson vindicate[s] Shakespeare from the charge of facility, which evidently still rankles him,' and that the poem constitutes 'Jonson's implied self-defense' (59), sums up one well-known line of interpretation. It is an interpretation whose central relevance Peterson acknowledges by focusing on the classical sources behind Jonson's discussion in the poem of creative facility and laboriousness (158ff). Peterson summarizes the various reactions to Jonson's poem from the seventeenth century to the present as a continuous debate on Jonson's own intentions, whether 'sincere' or not, but in any case one governed by the poet's perception of the differences between himself and Shakespeare as creative artists.

The eulogy in fact keeps before our eyes the significance and consequences of several explorations that proceed concurrently. These concern the poet's own authority to praise, the nature of praise itself, and Shakespeare's own merits – which turn out to be a version of the vera nobilitas argument. J.G. Nichols approaches the poem's true subject when he remarks that 'Jonson is simultaneously praising Shakespeare and deriding those who cannot praise him worthily' (128).[2]

From this perspective the sixteen-line introduction becomes integral to the poem's whole statement. That this introduction telescopes issues of prime concern to Jonson throughout his career can be seen by examining its high concentration of contrastive statements. The poem begins by discriminating two impressions that an amplitude of praise lavished on Shakespeare might make on the reader: it could appear excessive praise, or praise that however ample still falls short of being sufficient or adequate: 'To draw no enuy (*Shakespeare*) on thy name, / Am I thus ample to thy Booke, and Fame' (1–2). This couplet also points in a related direction, and seeks to forestall the possible charge that Jonson is trying to draw envy on Shakespeare by praising him so 'amply.'

The second line distinguishes 'Booke, and Fame,' where Jonson by an upgraded emphasis on *and* implies the distinction between reputation, which may or may not be valid, and the works themselves, to which alone true praise can be assigned. This is followed by another similarly evoked between the poet and his muse. The significance of this opposition, as the rest of the poem fills it out, depends on further distinctions between those who may or may not have the authority to judge, and between praise that flatters and that which tells the truth. Jonson asks the reader to recognize that the poet may have the authority to judge accurately but not the art or inspiration ('*Muse*') to articulate it verbally; or may possess the facility to write an epideictic text, but not the authority to judge correctly.

Combining these two binary oppositions (book/fame, man/muse), Jonson discriminates further two kinds of ill-justified or misdirected praise: 'But these wayes / Were not the paths I meant vnto thy praise: / For seeliest Ignorance on these may light, / Which, when it sounds at best, but echo's right; / Or blinde Affection, which doth ne're aduance / The truth, but gropes, and vrgeth all by chance' (5–10). There is in addition the praise of 'craftie Malice' (11), which may tacitly convey dispraise by praising the wrong things. Finally, Shakespeare and his works are invulnerable to fortune, to the need for praise, and consequently to casual or ill-founded praise. For Jonson, a person who needs praise discloses a need to compensate for a sense of inferiority.[3] The problem here is that Shakespeare is too easy to praise. Everyone does it (' 'Tis true, and all mens suffrage' [5]), and Jonson fears merely echoing the general consensus. Jonson's praise risks being seen to be either too little or too much, and secretly envious in either case. The poem, in short, runs the risk of being treated as trivial and insignificant – a risk that epideictic rhetoric has always run.

Jonson launches with a flourish into the body of the eulogy, but doesn't get very far: 'I, therefore will begin. Soule of the Age! / The applause! delight! the wonder of our Stage! / My *Shakespeare* rise' (17–19). The lines' ceremonial gesture leads the reader to expect a poem that never arrives, because the problems of writing it are insuperable. For what ensues is the question of what poets to 'lodge thee by' (19). Chaucer, Spenser, and Beaumont are not dismissed as lesser than Shakespeare, but rather found incomparable with him ('disproportion'd *Muses*,' 26). Jonson tests this notion by literalizing it and suggesting he might 'bid Beaumont lye / A little further, to make thee a roome' (20–1). How much room will Beaumont have to give up? How much is commensurate with Shakespeare's greatness? The absurdity of the question announces the difficulty in finding apt comparisons for Shakespeare.

Jonson foreshadows a post-Renaissance identification of the Shakespearean universal with the natural in the following lines: 'Nature her selfe was proud of his designes, / And ioy'd to weare the dressing of his lines! / Which were so richly spun, and wouen so fit, / As, since, she will vouchsafe no other Wit' (47–50). However, the art/nature topos in this poem does not merely set Shakespeare's native wood-notes wild off against Jonson's art. It moves rather toward an assertion of Shakespeare's art defined by Jonson's notion of true merit. With modifications appropriate to the distinction between the domains of the theatre and of sociopolitical structures, Jonson comes finally to praise Shakespeare for possessing vera nobilitas. The next lines on the art of turnings one's poem and one's ethical identity at the same time are a *locus classicus* of Jonsonian ethics, stating Jonson's ideal of the humanist who perfects his nature through the perseverant and conscious pursuit of art and learning:

Yet must I not giue Nature all: Thy Art,
   My gentle *Shakespeare*, must enjoy a part.
For though the *Poets* matter, Nature be,
   His Art doth giue the fashion. And, that he,
Who casts to write a liuing line, must sweat,
   (Such as thine are) are strike the second heat
Vpon the *Muses* Anuile: turne the same,
   (And himselfe with it) that he thinkes to frame;
Or for the lawrell, he may gaine a scorne,
   For a good *Poet's* made, as well as borne.   (55–64)

Peterson (160ff) develops Jonson's debt to Horace's *Ars Poetica* for the notion of 'turning' (*versus*) the self in the act of poetic creation. In the context of the vera nobilitas argument, however, these lines turn the Horatian allusion toward still more complex significances. Shakespeare may be 'gentle' in a purely honorific sense, but Jonson more probably alludes to the fact that Shakespeare was, after the 1596 purchase of a coat of arms from the College of Heralds, always referred to as William Shakespeare, gentleman (Schoenbaum 5, 36). The motto of the shield – which features the lance that Jonson has Shakespeare brandish 'at the eyes of Ignorance' (70) – is *non sanz droict*. The motto is self-reflexive, for it seems to justify the coat of arms itself against any who might challenge the right of the Shakespeare family to possess it. Shakespeare was no stranger to the vera nobilitas argument, as multiple passages, and at least one play (*All's Well That Ends Well*), devoted to the subject testify.[4] And Jonson in these lines agrees with Shakespeare: it is not without right that Shakespeare is called gentle, because he merited this status in the manner traditionally honoured by the vera nobilitas argument.

The sweat of the muse's anvil that turns the verse turns the poet as well. The labour of self-creation builds the achieved self on the foundation of natural talent at the same time as it fashions art out of the materials of nature. If it is true that Jonson praises in Shakespeare artistic practices that he values in himself, it is also true that in crediting him with the possession of vera nobilitas Jonson could give him no higher praise. Against the notion that scions of noble houses possess by biological inheritance the virtues of their ancestors, Jonson asserts a true genealogy, in which the well-turned and true-filed virtues of the father achieve their only appropriate reproduction: 'Looke how the fathers face / Liues in his issue, euen so, the race / Of *Shakespeares* minde, and manners brightly shines / In his well torned, and true-filed lines' (65–8).

For Jonson praiseworthiness always involves a paradox: those who are praiseworthy do not need praise, and those who need it are not praiseworthy. The central fact of this poem is that it achieves praise only by striving through its first half to refuse it. Because, as Jonson says early on, 'thy writings [are] such, / As neither *Man*, nor *Muse*, can praise too much' (the only time Jonson ever says such a thing), the major problem of praise, credibility, has been not so much solved as simply dissolved. Comparisons are not so much odious as irrelevant. The fusions of nature and art, of talent and achievement, of inner man and outer sign are such in Shakespeare's case that Jonson need not worry himself about either the credibility of the praise, the merits of the praised, or his own authority, because each has been validated by the other two.

2 Epideictic Rhetoric and Aristocratic Status

Jonson's treatment of epideictic rhetoric, and of praise in particular, as a theory of true nobility has significant antecedents in classical and Renaissance discussions of both. The major classical source is Aristotle, particularly the *Rhetoric* and *Nichomachean Ethics*, but Jonson would have found in Cicero an authority more directly relevant to his own concerns. Cicero judged that virtues achieved by personal labour were alone praiseworthy, as distinguished from gifts of birth and fortune, such as wealth and beauty. Cicero, however, did not develop this distinction any more than he developed a theory of epideictic rhetoric in his rhetorical treatises, where it claimed only a marginal place in his exposition of the rhetoric of the law courts. In the Renaissance, Sir Thomas Elyot's brief affirmation that 'nobility is not after the vulgar opinion of men, but is only the praise and surname of virtue' (106) summarized current opinion. Roger Ascham's insistence that noble status is increased by 'learning, virtue and their own deserts, which is true praise, right worthiness, and very nobility indeed' (59) makes the connection more direct, but is otherwise equally unelaborated. John Ferne in his treatise on heraldry is more explicit:

Some one, abounding in many outward graces and partes aboue the rest, and the same of his worthiness spread abroad, caused the multitude to yeeld an especiall honor vnto him, so that on such a one, were the eyes of many fixed, and he, for the vertues and worthy qualities knowne to all men to be in him, was chiefely honored, and thus at the first had nobleness her beginning, which that is thus, the Etymologie of the word *Nobilitas* will sufficiently approoue, which being a word of the Latines, is deriued of the verbe *Nosco*, to knowe ... (4)

In order to isolate the connection between the theory of epideixis and the vera nobilitas argument, however, it is necessary to distinguish two different objects of praise and blame as these were developed in current understanding of epideixis in the Renaissance. Elyot, Ascham, and Ferne, when they find virtue the object of praise, echo classical sources, and for this reason some Renaissance scholars have limited the purview of epideictic rhetoric to virtue and vice: to personal, private moral qualities.[5] And as long as 'virtue' and its cognates are understood in a strictly private ethical context, it is easy to see how epideixis could be thus narrowed in the range of its concerns.

Aristotle, however, opens his discussion of epideictic rhetoric with a distinction that moves it in a different direction: 'We have now to consider Virtue and Vice, the Noble and the Base, since these are the objects of praise and blame' (*Rhetoric* 1366A, p 56). Aristotle's subsequent discussion in the *Rhetoric*, as well as in the *Nichomachean Ethics*, conflates the virtuous and the noble, and finds only the truly virtuous are the truly noble. And when the distinction between the noble and the base enters the categorical distinctions historically developed in the vera nobilitas argument, 'virtue' comes to mean 'true nobility,' and its opposite is no longer 'vice' but the lack of true nobility.

Among Greek writers before Aristotle, Pindar explored most extensively praise as the reward of great personal achievement, and the intimate parallels he draws between the merits of praiser and praised foreshadow similar parallels drawn by Jonson. In Nemea 9, for instance, Pindar prays 'that with the Graces' aid I may sing his excellence and on many occasions / honor success, throwing my spear right close to the Muses' mark' (123). 'The uttermost of reputation' that the poet awards the winner 'lies in achievement,' and parity between both requires that the poet 'mount this occasion / for manifold praise, nor cast my words in falsehood' (Nemea 1:95). As Aristotle and Cicero will reiterate later, 'highest justice attends the saying: *Praise the good*' (Nemea 3:101).

It is in Aristotle's *Nichomachean Ethics*, however, that one finds the most expansive treatment among the Greeks of what constitutes the praiseworthy. Throughout this treatise Aristotle consistently tests the virtuous by what is and is not normally praised, and to what purposes in both cases. For instance, in a central statement of the mean as ideal virtue, he says:

> Now virtue is concerned with passions and actions, in which excess is a form of failure, and so is defect, while the intermediate is praised and is a form of success; and being praised and being successful are both characteristic of virtue. (1106b:958)

More immediately relevant to the history of the vera nobilitas argument is the honour deserved by virtue: 'For honour is the prize of virtue, and it is to the good that it is rendered' (1123b:992). Aristotle contrasts the man honoured for possessing the 'goods of fortune' with 'the good man,' who 'alone is to be honoured ... But those who without virtue have such goods are neither justified in making great claims nor entitled to the name of "proud"' (1124a:993). An even more direct contribution to the vera nobilitas argument is Aristotle's contention that justice demands that merit be rewarded: 'Further, this is plain from the fact that awards should be "according to merit"; for all men agree that what is just in distribution must be according to merit in some sense, though they do not all specify the same sort of merit' (1131a:1006).

The extent of Aristotle's consideration of the praiseworthy is unique in classical writing. Roman writing handles the subject with brevity, and outside of Pliny the Younger's *Panegyricus* tends to simplify Aristotle's distinctions. While most classical sources agree that vice is the proper object of dispraise, Marius in Sallust's *Jugurthine Wars* attacks those who possess the gifts of fortune in lieu of true nobility. And it is Cicero, a contemporary of Sallust, who develops the Aristotelian distinction between virtue as true nobility, and virtue as private moral quality. As the source of praiseworthy qualities, Cicero discriminates personal effort from external sources over which one has no control. In *De officiis* Cicero turns dispraise not only toward vice but toward the absence of virtue as well:

> [Men] respect and acclaim with the loudest praises those men in whom they believe they perceive certain outstanding and incomparable virtues, and conversely they reject and despise men whom they believe to possess no virtue, no spirit, no energy. (91)

Cicero makes it clear elsewhere that the virtues he considers praiseworthy are the four cardinal virtues of prudence, justice, temperance, and fortitude.[6] The identification of virtue in the Renaissance with this classical list, for instance in Montemagno (226), Elyot (Major 24), and Ferne (30), was part of the humanist version of the vera nobilitas argument. But in the Renaissance the virtues that dominate humanist demands for recognition and employment were intellectual virtues developed by study and mastery of eloquence: 'virtue' became less a moral matter than a matter of intellectual achievement. And Cicero, who in De officiis looks to the place of the cardinal virtues in the domain of public service, opposes virtue not to vice but to lack of 'spirit' and 'energy.' Cicero's spokesman in the De oratore gives this distinction expansive development:

> Well then, it is clear that the qualities that are desirable in a person are not the same as those that are praiseworthy: family, good looks, bodily strength, resources, riches and the rest of the external personal gifts of fortune do not in themselves contain any true ground for praise, which is held to be due to virtue alone; but nevertheless, as it is in the employment and wise management of these that virtue itself is very largely discerned, a panegyric must also treat of these goods of nature and of fortune in which the highest praise is not to have been puffed up in office or insolent in wealth, or to have put oneself in front of others because of fortune's bounty – so that wealth and riches may seem to have provided opportunity and occasion not for pride and licence but for beneficence and temperance. But virtue ... is praiseworthy in itself and is a necessary element in anything that can be praised ... (1:457–9)

The complaints of Sallust's Marius are echoed here, though with considerably less acerbity, as are the perennial conflicts between patricians and *equites* which were to lead finally to the downfall of the republic. The above passage fuses several distinct elements in a set of relations that transmit to the Renaissance the nexus between epideictic rhetoric and the vera nobilitas argument.

The first of these elements is Cicero's judgment that the gifts neither of nature (birth) nor of fortune are praiseworthy, but virtue alone.[7] Second, when Cicero opposes virtue to gifts of birth and fortune, he defines the former as the consequence of personal effort. For instance, in the 'Defence of Murena' he refers to his own rise to the consulship in terms of the same differential:

> When I had broken through the barrier, behind which nobility of
> birth had been entrenched these past thirty years, so that the ap-
> proach to the consulship would hereafter be, as it was in the era of
> our ancestors, not more accessible to nobility of birth than to ex-
> cellence of ability, I did not think that when a consul-designate,
> from an old and famous family was being defended by a consul,
> the son of a Roman knight, his accusers would speak out against
> the newness of his family origins. (*Nine Orations*: 173)

Finally, for Cicero the virtue/fortune differential likewise discriminates high office awarded on the basis of merit and patrician privilege
respectively. Cicero does not attack a decadent patriciate as did Sallust's
Marius before him or Juvenal after. Nevertheless, when the cluster composed of virtue, personal effort, and merit is set off against that comprising fortune and undeserved possession of inherited privilege, it is
clear that 'virtue' in Cicero's lexicon is opposed not only to 'vice' but
to false nobility as well.

The important thing for the study of praise in Jonson's poetry is that
Cicero linked praise to virtue, and virtue to true nobility. This set of
linkages, plus Aristotle's insistence that only the noble justly merit public praise, creates the foundation of Jonson's potentially explosive pre-
sumption that noble status is itself a form of epideictic rhetoric: that
aristocratic establishments are only the institutionalization of the praise
which those with the authority to praise justly bestow on those who
truly merit it.

When Quintilian distinguishes epideictic rhetoric and demonstrative
rhetoric, identifying the former with display and the latter with matters
of advice (1:395–7), he calls attention to the problem that epideixis confronted throughout the classical period: credibility. Aristotle looked upon
epideictic rhetoric as primarily a form of display, and therefore as something requiring no decision from the audience (Burgess 92). This may
well be the case where deliberative and forensic rhetorical ends have
by contrast real political significance. Cicero finds a place for epideictic
rhetoric in speeches that testify to a person's character in the law courts,
or in funeral orations (*De oratore* 1:457), and damned it among other
Asiatic forms of ornamented prose in his defence of Attic style in the
Orator (333–7). And the decline of Roman oratory during the first century of the principate into nothing but epideictic rhetoric became an
truism once Tacitus put his imprimatur on it in the *Dialogus* (119).[8]

Nevertheless, in finding a use for the epideictic in the service of the demonstrative, Quintilian nodded toward the usefulness of epideictic rhetoric as a means of applying leverage to an absolute prince. Just as Isocrates transmitted the vera nobilitas argument developed by the Sophists, so he also joined praise of the monarch with advice (Jaeger 3:86-7; Burgess 116). Similarly in the Renaissance Erasmus argued that praising the prince for virtues he did not possess could gently move him toward their possession (*Education* 5–6). And although Jonson in his poem addressed to Selden admitted that in sometimes praising 'Men past their termes' he had 'prais'd some names too much, / But 'twas with purpose to have made them such' (U14), Jonson's handling of epideixis throughout his poetry makes it clear that there he did not subscribe to the Erasmian justification.[9]

While the Isocratean panegyric praised the hereditary prince for virtues that he ought to possess if he were to rule successfully,[10] the conception of epideixis that highlighted praise as a matter of merit rather than birth positioned itself to probe more incisively the relations between noble status and praise. As a result epideictic rhetoric in the Renaissance developed a line of inquiry independent of the *de regimine principum* tradition traced by Garrison in seventeenth- and eighteenth-century English writing, and was for the same reason independent of epideixis conceived as ethical suasion, as seen by Hardison and Lewalski.

We find Jonson pursuing both forms of epideictic purposes: in the masques he seeks to instruct by praising (Orgel *Masque* 107), but in the nondramatic poetry aristocratic, if not royal, status is tested against the demands for just reward and recognition of true nobility that lie at the heart of the vera nobilitas argument. The fact that Jonson straddles both dimensions of the vera nobilitas argument, and encompasses in masques and poetry all four propositions constituting this argument, means that his is always an intrinsically unstable ideological and social situation. Like Pliny, Jonson found himself evoking both branches of the vera nobilitas argument: that which praises the aristocracy for being noble, and that which claims that true praise of true nobility alone constitutes aristocracy.

A thorny question at this level of consideration is whether and to what extent noble status is a function of others' praise, and, conversely, how much it depends upon qualities inherent in the individual. For instance, Nenna argued that nobility depends entirely on personal qualities and is independent of others' opinions (P1r and passim), and in this he echoes Cicero in *De officiis*: 'What we say about the good is correct: even if no one praises it, it is by nature praiseworthy' (10). On the other hand there is Robert Ashley's unpublished manuscript treatise *Of Honour* written in the late sixteenth century, which sees nobility entirely a function of others' praise, and in this echoes Aristotle's belief that 'men seem to pursue honour in order that they may be assured of their goodness' (1095b:938). Guillaume du Vair held the same position in the same century: 'True honour is the glittering and beaming brightnes of a good and vertuous action, which rebounds from our consciences unto the sight of them with whom wee live, and so by a reflexion in our selves, brings us a testimonie from others of the good opinion which they have of us, which make us to enjoy great comfort of minde' (quoted in C.B. Watson 11).[11]

This is a thorny question because it creates a dilemma typical of those generated by the vera nobilitas argument. For Jonson the dilemma came in this form: those who are truly noble do not require praise in order to make them so, which means that they do not require noble status in order to be noble. However, to praise someone for these qualities is to imply that they require praise, and by extension noble status, to establish their nobility. The problem was always one of sources and origins. Where did noble status originate, in the person honoured and praised, or in those who praise and bestow honours? Ferne cites the ubiquitous anecdote of the Emperor Sigismund, who said that he could make a man rich and privileged, but he could not make someone a gentleman who lacked 'vertue or noble desert' (61).[12] This anecdote was popular, I suspect, because it placed in the mouth of an emperor, who patently had the power to make anyone a nobleman, the insistence that despite this power only the person himself could make himself gentle. As Mervyn James' monograph establishes for England at least, the source of noble status shifted in the sixteenth century away from the honour community (governed by the code of chivalrous conduct) to the College of Heralds, and finally to the monarch himself or herself (18ff).

Along narrower lines of consideration, the notion that aristocratic status is a form of praise is vulnerable to the critique that Jonson launches in the poems discussed in chapter 3. There I showed how the semiotic structure of aristocratic status contained within itself the potentiality for both manifesting inner virtue and disguising its absence. Extended to the whole system of political hierarchy, this critique causes it to collapse from within like a house of cards. Just as praise becomes meaningless flattery when addressed to those who don't deserve it, so the institutionalization of public praise and recognition in aristocratic establishments whose members are among the 'ungentle gentle' retroactively invites renaming this public praise as public flattery.

The credibility of a poet with the ambitions of a Jonson depended radically on his success in guarding both his own praise and the aristocracy he praised from the charge of flattery and lack of credibility. Of course, in resting his career hopes on persuading an entrenched aristocracy that he deserved a place in it, by further persuading it that it must reform itself as an aristocracy of humanist virtue, Jonson implicitly cut the ground out from beneath himself. For the paradoxes of the vera nobilitas argument worked as inexorably against him in this connection as they worked against the Stuart aristocracy to which he applied the argument. And as I shall show in the final chapter, this radical ambivalence of the vera nobilitas argument was internalized in the poet's own fundamental ambivalence toward the object of his life's hopes: an ambivalence that at once raised aristocratic privilege as the object of desire and called it into question as illusory and meaningless.

3 Praise and Flattery

For Jonson, who declared to Drummond that were he to deliver a sermon to the king he would not flatter 'though he saw death,' flattery was a matter of prime concern. Jonson's poems and masques consistently argue the credibility of the humanist as counsellor to the rulers of the land. Consequently Jonson sought to rescue epideictic rhetoric from the perennial charge of flattery, because he recognized that the humanist poet's sole leverage with princes and aristocrats was the credibility of his own rhetoric. Establishing vera nobilitas as the criterion for judging public figures, and establishing epideictic rhetoric as the credible means for doing this, were for Jonson inseparable enterprises.[13]

The epigram 'To Thomas Earle of Svffolke' (E67) makes this connection overt, and states why flattery becomes for Jonson a major problem: 'Since men haue left to doe praise-worthy things, / Most thinke all praises flatteries' (1–2). By contrast, Suffolk was already praiseworthy before praise was given him: 'so thy vertue wrought, / As all thy honors were by them first sought: / And thou design'd to be the same thou art, / Before thou were it, in each good mans heart' (7–10). Jonson discriminates here between the man who seeks honour because he does not have it, and the man whose virtue refuses to seek honour mainly because he does not need it. Suffolk is praised for not needing praise because not lacking the virtues for which he is praised. In such a case praise is justly distinguished from flattery.[14]

Jonson's fear of flattery extends to what he takes to be flattery of himself. In an epigram addressed 'To Francis Beavmont' (E55), a response to Beaumont's 'Letter From the Country to Jonson' (H&S 11:374–6), Jonson says that in praising him lavishly Beaumont unwittingly draws attention to the excess of praise over deserving: 'At once you mak'st me happie, and vnmak'st; / And giuing largely to me, more thou tak'st. / What fate is mine, that so it selfe bereaues? / What art is thine, that so thy friend deceiues?' (5–10). Jonson admonishes Beaumont to be as conscious of the slippery ambiguities of epideictic rhetoric as is Jonson himself. Flattery has the appearance of 'giuing largely,' but the recipient of this equivocal gift must in looking within himself begin to suspect that he is 'not worth / The least indulgent thought thy pen drops forth' (3–4). The recipient suspects also that the praiser felt it necessary to flatter him because he thought him unworthy of judicious praise, which is why Jonson asserts that Beaumont's 'indulgent thought' takes away even as it gives. Jonson speaks here not false modesty, but the consciousness that the language of praise is a coin that must be employed sparingly, since it is easily debased by inflated usage.[15] Jonson is particularly upset in the last line when Beaumont says that he (Jonson) writes better than himself, even as Beaumont appears to claim judgment perpicuous enough to make such a discrimination. In this Beaumont seems to imply a superiority over Jonson at the very moment he is asserting the opposite.

If we are to believe Jonson's epigram addressed 'To William Camden' (E14), his teacher at the Westminster School, it was to him that the poet owed the kinds of discrimination he asks both of Beaumont and himself, along with 'All that I am in arts, all that I know' (2). Jonson finds a model in Camden of the ethos he projects for himself: 'What name, what skill, what faith hast thou in things! / What sight in searching the most antique springs! / What weight, and what authoritie in thy speech! / Man scarse can make that doubt, but thou canst teach' (7–10).

Denunciations of flattery both classical and Renaissance were easy to come by, and often they gave the finally trivial advice that one should always tell the truth. The notion that, in a context of political class stratification where pursuit of patronage was a necessity of life, one could tell the truth only by telling it slant was a minority opinion, limited to those, like Jonson, who understood that the rhetorical stance of 'truth-telling' was itself one of the oldest forms of flattery.[16] Erasmus leads us, as he may have led Jonson, back to one of the most incisive classical considerations of flattery, Plutarch's essay 'How to Distinguish a Friend from a Flatterer' (196). Plutarch warns specifically against the flatterer who mimics the unflattering language of the frank and truthful friend (1:277). The flatterer's 'aim is to get the name of a hater of iniquity, and to give the impression that he would not willingly abate his frankness to please others, nor do or say anything at all to curry favour' (319). The result is that 'the unscrupulous, being well aware that frankness is a great remedy for flattery, flatter by means of frankness itself' (327). So much for truth as a remedy against flattery.

Pliny the Younger's exposition of a strategy for overcoming this debility of praise I shall take up in the following section. Plutarch's and Dio Chrysostom's considerations of flattery, however, derive from observations of the same Roman world in which Pliny and Tacitus lived and wrote, and it is in Tacitus that Jonson would have noted the most trenchant criticism of a court in which truth-telling became the ultimate flattery: the courts of the Roman *principes*. In the opening of his *Histories* he complains of the difficulties attending attempts to write history under the principate, which are complicated by 'a passion for flattery, or else a hatred of autocrats.' The result is that 'adulation bears the ugly taint of subservience, but malice gives the false impression of being independent' (21). He repeats in the *Annals* (30) the same criticism of histories written during the reign of Augustus. Tiberius himself led the way in creating a political ambiance in which protestations of sincerity were instantly discredited and the 'show of independence was the only sort of flattery left' (34). The result was 'a degraded society' in which 'exaggerated servility is as dangerous as none at all,' and the only stances possible oscillated 'between perilous insubordination and degrading servility' (163).

The complicity between flatterer and flattered, trenchantly analysed by Tacitus, was recognized by Jonson in the *Discoveries*:

But flattery is a fine pick-lock of tender eares: especially of those, whom fortune hath borne high upon their wings, that submit their dignity, and authority to it, by soothing of themselves. For indeed men could never be taken, in that abundance, with the Sprindges of others' *Flattery*, if they began not there; if they did but remember, how much more profitable the bitternesse of *Truth* were, than all the honey distilling from a whorish voice; which is not praise, but poyson. (H&S 8:596–7)

The result is that the flattered allow themselves to be put in a passive position, and both lord and commoner become complicitous in the loss of inner virtue.[17]

In the Renaissance, Giovanni Della Casa in his courtier's handbook, the popular *Galateo*, lays out the structure of distrust built atop such political enervations, one that Jonson would have recognized:

> And albeit men be well pleased, that men doe give them worship & honour: yet when they find them selves cuningly courted, they be soone weary of it, and also disdaine it. For these glaverings, or flatteries I should say, to amend their knaveries & falsehoodes, have this fault withall: that these glavering fellowes doe plainly shewe, they count him whome they court in this sorte, but a vaine, and arrogant bodie, an asse of grose capacitie, and so simple, yt it should be an easie mater to baite him and take him too.   (58–9)

This is the level of analysis at which Jonson operates, and here choices become dilemmas. The difficulty of walking the narrow line between arrogance and sycophancy could be said to be the central problem of Jonson's career at court and as a poet. And the difficulty lay not only in the fact that these might well be the only options open to a man like Jonson, but particularly in the ways in which, following Tacitus, sycophancy could be interpreted as insubordination, and insubordination as a form of sycophancy.

In a poem apparently indebted to Plutarch's essay, 'Epigram. To a Friend, and Sonne' (U69), Jonson develops elaborate discriminations between friendship and flattery. The contrasts in the opening lines, induced by heavy pointing, distinguish finely the exact components of regard Jonson and his friend hold for each other: 'Sonne, and my Friend, I had not called' you so / To mee; or beene the same to you; if show, / Profit, or Chance had made us: But I know / What, by that name, wee each to other owe, / Freedome, and Truth' (1–5). The poet distinguishes the love between father and adopted son from the freedom and truth necessary for friendship. Freedom does not necessarily entail truth, though truth requires freedom: hence the comma which emphasizes the *and* and the nonimplicative relation between the two terms.

The rest of the poem extends this reciprocity by defining it negatively against flattery and the flatterer. The problem is one of perceiving differences within apparent likeness, something Jonson habitually confronts contrastively. The flatterer must keep true friends away from his victim, because in their presence the flatterer would himself be un-masked. The strategy of the poem becomes part of the poem's subject matter, and it is a strategy that the flatterer has an interest in thwarting. 'Painting' here (24) retains the notion of disguise, and so those who are susceptible to flatterers are like those who attempt 'the strife / Never so great to get them [pictures], and the ends, / Rather to boast rich hangings, then rare friends' (24–6). The flatterer becomes at once the poor painter and the false picture that he paints, and is in either case exactly like a rich hanging: something composed of mere externals. Jonson sees the flatterer as an Inigo Jones, one who strives to paint himself as the real thing, and the person who allows himself to be flat-tered is one who would prefer 'to boast rich hangings, then rare friends.'[18]

In dealing with the credibility of praise, however, he faces a still further though related problem: true praise, far from overstating the virtues of the person praised, can in fact fall short. In some early poems he strives to overcome the debilities of epideictic rhetoric by contrastive discriminations.

In praising William Lord Mounteagle (E60), the putative discoverer of the Gunpowder Plot, Jonson laments his country's failure to raise 'An obeliske, or columne to thy name,' only to conclude that the 'sauer of my countrey' 'exceeds' the very praise that the epigram attempts to render. A similar disclaimer is announced in E106, 'To Sir Edward Her-bert': 'If men get name, for some one vertue: Then, / What man art thou, that art so many men, / All-vertuous HERBERT! on whose euery part / *Truth* might spend all her voyce, *Fame* all her art' (1–4). The point seems to be that praise of all Herbert's specific virtues would have to be commensurate with the totality, which Jonson says is impossible. Like sentiments are declared in the epigram addressed 'To Alphonso Ferrabosco, on his Booke' (E130). Having catalogued Ferrabosco's mus-ical creations and accomplishments, Jonson concludes: 'I, yet, had vtter'd nothing on thy part, / When these were but the praises of the Art. / But when I haue said, The proofes of all these bee / Shed in thy Songs; 'tis true: but short of thee' (15–18).[19]

John Hoskins in his *Directions for Speech and Style* records two op-posite meanings of the figure of *hyperbole* (see chapter 1, section 2), one of which is a statement clearly in excess of the reality, and the other a statement at once great in its predications, and inadequate to what it is predicated of. Jonson sometimes uses *hyperbole*-as-inadequacy to dis-place *hyperbole*-as-exaggeration, and in this way disarm the reader's resistance (Friedberg). This strategy governs the epigram to Sir John

Roe (E27), when Jonson asserts that 'If any pious life ere lifted man / To heauen; his hath: O happy state! wherein / Wee, sad for him, may glorie, and not sinne' (6–8). One may praise him and not sin because any praise, including that which precedes these closing lines, must be inadequate and therefore immune to the charges of exaggeration.[20]

In fact, Jonson wrote a number of epitaphs where he makes epideictic capital out of calling into question the conventions of funerary praise. One of these is the epitaph inscribed on the tomb of Charles Cavendish at Bolsover Castle, 'Charles Cauendish to his posteritie' (M22). Jonson raises the question of where lies the true object of praise: 'Sonnes, seeke not me amonge these polish'd stones: / these only hide part of my flesh, and bones: / which, did they neere so neate, or proudly dwell, / will all turne dust, & may not make me swell. / Let such as iustly haue out-liu'd all prayse, / trust in the tombes, their care-full freinds do rayse' (1–6). Cavendish's answer from beyond the grave that the true object of praise lies in a man's life, not his monument, parallels the contrast between inner virtue and outer show: 'It [my lyfe (7)] will be matter lowd inoughe to tell / Not when I die'd, but how I liud' (11–12). Cavendish's life is contrasted with the conventional dates of birth and death, and the praise inscribed on the tomb below the poem (reproduced in H&S 8:387) is likewise called into question.

An even more explicit rejection of conventional epitaph forms occurs in M28, 'To the memorye of that most honoured Ladie *Jane*, eldest Daughter, to *Cuthbert* Lord *Ogle*: and Countesse of *Shrewsbury*':

> I could begin with that graue forme, *Here lies*,
> And pray thee *Reader*, bring thy weepinge Eyes
> To see (who'it is?) A noble *Countesse*, greate,
> In blood, in birth, by match, and by her seate;
> Religious, wise, chast, louing, gratious, good;
> And number Attributes vnto a flood ...   (1–6)

This is one of Jonson's wittiest poems and deserves to be better known. The perambulating visitor's idle curiosity is immediately challenged ('who'it is?'), and he is invited to inspect other epitaphs in the church if he is intrigued with 'ones *Descent*' and the '*Heralds* witt' (11, 12). This wry comment makes the point: such epitaphs open themselves up to the same kind of questioning as do all the panoply of titles, birth, and coats of arms. The remainder of the poem works out the lady's wooing of death after her husband's demise, but it is by assaulting the idle

reader's expectation of the standard form and topics of epitaphs that
Jonson seeks to establish Lady Jane's unique human value. These standard topics Jonson gives in an offhand catalogue, offering them in praise
which, though sincere enough, pricks the reader's assumption that such
praise is sufficient. We find here the conventions of epitaphs joining
other signs in the code of aristocratic semiosis, signs which if they are
to mean anything must be brought before the bar of true nobility and
tested for their significance.

Finally, there are two short epitaphs that call the purpose of epitaphs,
if not into question, at least to the reader's critical awareness. The first
is U16, 'An Epitaph on Master PHILIP GRAY':

> Reader, stay,
> And if I had not more to say,
> But here doth lie, till the last Day,
> All that is left of PHILIP GRAY,
> It might thy patience richly pay:
> > For, if such men as he could die,
> > What suretie of life have thou, and I?

This epitaph blithely refuses to be an epitaph, and deftly makes the
point that its brevity is a sign not of triviality, but of a significance so
profound that no more words than these can communicate it – in fact,
more words might trivialize it. The reader's 'patience' would indeed be
tried were he reading the kind of commonplace statement that Jonson
knows he expects to see on tombs. Instead, Jonson informs the reader
that the poem only exists to point past itself to the profound meaning
of death in the dead's community with the reader, and the writer.

The 'Epitaph {on ELIZABETH CHVTE}' (U35) appears on a tablet in
Sonning Church, Berkshire (H&S 8:188):

> What Beautie would have lovely stilde,
> What manners prettie, Nature milde,
> What wonder perfect, all were fil'd,
> Upon record, in this blest child.
> > And till the comming of the Soule
> > To fetch the flesh, we keepe the Rowle.

Keeping the roll means keeping this 'record,' this stone tablet which
registers the child's possession of these qualities. The concluding line –

'we keepe the Rowle' – foregrounds the memorial element in the epitaph. The legal point of this 'roll' is to keep a record of possession for the last day, which will enable the owner to reclaim possession.[21] This conceit ingeniously links these otherwise diverse elements: (1) the epitaph as a written record: (2) the written record, in the legal sense of 'record' and 'roll' registering what beauties the child has claim to; (3) the notion of future resurrection, a future of the sort against which records are made and kept. Thus the record of beauties lost has likewise become the record of beauties that must be or ought to be reclaimed. But it is a record that also calls attention to this loss, and registers in addition its own poverty as substitute, displacing even as it names the virtues of the dead child.[22]

4   The Merit of the Praised – Jonson and Pliny

Praise always runs the risk of diminishing its object even as it attempts to augment it. Flattery does this as a matter of course, and because praise so easily seems flattery it appears to take on the debilities of its perversion. Aristocratic status as a form of epideictic rhetoric replicates these problems, but in reversed form. Whereas epideixis' problem of credibility is quite simply the assumption that most praise is lies, the capacity of an aristocratic semiotic to disguise the lack of true nobility derives from the assumption that such signs tell the truth.

Since the signs of aristocratic status have the capacity to signify no true nobility at all, their relation to the latter can be at best supplementary, gaining their significance only from the inner virtues they refer to. Similarly, the credibility of praise finally must be tested on the merit of the praised, and in parallel fashion praise is just as supplementary to merit as is aristocratic status. And if this is the case, then the need for praise becomes as embarrassingly revealing as is the need for status: both declare people lacking in the very virtues which both status and praise declare them already to possess. In brief, those who are praiseworthy do not need praise, and those who need praise are not praiseworthy.

This is only one of the paradoxes and dilemmas that for Jonson flow from aristocratic status as a form of epideixis, and it generates others. For instance, to praise the virtues of true nobility in a noble person is to imply the possibility of its absence; not to praise such virtue is to imply the reality of its absence. As Jonson concludes U32, 'Another to [Thomas Lord Ellesmere]': 'He do's you wrong, that craves you to doe right' (16).[23] A still further dilemma demanding of the poet still further diplomatic discriminations is the notion that the poet confers aristocratic status on the nobility, in which case the poet's role substitutes for the herald's. In this case Jonson found himself on the edge of an abyss in which lived Tacitus' contorted double binds: the poet or rhetor at once presumptuous and servile. The poet who claims to have in his gift noble status is presumptuous in claiming implicit superiority over his betters, and servile in ministering to the latters' need to be dignified by his praise. Operative here is the paradox, already noted in Jonson's statement on flattery in the *Discoveries*, by which higher and lower classes become complicitous in upholding the established hierarchy and subverting it in the process of doing so.

These are the problems that Jonson confronts in the poetry to discussed in the last two sections of this chapter. Jonson's response brings them to consciousness, both his own and that of his readers, so as to open out their tangled logic, and by doing so to make possible predications of true nobility that are credible. Once again, Jonson establishes the meanings of his poems in the way outlined in chapter 1: by calling upon the reader to recreate the dialectics of choice and judgment constituting the poem's creation.

One of the epigrams addressed 'To Mary Lady Wroth' (E103) concludes with the following couplet: 'My praise is plaine, and where so ere profest, / Becomes none more then you, who need it least' (13–14). The poet's praise is indeed plain, since it consists entirely of restoring her family name of 'Sydney,' which she lost in marrying, and 'Which is, it selfe, the *imprese* of the great, / And glorie of them all, but to repeate!' (7–8). The name of the Sidney family becomes itself an impresa, a coat of arms summarizing virtues that Jonson does not name because they do not require naming. At this point one discovers that Jonson not only does not name the family's virtues, but makes praise out of his refusal. The crucial word here is 'need' – occurring twice in the poem – where Jonson denies that either Lady Mary or her family requires praise. Because both are complete in themselves Jonson says here that any addition is superfluous, and by implication insulting: 'Forgiue me then, if mine but say you are / A SYDNEY: but in that extend as farre / As lowdest praisers, who perhaps would find / For euery part a character assign'd' (9–12).

Called upon to supply a commendatory poem to a volume of verse by Sir John Beaumont, the brother of the playwright, Jonson responds with a carefully discriminated treatise on the implications of that request: 'On the honour'd Poems of his honored Friend, Sir *Iohn Beaumont*, Baronet' (M32). Jonson envisions pages of commendatory poems as military fortifications required when authors and printers 'sweat to fortifie a muse.' By contrast, 'Here needs no words expense / In Bulwarkes, Rau'lins, Ramparts, for defense' (3–4). The clear implication is that the 'fortification' supplied by such verse announces the lack of the virtues whose presence they putatively confirm. Such impertinence foresees attacks and tacitly admits doubts of defendability. Jonson insists that the book is itself a 'frontire,' and if so, then 'who dares offer a redoubt to reare? / ... where Enuy hath not cast / A Trench against it, nor a Battry plac't?' (11–14).[24]

If praise can be made out of critiques of praise's dyslogistic implications, then rejections of praise can be a significant component of the praiseworthy. In U26, 'An Ode' addressed to a man apparently wounded in a duel, Jonson advises that

> Your covetous hand,
> Happy in that faire honour it hath gain'd,
> Must now be rayn'd.
> True valour doth her own renowne command
> In one full Action; nor have you now more
> To doe, then be a husband to that store. (13–18)

This advice is presented as 'Physick' not for bodily wounds but 'for the mind' (9), and the mental wound Jonson seeks to cure is his addressee's appetite for more honour than he has already won. To covet more is to acknowledge a sense of lack that betrays what one already has.

A fuller statement of Jonson's point occurs in 'An Epigram. To WILLIAM Earle of Newcastle' (U59).[25] Jonson compares three notions of fencing. The first, which is decorous, gets a decorous statement: parallelism of syntax and line, and the zeugmas of lines 1, 2, and 6 – all these express the 'noble Science' that makes fencing into something that keeps 'with time; / As all defence, or offence were a chime!' (5–6). The second conception, again decorously described in asymmetrical alignments of syntactical and line units, contrasts with the first by being 'A quick, and dazeling motion.' And the third is introduced with the lines: 'No, it is the Law / Of daring not to doe a wrong, is true / Valour!' Whereas the second conception obeys the 'law of daring,' but does not necessarily dare not to do wrong, Newcastle knows when 'to sleight it [insult], being done to you! / To know the heads of danger! where 'tis fit / To bend, to breake, provoke, or suffer it! / And this (my Lord) is Valour!' (16–19). Newcastle and his family before him 'durst live great, 'mongst all the colds, and heates, / Of humane life! as all the frosts, and sweates, / Of fortune!' (21–3). Balancing between the first two conceptions of fencing has allowed them to be valiant in situations where mere duelling is useless.[26] Jonson says of Newcastle's ancestors that they 'valiant were, with, or without their hands' (24). Valour in duelling is true virtue only when it is more than valour in duelling, which means that Newcastle does not need duelling to manifest his valour or to coerce public recognition of it.[27]

As in the poem addressed to Francis Beaumont examined in a previous section, Jonson elsewhere displays sensitivity to false praise. In his 'Answer. The Poet to the Painter [Sir William Burlase]' (U52), Jonson genially tells the painter that in his portrait of the poet 'You made it a brave piece, but not like me' (15). The first four stanzas show Jonson at his occasional game of self-deprecation. He admits the vastness of his bulk and the difficulty the painter might have in painting him: 'Which if in compasse of no Art it came / To be describ'd by a *Monogram*, / With one great blot, yo'had formed me as I am' (10–12). The point is of course that in making Jonson look better than he is, the painter makes Jonson the kind of person that he inveighs against elsewhere: someone who needs praise to make up for deficiencies.

Clearly, Jonson's probing the nature of epideictic rhetoric took him far beyond the standard categories of analysis in classical and Renaissance examinations. To discover that praise may be a form of covert insult, and that the need for praise is a tacit confession of personal lack, is to turn the theory of epideixis away from ceremonial concerns, and toward a dialectical interplay among praise, the person who praises, and the person who is praised, always constrained by the decorums of a hierarchical, stratified society.[28] At this level of Jonson's consideration few writers can match him, and questions of influence are moot. Della Casa in *Galateo* is one such, and Pliny the Younger is another. The sophistication that enables such insights is not necessarily transmissible: if you have to read about it to discover it then it is probably beyond you.

In the *Panegyricus* addressed by Pliny to the emperor Trajan, Jonson found a document that alone among all classical texts he knew displays an analytic intelligence sufficient to grasp the pitfalls, rhetorical and ideological, that the vera nobilitas argument entails.[29] It stands behind one of his earliest treatments of the links between humanist poet and monarch: 'A Panegyre on the Happie Entrance of Iames, Ovr Soveraigne to His first high Session of Parliament in this his Kingdome, the 19. of March, 1603.'

The problem of making credible the assertion that Trajan's ascent to the principate is due to his eminent virtues lies in the fact that Trajan was destined for the office the moment Nerva adopted him. Pliny's difficulty was exactly that which Jonson was to confront: how to assert credibly that *de facto* heirs to high status are properly so by reason of personally achieved true nobility? The ingenious dialectical strategy by which Pliny reconciled imperial status with merit Jonson was to appropriate and put to identical uses.

This dialectic contains a negative and a positive component. Negatively, Pliny contrasts Trajan with earlier emperors who claimed the usual titles of the *Princeps* by inheritance or by military coup. Discriminating false titles from true opens up a new space for maintaining the latter's viability, and makes possible the positive argument which rests squarely on the assertion that only those who possess true nobility deserve imperial titles:

> Although your many outstanding merits surely called you to assume some title and honour, you refused the title of Father of your country, and it was only after a prolonged struggle between us and your modesty that in the end you were persuaded.   (369)[30]

The fact of merit precedes its public acknowledgment, and consequently Pliny can assert that 'in fact, you were emperor, but did not know it' (345). Having already ascended the imperial seat, Trajan continues to act as if he must continually merit it. As emperor *de facto*, Trajan insists on filling out the imperial titles by sedulously respecting republican forms, thereby meriting these titles *de jure*.

Pliny labours under two obstacles imposed by the past, and he makes his confrontation with these obstacles the substance of his oration.[31] The first is the history of the principate, wherein the cooptation of republican forms perverted senatorial assertions of republican independence into a warped allegiance to the principate. Any attempt to argue that Trajan joins imperial status with republican humility and respect for laws and customs has already been enervated by repetitions of the same argument from the time of Augustus on. Pliny responds by tying Trajan's ascendancy to republican ideals, and arguing that the republic alone awarded high status on the basis of merit.[32]

Secondly, related to this first cooptation is another: the fading of politically responsible rhetoric during the principate into empty panegyric (Syme, following Tacitus: 246). To call Trajan *Optimus* and *Princeps* (first citizen of the Senate) is instantly to risk total loss of credibility, since the same titles were routinely awarded past emperors – when, that is, as in the cases of Caligula and Domitian, they did not insist on the title *divus* (divine) as well.

Pliny transforms the mutual exclusion between inherited status and personal merit into mutual implication. The essential link between Pliny and Jonson lies in their both understanding that any argument for the separation of merit and status contains this potential for arguing their union as well. And like Jonson, Pliny saw that epideixis must always be itself at issue in any laudatory testimony, with the credibility of the second dependent wholly on the credibility of the first.

Burgess is partially correct then in viewing the *Panegyricus* in the tradition of the Isocratean oration *peri basileias*, a treatise *de regimine principum*: the text that teaches the prince as it praises him, that is, teaches him to be praiseworthy (137–8). But what exactly Pliny is lecturing the emperor on is not as obvious as it appears. The Isocratean genre, represented in the Renaissance by a host of handbooks typified by Erasmus' treatise (Gilbert), features straightforward advice on the dos and don'ts of monarchal power, heavily laced with catalogues of classical and Christian virtues. What links Jonson with Pliny over the centuries and differentiates both from the *de regimine principum* tradition is their insistence that the survival of any monarchal or aristocratic establishment depends on its members' consciousness of their own ideological vulnerability. And the vera nobilitas argument is at the core of this consciousness. For both Pliny and Jonson the powers that be must come to understand that their status rests on the originary virtues that historically gave rise to such political structures, or it rests on nothing at all. The signs of power can be used with security only as long as those who use them understand the power of signs to bear witness against them. Pliny's *Panegyricus*, like many of Jonson's poems of praise, is a treatise on praise, the purpose of which is to educate its addressee in the vertiginous semiotics of epideictic rhetoric and of aristocratic status. Understanding the pitfalls of the one is to understand those of the other. The monarch and aristocrat renew their authority by such understanding, and the authority of the epideictic rhetor (and poet) lies in his capacity to articulate the truth of these admonitions.[33] The self-reflexivity of Pliny's oration is intended to be a model for Trajan's own reflection on the foundations of his imperial status, and in this Pliny foreshadows Jonson's poetic practice.

In defending his praise against the charge of flattery, Pliny like Jonson was also defending himself against the charge of servility. It was a reasonable charge in Pliny's case, given the history of the *principes*' reduction of the patriciate to senatorial sycophancy recorded by Tacitus.[34] Jonson himself ran little risk of being seriously accused of sycophancy,[35] but he was open to the opposite criticism: of arrogating to himself the authority to determine who among the aristocracy possessed true nobility. In an epigram addressed 'To all, to whom I write' (E9) Jonson insists 'May none, whose scatter'd names honor my booke, / For strict degrees of ranke, or title looke: / 'Tis 'gainst the manners of an *Epigram*: / And, I a *Poet* here, no *Herald* am.' Officially of course a poet was not a herald. But a case could be made – and Jonson made that case – that the humanist poet claimed for himself the learning necessary for assigning the 'title' of vera nobilitas to those who deserved it, and by such a claim took over the office of a herald.

Beginning in the fifteenth century as an instrument of the titled class, but growing to power under the Tudors, the College of Heralds became the instrument by which the crown made itself the source of all titles of honour. As such it held the power of determining the rights of a family to titles and arms by reason of descent (James 23ff). In this respect the College of Heralds was the designated agency under the Crown for performing the very office which the humanist poet claimed for himself: determining who possessed true nobility. Ferne made the connection explicit when he wrote that 'the coate-armours ... [are] symbals or signes ... borne by them [Gentlemen] to signifie vertues in the bearers' (16).

Jonson, along with many others, had little respect for the College at the turn of the century and after, when the Stuarts sold titles to make up for financial ineptitude (Stone 23ff, 749). In 'A speach according to Horace' (U44) the decadent nobility claims its privileges by being 'Descended in a rope of Titles, be / From *Guy*, or *Bevis*, *Arthur*, or from whom / The Herald will' (80–2). And in M28, the epitaph for lady Jane Ogle discussed previously in this chapter, the poet laughs at tourists who search memorial tablets for records of '*Descent*' invented by 'a *Heralds* witt.' But these comments are just the point: the wit of the herald was dedicated to discovering genealogies on the premise that such established true nobility. When Jonson says that he is no herald he means two things: first, that he has little respect for such a premise; and second, that he in fact displaces the herald's office with his own.[36]

In the few poems addressed to King James, Jonson dealt tactfully with his similar conviction 'That *Poets* are far rarer births then kings' (E79). He does so in E4 'To King Iames,' where he praises James as both king and poet. At issue in the poem is the question who is testing whom. Jonson invites James to judge his volume of epigrams specifically in his capacity as poet. On such matters, Jonson suggests, the two are equals, and the test that James must pass is whether he can recognize that to be the case: 'Whom should my *Muse* then flie to, but the best / Of Kings for grace; of *Poets* for my test?' (9–10). E4 is a challenge to James similar to that delivered by Pliny to Trajan, and it says in effect: if you claim expertise in poetry by right of personal talent, just as you claim royal authority by divine decree, then you manifest both in the excellent judgment you display in gracing me as king, but testing my verse as a poet.

Jonson therefore does not flatter the king as long as the king refuses to demand more authority in either domain than he has earned: the credibility of the praise depends on the merit of the praised. And this is just Jonson's point in another epigram addressed to James, E36, 'To the Ghost of Martial,' specifically on the subject of flattery:

> MARTIAL, thou gau'st farre nobler *Epigrammes*
>   To thy DOMITIAN, that I can my JAMES:
> But in my royall subiect I passe thee,
>   Thou flatterd'st thine, mine cannot flatter'd bee.

Jonson alludes to epigram 72 from book X, where Martial exhibits the subtlest of flatteries:

> Blandishing Flatteries, in vain you present to me your lying lips; I will address no man as Master and God. There is no longer a place for you in this city; fly to the distant turbaned Parthians and, like vile suppliants, lick the sandals of painted kings. Here we have no master, but an emperor, the most just of senators, who has recalled from the Styx simple Truth with unadorned hair. If you are wise, Rome, forbear, under such a prince, to speak as formerly. (288–9)

This epigram also recalls Pliny, for it was against the precedent of just such inflation of praise lavished on Domitian that Pliny had to labour to establish the credibility of his own praise of Trajan. In the context of Jonson's criticism of Martial's disingenuous stance of unflattering frankness, the poet tests James by refusing to praise him, thereby challenging him, as Pliny challenged Trajan, to grasp the insidious logic that turns praise into flattery.[37]

A group of epigrams clustered at the end of the volume are particularly fitted to illustrate Jonson's strategies for confronting the rhetorical misprisions latent in praising true nobility in members of the aristocracy. E109, 'To Sir Henry Nevil,' explicitly contrasts those who 'toyle for titles to their tombes' (18), and Nevil's pursuit of neither 'fame, nor titles; but doth chuse / where vertue makes them both' (2–3). The standard Jonsonian antimonies appear here, posing inner worth against outer appearance. The object of praise, however, is not merely Nevil's true nobility but an awareness on his part matching the poet's that such nobility is to be preferred to pursuing titles and honours: 'Thou are not one, seek'st miseries with hope, / Wrestlest with dignities' (5–6). In other words, the discriminations that Jonson could have drawn in praising him he has already understood, and made his choices accordingly.[38]

E104 and E105, to the countess of Montgomery and Mary Lady Wroth respectively, both make praise out of a search for appropriate comparisons that is finally allowed to end in frustration. In the first instance Jonson raises the same question he had in E102 on the earl of Pembroke: how to make comparisons with other virtues and persons that do not implicitly diminish even as they attempt to augment? The next epigram (E105), on Lady Wroth, solves the problem by comparing the lady to herself, through the mediation of the various goddesses she has recently played in Jonson's masques at court. When wearing her wheaten hat she looks like Ceres; when dressed like a shepherdess, she reminds one of Oenone, Flora, or May; when dancing she is 'the Idalian queen,' Venus, an attribution that must be balanced by naming her Diana when she hunts, and Juno when she sits. Comparison implies difference, which implies a lack in the person praised. The poet nullifies the unwanted implication by a circular, tautological comparison in which the points of comparison turn out to be displaced elements in Lady Mary herself. The mythological goddesses take their identities from Lady Mary, from whom the poet alienates them just sufficiently to allow her own identity definition in terms of them.

Finally, in two poems Jonson confronts squarely the problem of praising true nobility in female friends who are also members of the aristocracy: 'On Lvcy Covntesse of Bedford' (E76) and 'To Elizabeth Covntesse of Rvtland' (F12). Jonson highlights the authority he claims for praising them and foregrounds the potential twin debilities of his own rhetoric: the implication of need on the ladies's part and arrogance on the poet's.

Jonson solves the problem in Lady Bedford's case by using a tactic of Pliny: praising her for the virtues of self-knowledge that make her capable of reading Jonson's praise in the right way. Having listed the virtues characterizing the 'kinde of creature I could most desire, / To honor, serue, and loue; as *Poets* vse' (3–4), to which he will at the end attach the name of '*Bedford*' (18), Jonson proceeds to catalogue some favourite qualities constituting true nobility: 'I meant to make her faire, and free, and wise, / Of greatest bloud, and yet more good than great; ... / I meant shee should be curteous, facile, sweet, / Hating that solemne vice of greatnesse, pride' (5–6, 9–10). The poem consistently links qualities that may exclude one another. What the lady is free of measures her strengths, and the former excludes any need for Ben Jonson's praise, which is fine with the poet since her freedom frees him from fear of misprision.

The epistle to the countess of Rutland (F12) has been partially examined in chapter 1 (section 4), where the opening lines illustrate Jonson's deployment of contrastivity in relatively extended passages. This is an early poem (1600; Donaldson *Ben Jonson* 677) and reflects Jonson's concern in *Cynthia's Revels* and *Poetaster* with the difficulties the humanist poet encounters in realizing his ambitions at court. Jonson makes the case in this poem for the sorts of virtues such as poetry can appropriately praise. Not surprisingly, among these is the aristocracy's recognizing that true nobility is constituted self-reflexively: by understanding itself as worthy of praise only by the poet who distinguishes true nobility from status residing in such things as birth, wealth, or coats of arms:

> Those other glorious notes,
> Inscrib'd in touch or marble, or the cotes
> Painted, or caru'd vpon our great-mens tombs,
> Or in their windowes; doe but proue the wombs,
> That bred them graues: when they were borne, they di'd,
> That had no *Muse* to make their fame abide. (43–8)

Jonson's promise to the countess of Rutland, which ends this unfinished fragment, he intends to be taken seriously:

> And show, how, to the life, my soule presents

Your forme imprest there: not with tickling rimes,
  Of common places, filch'd, that take these times,
But high, and noble matter, such as flies
  From braines entranc'd, and fill'd with extasies...   (86–90)

Poet, praise, and lady are bound together by a reciprocity in which the
candour of each enables that of the other two. Any failure of candour
necessarily discredits this reciprocity, evacuates from it all significance,
and turns it into just another exchange of self-serving bribes, such as
Jonson describes at the poem's beginning. Essential to preserving this
candour is the kind of discriminations which those prefacing lines serve
to make, which means that the poetry of praise, for Jonson at any rate,
must always confront overtly its own possible perversions.

5   The Authority of the Poet

In a stratified society dominated by a royal court where patronage is
sought and dispensed, there are fawns and there are satyrs. Fawns are
sycophants who place all hope of personal success in such patronage
and are willing to flatter in order to achieve it.[39] Satyrs are satirists (by
false etymology) who, having been disappointed in such aspirations,
turn envious and spiteful, attacking courtly favour, the fawns who receive it, and the whole panoply of hierarchical society as a mask behind
which lurk all human sins and vices (Kernan 135–40). Fawns and satyrs
tend to dance together, as in *The Faerie Queene* (1.6.7), and sometimes
a fawn is a satirist, as James Nohrnberg argues regarding Spenser's
Faunus in the *Mutabilitie Cantos* (749–53).

  Just as praise was historically discounted as flattery, so the dyslogistic
dimension of epideictic rhetoric was equally subject to dismissal as mere
envy and malice. Judgments that discriminate the truly noble and attack
those who undeservedly aspire to be recognized as such are vulnerable
to being called mere flattery and malice respectively. And this vulnerability manifests the larger, more radical vulnerability of the vera nobilitas argument to being dismissed as fraudulent and meaningless.[40]

  It is easy to see, then, why Jonson sought in his poetry to define a
credible epideixis against its perversions. For him, envious attack is to
true satire as flattery is to true praise.[41] Favourable and unfavourable
judgments stand or fall together, since both derive their credibility from
the authority of the judge.[42] All of this means that Jonson seeks his
readers' respect for the discriminations his judgments make by laying

out extensively defined distinctions between true and false praise, true and false blame. Once again, contrastivity validates the poet's judgments by making them the issue.

Poems in which Jonson argues these discriminations fall into two groups: poems addressed to fellow authors, whether directly or as commendatory prefaces to their books; and those addressed to critics who accuse him of being malicious in his satire. In both groups Jonson responds to the charge of partisanship by arguing that the credibility of praise and blame requires a personal relationship in which both are allowed and possible.

This is Jonson's point in 'An Epistle to a friend' (U37) which, as an apparently earlier version (M49) indicates, responds to a book submitted by an unnamed friend to Jonson for judgment. If M49 is indeed a draft of U37, a comparison shows that Jonson's later thoughts recognize the freedoms friendship allows, and indeed requires, for both favourable and unfavourable critical comment. In the *Vnder-wood* version Jonson advocates a 'comelie libertie' (20) that characterizes true friendship, which by refusing an abuse of 'faire leave' (24) avoids not only 'Licence' but the scanting of liberty implied by it. The liberty of true friendship also frees it from the perverse alternatives of praise that can only be flattery and criticism that appears arbitrary reproof. A clarifying extension of Jonson's point occurs in the earlier version. In reply to his friend's request that he 'Censure, not sharplye,' Jonson replies that accepting a priori constraints would impugn his friend's work, and the critic's censure as well. His point is the obvious one that when personal feelings dictate judgment neither praise nor blame carries any significance.

In his two epigrams addressed to John Donne, E23 and E96, Jonson deals respectively with his own judgment of Donne, and with Donne's judgment of his *Epigrammes*. As he says in E17, Jonson asks only for 'the learned Critick,' because he wishes for 'my poemes a legitimate fame' (3). In E23 Jonson insists that 'no' affection praise enough can giue' (6) to Donne's wit, 'All which I meant to praise, and, yet, I would; / But leaue, because I cannot as I should!' (9–10). The discriminations among 'meant,' 'would,' and 'should' unpack the earlier assertion that 'affection' could not praise Donne adequately. Affection might be expected to praise a friend hyperbolically, but in a typical assertion of inexpressibility Jonson says such praise here comes too short. This inexpressibility is then the subject of the interplay between intention and frustration in the closing lines already cited. By putting affection on the table and then trumping it with Donne's excessive deserving,

Jonson manages to discredit the possibility of a judgment vitiated by partisanship.[43]

In the second epigram Jonson desires no different consideration in Donne's judgment of his own poetry. Jonson claims a sort of self-validating confidence in sending his epigrams to Donne, founded on his confidence in Donne's sharing his own understanding of the detachment necessary to make critical judgment meaningful. Jonson expresses his confidence that Donne will 'take / As free simplicitie, to dis-auow, / As thou hast best authoritie, to'allow' (4–6). Free simplicity means that candour which extrapolates the dangers of criticism among friends that Jonson examines in this and similar poems. If Jonson finds 'but one [poem] / Mark'd by thy hand ... / My title's seal'd' (7–9), a conclusion Jonson confidently reaches because he knows that the value of Donne's praise is proportional to his freedom to criticize. On the other hand, those who write only for praise refuse adverse criticism, which means in turn that the praise they receive is meaningless (9–12). Jonson dismisses both judgments because the authority behind both is questionable:

To Foole, Or Knave (E61)

Thy praise, or dispraise is to me alike,
One doth not stroke me, nor the other strike.

In Jonson's many poems addressed to literary colleagues, a few of whom were also aristocrats, we find some of his most carefully weighed statements about literary judgment. Horace's *Ars Poetica* convinced him that critical judgments and ethical judgments were identical. Jonson would have been led to the same conclusion by reading the vera nobilitas argument as a theory of epideictic rhetoric, whereby the praise of true nobility is finally an ethical matter as well. The poem on Shakespeare becomes paradigmatic here, exemplifying versified literary criticism in which its own self-examination is as important as commentary on the author and work at hand.

For instance, in the poem contributed to William Browne's *Britannia's Pastorals* (M21), the second volume published in 1616, Jonson addresses the author's judgment of his own work, and that of the critic or reader. The opening couplet states in little the theme Jonson was to develop more exensively in the poem on Shakespeare: 'Some men, of Bookes or Friends not speaking right, / May hurt them more with praise, then Foes with spight' (1–2). Jonson lays part of the blame on the author himself:

> It must be thine owne iudgment, yet, that sends
> This thy worke forth: that iudgment mine commends.
> And, where the most reade bookes, on *Authors* fames,
> Or, like our Money-Brokers, take vp names
> On credit, and are cossen'd; see, that thou
> By offring not more sureties, then inow,
> Hold thyne owne worth vnbroke ...   (7–13)

The elaborate simile warns Browne not to publish more than has intrinsic worth. Publishing books is like other manifestations of self in society, such as clothes, speech, and the signs of status, in registering the level of one's self-knowledge. The flatterer has his counterpart in the one he praises, the deceiver of others whose self-deceiving flattery makes him receptive to false praise in turn.

Knowing himself accurately, the author neither craves praise nor fears criticism, and the object of the critic's praise is that self-knowledge. In linking together the truth of the praise, the merit of the praised, and the authority of the praiser, Jonson discriminates this from the parallel complex characteristic of false praise and blame, in which the self-deceiving author invites flattery (because fearing criticism), calling simultaneously into question author, critic, and text.[44]

In the long poem addressed to Michael Drayton (M30) it is the lack of just such critical discrimination that suggests a certain amount of condescension. In comparison with the poem on Shakespeare, Jonson refuses to worry his praise of Drayton and lauds each work in turn without evoking and setting aside any contrastively defined countertext. Drayton turns out to be all too easy to praise,[45] and while Jonson apparently considers Drayton's work worth reading, he does not consider it worth criticizing.[46]

Jonson was called upon to write commendatory poems for a number of translations, and he seized these occasions to make translation a test of a writer's authority. For Jonson, good translation requires that the translator achieve the correct perspective on his text (Gadamer's hermeneutics would speak of 'fusion of horizons' [273ff]). Jonson had implied as much in the very first poem of the *Epigrammes*. In a poem (M17) prefacing the anonymous *Cinthias Reuenge* (1613), Jonson explores various permissible levels of understanding. Some may simply wonder who the author is, others may 'roaue' through the pages (5), and still others may try to understand it. All receptions are acceptable with one essential proviso: 'Who cannot reade, but onely doth desire / To vnderstand, hee may at length admire' (9–10).

The willingness to take the appropriate perspective on a book is rare, and Jonson literalizes the problem in his poem prefacing Nicholas Breton's 1600 volume called *Melancholike humours* (M2). Reading this book properly requires a perspective on it replicating that demanded of those who would 'read' the human passions the book discusses. Reading both requires not being distracted by appearances, and readers that can do neither, because they 'looke asquint,' will read both 'wry' (7). Here 'the fault's not in the obiect, but their eyes' (8) which take 'a laterall viewe, / Vnto a cunning piece wrought perspective' (9–10), a picture that can be seen properly only from a specific location. Lacking the appropriate perspective they want 'facultie to make a censure true' (11).

Jonson praises Thomas May's reading of Lucan's *Pharsalia* in his translation of 1627 (M29) for having achieved a similar coincidence between the genius that wrote the poem and that which translates it (19–25). Translation as reading is extended to include reading men as well as books in another poem, prefixed to a translation by James Mabbe in 1622 of a Spanish picaresque tale, *The Rogue* (M24): 'Who tracks this Authors, or Translators Pen, / Shall finde, that either hath read Bookes, and Men: / To say but one, were single' (1–3). Readings of books and men 'chime' together when the reader discovers human nature in books written in different languages: 'When the old words doe strike on the new times, / As in this *Spanish Proteus*; who, though writ / But in one tongue, was form'd with the worlds wit' (4–6). Such translators liberate the universal from the particular for those who, like Jonson, cannot read the original, but who are nevertheless as capable of reading men as were the author and the translator. 'Such Bookes deserue Translators, of like coate / As was the *Genius* wherewith they were wrote' (11–12). All three must possess the same 'genius,' which entails on the reader's part the capacity to align his own perspectivally with that of author and translator.

Such alignment would appear to be for Jonson something quite other than partisanship, to the degree that the norm of judgment is not personal attachment but conformity of reader's perspective to the writer's.[47] As the modern truism has it, agreement means two people looking at the same thing from the same perspective, so that judgment does not consist finally of identifying the two perspectives, but must begin there in order to ensure a reading which, if finally not sympathetic, is not so by reason of missing the point.[48]

Jonson's poem prefacing George Chapman's translation of Hesiod in 1618 (M23) develops the metaphor of trade monopoly to praise Chapman's privileged position as translator of Greek classics. Chapman's translation of the *Iliad* had appeared in 1611, and the *Whole Works of Homer* appeared between 1614 and 1616 (Nicoll 2:xii). Chapman becomes an enterprising merchant plying his ships between ancient Greece and modern England:

> Whose worke could this be, *Chapman*, to refine
> Olde *Hesiods* Ore, and giue it vs; but thine,
> Who hadst before wrought in rich *Homers* Mine?
>
> What treasure hast thou brought vs! and what store
> Still, still, dost thou arriue with, at our shore,
> To make thy honour, and our wealth the more!   (1–6)

Jonson expands the concept of transmission into an allegory of merchant venturing. Common to all these poems is the notion of a perspectival 'line' whereby all see the same thing because all view within the same perspective. Here, the perspective which aligns reader with translator, and translator with original author, becomes a trade lane, replete with metaphorical transmutations of poetry into ore and treasure, with honour and wealth attending the 'passage' and 'return' (9) of the merchant ship.

Another extension of reading is copying, which is what Jonson says (U28) to Lady Mary Wroth he did with her sonnet sequence *Pamphilia to Amphilanthus* (see Wroth), the result being that he is 'become / A better lover, and a much better Poet' (3–4). He discriminates the different effects erotic verse may work on the reader: 'some, / But charme the Senses, others over-come / Both braines and hearts' (6–8). The line of transmission extends from erotic emotion, through Lady Mary's reading of this emotion, to Jonson's own rereading of her reading by rewriting her writing. In this way he telescopes his praise of her poetry with an act of reading that turns the praiser of the poetry into its writer. And once again true praise is presented as the almost tautological doubling in the praiser of the text praised.

Jonson's interest in verbal textualization of the erotic is more fully discovered in the preceding poem: 'An Ode,' U27, which lists classical and Renaissance poets and the lovers they have textualized in poetry:

> *Helen*, did *Homer* never see
> Thy beauties, yet could write of thee?
> Did *Sappho* on her seven-tongu'd Lute,
> So speake (as yet it is not mute)
> Of *Phaons* forme? or doth the Boy
> In Whom *Anacreon* once did joy,
> Lie drawne to life, in his soft Verse,
> As he whom *Maro* did rehearse?
> Was *Lesbia* sung by learn'd *Catullus*?
> Or *Delia's* Graces, by *Tibullus*?
> ...
> Hath *Petrarch* since his *Laura* rais'd
> Equall with her? or *Ronsart* prais'd
> His new *Cassandra*, 'bove the old;
> Which all the Fate of *Troy* foretold?
> Hath our *Sydney*, *Stella* set,
> Where never Star shone brighter yet?   (1–10, 21–6)

Jonson prefigures Roland Barthes' arguments that the erotic is a collection of rhetorical figures: 'beauty cannot assert itself save in the form of a citation' (*S/Z* 33). When Barthes elsewhere (*A Lover's Discourse* 77) cites Novalis – 'Love is mute ... only poetry makes it speak' – he offers support for a Jonsonian semiotic that privileges verbal discourse. This support is equivocal because, even though Barthes contended in his early, structuralist phase that nonverbal objects 'enjoy the status of systems only in so far as they pass through the relay of language' (*Elements* 10), erotic discourse in *S/Z* and *A Lover's Discourse* intimates a plenitude that is finally empty because it gestures toward an origin that exists nowhere outside of erotic discourse itself.

Being praised is Jonson's 'Celia,' whose beauty (and the poet's talent) allow her to join the classical list of poets-and-their-lovers. The list rehearses the convention of the list of poets and their lovers who are famous specifically for being part of the list. And the list is famous because it has a history of being referred to, each successive poet (like Jonson here) alluding to the list as he makes himself another addition to it. This recursivity even extends to the convention of 'following a convention,' producing poetry constituted wholly out of the act of writing poetry made out of references to poetic lists of other poets.

To repeat is not simply to say what has been said before: it is to repeat repetition, to make repetition itself a matter of regard. Erotic discourse is the practice of tautology (Barthes *A Lover's Discourse* 21): I love you because I love you. As praise such an assertion represents Jonson's insistence that the authority of the poet, like that of the reader, lies finally in reading the text (including the text of the beloved) with the same '*Genius* wherewith they were wrote.' 'An Ode' telescopes writing, reading, interpreting, judging, and praising with mock-serious literality.

If the poet's authority to praise is tested by charges of partisanship,[49] the authority of his adverse judgments is equally tested by the charge of malice. Ever since Kernan's study of satire's cankered muse, the complicity of the satirist in the vices he flays has become itself a test that critics must use in weighing the satirist's self-proclaimed ethical purity. Jonson was himself often attacked for exhibiting envy and spite in his dramatic and nondramatic satirical writing, and his replies either insisted that he attacked not individuals but types, or went on to accuse his accusers of disclosing themselves accurately touched by his satire. It is also true that Jonson could not under pressure always maintain the psychological and ethical independence that he found necessary ingredients of true nobility. His many quarrels early and late with those he saw usurping or perverting his agenda for the humanist poet, even the betrayal of his strictures on the desire for praise, of which Thomas Carew accuses him in his poem responding to Jonson's poem on the failure of *The New Inn*,[50] indicate his vulnerability to charges of inconsistency or worse.[51]

Counterbalancing the weight of these charges was and is Jonson's own unrelenting self-criticism, a form of negative narcissism imposed by his condition of aspiring new man of common birth, which dogged him throughout his career. Even the long-suffering Drummond, who had little reason to be sympathetic, was willing to grant that Jonson 'is passionately kind and angry, careless either to gain or keep, vindictive, but, if he be well answered, at himself' (Parfitt ed 479). It would seem that Jonson's anger at himself must have been a constant companion, since much of his poetry indicates that no one 'answered' him so often or so well as he himself.

The second poem in the *Epigrammes* (E2) extends the co-opting strategy of the first by seeking to finesse possible charges of malice. If E1 called for the understanding reader to do more than read well, Jonson here indicates that another virtue in request is self-knowledge. The opening lines of E2 mimic in free indirect discourse the charges of those who expect from him mindless malice: 'Thou should'st be bold, licentious, full of gall, / Wormewood, and sulphure, sharpe, and tooth'd withall; / Become a petulant thing, hurle inke, and wit, / As mad-men stones: not caring whom they hit' (3–6). Jonson sets a trap for his attackers in this mimicry, since if this is what they look for then their expectation is itself a sign of malice: 'Deceiue their malice, who could wish it so' (7).[52] Jonson's understanding readers receive their first lesson, in recognizing their own complicity in what they read. The book will read its readers, either through involving them in the contrastively structured process of the poem's creation, or – negatively – in mirroring back to malicious readers their own malice.

Jonson correctly understands that the charge of malice imputes to him the desire for praise won on the cheap, and this supposition elicits the *Epigrammes'* initial statement on the problem of praise: 'He that departs with his owne honesty / For vulgar praise, doth it too dearely buy' (E2:13–14). The following epigram (E3) indicates that Jonson does not want to be bought, either, by those who cannot understand him. He is willing to allow the bookseller's criterion of critical judgment – who 'Call'st a booke good, or bad, as it doth sell / Vse mine so, too' (2–3) but draws the line at wooing inappropriate customers such as 'termers, or some clark-like seruing-man, / Who scarse can spell th'hard names: whose knight lesse can' (9–10). The use once again of free indirect discourse to score the servant who can't read 'th'hard names' is a deft touch. We know immediately the kind of reader Jonson doesn't want. What he wants, it would appear, is all or nothing. Either sell to appropriate readers, Jonson tells his bookseller John Stepnith (Donaldson *Ben Jonson* 647), or send it off to the grocers' quarter to be used as wrapping paper.[53]

Jonson's poetical response to critics of his poetry generally takes the line that their criticism is literarily shallow and consequently morally suspect. E18, 'To my Meere English Censvrer,' responds to someone who has compared Jonson's epigrams unfavourably to those of Sir John Davies and John Weever. Jonson says that his critic would find his own epigrams praiseworthy were he to judge them as he judged those of his predecessors: if only 'thou'ldst but vse thy faith, as thou didst then, / When thou wert wont to'admire, not censure men' (7–8). In other words, such judgment is based on premises no more critical than liking what one likes.

This riposte is a version of E61, where he declares himself untouched by either the praise or the dispraise of the fool, and the implication is that he demands of his critic the same self-reflexive consciousness regarding norms of judgment that he develops at length in his own poems of praise and literary judgment. Lack of this consciousness is tantamount to lacking the authority to judge, and Jonson significantly identifies such intellectual callowness with courtly frivolity in E71 and E52, just as he had done in *Cynthia's Revels*.

He attacks the 'Covrt-Parrat' who 'To plucke downe mine ... sets vp new wits still, / Still, 'tis his lucke to praise me 'gainst his will' (E71), who, like 'Covrt-ling,' 'mak'st all wit / Goe high, or low, as thou wilt value it' (E72). Jonson refers to criticism passed on the poetry of a court coterie, such as Arthur Marotti describes as the context of Donne's poems. Jonson's poems, though addressed to individual members of the major and minor peerage, were not coterie poems. One reason is that, unlike those typical within the coteries Marotti describes, whether located at the Inns of Court or at the Court itself, Jonson's relations with courtiers were not predicated on ambition for preferment to bureaucratic offices in the gift of court favourites.[54] *Cynthia's Revels* and *Poetaster*, along with the poems that voice Jonson's criticism of the court, envision the poet as standing outside normal courtly bureaucratic categories, and in this Jonson's preoccupations differ decisively from Donne's.

The more pretentious, because more devious, courtly stance of damning with faint praise Jonson skewers in E52, 'To Censoriovs Covrtling,' whom he advises to 'vtterly / Dispraise my worke, then praise it frostily' (1–2), since this 'Would both thy folly, and thy spite betray' (6). Feigning 'a weake applause, / As if thou wert my friend, but lack'dst a cause' (3–4) 'thy judgement fooles' (5), but fools no one else. In these epigrams Jonson makes the case that these criticisms cannot be taken seriously because they are simply another topic of courtly table talk and banter. Jonson's position here is declared in E85, addressed 'To Sir Henry Goodyere,' which thanks him for an invitation to a hawking session, and refigures hawking as a metaphor for the judicious poet, who 'to knowledge so should toure vpright, / And neuer stoupe, but to strike ignorance: / Which if they misse, they yet should re-aduance / To former height, and there in circle tarrie, / Till they be sure to make the foole their quarrie' (6–10).

It is against this background that we must understand Jonson's responses to the more serious charge of malice brought against his satirical poems, as well as his ripostes to court butterflies. In both cases Jonson tests adverse criticism against the ethical purity of the critic, which is in turn decided on whether or not the critic uses criticism as a defence against his own sense of lack. E54, 'On Chev'ril,' picks up the charge Jonson reacts to in E2, namely that his satirical poems are in reality personal attacks: 'What are thy petulant pleadings, CHEV'RIL, then, / That quit'st the cause so oft, and rayl'st at men?' (3–4). Jonson turns the charge of personal attack back on his attacker, thereby raising a topic examined in chapter 3: satire that replicates the self-denigration directed by the satirized person against himself. E30 and E38 are both addressed 'To Person Gviltie,' those who announce their own guilt by protesting Jonson's satire.

Jonson registers his understanding that satire could easily be mistaken for libel in the early comical satires, where his own reputation was at stake, something he did not forget when he published the *Epigrammes* in the 1616 Folio. For instance, in *Every Man Out of His Humour* he distinguishes the true satirist from his envious perversion, by having Asper take on, and promise to put off, the character of Macilente (Grex 213–17; Wilkes 1:291).[55] Macilente is throughout that play presented as soured expounder of the vera nobilitas argument, whose envy discloses a fascination with the signs of noble status even as he attacks them.[56] Horace in *Poetaster* rejects a verson of Macilente, Crispinus, whose sycophantic envy of Horace's patron Maecenas Horace puts down with a true version of the vera nobilitas argument. At Maecenas' house 'There's no man griev'd, that this is thought more rich, / Or this more learned; each man hath his place, / And, to his merit, his reward of grace: / Which with a mutual love they all embrace' (3.1.228–31; Wilkes 2:157).

In the same play Virgil's distinction between true and false satire prefigures Jonson's most extensive statement on the subject, namely his preface to the Folio version of *Volpone*. Virgil says:

> 'Tis not the wholesome sharp morality,
> Or modest anger of a satiric spirit
> That hurts, or wounds the body of the state;
> But the sinister application
> Of the malicious, ignorant, and base
> Interpreter: who will distort, and strain
> The general scope and purpose of an author
> To his particular, and private spleen.
>
> (5.3.118–25; Wilkes 2:208)[57]

To accuse Jonson's satire of being malicious and envious is not merely to disclose the accuser's own malice and envy. It is also to call into question the norms of ethical judgment that alone justify epideixis, and by extension the norms of true nobility as well. Jonson rebuts his accusers by shrewdly expanding the range of implications such accusations are enmeshed in. In the preface to *Volpone* Jonson begins his defence by arguing 'the impossibility of any man's being the good Poet, without first being a good man' (Wilkes 3:xi). This point drawn from Quintilian (1:9–11) Jonson takes with a literal seriousness that is justified once one grants the humanistic spin he gives to the concept of the 'good man.' As I have shown, ethical probity is for Jonson indistinguishable from the capacity to make precise ethical discriminations, and for him the capacity to read Jonson's poetry – to recognize and respond to the contrasts that underpin their phonological and semantic surface structures – allies the reader with the poet's own capacity to make these discriminations. In that sense, only the 'good' person can read as well as write the kind of poetry Jonson espouses.

If this is the case, then who is it that accuses him of malice and envy – Jonson goes on to argue – unless it be the 'mimic, cheater, bawd, or buffoon, creatures (for their insolencies) worthy to be taxed? Yet, to which of these so pointingly as he might not, either ingenuously have confessed, or wisely dissembled his disease?' (xii) In short, those who attack Jonson's poetry are those who must necessarily misread it: the poetry reads and judges the reader, and the reader unwittingly corroborates that judgment by attacking it. Jonson goes on to insist that he knows 'that nothing can be so innocently writ, or carried, but may be made obnoxious to construction; marry, whilst I bear mine innocence about me, I fear it not.' Those who seek to apply generalized satire to individuals ('Application is now grown a trade with many; and there are that profess to have a key for the decyphering of everything') only succeed in disclosing 'their own virulent malice, under other men's simplest meanings.'

Application to individuals, whether intended by the satirist or interpreted as such by individuals themselves, characterizes malice and envy and distinguishes it from true satire.[58] In E115, 'On the Townes Honest Man,' Jonson anatomizes the motives guiding those who trade in scandal and gossip, which come down to self-denigrating sycophancy. He is 'A subtle thing, that doth affections win / By speaking well o' the company' it's in. / Talkes loud, and baudy, has a gather'd deale / Of newes, and noyse, to strow out a long meale' (7–10). Jonson unerringly traces the 'honest man's' course as he dodges and palters in the shifts of lowness. He 'watches / Whose name's vn-welcome to the present eare, / And him it layes on' (14–15). He attacks anyone not present, but if challenged 'It will deny all; and forsweare it too: / Not that it feares, but will not haue to do / With such a one' (19–21). In the 'honest man's' mouth praise and blame are finally interchangeable and indistinguishable: 'An inginer, in slanders, of all fashions / That seeming prayses, are, yet accusations' (31–2). The punctuation isolating *are* and suspending it in extended duration keeps the last line from saying merely that apparent praise is really accusation, although it says that too. What it says is that praises that appear are so in fact, but are also accusations. Lacking foundation in credible judgment because entirely a function of his play for popularity, his praise and blame derive entirely from observing who's in and out of favour with his present audience.

And this point adverts to the radical centre of Jonson's understanding of epideixis and its constitution of true nobility: that ungrounded praise is itself a form of dispraise, since it implies the personal lacks which it seeks to compensate for. To be accused of malice and envy in his satire was for Jonson to impugn his honesty just as surely as would charges of sycophancy and flattery. This is why he concludes E115 by insisting that '*The townes honest Man's* her erant'st knaue' (34). Flattery may pose as frankness just as honest criticism may appear malicious; and the credible exposition of both required of Jonson the careful and extensive discriminations of true epideixis that recur throughout his poetry.

CHAPTER FIVE

Jonson at Court

1 Jonson and Patronage

The fruit and conclusion of Jonson's vera nobilitas argument is the nobility of England transformed into an aristocracy of humanist virtue in which the hierarchical distinctions separating patron and client are superseded by an equality grounded upon possession of true nobility. Jonson's arguments on this score are heavily indebted to the *De beneficiis* of Seneca. Here the poet found the *officia* (obligations) binding patron and client transformed into an *amicitia* between equals, and a social structure characterized by class hierarchy displaced by personal bonds of benevolence and gratitude. The poems discussed in the first section of this chapter all project Jonson's vision of an aristocracy of true nobility defined in terms drawn from Seneca and Roman patronage practices in general. As such they articulate the intersection between private virtue and public status toward which all Jonson's poems were variously directed.

Jonson's career exhibited remarkable success in moving him into aristocratic inner circles and into friendship with King James himself. Nevertheless, because he never ceased to judge himself by the norms of the vera nobilitas argument that alone justified for him his own ambitions, Jonson strove, with varying success, to remain independent of courtly ambition, malice, and resentment, even as he sought status, recognition, and support there. The subject of section 2 are those poems where Jonson confronts directly the ambiguous position in which his aspirations placed him, and the *ressentiment* which tempted him, as it did so many of his colleagues and contemporaries. In these poems Jonson articulates the conditions under which a hierarchical political and social structure such as that of Stuart England could continue to exist and claim allegiance.

Nowhere do the full implications of Jonson's vera nobilitas arguments come to greater crisis than in the kind of relations he sought to establish with aristocratic friends and patrons. It is certainly true that he was at different times financially dependent on various aristocrats, including Esmé Stuart, the countess of Bedford, the earl of Newcastle, and the earl of Dorset among others, and came to rely on the largesse of both James and Charles, not to mention in his later years the City of London (for a city chronicle that he did not write). It is equally true that Jonson took care never to identify himself as client of a given patron in the same way that Michael Drayton did willingly and John Donne unwillingly, and as Spenser and Chapman (after the death of Prince Henry) sought unsuccessfully to do.[1] Werner Gundersheimer's comments on Erasmus seem equally applicable to Jonson:

> While willing to accept the occasional purse filled with golden coins, or a horse, or a case of some good wine, or even prolonged hospitality, he would not agree to the role of client as a definition of himself. ... His was the privilege, relatively rare in his time, of what might be called the cultural 'superstar.' This is a colloquial way of expressing the fact that an identification with him produced greater benefits for his patrons than he could derive from prolonged attachment to them. (5–6)[2]

Jonson in effect sought to expand and highlight one component of the patron-client relationship at the expense of others. This component was the mutual solidarity and equality between patron and client which historically has existed within the usual hierarchical patronage relation characterized by unequal power and status.[3] The vera nobilitas argument was historically never egalitarian when it came to comparing those possessed of true nobility and those without it. But one entailment of its investment in hierarchy is an equality among the former, an elitism in which the elite are themselves on a par by being so.[4]

Seneca's De beneficiis, which is the main source of one of Jonson's major statements on patronage, 'An Epistle to Sir EDWARD SACVILE, now Earle of Dorset' (U13), expounds at length a patronage model in which such is the case. Along with Pliny's Panegyricus, this longest of Seneca's moral essays is also a major source of Jonson's arguments on vera nobilitas. And because it develops these arguments in the process of discriminating the proper and improper ways of conducting a patronage relationship, its influence on Jonson is important for understanding the model of patronage the poet projected for his own career.

Those poems concerned with patronage focus on the same issues Seneca features in his essay: how to deal with a client who does not repay a patron for gifts either with gratitude or services. Seneca's reply is an extraordinarily discriminated, even casuistical,[5] exposition of social relations in which external bonds of services and commodities given and reciprocated are replaced by bonds of generosity and gratitude. In typical stoic fashion, Seneca displaces an economy of external acts and gestures with internal judgment and intention that determine all value. When financially straitened, Jonson requires all his diplomatic skill to defer repayment of borrowed money, while at the same time translating a debt relation with his patron-creditor onto a higher plane where monetary exchange becomes synecdoche for a patronage model characterized by equality of true nobility. Jonson is of course acutely aware of the cynicism such arguments invite, and he employs the resources of contrastivity to obviate debunking interpretations.

The Epistle to Sackville (U13) is one of Jonson's most complex poems, as well as being a major statement of his humanist perspective on what constitutes the ethically sound and viable society. It stands in this regard alongside 'An Epistle to a Friend, to perswade him to the Warres' (U15), 'A speach according to Horace' (U45), and 'To Penshvrst' (F2). The contrasts that it draws create a vertiginous circle of transformations, all aimed at reinscribing the monetary bonds of society as signifiers in a semiotic code of true nobility. Countering this circulation are its perversions, in which a feckless aristocracy subjugates itself not only to middle-class money-lenders, but to middle-class values as well. On the one hand, an aristocracy of Senecan generosity raises the humanist poet to an equality of friendship and thereby transforms the *noblesse oblige* of patronage into an endorsement of true nobility. In contrast, an aristocracy that insists – like Seneca's addressee in *De benefiiciis* – on quid-pro-quo repayment transforms itself downward into miserly bourgeoisie which battens on the prodigal scions of noble families. Money either can signify true nobility and the friendship among those truly noble, or it becomes a system of meanings wholly economic, governed entirely by a balance-sheet economy of demands and exchanges. Money becomes in this poem, along with clothes, genealogies, and coats of arms, another sign of aristocratic status with the dual capacity for signifying either the possession of true nobility or its absence.

The context of Seneca's arguments was the patronage practices in the late Republic and early Principate, and particularly the ambiguities characterizing the place of *utilitas* and *officium* within clientelistic relations also characterized by *amicitia* and *beneficium*.[6] As Richard Saller shows, the latter two terms summarize relations of equality and generosity respectively (11ff, 17ff), wherein friends exchanged goods and services putatively without the pressure of maintaining parity or exerting pressure for repayment. Utility and duty (*officium*) on the other hand likewise entered into such exchanges to the degree that it was understood on all sides that freely conferred benefits nevertheless implicitly called for reciprocation. Thus, as Saller points out, arises the paradoxical phrase *ingratus amicus*, the ungrateful friend who accepts benefits but does not reciprocate them – the subject of Seneca's treatise.[7] Saller says, regarding this paradox in general and Seneca's attitude toward it in particular:

> The Stoic wise man should not form *amicitiae* for the purpose of *utilitas*, yet *utilitas* inevitably results from *amicitia* – how can that *utilitas* not enter into the wise man's thoughts? The answer: what virtue does not have *utilitas* as a by-product? 'But that is said to be desired for its own sake which, even though it possesses some outside advantages, would still be pleasing even if those advantages were stripped off and removed.' Seneca's argument here would seem to underline the instrumental nature of Roman *amicitia*: even the self-sufficient wise man would be expected to exchange *beneficia*, and so it requires a logical argument to show that this would not be the aim of his friendships. (14–15)

This logical argument is the substance of Seneca's treatise, the conclusion of which is to take *beneficium* wholly out of the domain of *utilitas* in order to preserve it as the mark of *amicitia*. The fundamental distinction that underlies this argument is the stoic distinction between the inner domain of mental intentions and the outer domain governed by fortune:

> A benefit cannot possibly be touched by the hand; its province is the mind. There is a great difference between the matter of a benefit and the benefit itself; and so it is neither gold nor silver nor any of the gifts which are held to be most valuable that constitutes a benefit, but merely the goodwill of him who bestows it. ... The gifts that we take in our hands, that we gaze upon, that in our covetous-

ness we cling to, are perishable; for fortune or injustice may take them from us. But a benefit endures even after that through which it was manifested has been lost; for it is a virtuous act, and no power can undo it. (3:21).

What counts 'is, not what is done or what is given, but the spirit of the action, because a benefit consists, not in what is done or given, but in the intention of the giver or doer' (23). The purpose of these distinctions, as Seneca says at the beginning of the treatise, is to establish *beneficia* as signs and manifestations of relations between equal friends, not between debtor and creditor. Seneca tells his friend Aebutius Liberalis not to become upset if his liberality is not reciprocated, 'for if a benefit is acknowledged, it is returned' (5).

Those who give in the spirit of demands for reciprocation are themselves responsible for creating the ingratitude they criticize:

Can anyone be grateful to another for a benefit that has been haughtily flung to him, or thrust at him in anger, or given out of sheer weariness in order to save further trouble? ... A benefit is acknowledged in the same spirit in which it is bestowed. (5–7).

For Seneca *beneficia* are a set of outward gestures that have no meaning except that given them by the spirit and intentions of those involved. He seeks to keep benefits within the power of thought, judgment, and intention; and to view human relations as a function of inner freedom rather than the outward constraints of status, custom, or law (Seneca's addressee had raised the possibility of passing laws against ingratitude!). As Jonson makes explicit in the Epistle to Sackville and elsewhere, transfer of benefits will signify a purely economic bond of credit and debt, forming a semiotic system unto itself as do other signs of aristocratic status, unless overcoded with a different and countervailing set of meanings.

Jonson reoriented Seneca's arguments to his own uses with little difficulty. Implicit in Seneca's arguments, given their context in de facto Roman patronage practices, was a redefinition of the inequality between patron and client.[8] Seneca's example of the slave who confers a benefit on his master makes explicit a conclusion that is implied throughout: that the bond between patron and client, being free rather than coerced and a function of inner intention rather than outer status, places them on a parity, at least as regards the meeting of their minds. *Amicitia,* summing up the element of mutual solidarity and equality adduced by Eisenstadt and Roniger as a central element of clientelistic relations, gains dominance for Seneca over *officium*, which summarizes relations of duty and obligation between unequals.[9]

In the Epistle to Sackville and other poems concerned with Jonson's financial dependence on aristocratic and royal patronage, the poet transforms the patron-client relation implicit in financial dependence into one between equal friends. The basis of this equality is to be equal possession of true nobility, and the conferring of financial benefits is accordingly transformed from a sign connoting economic dependence into a signifier signifying an internal reciprocity of mutual esteem.[10]

The first two paragraphs and the opening lines of the third (1–42) essentially versify Seneca, whose discriminations are tailor-made for rendering in contrastive fashion. 'Benefits are ow'd with the same mind / As they are done, and such returns they find' (5–6), with the result that 'I, who freely know / this Good from you, as freely will it owe' (13–14). In contrast, 'Gifts stinke from some, / They are so long a comming, and so hard; / Where any Deed is forc't, the Grace is mard' (22–4). Reciprocities are defined contrastively at several levels and reinforce one another. The 'great and good turns' (2) of patronage unite two key terms of Jonson's vera nobilitas lexicon, when benefits are bestowed not only by the will but the desire of the patron, and not in response to petition. Jonson feels 'it done, as soone as meant' (12), Sackville's intention to prevent 'my blush' (11) of petition being the crucial quality defining the benefit. The tactful discriminations of the giver are reciprocated by the receiver, and these are what the latter remembers best: 'The memorie delights him more, from whom / Then what he hath receiv'd' (21–2).

The concluding lines of the first paragraph lead into an equally Senecan meditation in the second. For the bestowal of money to become an affirmation of parity and friendship, this semiotic transvaluation must be discriminated from its capacity to signify unequal status. Benefits offered grudgingly and with expectation of repayment call up a matching ingratitude and unwillingness to repay: 'Can I owe thankes, for Curtesies receiv'd / Against his will that do's 'hem? that hath weav'd / Excuses, or Delayes? or done 'hem scant, / That they have more opprest me, then my want?' (25–8). As for Seneca, intention determines meaning, just as it determines the relations between patron and client. The conferral of benefits becomes paradigmatic for Jonson of a society in which men face each other across a gulf of disproportionate power relations, and the intentions and significance each invests in these relations are reflected back to him in those of the other: 'Gifts and thankes should have one cheerfull face' (39).[11]

Grudging bestowal of benefits reasserts inequality of status, which in turn moves the poet toward familiar unmasking of simulated nobility on the part of the patron who 'doth sound a Trumpet, and doth call / His groomes to witnesse; or else lets it [the gift] fall / In that proud manner' which makes the poet regret receiving it (35–7). This corruption of true nobility turns clients into ungrateful prodigals and patrons into miserly money-lenders: the stuff of city comedy (Gibbons). And it is the potential of aristocratic patronage to transform itself into bourgeois money-grubbing that Jonson develops later on in the poem.[12]

The loftiness of Senecan generalization yields to Jonsonian detail, and the *amicus ingratus* of Roman patronage suddenly sprouts gestures, voice, and a con-man's patter. Having borrowed 'in corners' (44) and desirous of running 'from Conscience of it, if they could' (46), such types attempt to put the poet 'off the sent':

> Now dam'mee, Sir, if you shall not command
> My Sword ('tis but a poore Sword, understand)
> As farre as any poore Sword i' the Land.
> Then turning unto him is next at hand,
> Dam's whom he damn'd to, as the veriest Gull,
> Ha's Feathers, and will serve a man to pull.   (53–8)

By the fifth paragraph (59ff) Jonson is talking about money-lenders who refuse loans to any but new-made knights, who in turn bilk them (59–74). Jonson opens the paragraph by reiterating reciprocity as a major structure in society, but here the reciprocity between money-lenders and prodigals degenerates into mutual preying on each other: 'Are they not worthy to be answer'd so, / That to such Natures let their full hands flow, / And seek not wants to succor ...?' The 'Misterie' (profession: 97) of the town gallant as he bilks the 'Clownes' (89) who lend 'with a trembling zeale, / And superstition I dare scarce reveale' (85–6) becomes a religion, as Jonson develops it, replete with 'reverence' (98), 'sacrifice of drinke' (100), and 'certaine swearing rites' (102).

Young prodigal aristocrats borrow money to support noble pretensions, an act which in turn unmasks their pretensions and discloses their complicity with the money-lenders. By enabling false aristocrats to deck themselves in the luxuriant signs of noble status, money-lenders also become the flatterers Jonson inveighs against elsewhere. In other words, as Jonson develops the options, the aristocrat either lends money in the spirit of true nobility, or he borrows it in the spirit of false nobility.

Lines 109ff develop by contrast the kinds of self-knowledge whose 'ends are honestie, and publike good' (111). A dozen lines on, Jonson's knowledge of his own faults, and by extension of his own mind, leads to the conclusion: 'he must feel and know, that will advance. / Men have beene great, but never good by chance, / Or on the sudden' (123–5). Jonson questions whether men can go to bed fools, awaken wise, and 'Were the rack offer'd them [not know] how they came so' (130). Then follows a summary statement of the humanist ideal of laborious accomplishment: ' 'Tis by degrees that men arrive at glad / Profit in ought; each day some little adde, / In time 'twill be a heape; This is not true / Alone in money, but in manners too' (131–4). Accomplishment is 'the last Key-stone / That makes the Arch' (136–7):

> Then stands it a trimphall marke! then Men
> Observe the strength, the height, the why, and when,
> It was erected; and still walking under
> Meet some new matter to looke up and wonder!
> Such Notes are vertuous men! they live as fast
> As they are high; are rooted, and will last. (139–44)

These men 'need no stilts, nor rise upon their toes, / As if they would belie their stature; those / Are Dwarfes of Honours' (145–7). Having traced the reduction of money as signifier of nobility to one of its absence, Jonson recirculates it as a simile for the gradual process by which greatness is accumulated and built. The truly noble become their own monuments, triumphal arches that require the keystone of accomplishment to mark the completion of an edifice built on greatness. Rising as high as they are rooted, they contrast favourably with other high growths: cane which tapers off to nothing at the top.

Jonson says in conclusion that Sackville knows these things already: 'You that see / Their difference, cannot choose which you will be. / You know (without my flatt'ring you) too much / For me to be your Indice' (153–6). In other words, Sackville, cognizant of these Jonsonian discriminations, does not even need to make a choice, and also does not need Jonson's poem to praise him. The perfection of true nobility is exemplified in Sackville's 'curtesie' (159), by which 'you ... reckon nothing, me owe all' (164). And with this conclusion Jonson returns to

Seneca: 'the one should say, "I have received," the other, "I still owe"'
(3:493).

In several other poems Jonson offers his addressees portions of the
argument he develops fully in the Epistle to Sackville. In a poem dating
probably from about 1602, when Jonson went to live with Esmé Stuart,
Jonson addresses to him a epigram of gratitude (E127). Here gratitude
is (and for Jonson, must be) the only repayment: the poet's gratitude
and that of posterity. The dialectics of patronage are absent here, since
Jonson feels no need to insulate himself from charges, real or imagined,
of clientage. A similar innocence invests another epigram on the same
subject, E84, 'To Lvcy Covntesse of Bedford,' where Jonson contrasts
her unasked generosity with the refusal of a lord of whom the poet 'ask'd
... a buck, and he denyed me; / And, ere I could aske you, I was preuented'
(2–4). Such generosity provokes a poem in repayment ('how euery *Muse*
should know it' [7]), and a request that the countess turn her grant into
a gift, a legal bequest 'without any valuable conveyance' (William Hunter
ed *Complete Poetry* 35).

In a later poem, included like the Sackville epistle in *The Vnder-wood*,
Jonson feels the pinch both of financial constraint and of embarrassment
when he must fail to repay at the agreed-upon date. Unlike the two
epigrams, 'Epistle to a Friend' (U17) depends heavily on contrastive
emphases to make discriminations that will ease the poet's plight: 'They
are not, Sir, worst Owers, that doe pay / Debts when they can: good
men may breake their day, / And yet the noble Nature never grudge; /
'Tis then a crime, when the Usurer is Judge, / And he is not in friendship'
(1–5). The situation Jonson describes is simple economic necessity: owed
money which he has not collected, the poet cannot pay his debts in
turn. In a post-Renaissance culture of middle-class mores, such an explanation would be sufficient to cover a failure to pay, even if it does
not satisfy one's creditors. But Jonson wants more than that: he wants
to lecture his creditor, who is his friend, on the proper Senecan attitude
to take toward this failure: 'If you be / Now so much friend, as you
would trust in me, / Venter a longer time, and willingly: / All is not
barren land, doth fallow lie' (13ff). Jonson wants his friend to join him
in exploring the meanings debt can take on, which comes down to
treating money as a signifier in a set of overcodings within which the
bond of friendship supersedes the 'Band' of the cash nexus.

Forestalling criticism by preemptive strike is a move central for Jonson's dealing tactfully with the inequality thrust upon him by the
hierarchical society in which he lived. E101, 'Inviting a Friend to Svpper,'

reveals in detail Jonson's habit of thinking out beforehand the scenarios of his encounters with social superiors, and it is notable for making that planning the substance of his diplomatic address. In the poem Jonson and his 'poore house' (1) invite to dinner a person of honour, in the contemporary phrase, whose 'worth will dignifie our feast' (4) and 'whose grace may make that seeme / Something, which, else, could hope for no esteeme' (5–6). Jonson is unusually diffident and scrupulous in setting out point-by-point the fine disparities between degrees of worth. He hastens to forestall his guest's possible suspicion that the poet has forgotten the disproportion of dignity between them. But this humility only serves to preface disarmingly the true rhetorical purpose of the poem, which is to displace the inequality of social status with the parity founded on equal devotion to, and capacity for, true festivity (McCanles 'Festival'). Consequently, the limitations of the feast will be compensated by the 'worth' of the guest, which 'will dignifie our feast.'

The poem queries the origins of true worth, grace, and dignity, and goes about answering this question in typically Jonsonian fashion: by evacuating material signs of any meaning and value save those conferred by human intention: 'It is the faire acceptance, Sir, creates / The entertaynment perfect: not the cates' (7–8).[13] Jonson's admission that his meal lacks the full measure of luxury frees his guest to react with equal candour, to grace the meal in recognition that it is his worth that makes the feast valuable. This worth is, however, deftly conferred by the poet himself rather than by his guest's social rank, through the very impoverishment of the signs of luxury his feast exhibits. Jonson's refusal to pretend to more sumptuousness than he can afford is likewise to refuse complicity in the vanity (Chateaubriand's term) of social rank, as it is finally a tactful refusal to assign his noble guest the correlative role of the aristocrat who demands sumptuous entertainment to match and reflect back to himself his sense of worth. The supper's sparseness discloses the plenitude both host and guest bring to it, the lack of which the fullest meal could never supply.

However, lest the material substructure of the feast disappear altogether, Jonson recites the menu, freely admitting that he exaggerates: 'Ile tell you of more, and lye, so you will come: / Of partrich, pheasant, wood-cock, of which some / May yet be there' (17–19). The poet is candid about his candour, in distinguishing between what can be hoped and what not. Food is to be the nourishment of mind, having been raised to high value by the willingness of the guest to value it; thus the 'rich *Canary*-wine' (29) inspires poetry. And while Roman authors are read during the meal, one author who will not be read is Jonson himself: the only paper produced by the poet will be that on which the pastry rests (20–6).

Dinner parties that bring together social unequals seem to have been for Jonson paradigmatic of situations that reveal the equivocal space between social codes of noble status and the internal reality of true nobility. The chasm between the two – the fundamental complaint of the vera nobilitas argument – could generate either sycophancy or subversion, options that, extended from the personal to the historical sphere, yield reactionary conservatism and revolution respectively. 'To Penshvrst' (F2) – where Jonson is the guest rather than host – is similar to 'Inviting a Friend to Supper' in merging potentially antagonistic social strata, attitudes, and values, and in carefully eyeing the social frictions it seeks to exclude.[14]

In the context of this study the best place to begin is with the figure of the poet, 'whose bitter memories of unrecognized function and insulted dignity' make him, in Anthony Mortimer's memorable phrase, 'something of a spectre at the feast' (74). Jonson recalls fondly that at Penshurst he eats 'of thy lords own meate' (62), and he need not 'sit (as some, this day, / At great mens tables) and yet dine away' (65–6). The sources may be Juvenal and Martial (Donaldson *Ben Jonson* 672), but the occasion was provided by Robert Cecil, earl of Salisbury. That at least is the suggestion of Jonson's confidence conferred on Drummond:

Being at the end of my lord Salisbury's table with Inigo Jones, and demanded by my lord why he was not glad, said he 'You promised I should dine with you, but I do not,' for he had none of his meat; he esteemed only that his meat which was of his own dish.

(Parfitt ed *Ben Jonson* 469)

Several things are suggestive here, not the least of which was Salisbury's remarkable readiness to reenact a scene from classical satire. Whether fictional or not, a second element in the scene is Inigo Jones, with whom Jonson finds himself effectively equated as the object of his host's neglect. Jonson knows very well why they are being treated this way, for Juvenal tells him.

What Juvenal tells Jonson is that such invitations, delivered putatively in the spirit of fellowship, represent a false equality aimed at signifying a *de facto* superiority. Juvenal's friend may think himself 'a free man, a tycoon's / guest; he thinks you – / Not bad guesswork – a slave to his / kitchen's odor' (166ff). Such dinner invitations are issued 'to compel / you to pour out tears / Of rage and grind your squeaking / teeth too long' (Satire 5; Creekmore trans 161ff). Consequently, an appropriate context in which to examine 'To Penshvrst' is a group of four epigrams, three addressed to Robert Cecil and the fourth apparently a retraction, in which Jonson confronts and attempts to deal with four different facets of his predominantly negative reaction to Cecil's rise to aristocratic status.

Born in the minor gentry (Cecil 58ff), Robert Cecil was of course the paradigm of great place achieved by talent (Simon 295). In E63, 'To Robert Earle of Salisbvrie,' Jonson praises Cecil for 'what thy vertue on the times hath won, / And not thy fortune'; for seeking 'reward of thy each act, / Not from the publike voyce, but priuate fact'; for confronting envy with 'constant suffring of thy equall mind' (2–3, 5–6, 8). The poet finds it impossible not to praise him for his 'true worth' (12). In short, Cecil discloses the self-knowledge and consequent capacity to discriminate the prescripts of true nobility which Jonson praises throughout his poetry.

Significant is the tonal alteration of Jonson's address in the next poem, E64, 'To the Same. Vpon the accession of the Treasurer-ship to him.' Where Jonson's identification with the new man of merit rewarded is patent in E63, here Jonson also feels the sudden distance between them. The negative disclaimers disclose an unusual number of slurs Jonson feels himself vulnerable to, and he has to struggle somewhat to deny such subservience or resentment as might signify belligerence. Jonson insists, for instance, that he does not 'bring ... these early fruits / Of loue' because he has 'new hopes, or sutes, / With thy new place' (1–3). Exhibiting neither 'a fit / Of flatterie to thy titles. Nor of wit' (7–8), Jonson comes to celebrate a time 'Where good mens vertues them to honors bring' (11). Clearly, if Jonson sought the humanist goal of virtue rewarded all deserving new men, he likewise felt strong resentment if new men, having been rewarded, revealed qualities that might call that deserving into question. Such was the case with Inigo Jones during Jonson's declining years, and it would appear likewise to be the case with Robert Cecil.

Revealing in this connection is an epigram, also addressed to Cecil, that appears earlier in the *Epigrammes*: E43, 'To Robert Earle of Salisbvrie,' which may have been written when Cecil was created earl in 1605. Here the acts of choice are almost embarrassingly apparent, as Jonson declares what he will and will not say, what his relation to Cecil is not and is. Jonson feels compelled to praise him, since not praising him would appear to express hostility, while having the additional negative result of revealing the poet's sense of inferiority. Jonson makes overt his sense of being redundant and superfluous when confronted with a man who has truly risen to political heights on talent and energy alone, and he admits candidly his envy of Cecil: 'What need hast thou of me? or of my *Muse*? / Whose actions so themselues doe celebrate' (1–2). Being beyond the need for praise is usually for Jonson a sign of self-sufficient possession of true nobility. But here it conveys the poet's sense of his own redundancy when left behind by true nobility rewarded by promotion. If then the poet is 'covetous' (6) of Cecil, he makes a good show of conquering a sense of sour grapes, and declares his refusal of flattery. It is an honest poem, and a brave one, displaying at once Jonson's pique and his almost successful struggle to overcome it.

The final poem in the later sequence (E65), 'To My Mvse,' presuming it constitutes a retraction of the previous two epigrams, illuminates Jonson's sensitivity to the ricochet effect of suits for favour addressed to nobles unworthy of their titles. For Jonson perhaps the most galling consequence of misplaced praise is its retroactive transformation into flattery. He discovers that he has committed 'most fierce idolatrie / To a great image' of 'a worthlesse lord' (2–4). He comforts himself at the end by remembering that 'who e're is rais'd, / For worth he has not, He is tax'd, not prais'd' (15–16), but it is not Cecil's undeserved titles that bother Jonson so much as his complicity in debasing his own commitment to titles reflecting only true nobility. He has become despite himself a 'parasite' (14), and the moment of this discovery may well have been that dinner at which the poet found that 'the same beere, and bread, and selfe-same wine, / That is his Lordships' was not 'also mine' ('To Penshvrst' 63–4).

In the opening lines of 'To Penshvrst' Jonson rejects still another set of signs of noble status eviscerated from within by lack of true nobility: 'Thou art not, PENSHVRST, built to enuious show, / Of touch, or marble; nor canst boast a row / Of polished pillars, or a roofe of gold' (1–3). In a sense, the whole poem is an attempted exorcism of *ressentiment*. 'To Penshurst' coaches the Sidney family in the discourse of *noblesse oblige* which alone can maintain 'reverence' uncontaminated by the potential synonymic slide into 'grudge' (6). Part of Jonson's point is that the benign form of aristocratic hierarchy can be maintained only as long as its various perversions are recollected and deliberately rejected.[15]

The dangers of forgetfulness are the subject of Jonson's daring passage on the willingness of the estate's game to be killed to serve the house's table. Alastair Fowler reminds us that fish dying to be caught appear in Juvenal's Fourth Satire 'in a context of "gross flattery". May not Jonson intend that playful panegyric tone which depends on openly hyperbolic excess of flattery?' (274). This passage does not simply replicate the 'great chain of being' in which those lower in the chain gladly serve those above them (Cubeta 'A Jonsonian Ideal'), although that element is present as well.[16] If this is a joke that invites discounting, it cuts close to a serious reality, namely the whole hierarchical structure of society that Penshurst stands for.

Part of the message is clear: the Sidney family can no more expect their tenants to exist solely for their own benefit than they can expect fish and eels to leap into their nets for the sole purpose of being served up on their tables. The competition between the pikes who 'Officiously, at first, themselues betray' (36) and the eels 'that emulate them' (37) tropes courtly competitions for status. To 'betray' oneself to being 'caught' by a patron involves perhaps too many betrayals to discriminate here. Jonson instructs the noble reader capable of understanding him that the services fish, tenants, and servants rush to perform disclose and mask ambiguities of attitude, and finally of ideology, which the aristocracy has the sole responsibility to shape and control; for if they fail, the power to do so will be taken out of their hands.[17]

Jonson is in this poem, at any rate, only as serious as he has to be. It is a festive poem about festival, and in this respect makes its own contribution to the politics of mirth Leah Marcus predicates of James' attempted rustification of the aristocracy.[18] With the entrance of 'the farmer, and the clowne' (48) reciprocity signified by, but not reducible to, class distinction rules almost unchallenged. This temporary collapsing of hierarchy affirms it by contrast, by being precisely an exception to the normal routine.[19] As Jonson asserts in those plays where the nature of festival is at issue, the capacities for true festival and true rationality necessarily go together, the comedy of the first building on the second (McCanles 'Festival'). For a short time hierarchy is not so much a political structure inverted, as a mystery exfoliated and a semiotic revealed, whose meanings are always 'inner' and always in need of being readjusted to their signifiers. When the house's servants wait on Jonson 'As if thou [Penshurst], then, wert mine, or I raigned here' (74), *beneficia* ceases to signify only *officia* and represents *amicitia* as well. The signs of status bound up with the first term can be allowed to float freely, taking up residence with a humanist poet who, for the moment, takes up residence in a noble house.

The poem which follows 'To Penshvrst' in *The Forrest*, 'To Sir Robert Wroth' (F3), complements 'To Penshvrst' in several ways. First, hierarchy is maintained in the midst of, and because of, occasional transgressions of it: 'The rout of rurall folke come thronging in' and they can 'Sit mixt with losse of state, or reuerence' because the Wroths' freedom from ambition and snobbery 'doth with degree dispense' (53–8). This freedom leads to the second point this poem shares with 'To Penshurst': the Wroths' capacity to discriminate true nobility from its various perversions. If nobility were only a matter of shows and social snobbery, then those who seek to aggrandize themselves would be drawn to such. But Wroth is not tempted by 'The richer hangings, or crowne-plate' (8), nor does he throng to masques 'To view the iewells, stuffs, the paines, the wit / There wasted, some not paid for yet!' (11–12).

Rustification obviously meant something different under James than it did under Elizabeth, who banished obstreperous courtiers like Sidney and Harington to the country for displeasing her. A brief comparison with another version of the same genre, Jonson's translation of Horace's epode *beatus ille* (U85), indicates how Jonson redirects the virtues he praises in Wroth. The urban world that Alphius dreams (but only dreams) of escaping is defined at the beginning: 'Happie is he, that from all Businesse cleere, / As the old race of Mankind were, / With his owne Oxen tills his Sires left lands, / And not in the Usurers bands' (1–4). These lines collectively identify the active life with urban living and later with subjection to the storms of nature. 'Proud bords' and 'great lords' are as far as Horace goes in gesturing toward what concerns Jonson, namely the scramble for wealth and honourable place. What Alphius might be tempted to escape is little more than the constant pressure of getting his money in and lending it out again. In contrast, Wroth understands – or Jonson understands for him – that self-possession has nothing to do with geography. Unlike Alphius, whose vivid but momentary yearnings define at the same time acquiescence in their frustration, Jonson demonstrates for Wroth that it is the individual's reading of the semiotics of his own desire that determines his relative freedom from or enslavement to the powers of the court or the city.

This withdrawal gets almost as close to a stoic rejection of the active life as Jonson ever seriously propounds. This qualification is necessary because the poem that follows it in *The Forrest* is one of Jonson's central

stoic statements. Taken out of context of the whole of the poet's production, or – which is the same thing – in the context of a few other
poems,[20] 'To the World: A farewell for a Gentle-woman, vertuous and
noble' (F4) looks a likely candidate for summarizing the Jonsonian ethic.
The stoic withdrawal it praises, however, never was Jonson's way, and
we must be careful to note the limits of Jonson's identification with the
'Gentle-woman' for whom he speaks. One must be careful, in other
words, not to reverse his ventriloquizing for her, and misread her as
ventriloquizing for the poet.

Much of the poem is a process of renaming along a synonymical chain
typical of Jonson's epigrams, whereby true names for the snares of the
world are discriminated from the false. Forms are studied arts, subtlety
is constriction, courtesy inconstancy and gifts baits (9–12). The world is
a place 'Where euery freedome is betray'd, / And euery goodnesse tax'd,
or grieu'd' (51–2). In exemplary stoic fashion the speaker concludes 'But
I will beare these, with that scorne, / As shall not need thy false reliefe'
and 'make my strengths, such as they are, / Here in my bosome, and
at home' (63–8).

This gentle lady has been reading her Seneca, particularly the letters
to Lucilius. She has learned that freedom and slavery are a matter of
mental attitude (letter 28), that one must will the necessary (letter 54),
that one should withdraw within oneself (letter 56). Jonson was tempted
to retire from the stage, and even succumbed during the ten years separating Bartholomew Fair and The Staple of News (1616–26), as recorded
in 'An Ode. To himselfe' (U23). However, the court was something else
entirely, and we find him here versifying an attitude toward courtly
decadence that he could sympathize with, but with which finally he
could not identify. The lady has the right Jonsonian complaints, but
her attitude toward them is different. Certainly her innocence is not
Jonson's ('My tender, first, and simple yeeres / Thou did'st abuse, and
then betray' [41–2]). She is a victim, passive before the virulent fraud
and malevolence of the court, which she sees not as a perversion of
values but as its essence, and for which she envisions one remedy only:
withdrawal and flight.

As a satirist the lady lacks Jonson's bold intellectual energy, for in
poems and plays he penetrates farther than she into the twists of mind
and body courtly sycophancy demands.[21] But in lacking so much, she
also fails of Jonson's vision of what true nobility is and can be. I have
already suggested in chapter 2 the limits of Jonson's debt to Senecan
stoicism: Jonson's refusal to sunder along with Seneca inner virtue and

outer status. And this refusal illuminates the important modifications Jonson works on the ethic espoused in *De beneficiis*. Seneca sublimates the potential adversary relation between patrons and clients in an *amicitia* founded on internal intentions and beyond coercion by custom or law. Jonson appropriates this internalization, but locates it as the signified in a semiotic within which noble status is the necessary outer signifier. In short, neither Seneca's nor the gentle lady's stoicism in this regard in Jonson's.[22] If it may be said that Jonson erred it was rather in clinging to his court connections past the point where he was welcome and could respect his own honesty in doing so.

2 Jonson and the Arts of Courtship

The person to whom Jonson addressed by far the greatest number of his works was of course the king. Most of the masques were written with James in mind as the principal auditor. Jonson's friendship with the king was cemented by common interests: both were garrulous, loved learned discussion and capping literary tags among their cups, both wrote prodigiously (and were enormously touchy on the subject), and as the masques demonstrate, Jonson knew exactly the vein of earthy, grotesque humour that most tickled the king.[23] It was a match-up of sympathetic temperaments that required no labour to overcome the vast gulf of status that separated the two, a factor to be remembered in connection with the complex rhetoric of Jonson's addresses to the king. As we move chronologically from the early entertainments through the masques up to James' death in 1625, it becomes apparent that the closer Jonson's intimacy with the king, the more intricate the rhetorical strategies required for balancing familiarity of friendship with the diffidences to be accorded majesty. Clearly James could be played by those he loved, as his relations with the royal favourites Carr and Villiers demonstrate past the point of embarrassment. Jonson was infinitely more intelligent than either, and this is exhibited in the canny diplomacy with which he engineered a *rapprochement* between intimacy and royal status.

We must therefore distinguish two Jonsonian addresses to the king. The first is ceremonial, allegorical, distanced, highlighting the king's office and the responsibilities and majesty attending that office. The second, typified at its most extreme in an extemporary grace pronounced at meal before the king (M47), distils that intimacy between men of equal and sympathetic intellectual cultivation which is the essence of Jonson's vision of an aristocracy of true nobility:

Our King and Queen the Lord-God blesse,
The Paltzgrave, and the Lady Besse,
And God blesse every living thing,
That lives, and breath's, and loves the King.
God blesse the Councell of Estate,
And Buckingham the fortunate.
God blesse them all, and keepe them safe:
And God blesse me, and God blesse Raph.

Aubrey, whose account of Jonson is generally not to be trusted, comments on this occasion:

The King was mighty enquisitive to know who this Raph was. Ben told him 'twas the Drawer at the Swanne Taverne by Charing-crosse, who drew him good Canarie. For this Drollery his Majestie gave him an hundred poundes. (179)

The hundred pounds is fiction, though in 1616 Jonson was granted a lifelong pension of one hundred marks in recognition of his literary services to the court (Miles 166). The rest of the story, the essentials at any rate, can be deduced without Aubrey's help. Raph is a lower-class name, and Jonson in calling down blessings on the hierarchy of England does not neglect a representative of his own origins.

Hitting the right note of seriousness in discussing this revealing piece of nonce verse requires a tact matching Jonson's own. For tact is what this poem reveals, and concerns. The grace both acknowledges hierarchy and short-circuits it. At dinner not only with King James and Queen Anne, but their daughter Elizabeth and her husband Frederick v, elector of the Palatine, as well as the king's favourite the duke of Buckingham, Jonson preempts recognition of his own lower status by acknowledging it himself. But it is a preemption which also declares, as Jonathan Goldberg says, that 'Jonson participates in the court as he audaciously proclaims himself outside and equal' (222). To meet the members of the king's court as equals is to highlight at once his humble origins – signified by his acquaintance with tapsters – and his capacity to temper with knowledge of his own achievements the diffidence consequent on these origins. The problem here, as always, was to strike the right note between servility and independence, between participating in the court and being 'outside and equal.'

One of Jonson's early addresses to the king is 'A Panegyre on the

Happie Entrance of Iames Ovr Soveraigne, to His first high Session of
Parliament in this his Kingdome, the 19. of March. 1603,' which was
published in quarto in 1604 (HS 7:133–17). The title is indebted to Pliny
the Younger's oration to Trajan, but further influence is marked less
by citation of specific ideas (as in Jonson's use of Seneca's *De beneficiis*)
than in the overall strategy of the poem itself. Jonson's voice is displaced
by that of others, who speak to, through, and for the king in discriminating true kingship from its perversions. As in Pliny's case, Jonson
indicates that the precepts of the former must be internalized by the
king himself, must be spoken by him as if originating in him, even if
that origin is elsewhere: the collective voice of the Roman republic and
of Rome under the earlier *principes* in Pliny, the voice of the people,
of the goddess Themis, and finally of the king himself in Jonson's poem:

> She blest the people, that in shoales did swim
> To heare her speech; which still began in him
> And ceas'd in them. (133–5)

Jonson makes overt what is only implicit in Pliny's oration, namely
that he is writing a dramatic scenario – in effect, a masque in narrative
form – where the royal addressee plays a part along with the people,
and Jonson is giving both their lines. The diverse designations of who
spoke whose discourse to whom distances the texts of both panegyrics
from their respective authors, enabling more readily their free circulation among several speakers. This circulation is intended to draw together all speakers and audiences, thereby hopefully voiding potential
opposition. Pliny exhorts Trajan to repeat his own speech, by pretending
to repeat after the fact what Trajan has already said; and what he has
said he has spoken with the voice of the rejuvenated Roman republic.
Similarly, the above lines chart the circulation of the text of Jonson's
poem, the goal of which is that 'No age, nor sex, so weake, or strongly
dull, / That did not beare a part in this consent / Of hearts, and voices'
(58–60). As in Milton's 'At a Solemn Music,' where Voice and Verse are
exhorted

> to our high-rais'd fantasy present
> That undisturbed Song of pure concent,
> Aye sung before the sapphire-color'd throne
> To him that sit thereon,
> With Saintly shout and solemn Jubilee ... (5–9)

'consent' means also 'concent,' a harmony of voices. Jonson exhorts the perfect harmony of consent by narrating after the fact a harmony of voices achieved by each speaking what the others speak.[24]

The cons(c)ent binding king and people is doubled in the identification of people and nobility 'as doth the wike and wax, / That friendly tempered, one pure taper makes' (71–2). Following the lengthy advice of Themis the king speaks – or the poet speaks for him, noting 'That kings, by their example, more doe sway / Then by their power; and men doe more obay / When they are led, then when they are compell'd' (125–7). In putting his own exhortations first into the mouth of the mythical Themis, and then lecturing the king in wholesome recognitions that he 'knew already,' Jonson enacts the standard humanist role of adviser to princes. This advice urges the king to an act of verbal imitation, where the poet who speaks puts himself forth not as the origin of the text imitated, but only its medium and transmitter. The poet speaks for the people in urging the king to speak what the people speak: a concent of voices, Jonson argues, necessary for the consent that make monarchal rule possible.[25]

Two epigrams addressed to James have already been discussed: E4 and E36 in chapter 4. These raise issues of praise, and one (E4) relates Jonson to James as poet to poet. The two other epigrams addressed to the king, however, take up issues of power and equity central to the 'Panegyre' and call upon similarly diplomatic strategies.

The first of these, E35, 'To King Iames,' echoes both words and sentiments in a sonnet that James himself wrote as preface to *Basilikon Doron* (Brady 389ff). This poem repeats a significant point of the 'Panegyre': if the subject fears the king and his laws, it is not tyranny that imposes fear, but the laws which crimes have violated. This perspective instructs the king to let tyranny exist only in the eye of the (guilty) beholder. Because James is 'A Prince, that rules by'example, more than sway / Whose manners draw, more than thy powers constraine' (2–3), his subjects 'haue now no cause / Left vs of feare, but first our crimes, then lawes' (5–6).

The fears that subjects may have of kings Jonson seeks to transform into the fears that subjects may have for the king's safety in E51, 'To King Iames. Vpon the happy false rumour of his death, the two and twentieth day of March, 1607.' The discriminations here are sufficiently laboured as to call attention to the poet's evident concern lest James misinterpret them. The fact that 'terror' at the rumour turned out to be 'but *panick*' (3) leads Jonson to distinguish between the people's fears and the true invulnerability of king, guarded by the love that creates this fear. If this fear is 'farre beneath least pause of such a king' (4), still the subjects must ponder the king's escape from rumour 'No less than if from perill' (7). As a consequence they 'beg thy care vnto thy after-state' (8), but even in this the people's concern is due 'not [to] thy dangers, but our feares.' In other words, the people's fears reflected not the king's vulnerability but their own.

But what is the countertext to this text, which Jonson feels the evident need to obviate? The occasion is peculiar: not the king's danger (there was none), but the fear in the populace that he was in danger, a panic that in Freudian fashion recoiled from a threat to the monarch which the populace had itself created. And that is of course the point. Jonson here is, as always, indefatigable in preemptive scenario-writing, seeking out in order to forestall possible misinterpretations of even the apparently most innocent gestures.

After the accession of Charles in 1625, Jonson's stock at court fell drastically and notoriously. The ascendancy of Inigo Jones' influence on the art-conscious king (Parry 158–9 and passim), the lack in James' son of the father's tastes in learning and scurrility, and the passing in the court of the taste for Jonson's dramatic bents, all worked to make the poet an outsider. His incapacity to leave off attacking Inigo Jones finally earned him the censure of the court itself (Miles 250–1). Nevertheless, Jonson continued to turn out verse for state occasions as befitted the possessor of the laureateship, for which nevertheless he was but irregularly paid.

The Vnder-wood includes seventeen poems addressed to King Charles, members of his family, and two of his favourites, the Westons, father and son, which collectively in some respects represent the most embarrassing portion of Jonson's poetic output.[26] Significantly, among this group are to be found four poems dealing with Jonson's need for money (U62, U68, U71, U76), in which he unabashedly petitions for support. His dependence on the court for financial help only emphasizes by contrast how far he has fallen out of its favour. Added to this necessarily demeaning situation are Jonson's attempts to argue the king's increasingly untenable position vis-à-vis the growing disaffection in parliament and among the religious dissenters. Jonson's heart is in these poems only intermittently, something evident in their occasional prosodic limpness— betokening no invitation of critical response from the reader. We can, if anything, applaud the doggedness of his spirit, and even his wit and sense of humour, when we remember that after 1628 they were all written in the bed from which the poet, partially paralysed by a stroke, would remove only at death.

It is unnecessary and fruitless to examine these poems in detail, since their significance in the context of Jonson's total poetic output lies less in their intrinsic value, such as it is, than in the light which they throw on the poet's changing attitudes toward the court and his relations with it.

The poems appealing for money seem to mark success in the asking, if also the humiliation as well. Jonson keeps his wits about him in his straitened condition, sending doggerel in 1630 (U76) to ask Charles to increase his father's grant from one hundred marks to one hundred pounds. This request was successful (U62 registers the poet's thanks), and the grant was augmented by a further one of wine from the king's cellar, which nevertheless required a further squib of wit to pry loose from the Royal Household (U68) (Miles 245–6). The most affecting of the lot is the poem addressed 'To the Right Honourable the Lord high Treasurer of England. An Epistle Mendicant' (U71). Richard Weston, the first earl of Portland, became treasurer in 1628. He made few friends in the kingdom, but one of them was Ben Jonson, whom he apparently aided. U71 is notable for the proverbial grace under pressure, and it is a late revelation of the wit and diplomatic cunning that brought the poet to courtly favour in earlier days. Jonson compares his bed-rid state to that of a state under siege, and he begs for the 'succours, and supplies / Of *Princes* aides' (2–3). Jonson warms to the comparison, and, as in the love poems I shall examine later in this section, he labours successfully to turn liabilities into the motives of wit:

> *Disease*, the Enemie, and his Ingineeres,
> *Want*, with the rest of his conceal'd compeeres,
> Have cast a trench about mee, now, five yeares;
>
> And made those strong approaches, by *False braies*,
> *Reduicts*, *Halfe-moones*, *Horne-workes*, and such close wayes,
> The *Muse* not peepes out, one of hundred dayes;
>
> But lyes block'd up, and straightned, narrow'd in,
> Fix'd to the bed, and boords, unlike to win
> Health, or scarce breath, as she had never bin ...   (4–12)

What the king got for his money was poetry less epideictic than celebratory, and half-heartedly factious for royal claims of *divina juris* against the complaints of an unruly people. 'An Epigram. To our great and good K. CHARLES On his Anniversay Day' (U64) refers overtly to the king's problems with the 1629 parliament, whose dissolution marked the beginning of the 'eleven years' tyranny.' Jonson almost masters the Stuart note of querulous ideologizing; the king's subject would be 'happy' (1) if he only knew 'his owne good in you' (2); weighing 'the blessings of this day' he would 'For safetie of such Majestie, cry out' (4, 6); the king merely asks the people to live by the laws with which he binds himself (9–10); instead the people 'murmure' (14), are 'barren growne of love' (15), all of which climaxes with a brief echo of the old satire now dismayingly put to the service of royalist posturing:

> O Times! O Manners! Surfet bred of ease,
> The truly Epidemicall disease!
> 'T is not alone the Merchant, but the Clowne,
> Is Banke-rupt turn'd! the Cassock, Cloake, and Gowne,
> Are lost upon accompt! And none will know
> How much to heaven for thee, great CHARLES, they owe! (17–22)

The Ciceronian expletives were last heard in the fourth act of *Catiline*, in support of the learned new man's campaign against the blind malice of headstrong aristocracy. They have now, as it were, switched sides. In the 'Epigram Anniversarie' addressed 'To the King. On his Birthday' (U72) of 1632, Jonson catalogues at length the cannon salutes, drums, fireworks, and bells pealing out across the country, as if to hide the people's disaffection, something alluded to incongruously among all the joyous noise.

Jonson's commitment to Charles' quarrel with the people of England returns him to earlier concerns with the *vera nobilitas* argument, but the differences do not display him in a favourable light. These occur in the poems addressed to the Westons, where the old matter of merit and its vicissitudes is fought over again, but discloses a significant shift from Jonson's argument in 'To Penshvrst' (F2) and 'To Sir Robert Wroth' (F3). U73, U75, and U77 all confront the elder Weston's unpopularity by attempting to rewrite it as envy's hatred of true nobility. Jonson's linking Weston's rise to the people's criticism of the king brings these poems into the larger context of Jonson's apologia for the Stuart monarchy.[27]

'On the Right Honourable, and vertuous Lord Weston, L. high Treasurer of England, Vpon the Day, Hee was made Earle of Portland, To the Envious' (U73) attacks 'thou seed of envie' (1) which reads with 'narrow eyes' ... the *King* / In his great Actions' (2–3). Who would not sing for Portland? Only the 'sluggish spawne,' who is invited to 'Feed on thy selfe for spight, and shew thy Kind: / To vertue, and true worth, be ever blind' (8–10). The same note is struck incongruously in the 'Epithalamion' written for the wedding of Weston's son and the daughter of Jonson's old patron Esmé Stuart (U75). In U77 the poet praises Weston for having 'studied the arts of life; / To compose men, and manners' (17–18), which has a familiar ring. What does not is Jonson's castigating 'murmuring Subjects' (19) who refuse to 'know / What worlds of blessings to good Kings they owe' (19–20).

Whereas in 'To Penshvrst' and 'To Robert Wroth' Jonson sought to define the complex and delicate reciprocities necessary to make a hierarchical society operate, in these poems his position is simply that of royalist partisans in general: that the people are envious, malevolent in their attacks on Charles and ignorant of their own good.[28] In other words, Jonson in these poems confirms that erosion of communal reciprocity, duty, and regard he had obliquely warned against in the earlier poems. And he does so by verbalizing the monarchy's arrogant invective and recrimination that was to solidify the opposition and make it implacable in 1640–2. Particularly significant here is Jonson's turning the vera nobilitas argument to support this invective. By tying himself to the Stuart ideology Jonson transforms his role from that of humanist adviser to that of apologist, and in doing so he realizes the very perversion of this role his poetry has fought against earlier.

The prosodic complexity of the earlier poetry enforcing dialectical engagement is absent also, supplanted by a celebratory, and sometimes querulous, mood demanding unquestioning acquiescence. We have on the one hand prosodic irregularities which, lacking any significant point, quickly become fussy:

> Soone shoot thou up, and grow
> The same that thou are promis'd, but be slow,
> And long in changing. Let our Nephewes see
> Thee quickly come the gardens eye to bee,
> And there to stand so.
> ('An Epigram on the Princes birth' [U65] 5–9)

or perhaps even worse, the 'Epigram to the Queene, then lying in' (U66). After a polemic the poem conducts with itself about the propriety of

addressing Henrietta Marie the same greeting the angel delivered to the
Virgin, it concludes:

> Let it be lawfull, so
> To compare small with great, as still we owe
> Glorie to God. Then, Haile to *Mary!* spring
> Of so much safetie to the Realme, and King!   (11–14)

On the other hand, prosody exists to articulate no thought at all, as in
U74, addressed to Weston's son on a return from an embassy. Nature
graces his return: 'Such joyes, such sweet's doth your *Returne* / Bring
all your friends, (faire Lord) that burne / With love, to heare your
modestie relate / The bus'nesse of your blooming wit' (19–22).

There are, finally, two ceremonial poems that constitute libretti for
musical performance. With 'An Ode, or Song, by all the Muses. In
celebration of her Majesties birth-day' (U67), and U79, 'A New-yeares-
Gift sung to King CHARLES, 1635,' we cross over from nondramatic
poetry to masque, the latter poem being an adaptation of the masque
Pan's Anniversary originally written for Charles' father in 1620. This
means, in effect, that Jonson no longer feels himself constrained by the
protocols of epideictic rhetoric, but can celebrate the royal family in the
manner described by DeNeef: with 'a dogmatic attitude toward its subject,' Jonson need 'not explore, engage in a dialectical argument, or
question the value of [his] topic' (220). The allegory of Pan and Mira
is advanced and then with a flourish discarded, the veil of allegory
opening to disclose the monarch as he is: 'Our great, our good. Where
one's so drest / In truth of colours, both are best' (44–5). With Charles
now declared the true 'Chiefe of Leaders' (28), all the metaphorical crops
and flocks, previously adjunct to the figure of Pan, become intended
literally. It is of course part of the usual masque conclusion that the
sovereign literalizes the metaphors in the masque discourse and spectacle. Here, however, the difference between literal and metaphorical
collapses, and the physical person of the monarch fuses with the ideological, metaphorical trappings customary when evoking the myth of
monarchy.[29]

Clearly, Jonson did not look to Charles for the capacity to discriminate fine meanings. The simple fact is that Charles was dismayingly
too much the improper reader Jonson often addressed in his earlier
poems: the person of status whose lack of inner virtue and wisdom does
not match this status. Constrained by illness and poverty, out of fashion

with court and theatre, though supported by the latest of his patrons the earl of Newcastle (Miles 261ff), Jonson turned his talents to celebrating a monarch whose enthronement beyond criticism was confirmed not by the dialectics of epideictic rhetoric, but by the fiats of *divina juris*. This crucial difference is registered in praise that does not explore the grounds of its own justification, in prosodic flourishes without significance, and in a commitment of vera nobilitas motifs to defending factious partisanship. Marking the end of a superb literary career, these last poems present a sorry spectacle. Significantly, however, they demonstrate by contrast that the larger body of his poetry, written in better and more sanguine and combative days, cannot be justly described as flattery aimed at gaining patronage.[30] The poems addressed to the Caroline court, by telling us what Jonson looks like when he writes flattery, also tell us when he does not.[31]

Among the many treatments by his contemporaries, Jonson's best poetry exhibits the shrewdest and most thoroughgoing analysis of the dynamics of court life and behaviour, and of the humanist 'new man's' relations to the court in particular. He was also by far the most successful in reaping favour and reward from the court: from that of King James certainly, and to a diminished degree from that of his son (John Lyly of the previous generation was his only rival in this regard.)[32]

Jonson had little choice but to situate his acts of self-definition and self-valuation in the context of invidious comparison invited by a hierarchical society. There was nothing about frustrated desire for status, resentment, envy, the obsession with power that turns men into sycophants and satirists, and the consequent need to salve the wounds of rejection and failure that Jonson was unfamiliar with. Nevertheless, he sought to emphasize those aspects of the vera nobilitas argument which were not founded on invidious comparison but which valued the talented man, and woman, for their own sake. In this he waged perhaps the most important struggle in his life: against the kind of *ressentiment* described by Max Scheler, and fully developed in recent writing on the Renaissance poet at court as the dominant feature of courtly aspirants.[33]

That he was touchy, paranoid, boastful, arrogant, egotistical, quarrelsome; that he suffered ill the success of colleagues, that he levelled sarcasm in company at those present, could play the sycophant to noble lords while denigrating them behind their backs, complain at length about his ill treatment by theatre audiences, and be in fact capable of homicide: for all this there is contemporary evidence.[34] His hypersensitivity to criticism and attack is well documented. John Gordon Sweeney's recent book examines Jonson's quarrels with his theatre audiences, in which the playwright is torn between giving up his plays to their judgment, and attempting to coerce it. In chapter 4 I examined those poems in which he similarly attempts to forestall criticism of his encomiums and satires.

For our purposes, however, the kind of man Jonson was is less important than the kind of man Jonson saw himself to be; and to this perspective Drummond's comments are an informative introduction:

> He is a great lover and praiser of himself, a contemner and scorner of others, given rather to lose a friend than a jest, jealous of every word and action of those about him (especially after drink, which is one of the elements in which he liveth), a dissembler of ill parts which reign in him, a bragger of some good that he wanteth, thinketh nothing well but what either he himself or some of his friends and country-men hath said or done, he is passionately kind and angry, careless either to gain or keep, vindictive, but, if he be well answered, at himself. (Parfitt ed *Ben Jonson* 479)

This description catches up perfectly a man perhaps too conscious of his faults and narcissistically self-critical, whose main struggle is to avoid either turning on himself the full blast of loathing he reserves for his satires, or – the dialectical correlate of self-loathing – mounting pretensions with the end of disguising his lacks. In brief, Jonson had to struggle not to become the object of his own satire.

One imagines Jonson carrying on dialogues with himself, like the drunken Carlo Buffone at the end of *Every Man Out*, as he enacts both sides of a projected contest of voices. Such a dialogue of one is the 'Ode to Himself' written in anger against the poor reception elicited by his return to the stage and the production of *The New Inn*. He vows to give up the stage and return to poetry, to 'Strike that disdainful heat / Throughout, to their defeat' so that 'curious fools ... May blushing swear, no palsy's in thy brain' (47–50). He promises to sing 'The glories of thy king; / His zeal to God, and his just awe of men' (51–2), which may explain his willingness to contribute sedulously to the praise of a regime increasingly difficult to praise. In the 'Ode' Jonson strove to take the high road, but one response to it by R. Goodwin reminds Jonson of something he ought to have known without prompting: that the poet's angry readiness to respond to criticism by others discloses the criticism that has already echoed in the mind of the playwright himself (H&S 11:342, 61–4).

Late poems which display Jonson at his most embarrassingly un-hinged by anger and resentment include his response to Alexander Gill's attack on *The Magnetic Lady* (M39) and 'To my Detractor' (M37). Jonson answers Gill's attack on the faults of his last completed play in kind. He cites unsavoury details of Gill's career, calls him names ('thou bawling Fool,' 'poor wretched Tike'), and displays none of the judiciousness he demands of others and himself which give polemic credibility. M37 concerns one of Jonson's poems to Weston (U77, touched on above), and replies to accusations that the poet writes praise for money: 'These verses then, being rightly understood, / His lordship, not Ben Jonson, made them good' (Parfitt ed 349, lines 5–6). The harshness of Jonson's response is not surprising, when we remember how sensitive he shows himself to the vulnerability of the Senecan patronage relation to trans-formation into just such bargaining. The insult, as Jonson states, is a measure not of himself but of the detractor: 'ffoole, doe not rate my Rymes; I'haue found thy Vice / Is to make cheape, the Lord, the lines, the price' (5–6). But when Jonson goes on for over a dozen lines more with execrations such as 'A Mungrel Curre? Thou should'st stinck forth, and dye / Nameless, and noysome, as thy infamy!' (15–16), one senses a vast anger that reaches far beyond this petty enemy, and certainly breaks the bounds of judicious response the poet initially attempts to maintain.

Two epigrams, E81 and E112, manifest Jonson's capacity to skewer his targets with a deft wit that does not throw him off balance in the thrust. Both, however, address poetasters who steal from him, thereby confer-ring the proverbial compliment evinced by imitation. Jonson's scorn announces comfortable superiority, but also mediates through his scorned admirers perhaps some hidden self-contempt. This possibility opens up an avenue of approach to his inner thoughts and fears that Jonson otherwise took care to close off to the scrutiny of others. In this respect the concluding poem of *The Forrest*, 'To Heaven' (F15), reveals an un-wonted candour about his own personal motivations. In declaring that he knows his 'state,' 'both full of shame, and scorne' (17), the upgraded *and* separates and pairs off criticism of self with that of others, and elicits the recognition that scorn for others may reflect a scorn for oneself and therefore shame. The whole poem deals with Jonson's fear of being judged for having judged others, and this means that God, Jonson, and others who choose to judge Jonson are all implied observers in the opening lines.[35]

Jonson's adverse self-judgments, carefully calibrated and seasoned with a wit that lightens their intrinsic narcissism, become one of the main strategies by which he seeks to ingratiate himself with others. Significantly, Jonson deprecates his physical appearance often enough to suggest that he prefers this detrimental aspect of himself as a kind of lightning rod, to draw criticism away from facets of his personality on which he could less easily bear aspersions. In the 'Epistle. To my Lady COVELL' (U56), Jonson turns witty self-dispraise to advantage. Noting first that he is 'Laden with Bellie, and doth hardly approach / His friends, but to breake Chaires, or cracke a Coach' (9–10), in a move that he develops in A Celebration of Charis (U2), Jonson then contrasts the fat 'servant' with the nimble muse: 'Marrie the Muse is one, can tread the Aire, / And stroke the water, nimble, chast, and faire' (13–14).[36]

Jonson argues a contrast between outward ugliness and inner beauty in the manner allowed by the semiotics of the vera nobilitas argument, where the wit of mind compensates for and belies the lack of outer nobility.[37] If praise for Jonson means the public recognition of an inner true nobility, then he invites praise of himself – his talents and achievements – through the relay of dispraise of his outer appearance. He can thus disarm social hostility by making a public display of Jonsonian discriminations, hoping to charm with self-deprecating wit those he cannot charm with beauty. A Celebration of Charis (U2) focuses much of what I have been saying about Jonson, since it displays Jonson's most subtle and complex understanding of these tactical manoeuvres.

Before concluding with a consideration of this elusive set of poems I shall touch briefly on a few others which display individually the adroit moves that sequence embodies collectively. There are for instance several poems in which Jonson displays an unexpected humility of tone, some of which is imposed by the pinch of necessity. The wit of his enforced addresses to the royal household begging promised subsidies, discussed above, is evidenced in the Skeltonic couplets of U57, in which Jonson asks through an intermediary that the Exchequer be reminded of what is owed him. Another poem that finds Jonson in an unwontedly chastened mood is 'An Epitaph on Master VINCENT CORBET' (U12), where Jonson recognizes a moralist the force of whose rhetoric is significantly different from his own: ' 'Tis true, he could not reprehend; / His very Manners taught to'amend, / They were so even, grave, and holy; / ...

His lookes would so correct it, when / It chid the vice, yet not the Men' (21–3, 27–8).

Otherwise Jonson exploits the rhetorical resources of his unprepossessing appearance in those few poems, so difficult to incorporate into the concerns which his poetry generally evinces, that deal with love. In these poems we find Jonson at his most mellow and vulnerable, a true Cyrano de Bergerac whose physical unattractiveness is belied by the ardour and wit of his discourse.

Jonson opens *The Forrest* with a poem explaining 'Why I write not of Love' (F1), an explanation that implies a situation which is not quite the case. Jonson does write several love poems, although they make up a tiny percentage of the whole corpus. The implication is essentially accurate, however, because Jonson's love poetry is that of the failed, unsuccessful lover. To the question why Jonson does not write of love it could also be answered that in fact he writes of love all the time. Kenneth Burke's development of rhetoric as a form of courtship between those alienated by class distinctions, with all the transformations of the motifs of sexual desire into ambition appropriate to such troping (*Rhetoric* 177 et passim), suggests that Jonson's love poetry in effect parallels or replicates the poetry overtly concerned with vera nobilitas . The vera nobilitas argument is adapted to the stance of the poetic lover, when Jonson argues that his attractions were not inherited or the gift of fortune: the language of love rather than the looks of love. Jonson would accordingly want to redefine the rules of the courtship game in both instances, and to replace the one set of requirements for successful courtship with another: erotic attractiveness with intellectual, witty sophistication, where the latter is a version of true nobility argued against inherited nobility.[38]

The pathos of the conclusion to F1 – 'Then wonder not, / That since, my numbers are so cold, / When *Loue* is fled, and I grow old' (10–12) – is matched in only a few of Jonson's other love lyrics with love melancholy. In one of them, U11, 'The Dreame,' the poet wages an unequal battle against love because here, as in all the other poems on love, he is condemned quite unequivocally to love and not be loved in return. His attempts to guard himself against love are subverted by his own unconscious mind, which makes him fall in love in a dream. Motivated by a refusal of the self-pity found in the bulk of Renaissance love poetry, the pathos here lies in the speaker's attempts to avoid appearing pathetic, his gallant insistence on seeing his loving with balanced and self-knowing humour.

F7, 'Song. That Women are bvt Mens shaddowes,' is of Donnian inspiration both in wit and subject (cf 'A Lecture upon the Shadow')[39] and writes a perverse rule of courtship: 'Follow a shaddow, it still flies you; / Seeme to flye it, it will pursue: / So court a mistris, shee denyes you; / Let her alone, shee will court you' (1–4). Like shadows and substance that women and men replicate, one waxes in power as the other wanes. Power is the subject of the poem, and makes explicit the social dimension of courtship in which wooing and fleeing are devices for manipulation whether in bed or at court. In another poem (U10) Jonson reads the subservience and vulnerability of the lover as a version of similar vulnerabilities afflicting the subservient courtier. He rejects jealousy as the disease of 'doubting Men' (15), those unsure of their merits and therefore of the affections of a mistress. Jonson does not doubt his merits, partly because he has no illusions about the demerits of his physical bulk, but mainly because he refuses to play power games in the domains either of love or politics.[40]

As if in rehearsal for the *Charis* sequence, Jonson leaves his picture in Scotland (U9), and then laments, in terms recalling the Inigo Jones quarrel, that 'she' pays more attention to what she sees than to what she hears. Convinced that 'my language to her, was as sweet' as that of 'the youngest Hee, / That sits in shadow of *Apollo's* tree' (6, 9–10), Jonson yet fears that her ears have been stopped by seeing in his picture 'My hundred of gray haires ... seven and fortie years ... My mountaine belly, and my rockie face' (14–17). As if confronted with an emblem where picture and text are scrambled, the eye causes the ear to go deaf when inner merit is ignored in favour of the outer signifiers of merit empty of signification.[41]

In *A Celebration of Charis* (U2), Jonson seeks to love, and to be loved, for the right reasons, to define 'whom to love, and how' (U2.1:16). The dialectics that articulate these discriminations are identical with those discriminating true praise of true nobility from false versions of both. Most interpretations envision the sequence as detailing the vicissitudes of Jonson's relations with Charis, and within that perspective the question concerns the speaker's developing attitude toward these relations.[42] The perspective of this study would enclose most readings of the sequence that highlight the matter of erotic love, whether the tone be serious, cynical, or playful, since love is treated alternately in all these ways throughout. I am concerned with the sequence as a record less of Jonson's erotic success, or lack of it, than of the poet's unquestionable success in constructing for himself a persona and address to the lady, and the court at large, in which he credibly authorizes the extensive claims he makes for himself in the opening lyric.

I examined in the first section of chapter 1 the engaging play of contrasts initiated in the opening two lines of this poem. The forestalling strategy Jonson uses elsewhere to obviate criticism is, for once, here employed to invite laughter. Though the poet may now 'write fiftie yeares,'[43] he insists that 'it is not always face, / Clothes, or Fortune gives the grace; / Or feature, or the youth.' The catalogued items linked by the repeated 'or' comes off as an incremental set of conventional attractions merely extrinsic to the true virtue of one who has cultivated not only Language, but also Truth, not only Ardour, but also Passion: connectives evoked by the upgraded 'and' in the following lines (7–12). The conclusion of the poem praises the lady, who 'shall make the old man young, / Keepe the middle age at stay, / and let nothing high decay' (20–2). The matters of age, passage of time, and ultimately of death – all of which might be expected to militate against love – Jonson transforms into motives for love.

Sara Van Den Berg's characterization of the sophisticated play in the sequence is therefore correct when she notes that Jonson responds to the fact that he is 'an obviously unfit player in the game of love' with an 'increasingly bright wordplay' in which he 'grows unexpectedly' in 'his awareness of Charis, of himself, of wit and love and play' (30). When she says that Jonson must achieve 'the transformation through wit' of himself 'from hapless victim to accomplished artist, able to use language to his advantage' (31–2), one need only change the reference here from courtly love-play to the range of Jonson's ambitions as humanist poet, and gain in addition a capsule statement of Jonson's success in realizing these ambitions. The erotic wooing in the sequence supports an agenda in which the poet's capacity to fuse courtly wit and humanist wisdom in a successful marriage of inner virtue and outer status becomes its true subject and purpose.[44]

U2.2, 'How he saw her,' is an aetiological, or *pourquoi* tale, one that explains how something developed to its present state, as in Ovid's *Metamorphoses*, or the poems of Anacreon to which it alludes. Cupid's statue with a beard is an emblem of Jonson the middle-aged lover. But typical for this kind of tale, the emblem is treated literally and therefore demands an equally literal explanation. It must be shown, in brief, how Jonson has come to possess some of Cupid's identifying marks – the bow and arrows – when he so obviously doesn't look like Cupid. The answer to the riddle is the 'Lightning' of Charis' eyes (24), which makes

him stand 'a stone, / Mock'd of all ... / *Cupids* Statue with a Beard'
(27–8, 30). This poem, like the previous one, seeks to forestall the reader's
reactions by resisting the temptation to dissimulate the poet's anger and
make himself vulnerable to attack on this score as well. These poems
are object lessons in the deft and desperate art of deflecting mockery,
and in doing so Jonson refuses the pretences he satirizes in those who
inadvertently display their self-criticism in the act of dissimulating it.

The following poem, 'What hee suffered' (U2.3), similarly mythol-
ogizes the process by which the lady gives him back his eyes and the
use of his limbs, in order 'to hurt me more' (4). She does so only on
the condition that Jonson yield Cupid's bow and arrow to her, who
gives them back to Cupid, who in turn aims an arrow at Jonson's heart.
This frivolously elaborate mythologizing is all in the interest of explaining how the poet should be in love – the question asked at the beginning
of the first poem – and calls attention to its own pointlessness. It is a
pourquoi tale that explains nothing at all, the point being that no one
can give an acceptable account of why someone of Jonson's age, and
shape, should fall in love.

U2.4, the often anthologized 'Her Triumph,' balances carefully between the playful ironies initiated in the previous three poems, and a
serious exploration of a poetic mode unwontedly sensual in the Jonson
poetic corpus. The irony lies in the poet's rhapsodizing in the hyperbolic
manner which Charis' own haughty beauty seems to demand for itself.
He is protected from her possible remonstrances, which he would invite
only if Charis believes that he exaggerates, and evidently she doesn't.
The result is a poem where irony becomes sincerity without ceasing to
be ironic.[45]

Poems 5, 6, and 7 are compliment poems that, unlike 4, demand recompense for the compliment. The bargain seems struck less on Charis'
susceptibility to flattery than on Ben's mastery of 'the Language, and
the Truth, / With the Ardor, and the Passion' which 'Gives the Lover
weight, and fashion.' 'Weight' here is intended to displace the 'weight'
of the poet's bodily bulk, and is to be looked for only in the weightiness
of his poetic talent, which in courtly games of love is displayed in an
appropriate lightness of touch. This capacity these three poems demonstrate, which means that they exhibit a bricklayer's stepson not only
having educated himself in the classics – his learning being writ large
all over the sequence – but also having mastered the fine art of self-
praise by self-denigration, which is a sign of one who knows himself
possessed of true nobility.

Cupid in U2.5, 'His discourse with Cupid,' reads Ben's description of Charis and discovers in it his own mother Venus. So Charis is Venus, but as in the poet's case 'this Beauty yet doth hide / Something more then thou hast spi'd. / Outward Grace weake love beguiles' (49–51). The epideictic dimension of this sequence replicates its function in the discourse of the vera nobilitas argument, wherein praise is the public acknowledgment of inner virtue. What Charis is Ben can never be, the ideal fusion of outer beauty and inner nobility, but he can be the next best thing: the poet who confers on Charis what she would not possess otherwise, namely the status of a publicly acknowledged beauty. Which is the subject of the following poem, U2.6, 'Clayming a second kisse by Desert.' This poem turns on the wager the poet lays on whether Charis was judged by all more beautiful at a wedding party than the bride. The poet wagers that she will guess correctly – she does – and he wonders whether 'such a verse as this, / May not claime another kisse' (35–6). Uniting the virtues of the three goddesses Paris had to choose among, as the poet affirms at the conclusion of the previous poem, she is the cynosure of all eyes:

> Or, that did you sit, or walke,
> You were more the eye, and talke
> Of the Court, to day, then all
> Else that glister'd in *White-hall*;
> So, as those that had your sight,
> Wisht the Bride were chang'd to night,
> And did thinke, such Rites were due
> To no other Grace but you! (13–20)

The poise of pause and release, of unexpected isolation and connection in these lines marks the speaker as one who observes the articulations of his language about Charis with no less intensity than he observes the articulations of her body in movement and repose. And it is this articulation that justifies the second kiss. Jonson makes trifles whose mastery lies in their highlighting the art that makes them and therefore makes them cease to be trifles. Like the poet's capacity in the first poem to master his awkwardness in loving, the frivolity of his request here shows his knowledge of how little he asks of the lady, and therefore his powerlessness to bargain for more.

In U2.7, 'Begging another, on colour of mending the former,' the artifice of the argument – signalled in the title – enacts once again the speaker's mastery of language and thereby earns him a place in the ranks of bona fide lovers. The poem is disputative in the manner of Donne, but with this difference: where Donne's poetry tries to inveigle the lady within the toils of the argument, Jonson's here, as in the earlier poems in the sequence, makes the gallantry of the argument its own point. It is not that Jonson means what he says – he knows that Charis will not be moved to kiss him by the coercion of mere argument – but that he hopes to exhibit himself as a master of compliment. It is the language and the passion of the lover that he seeks to communicate: the ethos or authority of a lover whose mastery of the language of love communicates to the lady his willingness to recognize the limits of her compliance by his talent for saying beautiful nothings.

U2.8, 'Urging her of a promise,' is a *carpe diem* poem, though it doesn't look like one, or at least doesn't start out as one. The tidbits of idle behaviour from which the speaker summons Charis – idling at her window, critiquing the faces and dress of the passers-by, discussing cosmetics with her confidante – typify the trivia on which she spends her youth. The ironies of Charis judging others and putting on cosmetics when all her 'sweet of life is past' (28) are patent. What had begun for Charis an idle promise, which nevertheless 'set on fire / All that heard her, with desire' (5–6), a promise consistent with the idleness of her other activities, suddenly becomes an urgent thing: to declare 'What a man she could love well' (4). Life is passing her by, love is passing her by, and like Herrick's Corinna and all her Anacreontic and Horatian sisters she is passing into an old age the pains and longings of which the poet knows well.

The ideal manly lover Charis describes in U2.9 is deceptively quite different from Ben Jonson. The poet foregrounds his own urbanity as a fat and aging lover through his willingness to let her own predilections have such generous scope. Actually, however, as she proceeds her ideal lover turns out to be the ideal Jonsonian courtier. She 'would have him, if I could, / Noble; or of greater Blood: / Titles, I confesse, doe take me; / And a Woman God did make me' (3–6). Though with an eye to her poet lover she demands that he have a 'cheeke (withall) / Smooth as is the Billiard Ball: / Chin, as woolly as the Peach' (19–21), she describes a man who though noble fulfils one of Jonson's major desiderata by grounding his aristocratic rank on the inner virtues that make true nobility:

Valiant he should be as fire,
Shewing danger more then ire.
Bounteous as the clouds to earth;
And as honest as his Birth.
All his actions to be such,
As to doe no thing too much.
Nor o're-praise, nor yet condemne;
Nor out-valew, nor contemne;
Nor doe wrongs, nor wrongs receave;
Nor tie knots, nor knots unweave;
And from baseness to be free,
As he durst love Truth and me.   (41–52)

Charis is certainly one of Ben Jonson's most perceptive readers, for she describes in little the poet's ideal member of an aristocracy of humanist virtue. His valour, an honesty that matches his birth (or perhaps a birth that matches his honesty), his capacity to balance between excesses of bad epideictic rhetoric, and the rest: Charis describes a man who combines the qualities that Jonson most values with the youthful vigour and beauty of a younger man. The poet says in essence that if Charis had her wishes she would wish a young and beautiful lover with the soul of Ben Jonson.

Charis' sophisticated judgment and good taste are confirmed retroactively by contrast with the preferences of the lady in the final poem of the sequence, 'Another Ladyes exception present at the hearing' (U2.10). This lady prefers a man with the youth and beauty that Charis describes, but without a mind: 'That's a Toy, that I could spare' (2). Mention of the toy she can spare leads to consideration of the toy she cannot; indeed, the various good parts described by Charis are reduced to the 'one good part I'ld lie withall' (8). Clearly, this lady will not find attractive the elderly lover whose language and passion define the only true sources of love whether found in a young man or an old. Furthermore, her preference for a good face, a good title, and good clothes (3–5) clearly marks her as one of the types that Jonson would have satirized in the *Epigrammes*. Yet there is no satiric tone in this short poem. On the contrary, Jonson here as throughout the sequence takes care to maintain a remarkable equilibrium and urbane geniality. It is as if he saw quite clearly that a lover like himself could gain credibility only if he recognized his own debilities in the game of love, and did not allow himself scope to indulge his more hectoring predilections.

Ready admission of these debilities, however, is preface to our recognition that Jonson has in fact succeeded in wooing Charis when she speaks of an ideal lover that is a younger version of himself, even if this younger version possesses a physical beauty that Ben never claimed. The strategies of the Charis sequence recapitulate in little the master strategy of Jonson's life and literary career; and his success in transforming this charming court lady into willing spokeswoman for his most cherished ideal of himself may well have been worth his failure to seduce her. The strategy of forestalling criticism of the self by self-criticism, peculiar to these love poems, nevertheless replicates the larger Jonsonian strategy embodied in the prosody of his poetry in general. Contrastive emphasis in turn grounds in this poetry the discriminations between true and false nobility forced on the aspiring humanist poet by the political and social structures of Renaissance England. Jonson's poetry is the most clearly autobiographical of his productions, because in it Jonson literally wrote his own life, in the sense of constructing a life's career out of verbal dialogue with himself, with those around him, and not least with the centuries-long tradition of the vera nobilitas argument which governed his self-identity and yielded him the means of achieving it.

Notes

CHAPTER ONE

1 All citations of Jonson's nondramatic poetry, the masques, and the *Discoveries* are to C.H. Herford, Percy and Evelyn Simpson, eds *Ben Jonson* 11 volumes (Oxford: Clarendon P 1925–52). These citations are abbreviated in the text as H&S, followed by volume and page numbers. Citations of Jonson's plays are to G.A. Wilkes ed *The Complete Plays of Ben Jonson* 4 vols (Oxford: Clarendon P 1981), except for citation of the first version of *Every Man in His Humour*, which is to H&S. Poems are identified by letter and number. The letters refer to the four collections in which Jonson's poems are currently arranged. Two of these are authoritative: *Epigrammes* and *The Forrest*, both of which appear in the 1616 Folio. The third is *The Vnder-wood*, edited by Sir Kenelm Digby and brought out after Jonson's death, in 1640. The fourth is entirely a modern construction, miscellaneous poems published in plays, masques, and as commendatory poems solicited by authors or publishers, as well as a few existing in manuscript or as funereal inscriptions. In this study all poems will be cited by the following code: E = *Epigrammes*; F = *The Forrest*; U = *The Vnder-wood*; M = miscellaneous. Each poem is cited by letter, with a number attached derived from the numerical sequence in H&S.

2 Jonson's quarrels with his readers and his audiences are discussed by Carlson, Sweeney, Pearlman, and Donaldson ('Jonson and Anger').

3 Womack (81–2) comments on Jonson's suspicion of the reader evidenced in this opening epigram. 'There's no promise of a smooth confluence of thought uniting writer and reader: on the contrary, it seems all too possible that now, when the poet had done all he can and must perforce

leave his printed words to look after themselves, communication will still fail ... he doesn't trust the words. They have no presence, they merely designate thought, their sense is not in them but beyond them in a space where it must be repositioned by the reader ... the text eyes me narrowly because of its need for me. I could spoil everything.' Concentrating mainly on the plays, Womack's is the most intellectually challenging and critically incisive monograph to appear on Jonson in the last ten years.

4 The reader's participation in the process of discrimination that produces a Jonson poem has been noted in general terms before. J.G. Nichols (39) comments that 'Jonson's poems ... often read as though they were deliberately worked out, and they invite us to do the same. We are invited to pause and deliberate, to judge the worth of what is being said and of how it is being said, to criticize in fact ... Jonson ... wants [a reader] competent to judge and discriminate, one who is willing to learn from the poem how to judge and discriminate.' See also Beaurline ('Selective'), Gardiner (*Craftsmanship* 58), Edward Partridge ('*Epigrammes*'), Dutton (81), Marotti ('All about Jonson's Poetry' 226), and Winner (67). Rowe uses 'discrimination' (8) in the context of his argument that Jonson's career was driven by the need to distinguish himself from other writers, part of a larger new-historicist thesis that offers a revised version of Jonson victimized by the courtly lust for power.

5 'Emphasis' is used here rather than such cognate terms as 'stress' or 'accent' to name any form of phonological marking of syllable, word, or phrase. In this I follow the practice of Crystal (*Prosodic Systems* 120), who uses 'emphasis' to indicate phonological marking through loudness (stress), pitch (accent), duration, juncture, or any combination of these phonological parameters. Emphasis cued by punctuation through junctures, that is, pauses, will usually be rendered phonologically by a combination of increased stress and accent, and sometimes through extended duration as well. At the level of discussion I pursue here, the phonological components, other than juncture, are less important than the fact of phonological emphasis itself.

6 The edition I refer to is that edited in 1975 by Ian Donaldson. Donaldson (xviii–xix) recognizes that Jonson's punctuation 'is deliberate and systematic,' particularly in the 1616 Folio, and that 'to miss Jonson's points of punctuation is often to miss his points of meaning.' 'Yet,' Donaldson goes on to say, 'to modern eyes and ears, Jonson's punctuation is also at times intolerably heavy.' Donaldson's editorial practice is a confusing compromise: 'The punctuation of the present text is de-

signed to allow Jonson's lines to move more freely, but also to preserve something of their original weight, measure, and delicacy of transition.' A similar statement occurs in the reissue of that edition in the Oxford Authors Series (1985). My argument would militate directly against such compromises, as it would also against A.C. Partridge's reason for preserving original punctuation (*Orthography* 123), namely that it preserves 'the last touch of authenticity.' Stephen Booth justifies emendations of original punctuation in his edition of Shakespeare's Sonnets by making a similar, though more closely reasoned, compromise. Both a modernized and an unmodernized text risk confusing the modern 'plain reader,' though for different reasons (448). Booth's emendations presuppose that Renaissance punctuation is 'haphazard' and 'casually rhetorical,' and that the Renaissance reader 'was used to correcting printer's errors as he read' (451). My discussion shows that retaining Jonson's punctuation is a matter neither of taste nor of authenticity nor of reproducing the casual mistakes of compositors, but of determining meaning by marking juncture, emphasis, and contrast. There is in fact no completely satisfactory edition of Jonson's poetry available. The vagaries attending the printing of the 1640 Folio, which contains Jonson's third poetry collection, *The Vnder-wood*, are documented by Herford and Simpson (9:94ff). The only collections about which authorial intention is certain are in the 1616 Folio, which Jonson may or may not have seen through the press (Brock *Workes* Introduction [np]): the *Epigrammes* and *The Forrest*. Herford and Simpson collated several but not all extant copies of the 1616 Folio, and therefore, while their edition of these collections is the most definitive we have, it is not absolutely certain that the punctuation is authorial in every instance. I have done a spot collation of twenty-five poems from the *Epigrammes* and *The Forrest* among the Brock facsimile (Bodleian Library), the copy of the 1616 Folio at the University of Minnesota-Minneapolis Library, and the edition of George Burke Johnston (using his own copy of the 1616 and 1640 Folios [325]), and compared these with the versions in H&S 8, and have found no discrepancies in punctuation whatever. It is reasonable to assume that the 1616 Folio gives us a consistent rendering of the punctuation of the *Epigrammes* and *The Forrest*, while the punctuation of the poems in *Vnder-wood* and the poems printed in other books is less dependable. Finally the only argument for depending on the received versions is the consistency of punctuation practice itself throughout them all. The two other currently available editions of Jonson's poetry, in addition to Donaldson and Johnston, generally respect Jonson's punctuational practice, though at isolated spots they differ between themselves and with Herford and Simpson: those of William B. Hunter and George Parfitt.

7 For example, George Parfitt's assertion that the 'precision' of Jonson's ethical judgments costs the poet a 'reduction of moral complexity to simplified clarity' derives from Trimpi's notion of a plain style founded on and mediating a simple, straightforward ethical sincerity ('Ethical' 133; also 'Nature' 348–9). Parfitt's contention elsewhere ('Compromise' 119) that Jonson's poetry lacks resonance implicitly responds to W.V. Spanos' attempt to rescue Jonson's poetry from a surface of putative formality by discovering in it various forms of resonant allusion. Judith Gardiner attempts to move reading Jonson's poetry beyond echoes of New Critical thinking implied by these conclusions, when she notes that 'those who stress the esthetic pleasures of ambiguity often underrate the pleasures of self-righteousness' (*Craftsmanship* 147). All these remarks presuppose a conception of Jonson's poetic styles defined originally by Trimpi as conscious imitation of the classical 'plain style.' R.V. Young has successfully resisted Trimpi's thesis in an article that takes a perspective similar to that argued here. I would agree with him that 'the nature and *locus* of' the 'tension as it emerges in the Jonson epigram' lies neither 'in the historical situation nor in Jonson's psyche, but in the structure of figure and image and myth, and in the verbal texture of the individual poems. I further maintain that this view can reconcile Jonson the poet of irony and ambiguity with Jonson the poet of classical form and traditional morality' (203).

8 In the same vein Thomas Greene says: 'All of the poems depend upon a felt weight of personality, the plain, candid, blunt, but discriminating man, quick to size up, contemptuous of the ignorant and fraudulent, not given to fancy or sentimental expansiveness, alert, brusque, a famous character. Each poem modulates a recognizable moral style, what Leavis described as "the Latin judicial poise and conscious civilization ... curiously inseparable from a weighty and assertive personal assurance" ' ('Accommodations' 287).

9 A.C. Partridge says that Jonson is probably 'the earliest verse orthographer among practising poets' (80), and that his concern for punctuation is writ large and minutely throughout the 1616 Folio. The Folio punctuation is carefully discriminated, often eccentric, and even (Partridge says) 'fussy.' Herford and Simpson remark that 'the Folio, in contrast with the Quartos, shows a fully developed system of punctuation' (9:48).

10 I have chosen the version printed in the 1616 Folio *Volpone*, which differs in some respects from the version in *The Forrest* in the same vol-

ume: the former version is identical in punctuation with the latter, but also includes commas before 'in vaine' and before and after 'once.' As regards 'To Celia,' at least, the 1616 Folio faithfully reproduces the 1607 quarto of *Volpone*, which the Fountainwell text editor, Jay L. Halio, argues has greater authority than the Folio text, and which was in any case set from the Quarto text (7ff).

11 Contrastivity becomes an essential mark of new information for the following reason: In a passage of old information every specific word, phrase, or clause is predictable from the foregoing, and this means that within this passage no choices have been made between several possible and available units of information. All units of such a text appear tautologically or analytically – that is, predictably – to imply each other. New information, on the other hand, appears where there is a point of choice, where a word, phrase, or clause appears not to follow redundantly from the foregoing, but where instead the text approaches a crossroads, a moment of decision, and a new direction is taken. New information is not predictable from old information, which means that it is not logically entailed by old information, and the reason for this is that more than one possible unit is available to be chosen. For fuller development of this argument see McCanles 'Punctuation.'

12 Constrastive emphasis in Jonson's poetry was first examined and documented in Hubert M. English's Yale dissertation, 'Prosody and Meaning in Ben Jonson's Poems' (1954). With benefit of little linguistic theory, English understood that contrastivity is not only a matter of emphasis but also of meaning: 'Intensity, duration, and pitch are the building blocks from which resemblance or difference in metrical phrasing can be constructed' (119). For English, however, contrastivity only results from violating metrical set, and he limited Jonson's use of it to pairs of terms occurring in the same text (which I have called syntagmatic contrast). Richard Flantz notes Jonson's habit of upgrading otherwise downgraded syllables for thematic purposes, though he is mainly concerned with rhetorical and stylistic effect.

13 'Countertext' is a term defined in McCanles 'Dialectical Structure' 31ff and refers to a structuralist analysis of the semantic component of a text, in which semantic units present in a text binarily imply their (rejected) opposites in the semantic repertoire funding that text. Every text therefore has an indefinite number of 'countertexts' composed of the terms opposed to/rejected by/implied by the text itself.

14 In the interest of maintaining this study free of excessively technical exposition I direct the interested reader to my article 'Punctuation, Con-

trastive Emphasis, and New Information in the Prosody of Jonson's Poetry' listed in the bibliography. This article states the theoretical underpinnings of my argument in this section. In that article I take up (1) current thinking about the semantic import of contrastive emphasis, relying primarily on the work of M.A.K. Halliday, David Crystal, Noam Chomsky, and Morris Halle; (2) the works on punctuation, prosody, and meaning of writers roughly contemporary with Jonson, including Richard Mulcaster, Alexander Gill, Charles Butler, John Hart, Simon Daines, and George Puttenham. (3) The work of Percy Simpson, Walter Ong, and A.C. Partridge on Renaissance punctuation is cited. (4) On contrastivity I rely on that of Ferdinand de Saussure, Roman Jakobson and Morris Halle, Oswald Ducrot, Emile Benveniste, and Yury Lotman. (5) The work of the Birmingham, England school of linguistics (Malcolm Coulthard et al) and the magisterial *Grammar of Contemporary English* of Quirk, Greenbaum et al develop the import of contrastive emphasis for new information, as does that (6) of Umberto Eco, John Lyons, Eric Wanner, T.G. Bever, D.B. Fry, and Teun A. Van Dijk on information theory and its import for linguistics. (7) In the area of modern studies of prosody I am particularly indebted to the work of John Hollander, Seymour Chatman, Roger Fowler, D.W. Harding, George L. Trager, Henry Lee Smith, Edmund L. Epstein, Terence Hawkes, and Robert Ladd. Relevant to my argument here, though published after it, is Hardison *Prosody and Purpose.*

15 This distinction Jonson would seem to draw from Seneca's Epistle 102: 'When they say that renown is praise bestowed on the good by the good, what they refer to is not an utterance but a judgment. For a good man may remain silent; but if he decides that a certain person is worthy of praise, that person is the object of praise. Besides, praise is one thing, and the giving of praise another; the latter demands utterance also' (3:177). The distinction between renown and name is consistent with Jonson's understanding of epideictic rhetoric, to be discussed in chapter 4.

16 'Information focus' is described by Quirk, Greenbaum, et al as 'related to the difference between given and new information; that is to say, between information already supplied by context (perhaps by a preceding part of the discourse) and information which has not been prepared for in this way' (940). The notion of information focus is in turn indebted to the distinction in information theory between a section of a text that contains a message that is predictable from previous sections, and one

that contains a message that is unpredictable. As Crystal points out (*Prosodic Systems* 127): 'Only those features are recognized which are judged to be significant, i.e., contrastive; namely, those whose omission from an utterance would cause a linguistically untrained group of native English speakers to state that the utterance was 'different' in meaning from the original.'

17 Enjambment as trope in the Cary-Morison Ode is argued by Hollander (177–8). Seymour Chatman (Chatman and Levin 150) says that caesura and enjambment result not from a conflict between syntax and metre – the more traditional view – but from a conflict between metre and prose rhythm. This implies that enjambment works to specify meaning not through deviant boundary marking of normal syntactical units, but through the junctures and emphases appropriate to speech rhythm when these are imposed on metrical set. It is clear from Jonson's practice exemplified in these examples that he often followed before the fact Hollander's (101ff) and Chatman's recipes for upgraded emphasis before and after the enjambment: namely, sometimes placing the break within the most elementary phrase units.

18 As in Donaldson's edition; which has its uses to the degree that the editor renders quite often the 'normal' rhythm that Jonson's punctuation violates and which the reader is called (contrastively) to be cognizant of.

19 It is interesting to note how far Alfonso Ferrabosco observed the directions of Jonson's punctuation when he set this poem to music, very probably for the first performance of *Volpone* (see Chan 90ff). The metre is four quarters to the measure. The word 'proue' that ends the first line is given a whole note value, and 'while we may' is then set in the next measure to two quarter notes and one half note, thus isolating this clause exactly as it would be in a spoken rendition. Similar metrical isolation is given 'at length,' 'in vaine,' and 'with vs.' However, 'for euer,' 'that set,' and 'once' are set as part of larger musical phrases and consequently do not receive similar emphasis. Since the setting involves repetitions with variation of essentially the same melodic structure, these downgraded emphases are attributable to the exigencies of strophic melodic phrasing, as distinct from syntactical or contrastive phrasing.

20 Jonson's sensitivity to poetic rhythm as direct imitation of, and therefore direction for, a specific performance is indicated in U48, 'The Dedication of the Kings new Cellar. To Bacchus.' The unusual metrical play in this poem lends a sort of syncopation to a reading, something that might be taken as a kind of mimesis of drunkenness:

> For, *Bacchus*, thou art freer
> Of Cares, and over-seer
> Of feast, and merry meeting,
> And still begin'st the greeting (13–16)

Here Jonson deploys contrastive emphasis in a context generally devoid of serious meaning. Each line begins with an iamb and ends chiasmically with a trochee, which causes a juncture at the beginning of the next line in order to articulate its opening unaccented syllable. In addition, at line breaks Jonson often enforces enjambment, which reinforces upgrading the beginning syllable. As a mimesis of drunken discourse this mimicking of near-nonsense in the accents of significant statement has its own decorum.

21 Similar remarks are merited by U1.1, the first poem of the three religious poems that open *The Vnder-wood*, which is repetitive and predictable because Jonson is dealing with a static, undeveloping subject – the trinity itself and its various three-fold cognates.

22 See M41, 'The Reverse on the backe side,' which is appended to 'The Ghyrlond of the blessed Virgin MARIE' discussed earlier: 'to that most blessed *Trine*, Of Persons' (34–5). By isolating 'Of Persons' Jonson creates three possible logical and syntactical relations with the head of this phrase, '*Trine*': (1) contrastive – the trinity is a single thing, yet composed of different persons; (2) additive – the trinity is both a single thing, *and* separate persons. In this latter interpretation 'trine' and 'persons' are merely listed as distinct and unrelated things in some sort of otherwise unspecified relationship. And (3) analytic: 'trinity' implies 'persons,' which is the only meaning one gets when one drops Jonson's punctuation. When the punctuation seems equally to allow various words and phrases to be related in several ways the effect is always the same: an undecidability of syntactical and semantic relationships.

23 One can sympathize occasionally with Donaldson's intentions, for example in E39, 'On Old Colt':

> For all night-sinnes, with others wiues, vnknowne,
> COLT, now doth daily penance in his owne.

Donaldson omits all punctuation in the poem except the commas enclosing 'unknown.' The sense of the epigram is obscure, having to do probably with Colt's fantasied ('unknown') intercourse with others' wives (cf the epigrams on Sir Voluptuous Beast). Whatever its meaning, it depends on oppositions within several antithetical pairs; night/day;

[then]/now; others' wives/ his own; unknown/own (that is, known in the sexual sense). Jonson's isolating punctuation upgrades the emphasis on each unit in the first line, thereby setting it up for syntagmatic contrast with the appropriate matching term in the second. Donaldson's unpunctuated version allows and does not deny these match-ups, but neglects the primary focus on these which Jonson's punctuation enforces. A different effect results from another neglected point, this time in M24, the poem Jonson wrote to preface James Mabbe's translation of Matheo Aleman's 'Gusman de Alfarache' (1622): 'Such Bookes deserue Translators, of like coate / As was the *Genius* wherewith they were wrote (11–12). With the comma removed in line 11, 'of like coate' becomes simply a restrictive modifier of 'Translator.' With the comma in place, however, the line gives us a typically Jonsonian surprise continuation of a thought that was apparently concluded. Up to the comma the text says simply that such works deserve translators, a comment consistent with the preceding praise of the work itself. Isolation 'of like coate' now specifies 'translator' as one who writes with the same genius as the author.

24 Juncture usually creates emphasis, and emphasis is marked by one or more of three parameters of suprasegmentals: pitch, stress, and duration. However, emphasis involving these parameters can occur without juncture, as is illustrated in M9, the Epitaph on Cecilia Bulstrode, which finds Jonson uncharacteristically using extended duration to create or heighten emphasis (extended duration is indicated by wide spacing within individual words):

> S t a y, view this stone: A n d, if thou beest not such,
> Read here a little, that thou mayst k n o w much.
> It couers, first, a Virgin; and t h e n, o n e
> That durst be that in Court: a vertu' a l o n e
> To fill an Epitaph. But s h e had m o r e. ...
> ... She was e a r t h e s E y e: ...   (1–5, 9)

25 This contextual dimension of enjambment can be illustrated negatively by M16, 'A Speech Presented unto king James':

> Except your Gratious Eye as through a Glass
> made prospectiue, behould hym, hee must passe
> still that same little poynte hee was; but when
> your Royal Eye which still creates new men
> shall looke, & on hyme soe, then arte's a lyer
> yf from a little spark he rise not fier.   (11–16)

Except for the possible contrastive significance arising from the upgraded emphasis on 'your' in line 14, the enjambment here serves only
to maintain an unflagging high *sentence* appropriate to the ceremonial
nature of the occasion, a speech 'in the behalfe of the two noble Brothers sr Robert & sr Henrye Rich, now Earles of warwick and Hollande'
(H&S 8:382).

26 Herford and Simpson (11:64) cite in connection with this poem Jonson's
attack on Daniel and Campion in his conversations with Drummond.
It is not clear from either Campion's *Observations in the Art of English
Poesie* (1602) or Daniel's *Defence of Ryme*, that 'A Fit' quarrels with
either. Jonson's disagreement with Campion may have derived from the
latter's insistence that normal phrase rhythm never be violated by metrical set. All the verse cited by Campion exhibits this correspondence, and
Campion himself calls for this (53). In this respect Campion is regres-
sive, harking back to George Gascoigne's *Certayne Notes of Instruction
Concerning the Making of Verse or Ryme in English* (1575), which insists
on the same rule. John Thompson's informative but over-schematic notion of an evolution in the mid-sixteenth century from this rule toward
acceptance of an interplay between metrical set and phrase rhythm
would place Jonson alongside Sidney in exploiting the latter. Thompson's thesis is of limited interest in connection with Jonson, however,
and also misleading, since Thompson employs a metrical model in
which deviation occurs between the metrical set and normal speech
rhythm. As I have shown, the crucial deviance occurs in Jonson between normal speech rhythm and deviant speech rhythm, with the oc-
currence of the former signalled by its correspondence with metrical set.

27 D. Robert Ladd has shown that emphasis which is not part of a contrastive pair is possible. Ladd admits an essential rule of contrastivity,
namely that it comes into existence when the context of the utterance
demands it. When it does not demand it this means that emphasis remains, but is noncontrastive. Ladd's discussion allows me to distinguish
'normal' emphasis from deviant emphasis, and to avoid the assumption
that every emphasis is necessarily contrastive.

28 Similar remarks are invited by the verses appended to Alice Sutcliffe's
Mediation on Man's Mortalitie (1634) (M40):

> When I had read
>   your holy *Meditations*,
> And in them view'd
>   th'*uncertainty* of *Life*,

The *motives*, and the true *Spurres*
to all good *Nations*. (1–6)

These lines illustrate negatively the principle that enjambment, like medial juncture and emphasis, takes on significance only in a context
where thematic significance grants it to them, a principle also negatively
illustrated in the Elegies that Jonson (possibly) wrote in imitation of
Donne which have been included in *Vnder-wood*. The couplets are generally endstopped and do not work to reinforce or shift emphasis to
words otherwise left unforegrounded by syntax. Some of this results
from the poems' continued repetition of the same ideas: in U38, for example, the lady's anger, the speaker's repentance, his plea for mercy, his
insistence that in giving mercy she imitates God, etc. Such redundancies
make impossible the interplay between the expected and the unexpected
necessary for contrastive emphasis.

29 Compare the opening lines in M18, 'To the most noble, and aboue his
Titles, Robert, Earle of Somerset': 'They are not those, are present with
theyre face, / And clothes, and guifts, that only do thee grace / At these
thy Nuptials; but, whose heart, and thought / Do wayte vpon thee: and
theyre Loue not bought.'

30 M11, 'To the Right Noble Tom, Tell-Troth of his trauailes, the Coryate
of Odcombe,' illustrates Jonson's delight in reeling off strings of nonsense similar to the comic list. Here, the pretence to causal relevance
only serves to highlight its absence. The 'bonny bouncing booke' (86) is
brought forth like a 'daughter,' doubtless so that Jonson could rhyme it
with 'author,' which leads the poet to wonder whether the book is not
the author's son as well; which elicits the notion that Jove's son who
was Bacchus was carried in his thigh, while Minerva sprung out of his
head, which entails the injunction 'be / Ever his thighes male then, and
his braines *Shee*.' Which leads in turn to ... the end of the poem. U51,
'Lord BACONS Birth-day' gives us a similar list but put to serious purposes: 'Pardon, I read it in thy face, the day / For whose returnes, and
many, all these pray: / And so doe I. This is the sixtieth yeare / Since
Bacon, and thy Lord was borne, and here; / Sonne to the grave wise
Keeper of the Seale, / Fame, and foundation of the English Weale.' Paratactic structure here generates a sense of the greatness and fullness of
the event.

31 Compare the misogynist epigram 'To a Friend' (E83): 'To put out the
word, whore, thou do'st me woo, / Throughout my booke. 'Troth put
out woman too.'

32 Karcevskij introduced the structural linguistics of Saussure to the Russian formalist critics (P. Steiner 419). The standard expositions of Saussurian linguistics to which this, necessarily truncated, account is indebted include those of Hjelmslev, Benveniste, Greimas, and Jakobson and Halle.

33 The same slide from payment as remission of debt into payment as punishment or revenge occurs in Worcester's speech in *1 Henry IV* (1.3.28off): 'The King will always think him in our debt, / And think we think ourselves unsatisfy'd, / Till he hath found a time to pay us home: / And see already how he doth begin / To make us strangers to his looks of love.'

34 Compare E41, 'On Gypsee': 'GYPSEE, new baud, is turn'd physitian, / And get more gold, then all the colledge can: / Such her quaint practise is, so it allures, / For what she gaue, a whore; a baud, shee cures.' Two different meanings of 'practice' are here distinguished by the two meanings of 'quaint' in order for both to be linked ironically together: 'quaint' as female pudendum (cf *queynte* in Chaucer [Robinson ed 972]), and as unusual. E13, 'To Doctor Empirick,' offers a less resonant pun on 'scape' (escape), where the poet offers a cock to Aesculapius to celebrate a double freedom: 'From my diseases dangers, and from thee.'

35 The following epigram, E118, 'On Gvt,' displays similar transformations. The pun on which the epigram turns is the 'meate,' which Gut 'tasteth ouer, twise': both food for gluttony and object of lust. Gut's belly thus becomes a point of synonymic intersection: It can 'change a sin, / Lust it comes out, the gluttony went in' (5–6). Compare also E24, 'To the Parliament,' where Jonson appears both to charge that parliament has made men vile and to absolve it of this charge: 'There's reason good, that you good lawes should make: / Mens manners ne're were viler, for your sake.' The second line retroactively elicits a parallel double meaning in the first line: (1) one can expect parliament to make good law because it has not made men vile; (2) parliament should make good laws to compensate for the evil it has brought men to.

36 This epigram is one of several in which Jonson discusses the nature of reading and judging, and distinguishes improper versions of both. E94 accompanies a copy of Donne's own satires to the countess of Bedford, and E123, 'To the Same [Beniamin Rvdyerd],' distinguishes (and reunites) the functions of writer and critic.

37 Jonson was no lover of one sort of homonymic slide, namely the paradox, which makes 'A Song' (U36) rather anomalous. The Lover's argument that love is made best in the shade is reversed when the Mistress

says that love is the light of the world, 'Yet he himselfe is but a sparke' (8). Lovers die in order to live and live in order to die, and the Chorus concludes with other love paradoxes. A second meaning is generated by a first which yet contradicts it: this is the sequence of the poem.

38 Plutarch's *Consolation to Apollonius*: 'The gods have put life into our hands by a fatal necessity, and there is no prefixed time when what is so deposited will be required of us, as the brokers know not when their pawns will be demanded' (Briggs '*Epigrams* and *Forest*' 173). Jonson saw the possibilities of the loan repayment metaphor for both elegiac and satirical uses.

39 Such paradoxes are really form of the classical 'liar's paradox,' in that they exist to turn the resources of syllogistic reasoning back on themselves; see McCanles ('Paradox'); also Malloch and Colie ('Same Paradoxes').

40 For discussions of metaphor that turn the literal/metaphorical distinction into an unstable dialectic, see Jacques Derrida 'White Mythology,' Paul de Man *Allegories of Reading*, and Michael McCanles 'The Literal and the Metaphorical.' In this connection a commendatory poem appended to a book of translations (M33) by Edward Filmer (1629) exemplifies the unfolding of an argument as a series of tropes troping one another. Also M44, 'A Song of Welcome to King Charles,' where the king and the spring become metaphors for each other through the relays of various aspects of both.

41 On 'unmetaphoring' see Colie ('*Ecchoing Song*' 79, 84, and passim).

42 Cf the opening lines of E64, 'To the Same [Robert Earle of Salisbvrie]': 'Not glad, like those that haue new hopes, or sutes, / With thy new place, bring I these early fruits / Of loue, and what the golden age did hold / A treasure, art: contemn'd in th'age of gold.'

43 F6, 'To the Same [Celia],' explores a similar use-plus-denial of money metaphors to mediate the wealth of kisses lovers bestow on each other. The impulse to tabulation and statistical rigour, which the speaker attributes to 'the curious' (19), is played off against lovers who spend kisses lavishly. Here the speaker both exploits and discounts the metaphor of wealth. See also M4, 'The Phoenix Analysde,' where its subject is the turtle-dove metaphor itself. It is not '*Fable*, / If a *Bird* so amiable, / Do turne into a Woman' (2–4). This metamorphosis in turn means that the bird 'Proue(s) of his *Mistres*' Feature, / But a bare *Type* and *Figure*' (7–8). The lady proves the fable of the turtle-dove true, while the fable becomes in turn (mere) metaphor figuring inadequately the lady.

44 Comedy and pathos are both present in U8, 'The Houre-glasse,' an ex-

ample of that form of petrarchism called anti-petrarchism which takes lurid erotic metaphors literally. Thus 'The body ... / Of one that lov'd / And in his Mistress' flame, playing like a flye, / turn'd to cinders by her eye' is entombed as ashes in the hour-glass. The conceit that sees in restless dust a metaphor for (because caused by) erotic passion would seem to argue that any lover that loves so intensely that he risks incineration by the flames of passion must deservedly abide the droll logic of metaphysical conceit, by which anything can turn into anything.

CHAPTER TWO

1 In *The Case Is Altered* nobility is a matter of family relationship, and as such runs oblique to Jonson's perspective on the issue of vera nobilitas in his maturer work. When, for instance, nobly born sons and daughters throw off the 'clothing' of low status they reveal not true nobility but only blood affiliation.

2 Medieval writing contains extensive treatments of the nature of nobility couched often in the form of debate concerning the three estates (Mohl). A major source of medieval discussions is Boethius' *Consolation of Philosophy*, where later writers could find unexceptionable, mainstream versions of the vera nobilitas argument: honour is paid to men not because of their rank but because of their virtue, honour bestowed on the dishonourable only discloses their lack of honour (2: prose 6), and praise of noble status is praise of one's ancestors (3: prose 6). In addition to Mohl other guides and surveys of medieval treatments include Cameron, Vogt, and Baskerville. Jonson appears considerably less indebted to medieval than to classical formulations, nor do the former, with their emphasis on distinctions between honour awarded by man and God respectively, which Watson features in his study, appear to have any echoes in Jonson's writing.

3 The concept is usually mentioned in passing, and this marks its pale significance for Jonson's twentieth-century readers. Notable exceptions are Isabel Rivers' judicious discussion, and Gabriele Jackson's brief treatment. Unlike Jackson, who finds Jonson affirming the traditional notion that true nobility will always be found among scions of noble families (103–5), Rivers is cognizant of the ambiguities implicit in Jonson's allegiance to aristocratic patrons (21ff). My main deviation from Rivers' perspective – and it is radical – is that for me Jonson's concern with the vera nobilitas argument was by no means limited to the context of patron-client relations. On the contrary, Jonson specifically sought to dis-

tance himself from this sort of relationship, for reasons that this study
develops at large: in particular, his aspiration to equal treatment as a
member of an aristocracy of humanist virtue. See also Maclean 58 and
McEuen 52–3.

4 Kennedy in his studies of classical rhetorical theory treats the topic of
true nobility as something of little importance. He says at one point
(101) that 'in political oratory, if a man did not have ancestors to give
him a claim to good character he was allowed a good deal of freedom in
dilating on his personal virtues,' as if the latter tack were a rhetorical
option casually taken, instead of being a major point of argument for
new men like Marius (in Sallust's *Jugurthine Wars*) and Cicero.

5 By referring to the constituents of noble status – titles, coats of arms,
clothes, genealogies, manors and palaces, as well as privileges – as the
signs of a purported inner true nobility, I am giving these a significative
function within a social code. I am also presuming that such a code
would allow successful investigation into the minimal units and differences that define these units (which constitute any semiotic code), although I do not undertake such an investigation in this study.

6 G.K. Hunter in his study of the courtier poet John Lyly speaks without
further comment of 'the obsessive Humanist question about the nature
of true nobility' (Hunter 121), a relegation of the idea to the limbo of
clichés matched, more surprisingly, by C.L. Barber's sole parenthetical
mention of it embedded in one of the major studies of the idea of honour in the Renaissance (Barber 81). John E. Mason's examination of
Renaissance and eighteenth-century books of courtesy and advice to
princes notes repeatedly, and with apparent fatigue, the fact that such
books open with a 'usual' statement about the true sources of noble status (Mason 168). In 1905 A. Smythe-Palmer published a 516-page anthology of texts from earliest times down to the end of the nineteenth
century on gentility, nobility, and the vera nobilitas argument. As a survey this anthology's very extensiveness confirms the common view that
the history of the argument consists of a series of repetitions of the same
idea the very universality of which astonishes when it does not simply
bore. Such extracting suggests, however, that the real significance of the
vera nobilitas argument can only be discovered when read in the context
of whole texts, where the structural dialectics constituting the argument
can alone be disclosed.

7 H.I. Marrou confirms Jaeger's central judgment when he says that
'Greek culture was originally a privilege reserved for an aristocracy of
warriors' (24), and that 'almost to the end of its history, the education of

antiquity was to retain many of the features which it received from its knightly and aristocratic origin' (28).

8 Jaeger cites Theognis and Pindar as idealizers of an aristocratic norm already past, and both poets argue the superiority of inherited nobility against the encroachment of low-born upstarts (1:198ff). Jaeger sees Pindar as the champion of 'the aristocratic educational tradition' against 'the new rational spirit' inspiring the ascendant city states (218). A central question for him was 'whether the true virtue of men can be learnt, or only inherited by blood.' Pindar initiates one version of the vera nobilitas argument when he poses inborn talent against education. The latter takes on a negative connotation for Pindar, since it results from mere training, whereas talent he sees as transmissible from generation to generation in aristocratic families. Pindar exhibits a preference for 'the wise skill [that] will wax greater for its innocence' (Olympia 7; Pindar 21). 'Innocent' denotes, presumably, 'The wise man [who] knows many things in his blood; the vulgar are taught. / They will say anything. They clatter vainly like crows / against the sacred bird of Zeus' (Olympia 2; 8). Clearly 'If men are brave, or wise, ... by the divinity / in them' (Olympia 9; 28) then education alone cannot make a person a member of the *aristoi*: 'No thing, neither devious fox / nor loud lion, may change the nature born in his blood' (Olympia 11; 35).

9 John Ferne in *The Blazon of Gentrie* (1586), 4, adds a different perspective on the originary conferral of honours on founders of noble dynasties, one that highlights such honours as a form of praise, that is, of epideictic rhetoric.

10 Jaeger 2:247: 'If the rule of the best men and women is to be founded on the best education, the best education in its turn demands the best natural abilities. The age of Plato was familiar with that principle, chiefly from the sophists. But the sophists simply took *physis* as they found it, without thinking of producing it by the deliberate policy. Breeding for quality was really a relic of the aristocratic code of early Greece.'

11 The *de regimine principum* is the genre of oratory generally concerned with advice to princes and other rulers (Gilbert). Arguments regarding true nobility were sometimes made in such treatises, preeminently in the Renaissance in Erasmus' *Education of a Christian Prince* and Sir Thomas Elyot's *The Governour*, but they were not a dominant characteristic of the genre. Jonson's poetry generally lacks interest in the subject, though there are exceptions.

12 Isocrates (1:49): 'for it is through this training that you can soonest be-

come such a man as we have assumed that one must be who is to perform properly the duties of a king, and to govern the state as he should.'

13 See Beard and Crawford (49) for the transformation during the late republican period of the notion of *nobiles* from an inherited aristocracy to something attained by winning the consulship. Whereas members of patrician families achieved this highest office by reason of that fact, as Cicero showed one could achieve aristocratic status, in reverse, by achieving the consulship.

14 Plutarch in fact says that his orations argue 'him guilty of an uncontrollable appetite for distinction, his cry being evermore that arms should give place to the gown, and the soldier's laurel to the tongue' (Plutarch *Lives* 1071).

15 Seneca's debt to Cicero appears clear when he says in *De beneficiis* 'There are goods of the mind, goods of the body, and goods of fortune' (*Moral Essays* 3:327).

16 Seneca presents this position in *De constantia sapientis* (*Moral Essays* 1).

17 For this reason, various interpretations of the dominant outlines of Jonson's career and character that envision him directed by the stoic ideal of the 'centred self' are, I think, in need of qualification. Thomas M. Greene in an influential article has set the direction for other interpretations of Jonson's ethical ideal founded on stoic withdrawal ('Centered Self'). This influence is particularly strong in Richard Peterson's study of Jonson's poetry and in Stanley Fish's very suggestive but flawed study of Jonson's poetry as a key to his biography ('Authors-Readers'). There are certainly times when Jonson appears to believe that 'he that will honest be, may quitt the Court, / Virtue, and Soveraintie, they not consort,' as he translates from the *Pharsalia* in 'A speech out of Lucane' (M50:17–18). Disgust with the slippery promotions offered by the life of the courtier has an honourable history in sixteenth-century poetry, as Wyatt, Gascoigne, Sidney, Spenser, Chapman, Shakespeare, and Donne collectively tell us. *Cynthia's Revels* and Jonson's many satires of courtly pretences, particularly in the *Epigrammes*, tell us no less. Yet Jonson achieved something that none of these poets, except Wyatt, could claim: namely (at least under James) a prominence and welcome in aristocratic and royal circles that need to be remembered in judging both Jonson's praise of the virtues of true nobility and his attacks on their absence.

18 But see endnote 32, chapter 4.

19 See two articles in Hanning and Rosand: Javitch '*Il Cortegiano*' and Saccone '*Grazia*.' Javitch makes the argument – relevant to Jonson's

own adroitly handled relations with the royal court – that *sprezzatura* marks the flexibility necessary for the aspiring courtier to avoid offending his prince. Saccone says 'sprezzatura is the test the courtier must pass in order to be admitted to this club, to obtain the recognition of his peers' (60). Both approaches are faithful to Castiglione's own position, which is that *sprezzatura* is the art of appearing noble. Jonson's position is, on the other hand, that those who work only to appear noble always do it badly.

20 Frank Whigham's treatment of the values and motivations of social mobility in the late Renaissance entirely from the perspective of conduct handbooks skews his presentation toward this kind of disguise, one-up-manship and game-playing. Nevertheless, within the context of this bias his comments on such matters are often shrewd. Regarding Castiglione's *sprezzatura*, he sees how the nobility's adherence to an aristocracy founded on natural gifts denies efficacy to learning (Pindar's argument), while at the same time inadvertently allowing a space for education in noble graces to be opened up: 'The gentleman is presumed to act in certain ways; the limiting case would have it that only a gentleman *can* act in those ways. But the symbolic referent here is ascriptive identity, an identity that by definition cannot be achieved by human effort. As a result there arose a basic governing principle of the display of *effortlessness*, Castiglione's *sprezzatura*, designed to imply the natural or given status of one's social identity and to deny any earned character, any labor or arrival from a social elsewhere' (33).

21 See also *The English Courtier, and the Cuntrey-gentleman* (1586) in Hazlitt. Henry Peacham in 1622 could argue that nobility is inherited from one's ancestors (A4r), that it is public recognition of personal achievement (2), that it is a matter of political responsibility (2), and that it is inherent, natural and does not depend on noble titles (4) – thereby demonstrating either that he saw no contradictions among these various points, or that he yielded to ideological pressure to ignore such contradictions.

22 Major 241 is generally accurate in his comment on Sir Thomas Elyot, who 'like the other humanists ... seems to have regarded "virtue" simply as a term for certain fundamental principles of right conduct which, operating together, justify man's claim to rank high in the universal order.'

23 Kelso makes some distinctions important at this juncture. The first is between 'nobility' and 'gentility' (18ff), which by the end of the sixteenth century came to distinguish greater and lesser nobility. The former in-

cluded the ranks of king, prince, duke, marquess, earl, viscount, and baron; the latter, knight, esquire, and gentleman. Gentility was an inherited family relationship, and while noble title died with its possessor or could be revoked, it could also be inherited in some cases. The second distinction is between 'nobility native' and 'nobility dative' (21ff). The former is inherited, the latter conferred. In the context of this study I do not distinguish between nobility and gentility, since all these ranks participate in, and represent, aristocratic establishments in general, and as such fall indifferently within the purview of the vera nobilitas argument.

24 Selden touches on the vera nobilitas theme in passing. He says, for instance, of Sparta and Persia in classical times, that 'both states conclud[ed] *Nobilitie* from their *Ancestors worth*, which hath its ground in the naturall supposition of *likeness* twixt *Children* and those which *get them*' ([B4r]). Later Selden says, 'Virtue plainly ennobleth not civilly but is a deserving cause of it only, whereof the Prince must iudge. If *Honor* and deserving *Vertue* accompanie not each other, its his Fault or Error. They should alwaies so' (c1r). Chute (219) records that in the second edition Selden listed the honour of poet laureate, which he had neglected in the first: 'Thus have I ... performed a promise to you, my beloved Ben Jonson ... And so you both fully know what concerns it, and your singular excellency in the art most eminently deserves it.' On archaeological and antiquarian studies at this time see Woolf.

25 Ferry argues that Jonson's praise by citing 'the unornamented name' (140) is an attempt to ground this praise on historical fact external to the poem's statement, a strategy different from that of Petrarchan poetry, in which what is praised is the projection of the poet's own ideals. The epitaph 'On Margaret Ratcliffe' (E40) literalizes this notion by spelling out Margaret Ratcliffe's name as the opening letters of each line, that is, filling out her name with the text of her praise.

26 Compare E76, 'On Lvcy Covntesse of Bedford,' where a catalogue of unlocalized aristocratic virtues is first given, only to be attached to the countess at the poem's end: 'Such when I meant to faine, and wish'd to see, / My *Muse* bad, *Bedford* write, and that was shee' (17–18).

27 U22, 'An Elegie,' offers another example of Jonson's contrasting not individual terms but rather possible relations among them. The opening three stanzas develop an elaborate interplay between beauty and virtue, free choice and constraint. The speaker says that though he will speak of the lady's virtue not her beauty, the one turns out to constitute the other; and though this beauty 'move, / And draw, and conquer all mens

love, / This subjects you to love of one' (6–8). These conjunctions between terms that putatively exclude each other exemplify how Jonson contrasts such exclusion with the reciprocity of mutual implication.

28 See E93, 'To Sir Iohn Radcliffe,' the last remaining of several brothers militant, 'that art all their valour, all their spirit, / And thine owne goodnesse to encrease thy merit' (9–10). The contrastive relationships between the virtues of war and peace Jonson expounds in several other poems, including E95, 'To Sir Henrie Savile': 'Although to write be lesser then to doo, / It is the next deed, and a great one too' (25–6); and E110, 'To Clement Edmonds, on his Caesars Commentaries obserued, and translated': [Caesar] wrote, with the same spirit that he fought' (8).

29 Swinburne was offended by the poem's ending – as he was offended by most of Jonson's poetry – calling it 'a horrible jolt' (113). Swinburne's lack of appreciation is, I suppose, due to his not recognizing how central such isolated elements are to Jonson's poetic practice.

30 Also Epistle 32: 'what a noble thing it is to round out your life before death comes, and then await in peace the remaining portion of your time, claiming nothing for yourself, since you are in possession of the happy life; for such a life is not made happier for being longer' (1:231). In this connection see also Donaldson 'Jonson's Ode' 147.

31 Hollander, who has written incisively on enjambment (*Vision* 101ff), notes the thematic import of some of the run-on lines in this poem (177–8).

32 Peterson reads these lines against the background of classical topoi having to do with the work of art's displaying the labour that went into its construction (*Imitation and Praise* 160ff), and he is doubtless correct regarding the poem on Shakespeare. It is indicative of the subtlety of Jonson's wit that in the Cary-Morison Ode he can 'turn' the direction of his *versus* toward the literal turn of enjambment and make out of that conversion a wholly new set of meanings. See in this connection Susanne Woods' article on the poem, where she treats the three-part stanza groupings as reflecting in various ways the poem's content.

33 Paul Fry sees that the references to title and merit in the Cary-Morison Ode raise for Jonson not only the question of what truly constitutes nobility, but the concomitant question of what constitutes true poetry of praise (21–2).

34 Hollander (*Vision* 178) sees the enjambment as expressing the poet's 'private and public roles and duties.'

35 Jonson's close association with the Roe family is detailed by Miles; on William Roe see 131–2.

36 Machiavelli in his dedication of the *Discourses* to his friends Buondel-monti and Rucellai: 'I have chosen not those who are princes, but those who because of their countless good qualities deserve to be; not those able to load me with offices, honors, and riches, but those who, though unable, would like to do so. If men wish to judge justly, they must es-teem those who are liberal, not those who merely have the power to be so, and likewise those who know how to rule a kingdom, not those who, without knowing how, have the power to do it' (1:188–9).

37 'The fact that, in Horace's theory, the internal characteristics of the poem are determined largely, if not exclusively, by the external demands of the audience brings his theory very close to specifically rhetorical ap-proaches. In theories of this kind, the determining factor in the produc-tion of the work is not an internal principle of structural perfection, but rather an acceptance of the assumption that all those elements are in-cluded in the work that will be susceptible of producing the desired ef-fect upon the audience envisaged, arranged in an order calculated to achieve the maximum degree of that effect' (Weinberg 1:71–2).

38 Weinberg inaccurately says that 'the character of the orator (or poet)' 'is absent from Horace' (ibid). Actually, one can say that Jonson's transla-tion, read in the context of the rest of his poetry, makes the moral char-acter of the poet the central focus. It is easy to miss this dimension of the treatise if one's interest is drawn to matters properly the province of poetic form, genre, and decorum, as it was for Weinberg in his survey of Italian Renaissance criticism, or for W.K. Wimsatt, Jr, who finds the discussion of the poet almost an afterthought (Wimsatt and Brooks 94).

39 In order to minimize confusion, I adopt the following protocol for cita-tion: (1) Jonson's final version (derived from Heinsius' version) is usu-ally cited; (2) Heinsius's own Latin (H&S 8:304–36) is cited only in those cases where Jonson's translation of that Latin is at issue; (3) otherwise I cite the Latin text in the commentary of C.O. Brink (55–72).

40 Brink's commentary on this passage supports the identity between poetic and ethical discriminations central to Jonson's thinking: 'If it is asked how this notion [*quo virtus, quo ferat error.* 'Whether truth may, and whether error bring'] differs from the *deceat* of the first half of the verse, the answer, I suggest, is that poetic virtue (*areté*) need not differ at all from poetic appropriateness (*to prepon*). H[orace] however distinguishes, conveniently for him, between the approved effects of poetry and the ideal *uirtus* of the *perfectus poeta* and the error personified and carica-tured in the *usesanus poeta*' (337) [italics in original].

41 On this complex dimension of Horace's thought, see Manly 48ff.

42 Brink's paraphrase of this passage dovetails matters of poetic form with the discriminations required of the poet, and points in the direction of Jonson's own agenda: 'Instead of the need for artistry which enables the poet to create a whole, attention is concentrated on the condition that makes such artistry possible. The condition lies in the right choice of his task: he will fail to organize a whole unless such organizing lies in his power. The success of *ars* depends on the right choice of aim, and right choice depends on the degree of native talent. The untiring advocate of craftsmanship ends with a studied paradox by inculcating the need for talent, just as he reflected on the ideal of unity in terms of variety' (122).

43 E125, 'To Sir William Vvedale,' follows the Rudyerd epigrams by one and exhibits similar characteristics. Jonson juggles several differentials in this poem: nature/virtue, primitive times/modern times, soul/body, adoration/idolatry (or flattery), to the end of aligning a series of equivalences that apply to the addressee and negate their undesirable opposites. Thus Uvedale's soul exhibits qualities conferred by both nature and achieved virtue, returning him to primitive perfection, which the poet professes to adore this side idolatry.

44 The early masques up through *The Masque of Queens* (1609) were published with elaborate glosses citing Jonson's sources and the symbolical significance of the mythic figures he drew from these sources. The poems connected with *Loues Martyr* predate all these, but it is not at all uncharacteristic for Jonson to take serious in one work literary materials which he criticizes in others. For Jonson's sources see Talbert.

45 See G. Wilson Knight's discussion of the poems comprising *Loues Martyr* in *The Mutual Flame*.

CHAPTER THREE

1 'Genuine genealogy was cultivated by the older gentry to reassure themselves of their innate superiority over the upstarts; bogus genealogy was cultivated by the new gentry in an effort to clothe their social nakedness, and by the old gentry in the internal jockeying for position in the ancestral pecking order. A lengthy pedigree was a useful weapon in the Tudor battle for status' (Stone 23).

2 For Kenneth Burke, courtship is a form of appeal for acceptance across class lines. Burke's analysis makes overt the hostility that lurks within rhetorical appeals for acceptance, that is identification, and is therefore applicable to Jonson's case: 'Identification is affirmed with earnestness

precisely because there is division. Identification is compensatory to division. If men were not apart from one another, there would be no need for the rhetorician to proclaim their unity' (22). The identification between speaker and audience which rhetoric seeks to create depends on the former's taking on the perspective of the latter, speaking its language and seeing things from its viewpoint: 'You persuade a man only insofar as you can talk his language, by speech, gesture, tonality, order, image, attitude, idea, *identifying* your ways with his. Persuasion by flattery is but a special case of persuasion in general' (55).

3 Parfitt (*Complete Poems* 599) gives Erasmus' *Apophthegmata* as Jonson's immediate source.

4 Relevant here is E5, 'On the Vnion,' which celebrates the union of England and Scotland in the person of James I 'with more truth of state' (2), where the exterior ceremony ('state') truly reflects the union within – an outward symbol of inner unity implicitly defined against the possibility that outward 'state' can in fact disguise the lack of inner unity.

5 It will appear in this chapter that I disagree with Lawrence Danson's argument that Jonson despaired of a central and autonomous self behind the masks donned in society (189). On the contrary, I find that his extensive analysis of these masks necessarily implies the desirability of such a self and its reality as well.

6 Simulation and dissimulation are used here according to Bacon's description in his essay on the subject: 'There be three degrees, of this Hiding, and Vailing of a Mans Selfe. The first *Closenesse, Reseruation,* and *Secrecy*; when a Man leaueth himselfe without Obseruation, or without Hold to be taken, what he is. The second *Dissimulation,* in the *Negatiue*; when a man lets fall Signes, and Arguments, that he is not, that he is. And the third *Simulation,* in the Affirmatiue; when a man industriously, and expressely, faigns, and pretends to be, that he is not' (23).

7 On Jonson's debts to Martial and the differences between his epigrams and those of his contemporaries, see Bruce Smith, 'Ben Jonson's Epigrammes.'

8 Freud discusses censorship, with the correlative concepts of latent and manifest meaning, in chapter 4 of *The Interpretation of Dreams.* And he makes explicit in these connections the challenge to an interpreter similar to that which Jonson's epigrams present to their reader: 'The stricter the censorship, the more far-reaching will be the disguise and the more ingenious too may be the means employed for putting the reader on the

scent of the true meaning' (176). Jonson plays the Freudian analyst in making explicit not only what is concealed, but the logic of this concealment as well.

9 E30, 'To Person Gviltie': 'GVILTIE, be wise; and though thou know'st the crimes / Be thine, I taxe, yet doe not owne my rimes: / 'Twere madnesse in thee, be betray thy fame, / And person to the world; ere I thy name.

10 Guazzo's spokesman comments in a similar vein: 'For seeing others to make no account of them, they beginne to set by them selves, and stirred up with a foolishe disdaine, they put on a Lyons skin, and looke with a sterne and fierce countenance: By means whereof they become hatefull to all men. But if according to the Philosopher they knew that honour did consist, rather in him which honoureth, then in him which is honoured, they would never take upon them so bigly, nor set them selves out so arrogantly, knowing that it is not in their power to be honoured of them selves' (1:155).

11 For Jonson, the man who pretends to be something he is not displays self-contempt. In shunning self-examination he creates the false friendship of mutual flattery classically examined in Plutarch's essay 'How to Tell a Flatterer from a Friend.' Plutarch recognizes that the flatterer has no self to possess: 'But the flatterer, since he has no abiding-place of character to dwell in, and since he leads a life not of his own, but variable and many in one, and, like water that is poured into one receptacle after another, he is constantly on the move from place to place, and changes his shape to fit his receiver' (1:281). See E75, 'On Lippe, the Teacher,' which attacks the Puritans' dislike of plays and players. The Puritans attempt to displace their own 'playing' onto others, and in this they are no different from the rest of the world of phonies, cheats, and cranks that Jonson inveighs against, whose judgment is corrupted, and whose ability to know themselves – or knowing themselves, to acknowledge the information – is nil.

12 Jonson opposes painting and verbal language as distinct modes of mediating the interior person in several poems. M7, which prefaces Thomas Wright's 1604 treatise *The Passions of the minde*, argues that 'To iudge which Passion's false, and which is true, / Betweene the doubtfull sway of Reason', and sense; / 'Tis not your fault, if they shall sense preferre, / Being told there, Reason cannot, Sense may erre' (11–14). The short poem (M25) prefacing the 1616 Shakespeare First Folio that refers to the playwright's picture laments that the engraver 'but haue drawne his wit / As well in brasse, as he hath hit / His face; the Print would then sur-

passe / All, that was euer writ in brasse. / But, since he cannot, Reader, looke / Not on his Picture, but his Booke' (5–10). Jonson compares poetry and painting in *Discoveries* (H&S 8:610) and concludes 'Yet of the Two, the Pen is more noble, then the Pencill. For that can speake to the Understanding; the other, but to the Sense.' And if this is the case then it clear why in the poet's reply to Sir William Burlase (U52), who painted his portrait, he claimed 'You made it a brave piece, but not like me' (15).

13 Barthes *Elements* 10: 'As for collections of objects (clothes, food), they enjoy the status of systems only in so far as they pass through the relay of language, which extracts their signifiers (in the form of nomenclature) and names their signifieds (in the forms of usages or reasons) ... Finally, and in more general terms, it appears increasingly more difficult to conceive a system of images and objects whose *signifieds* can exist independently of language: to perceive what a substance signifies is inevitably to fall back on the individuation of a language: there is no meaning which is not designated, and the world of signifieds is none other than that of language.'

14 On Jonson's judgment of the relative value of the verbal and visual, see Livingston, Gordon, and Orgel and Strong. The latter's attempt to mend the quarrel between Jonson and Jones may be perfectly justified on philosophical grounds ('For the Renaissance artist, the relation between verbal statements and visual representations was direct and unquestioned ... Pictures, that is, expressed in a visual fashion a meaning that was conceived verbally' [1:31]), but this attempt steps around the ineluctable fact that for Jonson, when the spectacle came in performance to outweigh verbal translation, spectacle's subordination to verbal discourse was inverted.

15 On Inigo Jones' functions and offices under James I and Charles I, see Parry and Summerson, both of whom give accounts of Jones' very real architectural achievements to balance out Jonson's tendentious account. Jonson's attacks on Jones seem to have cost him any further court favour: 'He was never again asked to prepare a masque for the royal family. From this time forward Jones reigned alone. Although Jonson was still occasionally commissioned by old friends who offered him the writing of country entertainments from time to time, his twenty-seven year career as the royal masque-maker was over' (Miles 251).

16 'In an important sense, the Court masque under Jonson and Jones was a theatre of mysteries ... The element of wonder which was the essential accompaniment of these rites was incomparably provided by Inigo Jones

through his mastery of light and motion and the revelation of the transformation scene, when the stage revolved or the shutters opened to discover the masquers in a new landscape, radiant and sublime. Music and the intricacies of formal patterns of dance provided the harmony which coalesced with the visual magic to induce a state of consciousness that bordered on the visionary, a state in which truths concerning the power of majesty could be seen and known to be true, validated on the instant before the Court's believing eyes, and affirmed by the final dance of concord and assent in which all participated' (Parry 42–3).

17 The concept of supplementation is derived from Jacques Derrida's development of it in *Of Grammatology*. See also Culler (*Deconstruction* 102ff) and Harari ('Critical Factions' 34).

18 Norbert Elias in his discussion of the French aristocracy at the time of Louis XIV argues that aristocratic status had no meaning except in terms of the outer signs in which it was displayed, and that extravagant display was an indigenous constituent of such status.

19 Edward B. Partridge ('Symbolism') notes Jonson's attacks on clothing in his plays, but argues the conclusion that for Jonson 'the mind is more important than the body because the understanding is nobler than sense experience, and the reality which is eternal, more important than the appearances which are transitory' (409). Partridge takes the position argued often in the Jonson literature that the poet held to a simplistic value dichotomy, in which inner is 'good' and outer is 'bad.'

20 'For I do not regard the colour of the garments that clothe the body. In rating a man I do not rely upon eyesight; I have a better and surer light, by which I may distinguish the false from the true. Let the soul discover the good of the soul' ('Ad Gallionem de Vita Beata' *Moral Essays* 2:103).

21 The anonymous I.M., writer of *Health to the Gentlemanly profession of Seruingmen: or, The Seruingmans Comfort ...* (London 1598), challenges the reader 'yf he can rightly discipher the nature of euery golde Lace, and the vertue of euery silke Stocking at the first blush, nay, after long perusing the same, yf he can shew me by their royall Roabes, and gorgious Garmentes, the Noble man, and Gentleman, from the Verser, Setter, Cros bieter, and Cunnie-catcher, then I will yeelde to his saying, and learne some of his cunning, that I may euer hereafter know my duetie the better, and spare my Cappe & Legge from such mates of no merite, as many tymes I lende them vnto unknowne' (124–5).

22 E11, 'On Some-Thing, That Walkes Some-where,' literalizes in another way the distinction between inner and outer as courtly pretensions par-

ody it: 'At court I met it, in clothes braue enough, / To be a courtier; ... A lord, it cryed, buried in flesh, and blood' (1–2, 5). Burial inside one's body ('Good Lord, walke dead still,' 8) respects the distinction between inner and outer, making the body a grave signifying the death of the spirit within. E21, 'On Reformed Gam-ster,' on the other hand, gives us an outward conversion impelled by merely outward causes: having been beaten up, Gamester now affects Puritan behaviour, and the poet concludes 'The bodies stripes, I see, the soule may saue.' The outward appearance does not reflect any real internal conversion, but rather compensates for its lack.

23 'While the mystery of sex relations, which leads to the rhetoric of courtship, is grounded in the communication of beings *biologically* estranged, it is greatly accentuated by the purely *social* differentiations which, under the division of human labor, can come to distinguish the "typically masculine" from the "typically feminine." Similarly, the conditions for "mystery" are set by *any* pronounced social distinctions, as between nobility and commoners, courtiers and king, leader and people, rich and poor, judge and prisoner at the bar, "superior race" and underprivileged "races" or minorities ... And all such "mystery" calls for a corresponding rhetoric, in form quite analogous to sexual expression: for the relations between classes are like the ways of courtship, rape, seduction, jilting, prostitution, promiscuity, with variants of sadistic torture or masochistic invitation to mistreatment' (*Rhetoric* 115).

24 Courtship is the subject of a poem (M3) by Jonson that appears in the anthology *England's Parnassus* (1600). 'Gold is a sutor, neuer took repulse' opens the poem's allegory, which runs through the various obstacles it overcomes, concluding 'Where Gold's the Motiue, women haue no Nay' (18). Sexual seduction becomes a metaphor for the pursuit of courtly favour: 'It thawes the frostiest, and most stiffe disdaine: / Muffles the clearnesse of Election, / Straines fancie vnto foule Apostacie, / And strikes the quickest-sighted Iudgement blinde' (13–16).

25 Gilles Deleuze, writing about *A la Recherche du temps perdu* wherein the equation of social snobbism and erotic desire is explored in dense detail, speaks of the deceptions wrought by mysterious signs emitted indifferently by social superiors and desired women: 'We think that the "object" itself has the secret of the signs it emits. We scrutinize the object, we return to it in order to decipher the sign ... [The hero] thinks that those who emit signs are also those who understand them and possess their code' (26, 27). This pursuit is the desire to possess the illusory secret depth which the signs of aristocratic status meretriciously an-

nounce by concealing, a vertiginous attempt to simulate a mystery by covertly revealing its dissimulation.

26 Juliet Flower MacCannel and Jean-Louis Baudry have written essays which explore the illusory promise of an interior person which masquing and role-playing make. Both have made suggestions that I expand on in discussing Jonson and the semiosis of aristocratic establishments in general.

27 E29, 'To Sir Annval Tilter,' pillories the knight's 'late sharpe deuice' (3), that is, impresa, which Jonson finds as extrinsic to his witlessness as the wine that runs through city conduits during festivals is to the conduits themselves. See also E48, 'On Mvngril Esqvire': 'His bought armes MVNG' not lik'd; for his first day / Of bearing them in field, he threw 'hem away: / And hath no honor lost, our Due'llists say.'

28 In the dedication of *Volpone* Jonson disclaims attacks on specific individuals, and wonders aloud at him who, in accusing the playright, 'might not, either ingenuously have confessed, or wisely dissembled his disease?' (Wilkes 3:xii). The playwright's contract with the audience in the induction to *Bartholomew Fair* specifies that he intends 'to delight all, and to offend none. Provided they have either the wit or the honesty to think well of themselves' (4:9). Asper, the fictive author of *Every Man Out* and the poet's *alter ego* which he seeks to distinguish from the envious Macilente, claims that 'I do not this [present this play], to beg your patience, / Or servilely to fawn on your applause, / Like some dry brain, despairing in his merit' (1:287). Robert Wiltenburg argues that the major vice Jonson attacks is self-love, a position which ignores the evidence that for Jonson there are different kinds of self-love, one of which equals self-loathing.

29 Jonson extends this form of insult in the epigram addressed to Inigo Jones (M36), where Jonson assures him that he is too insignificant for him to attack. Like Martial, whose epigram (12.61) Jonson imitates here, the poet unmasks such fear as a projection of Jones' self-importance, which Jonson sees generated by an underlying sense of inferiority.

30 One poem takes up the critiques developed by these mid-century treatises, 'On a Robbery' (E8), in which a courtier, having robbed someone, is immune to prosecution because 'for this money was a courtier found' (3). His victim declares Jonson's own conclusion, namely that 'the courtier is become the greater thief' (6).

31 Gardiner and Epp employ a statistical analysis of Jonson's poems and plays to arrive at the conclusion that he exhibits a negative attitude to-

ward the 'lower classes' and a positive attitude toward the gentry. They discover a negative attitude toward the titled nobility in the plays, matched by a positive attitude in the poetry. Illustrating the weakness of their method, they conclude that poets were for Jonson included in the class of 'gentry' (73), and thereby confuse Jonson's humanist agenda for poets with the *de facto* class divisions, which of course denied poets (like himself) inclusion in the gentry.

32 In an epigram on the death of Jonson's friend Sir John Roe (E32), the distinction between foreign dangers of death and death at home turns out to be no distinction at all. One may find death in one's own bed as easily as becoming on foreign soil the victim of 'Seas, serenes, swords, shot, sickness' (10). The appearance of distinction hides the fact that it is appearance, the fact, in short, that it hides nothing at all. Simulation dissimulates simulation as well as dissimulation. To grasp the 'point' of this epigram is likewise to grasp the moral perspective that funds the epigram, and within which the ironic dissipation of difference announces itself.

33 Thus Mime in E129, a zany who is the talk of the town ('That, not a paire of friends each other see, / But the first question is, when one saw thee?' [1–2]), assumes that this notoriety is complimentary when it is not: 'O, runne not proud of this. Yet, take thy due. / Thou dost out-zany COKELY, POD; nay, GVE: / And thine owne CORIAT too. But (would'st thou see) / Men loue thee not for this: They laugh at thee' (15–18). Mime's mistake lies in his inability to 'see' that laughter can be a sign not only of approbation but of scorn.

34 Epigrams exhibiting a similar import include the following: E10, 'To my Lord Ignorant,' who believes that 'Poet' is 'a terme of shame,' being ignorant that 'Lord' may be unmasked as a signifier whose signified is – what else? – ignorance; and E100, 'On Play-wright': 'PLAY-WRIGHT, by chance, hearing some toyes I'had writ, / Cry'd to my face, they were th'*elixir* of wit: / And I must now beleeue him: for, to day, / Fiue of my iests, then stolne, past him a play.' 'Elixir' is an alchemical term for the philosopher's stone, which then becomes a 'stone' which the plagiarist 'passes.' Actually, *stone* is not mentioned in the epigram, leaving it up to the reader to demonstrate his or her intellectual superiority by perceiving the hidden potential second meaning to *elixir* that the poem's addressee had missed. Finally, there is E6, 'To Alchymists,' who boast their ability to turn base metal into gold, thereby claiming to create new wealth. Jonson turns this claim inside out by suggesting that the pursuit

of such wealth is really a 'willing poverty.' If the alchemists' boasts are not true, then their collection of junk makes them poor; and if their boasts are true then they are still poor: base metals that are transmuted and those that are not are both synonyms (by synecdoche) for poverty.

35 Sara Van Den Berg (*Action* 79ff) argues that Bess of Hardwick lies hidden behind Jonson's epitaph.

36 Jonson referred to Mary Sidney in his conversations with Drummond: 'Sir P. Sidney's mother, Leicester's sister, after she had the little pox, never showed herself in court thereafter but masked' (Parfitt *Complete Poems* 470). She died before her son's own death in 1587, and so it is possible that F8 may refer to her.

37 The ladies who are the subjects of these poems contrast with 'Fine Lady Wovld-Bee' (E62), who fears pregnancy because 'you liue at court: / And there's both losse of time, and losse of sport / In a great belly' (9–11).

38 A similar interplay between a ravaging disease and inner nobility appears in 'An Epitaph on HENRY L. La-ware. To the Passer-by' (U60). The young Henry West, thirteenth baron De La Warr, died at the age of twenty-five (H&S 11:92) from 'a Disease, that lov'd no light / Of honour, nor no ayre of good' and was 'Offended with the dazeling flame / Of Vertue, got aboue his name' (6–7, 9–10). This anthropomorphized disease is motivated by the sort of envy and resentment that Jonson seeks always to exorcise from his discussion of true nobility. And the nobility of the young baron died unimpaired and untouched by his disease. The only thing 'his great Soule envy'd' was that 'it durst have nobilier dy'd' (17–18).

39 Jonson would seem to take up, while altering its import, Castiglione's assertion (through Bembo in book 4 of *The Courtier*) that 'the outwarde beautie [is] a true signe of the inwarde goodnesse, and in bodies this comelines is imprinted more and lesse (as it were) for a marke of the soule, whereby she is outwardly knowne' (599). So, while Jonson might agree that 'the body, where that beautie shineth, is not the fountaine from whence beautie springeth, but rather ... beautie is bodilesse' (604), he clearly eschews any neo-Platonic progress from the physical to the spiritual. Jonson in *Eupheme* shows that contacting the spiritual dimension of Venetia's beauty entails a rejection of her physical beauty because such signs cannot mediate the former, not because, as Bembo suggests, they mediate it all too well.

40 A third poem in the same vein as *Eupheme* and the eulogy for the marchioness of Winchester, but written much earlier (printed in *Loues Martyr*, 1601), is M5, 'Ode *enthousiastikè*':

Her wit as quicke, and sprightfull
As fire; and more delightfull
Then the stolne sports of *Louers*
When night their meeting couers.

Iudgement (adornd with Learning)
Doth shine in her discerning,
Cleare as a naked vestall
Closde in an orbe of Christall. (5–12)

CHAPTER FOUR

1 In E111, one of the two poems Jonson writes to preface Clement Edmonds' translation of Caesar's Commentaries (1609 edition), Jonson concludes by linking the credibility of Caesar, Edmonds, and his own praise
to one another: 'To those [who criticize you] / CAESAR stands vp, as
from his vrne late rose, / By thy great helpe: and doth proclaime by
mee, / They murder him againe, that enuie thee' (11–14).
2 I would therefore disagree with the judgment of T.J.B. Spencer on the
poem, when he finds that it attempts to appear 'well-considered' (39),
'belongs to the minor genre of "Commendatory Poems"' (24), and was
written primarily to aid the sale of the Shakespeare First Folio (27).
3 Earl Miner (138) recognizes in the beginning of the poem on Shakespeare
that Jonson wants to avoid 'praise by the unqualified' because it 'ranks
as dispraise.' But he also thinks Jonson seems to be 'coming through the
door sideways when it is wide open,' which suggests that Miner does not
see how extensive or complicated are the problems of praise that Jonson
here seeks to obviate.
4 The vera nobilitas argument was not apparently a major obsession in
Shakespeare's life. There are, however, several plays in which it receives
more than usual emphasis. The *Henry IV* plays enact a Plinian *paideia*,
wherein the prince of the realm, already designated as the future king,
must yet come to earn his status just as the Son does in *Paradise Lost*:
by merit more than birthright. Two other plays, *King John* and *All's
Well That Ends Well*, likewise explore the argument. *King John* focuses
at the beginning on whether Falconbridge is any less noble for being
born on the wrong side of the blanket (a question Edmund asks in his
first act soliloquy on true nobility in *King Lear*). The vera nobilitas argument makes an extended appearance in the mouth of the king in *All's
Well That Ends Well*, after Helena has been rejected by Bertram because

she lacks gentle birth. The king's reply (2.3.124–38) is a brief compendium of traditional topics.

5 O.B. Hardison, Jr (*Enduring Monument*) has led the way in limiting the range of epideictic rhetoric as it was understood in the Renaissance to the praise and blame of private virtue and vice respectively (39–40 and passim). Barbara Kiefer Lewalski finds that Donne's contemporaries 'identify moral virtue as the proper object of praise' (38), and while James Garrison does not narrow epideixis so explicitly, his treatment of the rhetoric of praise in the seventeenth and eighteenth centuries assumes a similar emphasis. See also Vickers.

6 *De officiis* 10 and passim; *De partitione oratoria* 367–9; *De inventione* 327. Cf also the *Rhetorica ad Herennium* 175.

7 He makes this distinction also in *De partitione oratoria* 365–7; *De inventione* 343–5; *Tusculan Disputations* 467ff.

8 See Harry Caplan's two essays 'The Latin Panegyrics of the Empire' and 'The Decay of Eloquence at Rome in the First Century.'

9 Maus (65–6) holds that this position is dominant for Jonson: 'The moral impulse, the desire to "correct manners" and to "better men," prevails in panegyric over values like representational precision or absolute sincerity. Jonson's attitude here is not idiosyncratic. The Roman moralists appreciate the educational value as well as the dangers of underserved praise.' A similar assertion is made by Dutton (83). Such generalizations are possible only if one assumes that epideictic rhetoric had for Jonson simply the function defined for it by the typical treatise *de regimine principum*. Though Maus discusses the topic of true nobility in Jonson briefly (123ff), she does not see its connection with epideixis.

10 Erasmus put the problem facing a nation living under a monarchy with succinctness: 'The more difficult it is to change your choice, the more circumspectly should your candidate be chosen, or else the rashness of a single hour may spread its retributions over a lifetime. There is no choice, however, in the case of hereditary succession of princes ... Under that condition, the chief hope for a good prince is from his education, which should be especially looked to. In this way the interest in his education will compensate for the loss of the right of election.' (140).

11 H.I. Marrou's statement of the Homeric hero's longing for glory matches du Vair's statement: 'Now, glory, the renown recognized by those who know, the company of the brave, is the measure, the objective recognition, of valour. Hence the impassioned longing for glory, the longing to be hailed as the greatest, which was the mainspring of this knightly ethic. Homer was the first to represent this consciously' (32)

12 Romei cites the same anecdote (218), while Peacham cites a variant (4).

13 It was the link between epideixis and the vera nobilitas argument that lifted the former to a topic of major concern to Jonson. Outside of this context, Jonson's theory and practice of the rhetoric of praise has proved something of a puzzle to his critics. Don E. Wayne feels that the encomiastic epigrams perform only 'an official social function,' and that the 'satiric poems might be read as insertions of the way he really perceived his society' ('Power' 88). Gardiner (*Craftsmanship*) recognizes that for Jonson the value of the praise depends on the authority of the praiser and the merit of the praised (34), but the object of praise – merit rather than birth – she finds to be merely 'conventional humanistic ideals' (39–40). In the most extensive treatment of Jonson's epideictic practice, Peterson (*Imitation*) identifies praise with Jonson's 'distinctive brand of *imitatio*, the process of judicious gathering in, assimilation, and transformation or turning whereby a good writer, and by extension a good man, shapes an original and coherent work of art or a virtuous life' (xiv). Peterson limits the purview of Jonsonian epideixis to the topic of the poet's authority, but otherwise does not take up the implications of Jonson's obsessive consideration of the matter in the poems themselves. Displacements of both epideixis and vera nobilitas away from their central place in Jonson's poetry likewise seem to go together, and apparently for the same reason: there seems to be little to say about either because they both appear impoverished clichés about which little of interest or credibility can be said. Other considerations of praise in Jonson's poetry include those of Guibbory, Ferry, Friedberg, Medine ('Praise and Blame'), Fry (*The Poet's Calling*), and Brady ('Jonson's "To King James"'). Sackton has noted that praise began to be taken seriously as ethical judgment among some of Jonson's contemporary poets at the turn of the century.

14 In U5, 'In the person of Woman-kind. A Song Apologetique,' the female persona rejects praise addressed to a fiction constructed out of many women, which means that none of these women is being praised.

15 Dio Chrysostom's 'Third Discourse on Kingship' may have told Jonson what he knew already, when he said flattery 'debases a thing most beautiful and just, even praise, so that it no longer appears honest or sincere, and – what is most outrageous – it gives to vice the prizes of virtue. Flatterers, therefore, do much more harm than those who debase the coinage: for whereas the latter causes us to suspect the coinage, the former destroy our belief in virtue' (1:113).

16 Daniel Javitch's analysis of the power games at court and their debilitat-

ing effect on the truth and credibility of encomiastic rhetoric captures a set of conditions that Jonson knew well: 'The praise made necessary by such hierarchical relations cannot be disinterested; more often it is bestowed for political motives rather than for the actual worth of its recipients. As a result, flattery is inevitable. And it hardly needs saying that flattery is decried as the most pernicious of courtly vices ... the court's encomiastic needs, stemming from the very conditions that foster a scourge like flattery, create employment for poets whose original functions are, after all, to praise and celebrate' (*Poetry* 116). Unfortunately, Javitch's analysis never goes beyond the implication that the alternative to flattery is telling the truth (117–18). Evans' analysis of Jonson's career charges the poet with just the kinds of flattery he inveighs against, and reads poems as these as attempts to deflect such a charge (60ff).

17 Margaret Clayton notes and develops Jonson's debt to John of Salisbury's *Policraticus* in this passage, and discovers that Jonson significantly changed John's emphasis from the flatterer to the lord who is flattered: 'Jonson questions the apparent passivity of their [lords'] role, and suggests that, beneath these appearances, there must be an act on their side that allows the flattery' (403).

18 Guazzo represents current opinion on flattery, and foreshadows the liaison Jonson makes between flattery and clothes which hide the truth of the flattered person's inner condition: 'for a cunning flatterer, setteth the garmentes so artificially uppon the backe of him whom hee disguiseth withall, that the seames shall not bee seene: and betaketh him selfe in suche sorte to things like to bee true, that hee maketh them taken for true in deede' (1:83).

19 The subject of F9, 'Song. To Celia,' is the incapacity of its metaphors to express the singer's emotions and those he elicits from her. Another version of the inexpressibility topos occurs in E126, 'To his Lady, then Mrs. Cary,' where speaker and Apollo quarrel over who will award the lady the laurel. The wit of the poem lies in telling Mrs Cary that the poet cannot praise her because Phoebus has prevented him, seizing her for his: 'CARY my loue is,' says Apollo, 'DAPHNE but my tree' (8).

20 The Elegies published in *The Vnder-wood* which Jonson wrote in imitation of Donne – several of which may even be by the latter – show the limits of Jonson's use of *hyperbole*. One elegy that seems to be authentically Jonsonian is U41, where he stakes out typically Donnian territory: hyperbolic expressions of the sorrow of parting. It is not a very successful poem, mainly because Jonson, unlike Donne, has not the knack for ingenious hyperbole that at once affirms and discounts itself. Hyperbolic

metaphor that runs out to extravagant lengths the entailments of its argument, for instance, is not Jonson's métier, probably because such figures do not generate precise terms and judgmental standpoints, which is what Jonson usually looks for.

21 Another epitaph, on Katherine, Lady Ogle (M31), employs the legal record conceit to less success because it spells out the conceit's ramifications, rather than leaving them to the reader's imagination. Thus 'Her right, by gift, and purchase of the Lambe: / Seal'd, and deliuer'd to her, in the sight / Of Angells, and all witnesses of light, / Both Saints, and Martyrs, by her loued Lord. / And this a coppie is of the Record' (36–40)

22 The 'Epitaph on S[alomon] P[avy] a Child of Q. El[izabeth's] Chappel' (E120) displays a similar playfulness. Jonson's humorous conceit has Salomon playing old men perhaps too well for his own good: for he 'did act (what now we mone) / Old men so duely, / As, sooth, the *Parcae* thought him one, / He plaid'd so truely' (13–16). But there is a serious truth behind the joke: the Parcae and death in seizing him obey blindly the decorum that matches death with old age.

23 An example of a poem that cites its own redundancy as a motive of praise is U50, 'An Epigram. To the honour'd —— Countesse of ——': 'And though all praise bring nothing to your name, / Who (herein studying conscience, and not fame) / Are in your selfe rewarded' (13–15). This may have been addressed to the countess of Rutland (Donaldson *Ben Jonson* 699).

24 My discussion of Jonson's commendatory poetry here and elsewhere rejects T.J.B. Spencer's dismissal: 'Nor did it greatly matter if there was some discrepancy between the genuine literary judgments uttered elsewhere and the panegyric fulsomely expressed in the commendatory poem. "In lapidary inscriptions," said the wise and tolerant Dr. Johnson, "a man is not upon oath." We can grant the same indulgence to the author of a commendatory poem.' (28).

25 Jonson addressed another epigram to Newcastle (U53), in which he praises his horsemanship. Like Sidney at the beginning of the *Apology for Poetry*, Jonson says he 'began to wish my selfe a horse' (12) so that he might live in Newcastle's stable, at whose 'Immortall Mangers *Virgil* fed' (20). The tone of this is problematic, although it is apparent that the poet makes equivalent the spirit of the great horse and that of the great poet.

26 Unlike Bobadil of *Every Man in His Humor*, but like Lovel in *The New Inn*, Jonson defines a conception of bravery that does not need a mastery of fencing to show itself. Duelling coerces esteem from others and

therefore discloses a sense of lack. Lovel in defining false valour makes a typical Jonsonian discrimination: 'in the form, / 'Tis carried rashly and with violence: / Then i' the end, where it respects not truth, / Or public honesty; but mere revenge ... then i'the end, which is the victory, / And not the honour' (4.4.91–4, 99–100; Wilkes 4:449).

27 Valour inspired by ignorance is worthy only of ridicule, as appears in the epigram 'On Play-wright' (E68). Having been beaten privately for the wrongs he does men publicly in his plays, he displays 'Two kindes of valour ... / Active in's brain, and passiue in his bones' (3–4). Being unable to understand the reason for these attacks, Playwright's 'active' virtue turns into a kind of foolhardiness, since, having taken 'priuate beatings' (2), Playwright can only begin again, thereby proving at once doubly brave and doubly ignorant.

28 In this I disagree with Leigh DeNeef's account of the epideictic lyric in the Renaissance: 'it may be assumed that epideictic lyric is characterized by a dogmatic attitude toward its subject: it does not explore, engage in a dialectical argument, or question the value of its topic. This assumption can be drawn from the common tendency of the rhetorics to exclude from an epideictic oration all parts of a discourse normally given to proof or refutation' (220). DeNeef admits that his description does not apply 'to the more subjective, impressionistic, or dialectical lyrics,' but rather to the epideictic poem that 'purports to be the final word on the subject by virtue of its dogmatic, celebratory tone and its representational, emblematic form' (222).

29 Betty Radice, the translator of Pliny's works for the Loeb Library, points out that '[the *Panegyricus*], then, is no idle flattery in conventional form; it is rather a sort of manifesto of the Senate's ideal of a constitutional ruler, one chosen to rule because he is qualified to do so, with emphasis on his *obsequium* to the people's will and his sense of service to his country' (168).

30 A judicious consideration of the historical truth of Pliny's praise is given by Mason Hammond.

31 See Giusto Picone for a summary of the rhetorical and political problems Pliny faced in composing the *Panegyricus* (167–71).

32 That this was not necessarily the case in fact is indicated by the rise of new men under Augustus and even of freed slaves under Claudius (Jones 178–80; Stevenson 184–86; Charlesworth 700; all in *Cambridge Ancient History* 10).

33 In one of his letters Pliny lays out his thoughts when preparing the *Panegyricus*, and insists that the freedom of speech the emperor has insti-

tuted both makes possible an oration of true praise, and becomes the proper object of that praise: 'A speech of thanks, which used to bore us after the first minute – even in the Senate, where we had to endure it – can now find a reader and an audience willing to listen for three days on end, not through any improvement in our standard of eloquence, but because greater freedom of speech makes writing more of a pleasure. This is yet another tribute to our Emperor: a type of speech which used to be hated for its insincerity has become genuine and consequently popular today' (letter to Vibius Severus; 1:225–7).

34 The literary relations between Tacitus' works and Pliny's *Panegyricus* are complex. Tacitus' early works – *Germania*, *Agricola*, and possibly *Dialogus* – served as sources of the *Panegyricus*. On the other hand, the *Panegyricus* served as a source for the *Histories* and the *Annals*. See Bruère 161. Giraldi Cinthio in the Renaissance attacks Pliny as a flatterer (165), while Edward Gibbon in the eighteenth century contrasted the 'doubtful light' of Pliny's oration with another 'far removed beyond the suspicion of flattery' on Trajan delivered 250 years later (1:67). Garrison speaks of the *Panegyricus* as 'an elaborate idealization of Trajan' (9). Harry Caplan calls it the 'best Roman panegyric' and goes on to say 'though you will find it in part dull and dry, though to Trajan are as-signed all the blessings and virtues, you will clearly see the orator's high-minded sincerity and noble purpose, some dignity and force, and at least decency in the relations of orator and patron' (37). Caplan com-pares it favourably with the collection of fourth-century panegyrics with which Pliny's production was bound in manuscript and transmitted to the Renaissance. However, the editor of the oration's single full schol-arly edition, Marcel Durry, judges that on balance Pliny's account of Trajan's virtues is reasonably accurate (19–21).

35 It has been left to recent new historicist discussions by Rowe, Evans, and Riggs to accuse Jonson of sycophancy, a matter I take up in the notes to the final chapter below.

36 Jonson's attitude is perfectly consistent with his applying for and receiv-ing the coat of arms of the Johnstone family of Annandale some time before 1606, something that Riggs suggests was aided by his teacher Camden who had become a member of the College in 1597 (Riggs 16, 116). This is an indication less that 'he had decided to refashion himself in the image of a Jacobean courtier' (Riggs 116), than that he thought himself worthy of such honour.

37 The epigram that follows this one, E37 'On Chev'rill the Lawyer,' turns inside out – appropriate for cheverel gloves – the point of the previous

epigram. The lawyer can argue for both sides of a case, and that side wins 'for whom he holds his peace' (4). Chev'rill is to the law what the flattering poet is to the flattered prince: he can make any argument the prince prefers, but he serves him best when he is silent.

38 E98 'To Sir Thomas Roe' makes some similar points to a similar purpose. Roe's 'gather'd selfe' 'nobly ... defend[s] / With thine owne course the iudgement of thy friend' (7–9), so that the poet's praise is justified by Roe's merit, who properly 'studie[s] conscience, more then thou would'st fame' (10). Being 'round within himselfe, and streight' he need 'seeke no other strength, no other height' (3–4), and the things he does not need include the poet's praise. Jonson makes this identical point in E131 'To the Same [Alphonso Ferrabosco]': 'Then stand vnto thy selfe, not seeke without / For fame, with breath soone kindled, soone blowne out' (13–14). On the 'gathered self' as a central thematic image in Jonson, see Greene ('Centered Self') and Peterson (*Imitation*).

39 See John Marston's play *The Fawn*, and Gerald A. Smith's introduction to the Regents Renaissance Drama edition of the play (xiii–xiv).

40 Frank Whigham's work analyses these attitudes as they were held in the Renaissance, and is indeed an expression of such attitudes. His demystification of courtly games of power takes the satirist's perspective, and extends to the vera nobilitas argument his critique of such games, with which he identifies it: 'Meritocratic arguments for social elevation tend to ground such status in substantive powers such as martial force or organizational ability. Such arguments legitimate social mobility by positing a prior hierarchy of merit; the meritorious inferior can then claim the right to relocate. Aristocratic ideology had to deal with this disruptive fact; he who would occupy exclusively the position of established aristocrat must de-emphasize not only his own efforts at self-manifestation but the substantive efforts of those below' (34). Cf also p 73ff where Whigham argues the demonstrably incorrect conclusion that Ferne (in *The Blazon of Gentrie*) 'repudiates the argument from merit.'

41 In the *Discoveries* Jonson says: 'yet I know not truly which is worse; hee that malignes all, or that praises all. There is as great a vice in praising, and as frequent, as in detracting' (H&S 8:613).

42 The need to avoid the extremes of flattery and brutality was recognized by Plutarch: 'Since, therefore, it is a shameful thing to fall into flattery in aiming to please, and a shameful thing also, in trying to avoid flattery, to destroy the friendly thoughtfulness for another by immoderate liberty of speech, we ought to keep ourselves from both the one and the

other extreme, and in frankness, as in anything else, achieve the right from the mean' (1:358).

43 A similar inexpressibility concludes the epigram 'To William Camden' (E14): 'Pardon free truth, and let thy modestie, / Which conquers all, be once ouer-come by thee. / Many of thine this better could, then I, / But for their powers, accept my pietie' (11–14). Jonson's 'pietie,' which would normally be taken to signify partisan judgment, becomes 'free truth' instead.

44 Compare the opening lines of M20, which prefaces the anonymous 1614 volume entitled *The Husband*: 'It fits not onely him that makes a Booke, / To see his worke be good; but that he looke / Who are his Test, and what their iudgement is: / Least a false praise do make theyr dotage his' (1–4).

45 A similar point might be made about the poem Jonson contributed to Thomas Palmer's *The Sprite of Trees and Herbes* (M1), which was never published. Jonson invents a complex conceit involving expanding circles in a pool, which throws him in a trance absolving him from having to say any more about Palmer's vegetative emblems. This poem is noteworthy because it defines negatively how Jonson's commendatory poems usually work. The fact of the matter is that he contrives to say as little about Palmer's work as possible.

46 The slightly embarrassed quality about Jonson's poem suggests the truth of Donaldson's observation that 'the extravagance of the poem may perhaps merely reflect Jonson's anxiety to make lavish amends to an unexpected admirer' (*Ben Jonson* 720). For Jonson's relations with Drayton, see Newdigate (136ff), where he comments on Jonson's poem: 'He [Jonson] proceeds to catalogue Drayton's poems in language too fulsome to be taken seriously. Most of the *Vision* reads like a bit of good-tempered leg-pulling, in which Ben burlesques with deliberate and luxuriously exaggerated pompousness the common run of commendatory verses.'

47 One kind of claim that supports this conformity is that the reader has read 'And weigh'd your *Play*: untwisted ev'ry thread / And know the woofe, and warpe thereof; can tell / Where it runs round, and even' ('To my deare Sonne, and right-learned Friend, Master JOSEPH RVTTER' [M42], 14–16). Similar claims occur in the earlier version of 'An Epistle to a Friend' (M49), and in the epistle to John Selden (U14): 'I turne a sharper eye / Upon my selfe, and aske to whom? and why? / And what I write? and vexe it many dayes / Before men get a verse: much lesse a Praise' (23–6). See also E33 and E34, where Jonson's refusal to mourn the dead Sir John Roe (in hope of the resurrection) is tested on himself:

'And I, now, / Breathe to expect my when, and make my how' (E33, 3–4). On classical versions of the twin labours of creation and criticism, see Peterson *Imitation* 155ff.

48 Jonson raged throughout his career against playgoers who refused to take his own perspective on his own plays. (See Sweeney 11 and passim.) He takes a similar tone in his poem [M8] prefacing the printed version of John Fletcher's *The Faithfull Shepherdesse*, whose audience was critical: 'Their motiues were, since it had not to do / With vices, which they look'd for, and came to' (9–10).

49 Jonson relates problems of perspective and nonpartisan praise in a poem on Josua Sylvester's translation of Du Bartas' *Divine Weeks and Works* (E132). He distinguishes admiration and commendation, insisting that while he may appreciate Sylvester's translation he cannot judge it because he has not compared it to the original. (To Drummond he admitted that when he finally did so after the poem was written, he found it a poor translation.) Jonson refuses to advance an inch beyond the point where his informed judgment stops, even if it means saying as little as he does here. Jonson's scrupulousness extends to his refusal to praise in detail a work that already has garnered a large collection of commendatory poems, as in Christopher Brooke's *The Ghost of Richard the Third* (1614): 'When these, and such, their volces haue employd; / What place is for my testimony void? ... Yet / If Praises, when the'are full, heaping admit, / My suffrage brings thee all increase' (M19; 1–2, 4–6).

50 Carew asks: 'Why should the follies then of this dull age / Draw from thy Pen such an immodest rage / As seems to blast thy (else-immortall) Bayes, / When thine owne tongue proclaimes thy ytch of praise?' ('To Ben. Iohnson. Vpon occasion of his Ode of defiance annext to this Play of the new Inne' 23–26).

51 I therefore would want to qualify Ian Donaldson's conclusions in 'Jonson and Anger,' where he argues that for Jonson satiric anger and the aggression it produced were an unqualified good; and the poems I survey in the rest of this section certainly will not support Donaldson's contention that Jonson was not concerned to 'reconcile the conflicting demands of truth and plain-dealing with those of good manners, good humour, and a Christian consideration for the feelings of others; how to combine the force of Juvenal with the civility of Horace' (70).

52 E49, 'To Play-wright,' amusingly reverses the direction of Jonson's response to meet the charge that he 'want[s] the tongue of *Epigrammes*; / I haue no salt: no bawdrie he doth meane' (2–3). Jonson correctly diag-

noses the mentality that underlies charges of obscenity as being that which also demands it where it is not: 'PLAY-WRIGHT, I loath to haue thy manners knowne / In my chast booke: professe them in thine owne' (5–6).

53 In later life Jonson could contemplate complaints about his books to his booksellers with better humour if not with more complacency. In an epigram included in *The Vnder-Wood*, 'to my Book-seller' (U58), Jonson does not bother to hide his conviction that only those who are wise will praise (5). Those who do not are 'Like a rung Beare, or Swine: grunting out wit / As if that part lay for a [ ] most fit!' (11–12). The deleted word in the 1640 Folio would seem to be the intersection of several phonemes in the immediate vicinity: part + for + fit = fart.

54 Marotti (*John Donne*) notes that 'Inns men learned and practiced the modes of behavior, speech, and writing, appropriate in the Court itself,' and that 'they collected courtly verse and prose in commonplace books as both literary and behavioral models. They acquired the courtly skills of dancing, singing, and the writing of love lyrics' (33). Nevertheless, 'At the same time there was a strong anticourtly impulse shared by many Inns men, reinforced by their common frustration in their search for preferment. Like disappointed courtiers, they attributed the envied success of others to the whims of Fortune or to influence-peddling, and viewed their own condition as that of injured merit. This led to a kind of moral or satiric disengagement from the courtly world, a stance of (sometimes openly cynical) criticism of its rules, of its styles, and of its (deliberately exaggerated) corruptions, the typical reactions of ... the "alienated intellectuals" of Elizabethan England.'

55 I would agree with Robert N. Watson that Macilente is the envying and loathing satirist, 'a green-eyed monster that mocks the meat it feeds on, and continues to waste away' (74).

56 Jackson (43–4) argues that Jonson assigns Horatian satire to Asper and Juvenalian satire to Macilente: 'To Asper belongs the frank, open, indignant attitude of the good man who is capable of being the good poet ... Jonson has endowed him with the forceful language and typical imagery of the satyr-satirist, but has reserved the normally concomitant moral blemishes to Macilente, into whom Asper turns himself for the purpose of taking part in the play itself, to purge its extravagant characters of their humors.' See also Thayer 30–1.

57 See E59, 'On Spies': 'Spies, you are lights in state, but of base stuffe, / Who, when you'haue burnt your selues downe to the snuffe, / Stinke, and are throwne away. End faire enough.' Gross misconstrual is a haz-

ard of the profession, as Jonson shows in the character Sir Politick Would-Be in *Volpone*. Vicious spies include Crispinus in *Poetaster* and Sejanus' henchmen in *Sejanus*. Cicero suborns spies in the service of the state in *Catiline*.

58 Jonson evokes the allegorical figure of Envy to open *Poetaster*, which has the following to say about itself: 'For I am risse here with a covetous hope, / To blast your pleasures, and destroy your sports, / With wrestings, comments, applications, / Spy-like suggestions, privy whisperings, / And thousand such promoting sleights as these' (22–6; Wilkes 2:125–6).

CHAPTER FIVE

1 Spenser's work deals extensively with various facets of the vera nobilitas argument, mainly in book 6 of *The Faerie Queene*. He wrote a commendatory sonnet for the English translation of Nenna, and complained of the unjust neglect of poets by aristocratic patrons in *The Teares of the Mvses* and *Mother Hvbberds Tale*. Chapman's search for patrons can be traced through the dedications of his poems in Bartlett's edition and in such poems as *Evthymiae Raptus; or The Teares of Peace* and *Petrarchs Seven Penitentiall Psalms*. In his dediction of his translation of the *Iliad* to Prince Henry he asserts that Homer should be read as an adviser to princes (Nicoll 1:4, 43–5, 8off). On Drayton see Newdigate.

2 Helgerson (166) lists those from whom Jonson received help during his lifetime, and argues that Jonson sought not only financial support but also the courtly status that patronage conferred: 'But patronage meant far more to Jonson than money, more even than the hospitality and protection he so frequently acknowledges. Entry into the system of patronage was a sign of his poetic elevation, testimony to his attainment of that laureate status for which he strove. Patronage associated him with the gentlemen amateurs, whose nonliterary advancement depended equally on the assistance of the wealthy and well-placed, and it dissociated him from the mere professionals, particularly the play-writing professionals.' Helgerson's argument assumes that patronage relations were necessarily confined to a hierarchical inequality of patron to client, and as such were sought by Jonson as a means of lifting himself to a prestigious position. However, it was just this narrow definition of patronage relations that Jonson, with the help of Seneca's *De beneficiis* and

the flexibility of Roman patronage practices which this treatise mediated to him, sought to abrogate in his poems on the subject discussed in this section. U49, 'An Epigram on The Court Pucell,' glosses Helgerson's argument in terms that I am inclined to accept as accurate: 'I never stood for any place: my wit / Thinkes it selfe nought, though she should valew it. / I am no States-man, and much lesse Divine (23–5).

3 Eisenstadt and Roniger, in their survey and summary of current patronage studies, name this combination as the first of several paradoxes to be discovered universally in all personal 'clientelistic' patronage relations: 'The most important contradictions are first, a peculiar combination of inequality and asymmetry in power with seeming mutual solidarity expressed in terms of personal identity and interpersonal sentiments and obligations; second, a combination of potential coercion and exploitation with voluntary relations and compelling mutual obligations; third, a combination of the emphasis on these obligations and solidarity with the somewhat illegal or semi-legal aspect of these relations' (50–1).

4 Mervyn James shows how before the institutionalization of honours in the College of Heralds (in the sixteenth century), the honour community was self-authenticating, that is, its own members decided who did and did not belong to it (18). The College itself, in making such judgments, consulted 'noble men worthy of belief' (22). Though there was a hierarchy within the nobility ranking major and minor nobility (Kelso 18–19), membership in the honour community established a parity among its members when defined against those ranks not admitted into the community.

5 The Loeb translator says that De beneficiis concerns the 'morality of giving and receiving – the casuistry of benefaction and gratitude' (3:vii).

6 Eisenstadt and Roniger give the name 'clientelistic' to patronage structures involving personal relations outside more general social structures and practices (55).

7 Saller finds Seneca 'a good source for the ideals of friendship in our period because most of his ideas are not uniquely Stoic; rather they represent the common philosophical currency of the aristocracy of his day, as shown by their repetition in the works of orators such as Pliny and Fronto' (12).

8 In citing the circumstances surrounding and governing Seneca's treatise, as well as those implied by Pliny's Panegyricus, as contributing to Jonson's meanings, I agree with Leah Marcus' insistence that 'Jonson's clas-

sicism needs to be thoroughly historicized: we need to apply the same methodological sophistication to our view of Roman and Greek writers and to Jonson's use of them as we do to Jonson himself' ('Report' 144).

9 Saller 14ff. Saller notes also that *beneficium* and *officium* overlapped in meaning: 'A survey of the usages listed in the *Thesaurus Linguae Latinae* shows that for every one use of *beneficium* which might qualify as a "spontaneous favour" three refer to exchanges in established *amicitia* relationships' (18).

10 Patricia Thomson distinguished Jonson as a professional poet who sought print for his works from Donne who was an amateur and who did not. In this she classifies Jonson with Daniel (310). It is necessary, however, to make a further distinction in order to take account of Jonson's conception of patronage in general and of his own situation in particular: one between poets who unabashedly sought patronage in return for literary production that in some way honoured the patron, and Jonson who sought, and presumably succeeded in receiving, patronage support while claiming a form of intellectual equality with his patrons.

11 The poem Jonson addressed 'To my old Faithfull Seruant: and (by his continu'd Vertue) my louing Friend: ... M. Rich. Brome' (M38) delineates the reverse situation, in which Jonson played the role of patron to his servant, later playwright, Richard Brome. The poem calls upon several arguments to reinforce each other: (1) Brome has moved up the ladder from servant through apprenticeship to 'Fellowship' (4) with the poet; (2) this ascent has been by Brome's honest labour ('You learn'd it well; and for it, seru'd your time / A Prentise-ship' [9–10]); (3) Brome contrasts favourably with those who do not merit such praise: 'each court-Hobby-horse will wince in rime; / Both learned, and vnlearned, all write *Playes*' (11–12).

12 My perspective on Jonson's attitudes toward economic practices is different from that of L.C. Knights, who is concerned with the contemporary dislocations of economic values toward monopolistic capitalism, and Jonson as a spokesman for traditional, medieval, pre-capitalistic ideals. These two perspectives are not incompatible, but I believe that Knights' argument must be modified by the semiotic interpretations which Jonson gives the economic practices contemporary with him: he was not, as Knights suggests, a straightforward commentator on economic matters for their own sake.

13 Gardiner (*Craftsmanship* 27): 'The merits of the guest are set against the speaker's unworthiness, which is gradually modified to adjust the values of the banquet of those of the guest.'

14 It is, however, the poem in which these sorts of multivalent relations have been most generally discerned: Cain; Williams; Wayne *Penshurst*; Pearlman 384. How far one goes in discovering what is excluded by what is included is a matter of choice, since other readers have found the poem a relatively placid matter, celebrating the harmony of man with nature, and of man with man in mutually beneficent reciprocity. See Rivers 40ff; Friedberg 130ff; Knapp; McGuire; Gayle Edward Wilson; Cubeta 'A Jonsonian Ideal'; Parfitt *Public Poet* 147–8.

15 Jonson's praise of Sidney's comparative modesty of self-advertisement may have a more topical motive as well. Rathmell calls attention to his financial difficulties, and speculates that Jonson's poem is intended 'as a tactful means of reconciling Lord Lisle to living within his means and of persuading him that his inability to emulate the magnificence of wealthier courtiers, so far from being a cause for shame, is in fact a matter for congratulation' (256).

16 Wayne's subtly articulated analysis of this poem takes the measure of Jonson's identification with the social and political values Penshurst stands for and concludes that 'a poem like "To Penshurst," despite its traditional, aristocratic theme, can be said to liberate a potential for future social praxis along bourgeois egalitarian lines; (*Penshurst* 154). The basis of Wayne's nascently middle-class Jonson is the vera nobilitas argument ('Although he did not, or could not, abandon Renaissance notions of hierarchy, his texts do give forceful articulation to the idea of intellectual merit as the standard of an individual's worth'), but Wayne directs this argument to a conclusion that seems to assume that rejection of hegemonic aristocracy necessarily entails embracing middle-class values as their alternative. Lacking a survey of the whole of Jonson's poetry, and an analysis of the vera nobilitas argument, Wayne's position can take account neither of Jonson's rejection of middle-class values in other poems (as well as in such plays as *Bartholomew Fair* [Haynes 652]), nor of the vera nobilitas argument's identification with hierarchical political structures and its rejection of egalitarianism. Also see McClung 61.

17 From Jonson's perspective the source of grudging and envy was not what a Marxist critic such as Raymond Williams thought it ought to be: the exploitation of tenants for the material support of Penshurst, matched by the obliteration of the marks of that support. Its source was rather the signs of noble status minus its justification. For him 'social justice' did not lie in equitable distribution of property, but in a social order that justly reflected the merits of its members. It was a matter less

of economics than of semiotics. Nor was Jonson's perspective as socially irrelevant as a Marxist view might hold. Lawrence Humphrey's 1563 treatise *The Nobles or of Nobilitye* is in effect a lengthy gloss on Jonson's poem in several respects, not least in locating where the source of class friction lay for those born below gentle status. Humphrey's declared reason for writing is to reform the vices of those born into noble families, and his position is squarely within the vera nobilitas tradition not least in the argument from justice with which he attacks the nobly born who do not merit their noble status. Jonson echoes Elyot as well: 'The most sure foundation of noble renown is a man to be of such virtues and qualities as he desireth to be openly published. For it is a faint praise that is gotten with fear or by flatterers given. And the fame is but fume which is supported with silence provoked by menaces' (Elyot 97).

18 Jonson praises festivals that James sought to revive in 'An Epigram to my Ioviall Good Freind *Mr. Robert Dover*, on his great Instauration of his Hunting, and Dauncing at *Cotswold*' (M43) in terms that echo those of 'To Penshurst.' Such festive rituals 'advance true Love, and neighbourhood, / And doe both *Church*, and Common-wealth the good, / In spite of *Hipocrites*, who are the worst / Of Subiects; Let such envie, till they burst' (7–10).

19 Marcus (*Politics* 7) advocates for modelling the Stuart politics of mirth a conception of festival that includes 'both normative and revisionary impulses. Its seeming lawless topsy-turvydom can both undermine and reinforce – it can constitute a process of adjustment within a perpetuation of order.'

20 In 'An Epistle answering to one that asked to be Sealed of the Tribe of BEN' (U47) Jonson takes the occasion to vent a mood of withdrawal from many irritations: noisy, gossiping, and bragging dinner companions (9ff), obsession with foreign news (31ff), the court's love of Inigo Jones (47ff), and the court itself: 'Live to that point I will, for which I am man, / And dwell as in my Center, as I can' (59–60).

21 In U61, 'An Epigram,' Jonson gives us something of the lady's perspective, when he addresses one who has 'seene the pride, beheld the sport, / And all the games of Fortune, plaid at Court,' and who has yet 'got off thence, with cleare mind, and hands / ... set apart, thus, from the rest' (1–2, 7, 10). Significantly, Jonson felicitates someone else for his escape from court.

22 See Rivers (31–2) for a judicious statement of Jonson's stoicism in this poem and in general, and of his refusal to be led by it into total withdrawal matching that of the gentle lady of F4.

23 Marcus (*Politics* 12–13) summarizes these and other points of similarity between Jonson and James. Willson comments on James' love of learned conviviality: 'His learned repasts are well known ... "That King's table was a trial of wits", wrote Hacket. The reading of some books before him was very frequent while he was at his repast. Otherwise he collected knowledge by the variety of questions which he carved out to the capacity of those about him. He was ever in chase after some disputable doubts which he would wind and turn about with the most stabbing objections that ever I heard, and was as pleasant and fellow-like in all these discourses as with his huntsmen in the field' (228–9). Also: 'He liked to mimic the grave and the sententious, as in his humorous interpretation of an eclipse, and he loved a tone of intimate banter and of calculated impudence. A part of his humour was the homely bluntness of the Scot who spoke the truth with amusing directness. For piquant phrases he never lacked. His was a true wit, he loved a jest for its own sake, and he told it well. "He was very witty ... and had as many ready jests as any man living, at which he would not smile himself but deliver them in a grave and serious manner"' (189).

24 Jonathan Goldberg's persuasive case for Jonson's strategies in 'A Panegyre' and throughout his many productions addressed to King James is one whose details I can often agree with, without agreeing with its overall purport. Goldberg says about this poem: 'Jonson depends upon the king's proclamation of his own transparency and the stoic politics that lies behind it. Ostensibly a poem of outright praise, Jonson's verse carefully uses James's own vision of himself trapped between two audiences to glance at a mode of mediative reconciliation that James could not entirely sanction. Jonson's protection, in speaking in ways that carry half of James's thought beyond the point that he would have allowed, lies in presenting the king in the position of the double calling that he had used to describe himself' (120). However, it is certainly true that in 'A Panegyre' and elsewhere Jonson's speaks James' own language, and with tactical purposes that Goldberg is correct in perceiving, namely to marshal the king the way he was (sometimes) going. Whether such mimicry implies alienation rather than identification is a question that could be argued either way; more correctly, I think, the second rather than the first.

25 There is finally no privileged origin of this text, as Jonson illuminates (or obscures) the matter. Certainly James himself does not originate it, since it is delivered by the goddess Themis, who descends from heaven to do so; and therefore the situation is not so simple, nor so simply unmasked, as Jonathan Goldberg argues in the liminal presentation of his

discussion of the discourse of monarchal power. Goldberg's demystifying analysis would apply were Jonson merely replicating the ascriptions that James produced in *Basilikon Doron* and throughout his reign, which drew royal prerogative from the throne of God. The reciprocity Jonson envisions, across the gulfs separating men and classes, no more originates from any single authority, than the meaning of royal (and noble) status derives from the *de facto* existence, that is, the signs, of that status itself. On the contrary, for Jonson both royal status and the reciprocity it exists to nurture (as well as the royal status that must be nurtured by reciprocity) come into existence together, or not at all.

26 This group includes U62, U63, U64, U65, U66, U67, U68, U71, U72, U73, U74, U75, U76, U77, U79, and U82. U81 is accepted by Herford and Simpson as by Sir Henry Wotten.

27 U63, addressed 'To K. CHARLES, and Q. MARY. For the losse of their first-borne, An Epigram Consolatorie,' defines a relation between God and the bereaved parents that is analogous to that between monarch and people. As in 'To Penshvrst,' justice runs in both directions: the opening couplet states that 'all first-fruits are due / To God,' while the second couplet asserts the *noblesse oblige* of a God who will recompense what he has taken away. (God fulfils the mandate of the vera nobilitas argument by having both 'his greatnesse, and his goodnesse too' [9].) Higher and lower are linked by a reciprocity in which justice in either direction depends on its moving in both: a significant piece of advice to a king whose notion of *divina juris* was edging increasingly toward denying such reciprocity.

28 U82, 'To my L. the King, On the Christening His second Sonne, IAMES,' evokes *divina juris* as the sanction revealed in the birth of a second son to support the succession: 'And by thy blessing, may thy *People* see / How much they are belov'd of God, in thee; / Would they would understand it!' (3–5). Here, the House of Stuart is revealed as burdened with a typically Jonsonian malady: lack of true 'understanders.'

29 A similarly circular play of eulogistic metaphor is suggested in M44, which appears to be a fragment of an early entertainment. The king initiates the spring, which produces the flowers that, woven into a garland, become a crown which encircles the obelisk that is in turn identified with the king.

30 Parry (42) calls Jonson 'an inveterate moralist and flatterer'; M.C. Bradbrook remarked that 'at court he was silken, bland; in the theatre he mercilessly satirized upstart courtiers,' quoted by Martines *Society and History* 91 with apparent approval.

31 Jonson's fear of flattery is a commonplace in the criticism: Barton (314), Wayne *Penshurst* 152–3), Fish (43), Beaurline (*Jonson* 167–8), Dunlap (143), Brady (386).

32 G.K. Hunter's account of Lyly's career indicates some parallels with Jonson's. Hunter attributes to Lyly the desire to wield influence with the queen (69–70), and his string of court dramas produced in the late 1580s were aimed at this end, much as were Jonson's masques. Lyly also suffered an eclipse of favour in his later years, and was even, like Jonson, awarded the reversion of the office of Master of the Revels (77–8). The work for which Lyly is most remembered, *Euphues*, is essentially a humanist treatise on the need to supplement natural talents by education, nature by nuture (51–2).

33 The person whose life is controlled by *ressentiment* is for Scheler one who has already brought in a verdict on himself of irredeemable inferiority and weakness, which in turn sets himself off against all values perceived as positive. *Ressentiment* is addressed to nothing and no one in particular, nor does it look for – because despairing of – redress. The elements constituting *ressentiment* relevant to those ambitious for status at the Renaissance court are the following: (1) it 'is chiefly confined to those who serve and are dominated at the moment, who fruitlessly resent the sting of authority' (48); (2) it includes 'strong pride coupled with an inadequate social position' (50); (3) 'it does not seriously desire that its demands be fulfilled ... the evil is merely a pretext for the criticism' (51); (4) the man of *ressentiment* only values himself to the degree that he is valued by others, and is therefore in social terms an '*arriviste*.' 'The ultimate goal of the *arriviste's* aspirations is not to acquire a thing of value, but to be more highly esteemed than others' (54–5). The work of Javitch, Greenblatt, Helgerson, Goldberg, Fish, Whigham, Marotti, and Wayne in rich individual detail collectively describes the Renaissance poet's commitment to aspirations to courtly place and patronage. Particularly relevant to Jonson is the work of Rowe and Evans, as well as Riggs' recent biography. For my commentary on Evans and Riggs, see my review in *Criticism* listed in the bibliography. It is patently inaccurate to risk anything but the broadest generalizations about this work as a whole, but if there is a common point of reference dominating all of it, it lies in viewing the poets as subject to the same ambitions, frustrations, and resentments that characterized all the younger sons and university and Inns-of-court men who aspired to courtly place and favour; as subject in short to *ressentiment* as Scheler describes it. But for a dissenting view of new historicist treatments of Renaissance patronage,

see Dubrow. A Jonsonian perspective on the courts of Elizabeth, James, and Charles, given exposition in the first four chapters of this study, yields much of the negative critique which these latter-day scholars have restated. More important, this critique grows out of Jonson's detailed development of the vera nobilitas argument, which also generates a positive analysis of the court and the political hierarchy it served that is generally absent from these studies. Also absent, with the exception of Whigham and Wayne, who give it subordinate emphasis, is any recognition of this argument's importance, either in funding Jonson's own work, or in setting the intellectual and ethical context for courtly aspirations in general.

34 Contemporary evidence of Jonson's habits and characteristics appears in *The Jonson Allusion-Book* and H&S 11:307–569. The central documents 'for the prosecution' include the portrayals of 'Horace' in Dekker and Marston's *Satiromastix*, a manuscript poem by Inigo Jones (H&S 385–6), a lengthy piece of poetic invective by George Chapman (406–11), some letters of a friend, the essayist James Howell, which records the criticism of others (416–19), and finally Jonson's Conversations with William Drummond of Hawthornden. Jonson is known to have killed two men, one in single combat while serving in the Netherlands, the second, a fellow actor Gabriel Spencer, in 1598, for which act Jonson carried the brand of felon (Miles 38–9). Modern attacks include Edmund Wilson's essay 'Morose Ben Jonson,' which finds in him the characteristics of the anal retentive, and the more balanced and insightful appraisal of Pearlman. Both essays are psychologistic, but the latter rises beyond the behaviouristic bias of the former, to note Jonson's refusing 'the option of a revolutionary stance' and his internalizing 'a form of self-expression compounded of the detritus of aristocratic feudal morality, and stressing such values as physical courage, reputation, honesty, command, status, generosity' (375). See also Gardiner, ' "A Wither'd Daffodill." ' The most recent attacks on Jonson, those of Rowe, Evans, and Riggs, view him in new historicist fashion as driven by the same kinds of self-loathing, *ressentiment*, and obsession with power ascribed to court life in general by Whigham. The present study implicitly responds to these attacks, since it was conceived and mostly written before these books appeared.

35 Kerrigan insists that the poem concerns only the poet's relations to God and not to unspecified friends or onlookers who question the sincerity of his religious melancholy, an interpretation advanced by Swinburne. Viewing another of Jonson's few religious lyrics in the context of his social self-presentation lends significance to what appears otherwise con-

ventional breast-beating. In U1.2, 'A Hymne to God the Father,' Jonson praises God's having 'Been sterne to mee' (8), 'For, sin's so sweet, / As minds ill bent / Rarely repent, / Untill they meet / Their punishment' (12–16). The melancholy of 'To Heaven,' which Jonson seeks to use rightly, is matched here with a willingness to submit to the pain of 'A broken heart' (2) in order not to lose the salutary consequences of self-knowledge.

36 Poems in a similarly good-humoured and self-deprecative mood include U54, 'Epistle to Mr. ARTHUR SQUIB,' which begs a loan to make up the supposed deficiencies in Jonson's bulk: weighing 'Full twentie stone' he nevertheless lacks 'two pound' (12), and he begs Squib to 'make me good, in weight, and fashion' (17); U55, 'To Mr. IOHN BURGES,' which begs pardon for the poet's inability owing to a hangover to mount a satisfactory thanks for a gift ('But since the Wine hath steep'd my braine, / I only can the Paper staine' [5–6]); and Jonson's reply (M46) to a sympathetic quatrain on the poverty of the poet which necessitated the journey to Scotland, and which encapsulates at once the poet's sang-froid and his acceptance of the pains of his condition.

37 In this, Jonson becomes like the Silenus to which Alcibiades compares Socrates in the *Symposium*, which 'when you open them down the middle there are little figures of the gods inside' (215b) (Hamilton and Cairns 566). In a study of the mock encomium in the Renaissance, Walter Kaiser links the Silenus figure with the Stultitia of Erasmus in *The Praise of Folly*, where the foolish and the ugly are praised for reasons that appear at first absurd, only later to disclose justification, just as the ugly Silenus is opened to disclose the divine within (36, 54, 60–1). Raymond Waddington has noted the relevance of the Silenus figure in connection with *A Celebration of Charis* (U2) (133–5).

38 Lemly notes that 'in many late poems Jonson's persona intrudes like an antimasque, a physical problem of visual disorder and gross imperfection for which the poetry seeks a solution ... As the facts of his actual condition grow more painful, Jonson's disdain for the visual arts becomes a common preliminary to whatever ideals the poems attempt to express' (251–2).

39 It was also inspired, so Jonson told Drummond, by a debate involving the earl of Pembroke and his wife on the question: 'Pembroke and his lady discoursing, the Earl said that women were men's shadows, and she maintained them. Both appealing to Jonson, he affirmed it true; for which my lady gave a penance to prove it in verse, hence his epigram' (Parfitt ed 471).

40 A revealing piece of aubiography occurs in *Discoveries* (H&S 8:604–5, lines 1323–72), where Jonson recounts attacks against him at court and the various charges that spearheaded them: 'It is true, I have beene accus'd to the Lords, to the *King*, and by great ones' (1333–5). Accusers neglected to note their own guilt in the matter of their accusations ('my accusers had not thought the Accusation with themselves' [1335–6]), or employed cat's-paws and surrogates. They slandered Jonson's profession (1343), but the poet easily sloughed these off, considering the accusers incapable of reading his poetry: 'They objected, making of verses to me, when I could object to most of them, their not being able to reade them, but as worthy of scorne' (1349–51). Quoting fragments of his writing out of context produced 'Calumnie, which read entire, would appeare most free' (1357–8), and finally 'they upbraided my poverty' (1358–9). Evans' dogmatic insistence that all assertions of self-possession mask self-loathing blinds him to Jonson's own analysis of weak men's complicity with their own oppression.

41 It is clear that Jonson's not writing extensively of love was not because of moral qualms (Venuti), since he insisted on regaling Drummond with his conquests. We know that he preferred married women to virgins, that a husband put his wife to courting him for two years, that he knew a woman who was a sexual tease (Parfitt ed 468–9). In the context of Jonson's general self-aggrandisement with Drummond, and the clear need evinced in the Conversations to plume himself before this provincial lord, such sexual bragging is not surprising. The tales may even be true, given their circumstantiality (which may also call them into question). The point is that in bragging of his sexual conquests Jonson was delivering more than one message: that despite his physical debilities he was attractive to women, a message in turn that conveys others, such as his conviction that he will be believed, or perhaps his equal conviction that he needs to make this point against the fear that he will not be believed.

42 Trimpi's neo-platonizing interpretation is matched inversely by Weinberger's reading as mock encomium. Peterson ('Virtue Reconciled') believes that Jonson consummates his love with Charis, a conclusion not ventured by other readers, while Strout suggests that '"A Celebration," ... presents not the exciting mutual discovery of a unity in love, not a chronicle of a mutually rewarding emotional relationship, but the conflicting views on love of its three speakers, views that conflict within themselves as well as with each other' (139). Waddington treats the sequence as 'an exercise in stylistic and generic mixture' (121) with the re-

sult that it leaves unanswered the question 'which Silenus is Ben –
Socrates or Anacreon?' (135). Sara Van Den Berg's argument that the
poet plays with 'the self-mocking role he adopts as the "Celebration" begins' and that he displays 'his ambivalent attitudes about himself as poet
and as man' approaches my own. I would agree with her that 'playfulness, based on self-awareness, is essential to his success' ('Play' 28).

43 His fiftieth seems to have been for Jonson the traumatic birthday. In his
translation of Horace's 4.1, 'To Venus' (U86), he begs the goddess 'Re-
fraine, / Sower Mother of sweet Loves, forbeare / To bend a man, now
at his fiftieth yeare / Too stubborne for Commands so slake' (4–7).

44 Waddington sums up critical responses to *A Celebration of Charis* as a
sequence of love poems: 'How seriously does "Ben" attempt to live up
to the Neoplatonic ideal of the old lover? How does he "revenge" himself on Charis? Is Ben accepted or rejected as Charis' lover? Is Charis
satirized as a shallow coquette, not different essentially from the grossly
sensual lady who has the last word, or does she represent a reasoned
mean between the poet's unworldly idealism and the lady's cynical real-
ism?' (121). If U40, 'An Elegie,' is genuinely Jonson's, it represents an
apologia in Donnian style for the 'merrie' lover (25) who, unlike the
'grave Lover' (32) that betrays his amorous secret through 'his Dark-lan-
terne face' (23) behind which he putatively hides it, 'Moves like a
sprightly River, and yet can / Keepe a secret in his Channels what he
breedes, / 'Bove all your standing waters, choak'd with weedes' (26–8).
Jonson's declared stance as a wooer is one always of wit and light-heart-
edness.

45 Cubeta ('A Celebration') points out that 'although "Her Triumph" ... has
cast about it an aura of high comic irony, the lyric itself is not a parody
of Elizabethan love poetry. Instead Jonson writes sympathetically here
in the finest traditions of the mode' (169).

Bibliography

Aristotle *Nichomachean Ethics*. Trans W.D. Ross. *The Basic Works of Aristotle*. Ed Richard McKeon. New York: Random House 1941
– *Rhetoric* (trans W. Rhys Roberts) and *Poetics* (trans Ingram Bywater). New York: Modern Library 1954
Ascham, Roger *The Schoolmaster (1570)*. Ed Lawrence V. Ryan. Ithaca: Cornell UP 1967
Ashley, Robert *Of Honour*. Ed Virgil B. Heltzel. San Marino: Huntington Library 1947
Aubrey, John *Aubrey's Brief Lives*. Ed Oliver Lawson Dick. Ann Arbor: U of Michigan P 1957
Bacon, Francis *Essays*. London: Oxford UP 1937
Barber, C.L. *The Idea of Honour in the English Drama, 1951–1700*. Gothenburg Studies in English 6. Göteborg 1957
Barish, Jonas A. 'Jonson and the Loathèd Stage.' In *A Celebration of Ben Jonson* ed William Blisset, Julian Patrick, R.W. Van Fossen. Toronto: U of Toronto P 1973
Baron, Hans *The Crisis of the Early Italian Renaissance*. 2 vols. Princeton: Princeton UP 1955
Barthes, Roland *A Lover's Discourse*. Trans Richard Howard. New York: Hill & Wang 1978
Barthes, Roland *S/Z*. Trans Richard Miller. New York: Hill & Wang 1974
– *Writing Degree Zero* and *Elements of Semiology*. Trans Annette Lavers and Colin Smith. Boston: Beacon P 1970
Barton, Anne *Ben Jonson, Dramatist*. Cambridge: Cambridge UP 1984
Baskerville, Charles R. 'Conventional Features of Medwall's *Fulgens and Lucrece*.' *Modern Philosophy* 24 (1928) 419–42

Baudry, Jean-Louis 'Ecriture, fiction, idéologie.' *Théorie d'ensemble.* Paris: Seuil 1968

Beard, Mary, and Michael Crawford *Rome in the Late Republic.* Ithaca: Cornell UP 1985

Beaurline, L.A. *Jonson and Elizabethan Comedy: Essays in Dramatic Rhetoric.* San Marino: Huntingdon Library 1978

– 'The Selective Principle in Jonson's Shorter Poems.' In *Ben Jonson and the Cavalier Poets: Authoritative Texts and Criticism* ed Hugh Maclean. New York: Norton 1974

Becker, Marvin B. *Florence in Transition.* 2 vols. Baltimore: Johns Hopkins UP 1967–8

Benveniste, Emile *Problèmes de linguistique générale.* Paris: Gallimard 1966

Bever, T.G., J.R. Lackner and R. Kirk 'The Underlying Structures of Sentences Are the Primary Units of Immediate Speech Processing.' In *On Noam Chomsky: Critical Essays* ed Gilbert Harman. Garden City, NY: Anchor Books 1974

Bevington, David *Tudor Drama and Politics: A Critical Approach to Topical Meaning.* Cambridge: Harvard UP 1968

Boethius *The Consolation of Philosophy.* Trans Richard Green. Indianapolis: Liberal Arts 1962

'A Book of Precedence.' In *Queene Elizabethes Achademy; A Booke of Precedence* ... Early English Text Society, extra series 8, ed F.J. Furnivall. London 1869

Booth, Stephen, ed *Shakespeare's Sonnets.* New Haven and London: Yale UP 1977

Bradley, Jesse Franklin, and Joseph Quincy Adams *The Jonson Allusion-Book: A Collection of Allusions to Ben Jonson from 1597 to 1700.* New Haven: Yale UP 1922

Brady, Jennifer 'Jonson's '"To King James": Plain Speaking in the *Epigrammes* and the *Conversations.*' *Studies in Philosophy* 82 (1985) 380–98

Briggs, William Dinsmore 'Source-Material for Jonson's *Epigrams* and *Forest.*' *Classical Philology* 11:2 (1916) 169–90

Brink, C.O. *Horace on Poetry: The "Ars Poetica."* Cambridge: At the UP 1971

Brock, D. Heyward, ed *The Workes of Benjamin Jonson (1616).* London and New York: Scolar P 1976

Bruère, Richard T. 'Tacitus and Pliny's "Panegyricus."' *Classical Philology* 49 (1954) 161–79

Burgess, Theodore C. *Epideictic Literature.* Chicago: U of Chicago P 1902

Burke, Kenneth *A Rhetoric of Motives.* New York: Braziller 1955

Burton, Robert *The Anatomy of Melancholy.* Ed Floyd Dell and Paul Jordan-Smith. New York: Tudor 1955

Butler, Charles *English Grammar* (1634). Ed A. Eichler. Halle: Max Niemeyer 1910

Cain, William E 'The Place of the Poet in Jonson's "To Penshurst" and "To My Muse."' *Criticism* 21 (1979) 34–48

Cameron, Kenneth Walter *Authorship and Sources of 'Gentleness and Nobility': A Study in Early Tudor Drama*. Raleigh, NC: Thistle Press 1941

Campion, Thomas *The Works of Thomas Campion*. Ed Percival Vivian. Oxford: Clarendon P 1909

Caplan, Harry *Of Eloquence: Studies in Ancient and Mediaeval Rhetoric*. Ed Anne King and Helen North. Ithaca: Cornell UP 1970

Carew, Thomas *The Poems of Thomas Carew*. Ed Rhodes Dunlap. Oxford: Clarendon P 1949

Carlson, Peter 'Judging Spectators.' *ELH* 44 (1977) 43–57

Caspari, Fritz *Humanism and the Social Order in Tudor England*. Chicago: U of Chicago P 1954

Castiglione, Baldassare *The Book of the Courtier*. Trans Sir Thomas Hoby. *Three Renaissance Classics*. Ed Burton A. Milligan. New York: Scribners 1953

Cecil, David *The Cecils of Hatfield House: An English Ruling Family*. Boston: Houghton Mifflin 1973

Chan, Mary *Music in the Theatre of Ben Jonson*. Oxford: Clarendon P 1980

Chapman, George *The Poems of George Chapman*. Ed Phyllis Brooks Bartlett. 1941; New York: Russell 1962

Charlesworth, M.P. 'Gaius and Claudius.' In *The Cambridge Ancient History*. Vol. 10: *The Augustan Empire 44 B.C.–A.D. 70* ed S.A. Cook, F.E. Adcock, M.P. Charlesworth. Cambridge: At the UP 1966

Charlton, Kenneth *Education in Renaissance England*. London: Routledge and Kegan Paul 1965

Chateaubriand, François-René de *Memoirs*. Trans and ed Robert Baldick. New York: Knopf 1961

Chatman, Seymour *A Theory of Meter*. The Hague: Mouton 1965

Chatman, Seymour, and Samuel R. Levin, eds *Essays on the Language of Literature*. Boston: Houghton Mifflin 1967

Chaucer, Geoffrey *The Works of Geoffrey Chaucer*. 2nd ed. Ed F.N. Robinson. Boston: Houghton Mifflin 1957

Chomsky, Noam, and Morris Halle *The Sound Pattern of English*. New York: Harper 1968

Chute, Marchette *Ben Jonson of Westminster*. New York: Dutton 1953

[Cicero] *Ad C. Herennium De Ratione Dicendi (Rhetorica ad Herennium)*. Trans Harry Caplan. Loeb Classical Library. Cambridge: Harvard UP 1954

Cicero *Brutus and Orator*. Trans G.L. Hendrickson and H.M. Hubbell. Cambridge: Harvard UP 1939
– *De Inventione; De optimo genere oratorum; Topica*. Trans H.M Hubbell. Loeb Classical Library. London: Heinemann 1949
– *De officiis/On Duties*. Trans Harry G. Edinger. Indianapolis: Bobbs-Merrill 1974
– *De oratore and De partitione oratoria*. Trans E.W. Sutton and H. Rackham. Loeb Classical Library. 2 vols. Cambridge: Harvard UP 1942
– *Nine Orations and the Dream of Scipio*. Trans Palmer Bovie. New York: New American Library 1967
– *Tusculan Disputations*. Trans J.E. King. Loeb Classical Library. Cambridge: Harvard UP 1950
Cinthio, Giraldi *On Romances*. Trans Henry L. Snuggs. Lexington: U of Kentucky P 1968
Claudian Trans Maurice Platnauer. Loeb Classical Library. 2 vols. London: William Heinneman 1922
Clayton, Margaret 'Ben Jonson, "In Travaile with Expression of Another": His Use of John of Salisbury's *Policraticus* in *Timber*.' *Review of English Studies* ns 30(120) (1979) 397–408
Colie, Rosalie L. *'My Ecchoing Song': Andrew Marvell's Poetry of Criticism*. Princeton: Princeton UP 1970
– 'Some Paradoxes in the Language of Things.' *Reason and the Imagination: Studies in the History of Ideas 1600–1800*. Ed J.A. Mazzeo. New York: Columbia UP 1962
Commager, Steele *The Odes of Horace: A Critical Study*. New Haven and London: Yale UP 1962
Coulthard, Malcolm, Martin Montgomery, and David Brazil *Studies in Discourse Analysis*. London: Routledge & Kegan Paul 1981
Crystal, David *The English Tone of Voice: Essays in Intonation, Prosody and Paralanguage*. New York: St Martin's 1975
– *Prosodic Systems and Intonation in English*. Cambridge: Cambridge UP 1966
Cubeta, Paul '"A Celebration of Charis": An Evaluation of Jonsonian Poetic Strategy.' ELH 25 (1958) 163–80
– 'A Jonsonian Ideal – "To Penshurst."' *Philological Quarterly* 42 (1963) 14–24
Culler, Jonathan *On Deconstruction: Theory and Criticism after Structuralism*. Ithaca: Cornell UP 1982
Curtius, Ernst Robert *European Literature and the Latin Middle Ages*. Trans Willard R. Trask. New York and Evanston: Harper 1963

Daines, Simon *Orthoepia Anglicana: or, the First Principall Part of the English Grammar.* London 1640

Daniel, Samuel *A Defence of Ryme. Poems and A Defense of Ryme.* Ed Arthur Colby Sprague. Chicago: U of Chicago P 1965

Danson, Lawrence 'Jonsonian Comedy and the Discovery of the Social Self.' *PMLA* 99 (1984) 179–93

Dante's Convivio. Trans William Walrond Jackson. Oxford: Clarendon P 1909

Deleuze, Gilles *Proust and Signs.* Trans Richard Howard. London: Allen Lane 1973

Della Casa, Giovanni *Galateo of Manners and Behaviours.* Trans Robert Peterson (1576). Ed J.E. Spingarn. Boston: Merrymount 1914

de Man, Paul *Allegories of Reading: Figural Language in Rousseau, Nietzsche, Rilke, and Proust.* New Haven and London: Yale UP 1979

DeNeef, A. Leigh 'Epideictic Rhetoric and the Renaissance Lyric.' *Journal of Medieval and Renaissance Studies* 3 (1973) 203–31

Derrida, Jacques *Of Grammatology.* Trans Gayatri Chakravorty Spivak. Baltimore: Johns Hopkins UP 1976

– 'White Mythology: Metaphor in the Text of Philosophy.' *New Literary History* 6 (1974) 5–74

de Saussure, Ferdinand *Course in General Linguistics.* Ed Charles Bally and Albert Sechehaye. Trans Wade Baskin. New York: Philosophical Library 1959

Dio Cassius *Roman History.* Loeb Classical Library. 9 vols. Trans Ernest Cary. Loeb Classical Library. London: Heinemann 1914–27

Dio Chrysostom. 5 vols. Trans J.W. Cohoon. Loeb Classical Library. Cambridge: Harvard UP 1949

Donaldson, Ian 'Jonson and Anger.' In *Yearbook of English Studies.* London: Modern Humanities Research Assn 1984

– 'Jonson's Ode to Sir Lucius Cary and Sir H. Morison.' *Studies in the Literary Imagination* 6:1 (1973) 139–52

Donaldson, Ian, ed *Ben Jonson: Poems.* London: Oxford UP 1975

– ed *Ben Jonson.* Oxford Authors. Oxford: Oxford UP 1985

Donne, John *the Elegies and the Songs and Sonnets of John Donne.* Ed Helen Gardner. Oxford: Clarendon P 1965

– *The Poems of John Donne.* Ed Herbert J.C. Grierson. 2 vols. Oxford: Oxford UP 1912

Donno, Elizabeth Story, ed *Elizabeth Minor Epics.* London: Routledge & Kegan Paul 1963

Dubrow, Heather '"The Sun in Water": Donne's Somerset Epithalamium and the Poetics of Patronage.' In *The Historical Renaissance; New Essays on Tudor and Stuart Literature and Culture.* Ed Heather Dubrow and Richard Strier. Chicago: U of Chicago P 1988

Ducrot, Oswald 'Le structuralisme en linguistique.' In *Qu'est-ce que le structuralisme.* Paris: Seuil 1968

Dunlap, Rhodes 'Honest Ben and Royal James: The Poetics of Patronage.' *Iowa State Journal of Research* 57 (1982) 143–51

Durry, Marcel, ed *Pline le jeune: Panégyrique de Trajan.* Paris: Société d'édition 'Les Belles Lettres' 1938

Dutton, Richard *Ben Jonson: To the First Folio.* Cambridge: Cambridge UP 1983

Eco, Umberto *A Theory of Semiotics.* Bloomington: Indiana UP 1976

Elias, Norbert *The Court Society.* Trans Edmund Jephcott. New York: Pantheon Books 1983

Eliot, T.S. *Ben Jonson.* Rptd in *Ben Jonson: A Collection of Critical Essays.* Ed Jonas A. Barish. Englewood Cliffs, NJ: Prentice-Hall 1963

Eisenstadt, S.N., and Louis Roniger 'Patron-Client Relations as a Model of Structuring Social Exchange.' *Comparative Studies in Society and History* 22 (1980) 42–77

Elyot, Sir Thomas *The Book named The Governor.* Ed S.E. Lehmberg. London: Everyman's Library 1962

English, Hubert M. 'Prosody and Meaning in Ben Jonson's Poems' PH D Dissertation, Yale U 1954

The English Courtier, and the Cuntrey-gentleman: A pleasaunt and learned Disputation betweene them both: very profitable and necessaries to be read of all Nobilitie and Gentlemen. London 1586. Anonymous. In *Inedited Tracts* ed Hazlitt

Epstein, Edmund L., and Terence Hawkes 'Linguistics and English Prosody.' In *Studies in Linguistics: Occasional Papers #7.* Buffalo: U of Buffalo 1959

Erasmus, Desiderius *The Education of a Christian Prince.* Trans with intro by Lester K. Born. 1936; New York: Octagon Books 1965

Evans, Robert C. *Ben Jonson and the Poetics of Patronage.* Lewisburg: Bucknell UP 1988

Ferne, John *The Blazon of Gentrie.* London 1586. Rptd Amsterdam: Theatrum Orbis Terrarum 1973

Ferry, Anne *All in War with Time: Love Poetry of Shakespeare, Donne, Jonson, Marvell.* Cambridge: Harvard UP 1975

Fish, Stanley E. 'Authors-Readers: Jonson's Community of the Same.' *Representations* 7 (1984) 26–58

Flantz, Richard 'The Authoritie of Truth: Jonson's Mastery of Measure and the Founding of the Modern Plain-Style Lyric.' In *Classic and Cavalier: Es-*

says on Jonson and the Sons of Ben ed C.J. Summers and T.-L. Pebworth. Pittsburgh: U of Pittsburgh P 1982

Fowler, Alastair 'The "Better Marks" of Jonson's To Penshurst.' RES ns 24:95 (1973) 266–82

Fowler, Roger The Languages of Literature: Some Linguistic Contributions to Criticism. New York: Barnes and Noble 1971

Freud, Sigmund The Interpretation of Dreams. Trans James Strachey. New York: Avon 1965

Friedberg, Harris 'Ben Jonson's Poetry: Pastoral, Georgic, Epigram.' English Literary Renaissance 4 (1974) 111–36

Fry, D.B. 'Speech Reception and Perception.' In New Horizons in Linguistics ed John Lyons. Harmondsworth: Penguin 1970

Fry, Paul H. The Poet's Calling in the English Ode. New Haven: Yale UP 1980

Gadamer, Hans-Georg Truth and Method. New York: Crossroad 1985

Gardiner, Judith Kegan Craftsmanship in Context: The Development of Ben Jonson's Poetry. The Hague: Mouton 1975

– '"A Wither'd Daffodill": Narcissism and Cynthia's Revels.' Literature and Psychology 30 (1980) 26–43

Gardiner, Judith K., and Susanna S. Epp 'Ben Jonson's Social Attitudes: A Statistical Analysis.' Comparative Drama 9 (1975) 68–86

Garrison, James D. Dryden and the Tradition of Panegyric. Berkeley: U of California P 1975

Gascoigne, George Certayne Notes of Instruction Concerning the Making of Verse or Ryme in English. In English Literary Criticism: The Renaissance ed O.B. Hardison, Jr. New York: Appleton 1963

Gibbon, Edward The Decline and Fall of the Roman Empire. 3 vols. New York: Modern Library nd

Gibbons, Brian Jacobean City Comedy: A Study of Satiric Plays by Jonson, Marston, and Middleton. Cambridge: Harvard UP 1968

Gilbert, Allan H. Machiavelli's 'Prince' and Its Forerunners: 'The Prince' as a Typical Book 'De Regimine Principum.' Durham, NC: Duke UP 1938

Gill, Alexander Logonomia Anglica (1619). Notes by Bror Danielsson and Arvid Gabrielson. Trans Robin C. Alston. Acta Universitatis Stockholmiensis, Stockholm Studies in English, no 27. 2 vols. Stockholm: Almqvist & Wiksell, 1972

Goldberg, Jonathan James I and the Politics of Literature: Jonson, Shakespeare, Donne, and their Contemporaries. Baltimore: Johns Hopkins UP 1983

Gordon, D.J. 'Poet and Architect: The Intellectual Setting of the Quarrel between Ben Jonson and Inigo Jones.' In *The Renaissance Imagination: Essays and Lectures by D.J. Gordon* ed Stephen Orgel. Berkeley, Los Angeles, London: U of California P 1975

Greenblatt, Stephen *Renaissance Self-Fashioning from More to Shakespeare.* Chicago: U of Chicago P 1980

Greene, Thomas 'Accommodations of Mobility in the Poetry of Ben Jonson.' In *The Light in Troy: Imitation and Discovery in Renaissance Poetry.* New Haven and London: Yale UP 1982

– 'Jonson and the Centered Self.' In *The Vulnerable Text: Essays on Renaissance Literature.* New York: Columbia UP 1986

Greimas, A.J. *Du sens: Essais sémiotiques.* Paris: Seuil 1970

Guazzo, Stefano *The Civile Conversation of M. Steeven Guazzo.* Books I–III trans George Pettie (1581); book IV trans Barth. Young (1586). Introduction by Sir Edward Sullivan, Bart. 2 vols. London: Constable; New York: Knopf 1925

Guibbory, Achsah 'The Poet as Myth Maker: Ben Jonson's Poetry of Praise.' *CLIO* 5:3 (1976) 315–29

Gundersheimer, Werner L. 'Patronage in the Renaissance: An Exploratory Approach.' In *Patronage*, ed Lytle and Orgel

Halliday, M.A.K. 'Intonation in English Grammar.' In *Transactions of the Philological Society.* Oxford 1964

Hamilton, Edith, and Huntington Cairns, eds *The Collected Dialogues of Plato.* New York: Pentheon Books 1963

Hammond, Mason 'Pliny the Younger's Views on Government.' In *Harvard Studies in Classical Philology* 49. Cambridge: Harvard UP 1938

Hanning, Robert W., and David Rosand, eds *Castiglione: The Ideal and the Real in Renaissance Culture.* New Haven and London: Yale UP 1983

Harari, Josue V. 'Critical Factions/Critical Fictions.' In *Textual Strategies* ed Harari

– ed *Textual Strategies: Perspectives in Post-Structuralist Criticism.* Ithaca: Cornell UP 1979

Harding, D.W. *Words into Rhythm: English Speech Rhythm in Verse and Prose.* Cambridge: Cambridge UP 1976

Hardison, O.B., Jr *The Enduring Monument: A Study of the Idea of Praise in Renaissance Literary Theory and Practice.* Chapel Hill: U of North Carolina P 1962

– *Prosody and Purpose in the English Renaissance.* Baltimore: Johns Hopkins UP 1989

Hart, John *The Opening of the Unreasonable Writing of Our Inglish Toung. John Hart's Works on English Orthography and Pronunciation (1551–1569–*

1570). Part 1: Biographical and Bibliographical Introductions, Texts, and Index Verborum by Bror Danielsson. Stockholm: Almqvist & Wiksell 1955

Haynes, Jonathan 'Festivity and the Dramatic Economy of Jonson's *Bartholomew Fair.*' *ELH* 51 (1984) 645–68

Hazlitt, W.C., ed *Inedited Tracts: Illustrating the Manners, Opinions, and Occupations of Englishmen During the Sixteenth and Seventeenth Centuries: Now First Republished from the Original Copies with a Preface and Notes.* 1868; New York: Burt Franklin nd

Helgerson, Richard *Self-Crowned Laureates: Spenser, Jonson, Milton and the Literary System.* Berkeley: U of California P 1983

Herford, C.H., and Percy and Evelyn Simpson, eds *Ben Jonson.* 11 vols. Oxford: Clarendon P 1925–52

Hibbard, G.R. 'The Country-House Poem of the Seventeenth Century.' *Journal of the Warburg and Courtauld Institutes* 19 (1956) 159–74

Hjelmslev, Louis *Prolegomena to a Theory of Language.* Trans Francis J. Whitfield. Rev English ed. Madison: U of Wisconsin P 1969

Hofmannstal, Hugo von *Der Rosenkavalier.* Libretto for Angel label recording of the opera SDLX-3970

Hollander, John *Vision and Resonance: Two Senses of Poetic Form.* New York: Oxford UP 1975

Holmes. George *The Florentine Enlightenment 1400–50.* New York: Pegasus 1969

Hoopes, Robert *Right Reason in the English Renaissance.* Cambridge: Harvard UP 1962

Horatius Flaccus, Q. *Opera.* Ed Fridericus Klingner. Leipzig: Teubner 1959

Hoskins, John *Directions for Speech and Style.* Ed Hoyt H. Hudson. Princeton: Princeton UP 1935

Humphrey, Lawrence *The Nobles, or of Nobilitye.* London 1563; New York: Da Capo P 1973

Hunter, G.K. *John Lyly: The Humanist as Courtier.* Cambridge: Harvard UP 1962

Hunter, William B., ed *The Complete Poetry of Ben Jonson.* Garden City, NY: Anchor Books 1963

I.M. *Health to the Gentlemanly profession of Seruingmen: or, The Seruingmans Comfort:* ... London 1598. In *Inedited Tracts* ed W.C. Hazlitt

Institucion of a Gentleman (1555). The English Experience, no 672. Amsterdam: Theatrum Orbis Terrarum; Norwood, NJ: Walter J. Johnson 1974

Isocrates. Trans George Norlin. 3 vols. Loeb Classical Library. London: Heinemann 1928

Jackson, Gabriele Bernhard *Vision and Judgment in Ben Jonson's Drama.*

New Haven and London: Yale UP 1968

Jaeger, Werner *Paideia: The Ideals of Greek Culture.* 3 vols. Trans Gilbert Highet. Oxford: Oxford UP 1939–44

Jakobson, Roman, and Morris Halle *Fundamentals of Language.*'s-Gravenhage: Mouton 1956

James, Mervyn *English Politics and the Concept of Honour 1485–1642. Past and Present* supplement 3. Oxford: Oxford UP 1978

Javitch, Daniel '*Il Cortegiano* and the Constraints of Despotism.' In *Castiglione* ed Hanning and Rosand

– *Poetry and Courtliness in Renaissance England.* Princeton: Princeton UP 1978

John, Lisle Cecil 'Ben Jonson's "To William Sidney, on His Birthday."' *Modern Language Review* 52 (1957) 168–76

Johnston, George Burke, ed *Poems of Ben Jonson.* Cambridge: Harvard UP 1954

Jones, Sir Henry Stuart 'The Princeps.' In *The Cambridge Ancient History, Vol 10: The Augustan Empire 44 B.C.–A.D. 70* ed S.A. Cook, F.E. Adcock, M.P. Charlesworth. Cambridge: At the UP 1966

Jonson, Ben *Volpone.* Ed Jay L. Halio. Berkeley and Los Angeles: U of California P 1968

Juvenal *The Satires of Juvenal.* Trans Hubert Creekmore. New York: New American Library 1963

Kaiser, Walter *Praisers of Folly (Erasmus, Rabelais, Shakespeare).* Cambridge: Harvard UP 1963

Karcevskij, S. 'Du dualisme asymétrique du signe linguistique.' *Travaux du Cercle Linguistique de Praque* 1 (1929) 88–93

Kelso, Ruth *The Doctrine of the English Gentleman in the Sixteenth Century.* Illinois Studies in Language and Literature 14, nos 1–2. Champaign-Urbana: U of Illinois P 1929

Kennedy, George *The Art of Rhetoric in the Roman World: 300 B.C.–A.D. 300.* Princeton: Princeton UP 1972

Kernan, Alvin *The Cankered Muse: Satire of the English Renaissance.* New Haven: Yale UP 1959

Kerrigan, William 'Ben Jonson Full of Shame and Scorn.' *Studies in the Literary Imagination* 6:1 (1973) 199–217

Knapp, Peggy 'Ben Jonson and the Publicke Riot.' *ELH* 46 (1979) 577–94

Knight, G. Wilson *The Mutual Flame.* New York: Macmillan 1955

Knights, L.C. *Drama and Society in the Age of Jonson.* 1937; New York: Barnes and Noble 1968

Lacan, Jacques 'The Insistence of the Letter in the Unconscious.' In *The*

Structuralists: From Marx to Lévi-Strauss ed Richard T. De George and Fernande M. De George. Garden City, NY: Anchor Books 1972

– *The Language of the Self: The Function of Language in Psychoanalysis.* Trans with commentary by Anthony Wilden. New York: Delta Books 1975

Ladd, D. Robert *The Structure of Intonational Meaning: Evidence from English.* Bloomington: Indiana UP 1980

Latini, Brunetto *Li Livres Dou Tresor.* Ed Francis J. Carmody. Berkeley: U of California P 1948

Lemly, John 'Masks and Self-Portraits in Jonson's Late Poetry.' *ELH* 44 (1977) 248–66

Lewalski, Barbara Kiefer *Donne's 'Anniversaries' and the Poetry of Praise: The Creation of a Symbolic Mode.* Princeton: Princeton UP 1973

Livingston, Mary L. 'Ben Jonson: Poet to the Painter.' *Texas Studies in Literature and Language* 18 (1976) 381–92

Lotman, Yury *Analysis of the Poetic Text.* Trans D. Barton Jones. Ann Arbor: Ardis 1976

Lyons, John *Semantics, Volume One.* Cambridge: Cambridge UP 1977

Lytle, Guy Fitch, and Stephen Orgel, eds *Patronage in the Renaissance.* Princeton: Princeton UP 1981

MacCannel, Juliet Flower 'Fiction and the Social Order.' *Diacritics* 5:1 (1975) 7–20

Machiavelli, Niccolò *The Chief Works and Others.* 3 vols. Trans Allan Gilbert. Durham, NC: Duke UP 1965

Maclean, Hugh 'Ben Jonson's Poems: Notes on the Ordered Society.' In *Essays in English Literature from the Renaissance to the Victorian Age* ed Millar MacLure and F.W. Watt. Toronto: U of Toronto P 1964

Major, John M. *Sir Thomas Elyot and Renaissance Humanism.* Lincoln: U of Nebraska P 1964

Malloch, A.E. 'The Techniques and Function of the Renaissance Paradox.' *Studies in Philology* 53 (1956) 191–203

Manley, Lawrence *Convention 1500–1750.* Cambridge: Harvard UP 1980

Mannheim, Karl *Ideology and Utopia: An Introduction to the Sociology of Knowledge.* Trans Louis Wirth and Edward Shils. New York: Harcourt nd

Marcus, Leah S. *The Politics of Mirth: Jonson, Herrick, Milton, Marvell, and the Defense of Old Holiday Pastimes.* Chicago and London: U of Chicago P 1986

– 'Report from the Opposition Camp: Jonson Studies in 1980s.' *John Donne Journal* 4:1 (1985) 121–44

Marotti, A.F. 'All about Jonson's Poetry.' *ELH* 39 (1972) 208–37

– *John Donne, Coterie Poet.* Madison: U of Wisconsin P 1986

Marrou, H.I. *A History of Education in Antiquity.* Trans George Lamb. New York: Mentor 1964

Marston, John *The Fawn.* Ed Gerald A. Smith. Regents Renaissance Drama. Lincoln: U of Nebraska P 1965

Martial *Epigrams in Fifteen Books.* Trans anonymous. Privately printed 1921

Martines, Lauro *Power and Imagination: City-States in Renaissance Italy.* New York: Knopf 1979

– *Society and History in English Renaissance Verse.* Oxford: Blackwell 1985

– *The Social World of the Florentine Humanists 1390–1460.* Princeton: Princeton UP 1963

Martin, Graham Dunstan *Language Truth and Poetry: Notes towards Philosophy of Language.* Edinburgh: Edinburgh UP 1975

Mason, John E. *Gentlefolk in the Making: Studies in the History of English Courtesy Literature and Related Topics from 1531 to 1774.* Philadelphia: U of Pennsylvania Press 1935

Maus, Katharine Eisaman *Ben Jonson and the Roman Frame of Mind.* Princeton: Princeton UP 1984

McCanles, Michael 'Conventions of the Natural and the Naturalness of Conventions.' *Diacritics* 7:3 (1977) 54–63

– *Dialectical Criticism and Renaissance Literature.* Berkeley: U of California P 1975

– 'The Dialectical Structure of Discourse.' *Poetics Today* 3:4 (1982) 21–37

– *The Discourse of 'Il Principe.'* Center for Medieval and Renaissance Studies, University of California–Los Angeles. Humana Civilitas Series no. 8. Malibu: Undena Publications 1983

– 'Festival in Jonsonian Comedy.' *Renaissance Drama* ns 8 (1977) 203–19

– 'The Literal and the Metaphorical: Dialectic or Interchange.' *PMLA* 91 (1976) 279–90

– 'Love and Power in the Poetry of Sir Thomas Wyatt.' *Modern Language Quarterly* 29 (1968) 145–60

– 'Mythos and Dianoia: A Dialectical Methodology of Literary Form.' In *Literary Monographs 4* ed Eric Rothstein. Madison: U of Wisconsin P 1971

– 'Paradox in Donne.' In *Essential Articles for the Study of John Donne's Poetry* ed John R. Roberts. Hamden: Archon 1975

– 'Punctuation, Contrastive Emphasis, and New Information in the Prosody of Jonson's Poetry.' *Language and Style* 19 (1986) 74–98

– Review of Evans and Riggs. *Criticism* 32:1 (1990) 129–33

– 'The Rhetoric of the Sublime in Crashaw's Poetry.' In *The Rhetoric of Renaissance Poetry* ed Thomas O. Sloan and Raymond B. Waddington. Berkeley: U of California P 1974

McClung, William A. *The Country House in English Renaissance Poetry.*
Berkeley: U of California P 1977

McEuen, Kathryn Anderson *Classical Influence upon the Tribe of Ben: A
Study of Classical Elements in the Non-dramatic Poetry of Ben Jonson and
his Circle.* 1939; New York: Octagon Books 1968

McGuire, Mary Ann C. 'The Cavalier Country-House Poem: Mutations
on a Jonsonian Tradition.' *Studies in English Literature* 19 (1979)
93–108

Medine, Peter M. 'Praise and Blame in Renaissance Verse Satire.' *Pacific
Coast Philology* 7 (1972) 49–53

Miles, Rosalind *Ben Jonson: His Life and Work.* London and New York:
Routledge & Kegan Paul 1986

Milton, John *Complete Poems and Major Prose.* Ed Merritt Y. Hughes. New
York: Odyssey 1957

Miner, Earl *The Cavalier Mode from Jonson to Cotton.* Princeton: Princeton
UP 1971

Mohl, Ruth *The Three Estates in Medieval and Renaissance Literature.* New
York: Ungar 1962

Montemagno, Buonaccorso da *The Declamacion of Noblesse (Controusersia
De Nobilitate).* Trans John Tiptoft. In R.J. Mitchell, *John Tiptoft
(1427–1470).* London: Longmans 1938

More, Thomas *Utopia.* Trans H.V.S. Ogden. New York: Appleton-Century-
Crofts 1949

Mortimer, Anthony 'The Feigned Commonwealth in the Poetry of Ben Jonson.' *Studies in English Literature* 13 (1973) 69–79

Mulcaster, Richard *The First Part of the Elementary.* London 1582

Neilson, W.A., and C.J. Hill, eds *the Complete Plays and Poems of William
Shakespeare.* Boston: Houghton Mifflin 1942

Nenna, Giovanni Battista *Nennio, or a Treatise of Nobility.* Trans William
Jones. London 1595. Rptd London: H.A. Humphrey 1967

Newdigate, Bernard H. *Michael Drayton and His Circle.* Oxford: Blackwell
1941

Nichols, J.G. *The Poetry of Ben Jonson.* New York: Barnes & Noble 1969

Nicoll, Allardyce, ed *Chapman's Homer.* 2 vols. Bollingen Series 41. Princeton: Princeton UP 1956

Nohrnberg, James *The Analogy of 'The Faerie Queene'.* Princeton: Princeton
UP 1976

Ong, Walter, 'Historical Backgrounds of Elizabethan and Jacobean Punctuation Theory.' *PMLA* 59 (1944) 349–60

Orgel, Stephen *The Jonsonian Masque.* Cambridge: Harvard UP 1967

Orgel, Stephen, and Roy Strong *Inigo Jones: The Theatre of the Stuart Court.*
2 vols. Berkeley: U of California P 1973

Paine, Tom *Pennsylvania Magazine* May 1775. In *The Spirit of 'Seventy-Six: The Story of the American Revolution as Told by Participants* ed.
Henry Steele Commager and Richard Morris. New York: Harper &
Row 1958

Parfitt, G.A.E. 'Compromise Classicism: Language and Rhythm in Ben Jonson's Poetry.' *Studies in English Literature* 11 (1971) 109–23

– 'Ethical Thought and Ben Jonson's Poetry.' *Studies in English Literature*
9:1 (1969) 123–34

– 'The Nature of Translation in Ben Jonson's Poetry.' *Studies in English Literature* 13 (1973) 344–59

– *Ben Jonson: Public Poet and Private Man.* London: Dent 1976

– ed *Ben Jonson: The Complete Poems.* Harmondsworth: Penguin 1975

Parry, Graham *The Golden Age Restor'd: The Culture of the Stuart Court,
1603–42.* New York: St Martin's P 1981

Partridge, A.C. *Orthography in Shakespeare and Elizabethan Drama: A
Study of Colloquial Contractions, Elision, Prosody and Punctuation.* Lincoln: U of Nebraska P 1964

Partridge, Edward B. 'The Symbolism of Clothes in Jonson's Last Plays.'
Journal of English and Germanic Philosophy 56 (1957) 396–409

– 'Jonson's *Epigrammes*: The Named and the Nameless.' *Studies in the Literary Imagination* 6:1 (1973) 153–98

Pascal, Blaise *Thoughts and Minor Works.* Harvard Classics 48. New York:
P.F. Collier & Son 1938

Patterson, Annabel 'Lyric and Society in Jonson's *Under-wood.*' In *Lyric Poetry Beyond New Criticiam* ed Chaviva Hosek and Patricia Parker. Ithaca
and London: Cornell UP 1985

Peacham, Henry *The Compleat Gentleman.* London 1622. Amsterdam: Theatrum Orbis Terrarum 1968

Pearlman, E. 'Ben Jonson: An Anatomy.' *ELR* 9 (1979) 364–93

Peterson, Richard S. *Imitation and Praise in the Poems of Ben Jonson.* New
Haven and London: Yale UP 1981

– 'Virtue Reconciled to Pleasure: Jonson's "A Celebration of Charis."' *Studies in the Literary Imagination* 6:1 (1973) 219–68

Picone, Giusto *L'eloquenza di Plinio.* Palumbo 1977

Pindar *The Odes of Pindar.* Trans Richmond Lattimore. Chicago: U of Chicago P 1947

Pliny, the Younger *Letters and Panegyricus.* Trans Betty Radice. Loeb Classical Library. Cambridge: Harvard UP 1969

Plutarch *Lives*. Trans (attributed) John Dryden, rev A.H. Clough. New York: Modern Library nd

– *Moralia*. Trans Frank Cole Babbitt. 14 vols. Loeb Classical Library. Cambridge: Harvard UP 1927

Puttenham, George *The Arte of English Poesie*. Kent: Kent State UP 1970

Quintilian *The Institutio Oratoria*. Trans H.E. Butler. 4 vols. London: Heinemann 1921

Quirk, Randolph, Sidney Greenbaum, Geoffrey Leech, and Jan Svartnick *A Grammar of Contemporary English*. London: Longman 1972

Radice, Betty 'Pliny and the *Panegyricus*.' *Greece and Rome* 15 (1968) 166–72

Rathmell, J.C.A. 'Jonson, Lord Lisle, and Penshurst.' *English Literary Renaissance* 1 (1971) 250–60

Riggs, David *Ben Jonson: A Life*. Cambridge and London: Harvard UP 1989

Rivers, Isabel *The Poetry of Conservatism, 1600–1745*. Cambridge: Rivers P 1973

Romei, Count Annibale *The Courtiers Academie* Trans I.K. 1598; Amsterdam and New York: Da Capo 1969

Rowe, George E. *Distinguishing Jonson: Imitation, Rivalry, and the Direction of a Dramatic Career*. Lincoln and London: University of Nebraska P 1988

Russell, D.A. 'Ars Poetica.' In *Horace* ed C.D.N. Costa. London: Routledge 1973

Saccone, Eduardo '*Grazia, Sprezzatura, Affettazione* in the *Courtier*.' In *Castiglione* ed Hanning and Rosand

Sackton, Alexander 'The Rhetoric of Literary Praise in the Poetry of Raleigh and Chapman.' *Texas Studies in Literature and Language* 18 (1976) 409–21

Saller, Richard F. *Personal Patronage under the Early Empire*. Cambridge: Cambridge UP 1982

Sallust *The Jugurthine War* and *Conspiracy of Catiline*. Trans S.A. Handford. Harmondsworth: Penguin Books 1963

Scheler, Max *Ressentiment*. New York: Free Press 1961

Schelling, Felix S. 'Ben Jonson and the Classical School.' *PMLA* 13; rptd in *Publications of the University of Pennsylvania*

Schoenbaum, S. *Shakespeare's Lives*. Oxford: Clarendon P 1970

Selden, John *Titles of Honour*. London 1614

Seneca *Ad Lucilium Epistulae Morales*. Trans Richard M. Gummere. Loeb Classical Library. 3 vols. Cambridge: Harvard UP 1917–25

– *Morals Essays*. Trans John W. Basore. 3 vols. Loeb Classical Library. London: Heinemann 1928

Shakespeare, William *The First Part of King Henry IV*. Ed A.R. Humphreys. Arden Shakespeare. London: Methuen 1961

Sidney, Sir Philip *The Prose Works of Sir Philip Sidney.* Ed Albert Feuillerat. 4 vols. Cambridge: At the UP 1965

Simon, Joan *Education and Society in Tudor England.* Cambridge: At the UP 1966

Simpson, Percy *Shakespearian Punctuation.* Oxford: Clarendon P 1911

Skinner, Quentin *The Foundations of Modern Political Thought.* 2 vols. Cambridge: At the UP 1978

Smith, Bruce R. 'Ben Jonson's Epigrammes: Portrait-Gallery, Theater, Commonwealth.' *SEL* 14:1 (1974) 91–109

Smith, Hallett *Elizabethan Poetry: A Study in Conventions, Meaning, and Expression.* Cambridge: Harvard UP 1952

Smythe-Palmer, A. *The Ideal of a Gentleman, or A Mirror for Gentlefolks: A Portrayal in Literature from the Earliest Times.* London: George Routledge & Sons nd [1905]

Spanos, W.V. 'The Real Toad in the Jonsonian Garden.' *Journal of English and Germanic Philology* 68 (1969) 11–23

Spencer, T.J.B. 'Ben Jonson on his beloved, The Author Mr. William Shakespeare.' *Elizabethan Theatre* 4 (1974) 22–40

Steiner, Peter 'In Defense of Semiotics: The Dual Asymmetry of Cultural Signs.' *New Literary History* 12 (1981) 415–35

Steiner, Wendy 'Language as Process: Sergej Karcevskij's Semiotics of Language.' In *Sound, Sign and Meaning: Quinguagenary of the Prague Linguistic Circle* ed Ladislav Matejka. Michigan Slavic Contributions, no. 6. Ann Arbor: U of Michigan 1978

Stevenson, G.H. 'The Imperial Administration.' *The Cambridge Ancient History.* Vol. 10: *The Augustan Empire 44 B.C.–A.D. 70.* Ed. S.A. Cook, F.E. Adcock, M.P. Charlesworth. Cambridge: At the UP 1966

Stone, Lawrence *The Crisis of the Aristocracy, 1558–1641.* Oxford: Clarendon P 1965

Strout, Nathaniel 'Reading "A Celebration of Charis" and the Nature of Jonson's Art.' *Texas Studies in Literature and Language* 26 (1984) 128–43

Summerson, John *Inigo Jones.* Harmondsworth: Penguin Books 1966

Sweeney, John Gordon, III *Jonson and the Psychology of Public Theater: To Coin the Spirit, Spend the Soul* Princeton: Princeton UP 1985

Swinburne, Algernon Charles *A Study of Ben Jonson.* Ed Howard B. Norland. Lincoln: U of Nebraska P 1969

Syme, Ronald *The Roman Revolution.* Oxford: Clarendon P 1939

Tacitus *The Annals of Imperial Rome.* Trans Michael Grant. Baltimore: Penguin 1959

– *Dialogus; Agricola; Germania.* Loeb Classical Library. Cambridge: Harvard UP 1914

– *The Histories*. Trans Kenneth Wellesley. Baltimore: Penguin 1964

Talbert, Ernest William 'New Light on Ben Jonson's Workmanship.' *Studies in Philology* 40 (1943) 154–85

Thayer, C.G. *Ben Jonson: Studies in the Plays*. Norman: U of Oklahoma P 1963

Thompson, John *The Founding of English Metre*. London: Routledge 1961

Thomson, Patricia 'Donne and the Poetry of Patronage: The Verse Letters.' In *John Donne: Essays in Celebration* ed A.J. Smith. London: Methuen 1972

Trager, George L., and Henry Lee Smith 'An Outline of English Structure.' *Studies in Linguistics: Occasional Papers #3*. Norman, Oklahoma: Battenburg P 1951

Trimpi, Wesley *Ben Jonson's Poems: A Study of the Plain Style*. Stanford: Stanford UP 1962

Van Den Berg, Sara *The Action of Ben Jonson's Poetry*. Newark: University of Delaware P 1987

– 'The Play of Wit and Love: Demetrius' *On Style* and Jonson's "A Celebration of Charis."' *ELH* 41 (1974) 26–36

Van Dijk, Teun A. 'Text Grammar and Text Logic.' In *Studies in Text Grammar* ed J.S. Petöfi and H. Rieser. Dordrecht: D. Reidel Pub 1973

Venuti, Lawrence 'Why Jonson Wrote Not of Love.' *Journal of Medieval and Renaissance Studies* 12 (1982) 195–220

Vickers, Brian 'Epideictic and Epic in the Renaissance.' *New Literary History* 14 (1983) 497–537

Vogt, George McGill 'Gleanings for the History of a Sentiment: Generositas Virtus, non Sanguis.' *Journal of English Germanic Philology* 24 (1925) 102–124

Waddington, Raymond B. '"A Celebration of Charis": Socratic Lover and Silenic Speaker.' In *Classic and Cavalier: Essays on Jonson and the Sons of Ben* ed Claude J. Summers and Ted-Larry Pebworth. Pittsburgh: U of Pittsburgh P 1982

Waith, Eugene 'The Poet's Morals in Jonson's *Poetaster*.' *Modern Language Quarterly* 12 (1951) 13–19

Wanner, Eric 'Do We Understand Sentences from the Outside-In or from the Inside-Out?' *Daedalus* 102 (1973) 163–83

Watson, Curtis Brown *Shakespeare and the Renaissance Concept of Honor*. Princeton: Princeton UP 1960

Watson, Robert N. *Ben Jonson's Parodic Strategy: Literary Imperialism in the Comedies*. Cambridge; and London: Harvard UP 1987

Wayne, Don E. *Penshurst: The Semiotics of Place and the Poetics of History*. Madison: U of Wisconsin P 1984

– 'Poetry and Power in Ben Jonson's *Epigrammes*: The Naming of "Facts" or the Figuring of Social Relations.' *Renaissance and Modern Studies* 23 (1979) 79–103

Weinberg, Bernard *A History of Literary Criticism in the Italian Renaissance*. 2 vols. Chicago: U of Chicago P 1961

Weinberger, G.J. 'Jonson's Mock-Encomiastic "Celebration of Charis."' *Genre* 4 (1971) 305–28

Whigham, Frank *Ambition and Privilege: The Social Tropes of Elizabethan Courtesy Theory*. Berkeley: U of California P 1984

Wilkes, G.A., ed *The Complete Plays of Ben Jonson*. 4 vols. Oxford: Clarendon P 1981

Williams, Raymond *The Country and the City*. New York: Oxford UP 1973

Willson, D. Harris *King James VI and I*. New York: Holt 1956

Wilson, Edmund 'Morose Ben Jonson.' 1938; rptd in *Ben Jonson: A Collection of Critical Essays* ed Jonas A. Barish. Englewood Cliffs, NJ: Prentice-Hall 1963

Wilson, Gayle Edward 'Jonson's Use of the Bible and the Great Chain of Being in "To Penshurst."' *Studies in English Literature* 8 (1968) 77–89

Wilson, Thomas *The Arte of Rhetorique*. Ed G.H. Mair. Oxford: Oxford UP 1909

Wiltenburg, Robert *Ben Jonson and Self-Love: The Sublest Maze of All*. Columbia and London: U of Missouri P 1990

Wimsatt, William K., Jr, and Cleanth Brooks *Literary Criticism: A Short History*. New York: Knopf 1965

Winner, Jack D. 'Ben Jonson's *Epigrammes* and the Conversations of Formal Verse Satire.' *Studies in English Literature* 23 (1983) 61–76

Womack, Peter *Ben Jonson*. Oxford: Basil Blackwell 1986

Woods, Susanne 'Ben Jonson's Cary-Morison Ode: Some Observations on Structure and Form.' *Studies in English Literature* 18 (1978) 57–74

Woolf, D.R. 'Erudition and the Idea of History in Renaissance England.' *Renaissance Quarterly* 40 (1987) 11–48

Wright, Louis B. *Middle-Class Culture in Elizabethan England*. Chapel Hill: U of North Carolina P 1935

Wroth, Lady Mary *The Poems of Lady Mary Wroth*. Ed with intro Josephine A. Roberts. Baton Rouge and London: Louisiana State UP 1983

Young, R.V. 'Style and Structure in Jonson's Epigrams.' *Criticism* 17 (1975) 201–22

General Index

Index of Jonson's Works

The Forrest